THE AMERICAN ADVENTURE!

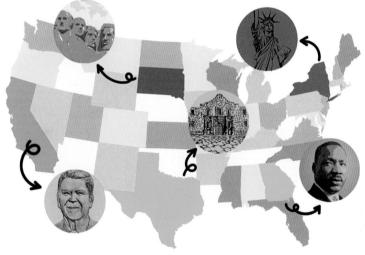

A Conservative Christian Kids' Guide to US History and the 50 States

TRACY M. SUMNER

BARBOUR kidz
A Division of Barbour Publishing

T0012456

© 2024 by Barbour Publishing, Inc.

ISBN 978-1-63609-892-0

All rights reserved. No part of this publication may be reproduced or transmitted for commercial purposes, except for brief quotations in printed reviews, without written permission of the publisher. Reproduced text may not be used on the World Wide Web. No Barbour Publishing content may be used as artificial intelligence training data for machine learning, or in any similar software development.

Churches and other noncommercial interests may reproduce portions of this book without the express written permission of Barbour Publishing, provided that the text does not exceed 500 words and that the text is not material quoted from another publisher. When reproducing text from this book, include the following credit line: "From *The American Adventure!* published by Barbour Publishing, Inc. Used by permission."

All scripture quotations are taken from the King James Version of the Bible.

Published by Barbour Publishing, Inc., 1810 Barbour Drive, Uhrichsville, Ohio 44683, www.barbourbooks.com

Our mission is to inspire the world with the life-changing message of the Bible.

ecpa Member of the
Evangelical Christian
Publishers Association

Printed in India.

002048 0624 TP

HEY, KIDS. . .

IT'S A GREAT COUNTRY.
HERE'S WHY YOU
CAN AND SHOULD LOVE IT!

The American Adventure! *A Conservative Christian Kids' Guide to US History and the 50 States* covers the whole range of the American experience. Inside, you'll find two complete books, each containing fascinating details on the good old U.S. of A.

The kids' guide to US history begins on page 5. On its pages, you learn about

- explorers, like **Christopher Columbus, Henry Hudson,** and **Sacagawea**
- presidents, from **George Washington** to **Joe Biden**
- inventors and industrialists, such as the **Wright brothers, Thomas Edison,** and **Henry Ford**
- religious and social leaders, including **Jonathan Edwards, Harriet Beecher Stowe,** and **Martin Luther King Jr.**

Then, starting on page 161, you'll find a fascinating (and often funny) collection of facts about the 50 states, Washington DC, and the US territories.

Honest about tough issues like slavery, but upbeat on the faith and freedom that have made the United States the envy of the world, this book celebrates the USA. It's a great country—the freest, most prosperous, and most generous ever—a nation that by God's grace has shined the light of hope on the world.

THE
AMERICAN
ADVENTURE!

A Conservative Christian
Kids' Guide to US History

WHAT'S IN THIS BOOK

BEFORE YOU GET STARTED

Have you ever sat in your social studies or history class at school, wishing you knew more about how the United States came to be the country it is today? If you have, then this book is for you! (If you haven't, it's still a pretty cool book anyway.)

As you read through this book, you'll learn the basics of US history, starting with European explorations of North America that started as far back as about 1,000 years ago. You'll also learn about the brave people who started coming here from Europe about four centuries ago and began setting up 13 communities called *colonies*. You'll also learn the exciting story of how those colonies eventually became the original 13 states of the United States of America.

If that's not enough—and we hope it won't be!—you'll also learn about how Americans began moving west from the original 13 colonies to explore and settle the rest of the country.

And, of course, you'll learn that many of the people who played important parts in American history were people who believed in God and believed that He had a purpose in allowing the United States of America to get its start *and* expand to become the nation you live in today.

But there's even more! This book also includes fun and informative features with facts, figures, and profiles of important people in American history. Here is a list of those features:

Historic Happenings:
Events in American history that are worth remembering

History Makers: Stories about
important people in American history and the things they did to become famous

Worth Repeating: Interesting
things that people in the past said about America

Interesting!: Good-to-know facts
about the people, places, and events in the history of the United States

Before you get started, here are some things to keep in mind:

First of all, this book won't teach you everything there is to know about US history. Entire books have been written about many of these important people and events, and it wasn't easy deciding what to include and what to leave out.

Our hope is that this book will give you a good idea of how the United States started and grew to become the great nation it is today. Then, through your own studies, you can build on what you've learned. You will also have a great head start when you study American history at school!

Second (and this is kind of a warning), some of the things that have happened in our country aren't very pleasant to read or think about. There have been several big wars, and a lot of people died to protect our freedom. You'll also find some stories about people who went through some really hard times—and some who even died because they didn't have enough to eat or because they got sick. And because people aren't perfect, you'll read about some of the mistakes the United States made along the way.

About now, you might be thinking, *Why would I want to read about wars and about people suffering and dying? That doesn't sound like fun to me.* Look at it this way: If you understand what some people had to give up in order to build such a great nation as the United States, it will make you more thankful for the freedom we have today.

When you're finished reading this book, you won't know everything there is to know about American history. But you'll understand most of the important events and how a lot of people had to depend on God, be brave, and not give up in order to make the United States of America the great nation it is today.

And maybe—*just maybe*—you'll find that learning about history is not only interesting but a lot of fun, too! ❌

CHAPTER 1

A Time of "New World" Discovery

The Pre-Colonial Period of American History

If you could travel back in time to see what the United States looked like 500 or 600 years ago, what do you think you'd find? Obviously, it wouldn't look anything like it does today. There were no cities or roads back then, and the only people you would see were the Native Americans—which some people call Indians—who had lived here for generations.

In those days, most of our ancestors were living in Europe, Asia, or Africa, and they didn't know much about the unexplored territory that would come to be known as the New World. In fact, very few of them even knew it existed!

But that began to change toward the end of the fifteenth century (the 1400s) when brave and curious men like Christopher Columbus, John Cabot, Ponce de León, and many others started sailing west in search of discovery.

There was a huge "New World" out there for the European explorers to discover.

Christopher Columbus Sails West

In fourteen hundred and ninety-two, Columbus sailed the ocean blue.

That little poem probably helps you remember that way back in 1492, an Italian sailor named Christopher Columbus set sail from Spain and eventually landed on some islands near two big continents that would come to be

HISTORY MAKERS

Even though Christopher Columbus is credited with "finding" North America, he wasn't the first European to land on the continent. Around the year 1001, almost 500 years earlier, an explorer from Norway named Leif Eriksson is said to have set up a settlement in a place he called Vinland. We don't know exactly where this settlement was, but it was probably located in what today is Newfoundland, Canada.

known as "the Americas" (North America, which is where the United States, Canada, and Mexico are located; and South America, which today has 12 countries, including Brazil, Argentina, Peru, and Chile).

What you might not know is that Columbus's real claim to fame is that he discovered the Americas *by accident.* In fact, he wasn't even trying to discover anything—except an easier, safer way for sailors back then to travel to India.

Christopher Columbus was born in the Republic of Genoa in northwestern Italy in 1451. His father was Domenico Colombo (*Columbus* is the English spelling of the Italian name Colombo), who made a living for his family by working as a wool weaver. He also owned a cheese stand, which young Christopher helped run. Christopher's mother was Susanna Fontanarossa, and he had three brothers—Bartolomeo, Giovanni Pellegrino, and Giacomo—and a sister, Bianchinetta.

Christopher Columbus didn't get much of an education when he was young. Instead of studying, he began sailing. He traveled around the Mediterranean Sea and even traveled as far as England and Ireland. When Columbus was about 25 years old, he was shipwrecked and made his way ashore in Portugal. He later lived there with his brother Bartolomeo.

Finding a New Way to India

Like other sailors in his day, Columbus knew that traveling around the southern tip of Africa to reach India was very dangerous and difficult. Not only that, it took a long time! He believed he could find a new route to India by sailing west across the Atlantic Ocean. He didn't know there were two big continents in the way (that would one day be called the Americas). He thought if he just sailed west, he would circle the globe and eventually end up in eastern Asia.

Columbus spent seven years traveling across Europe looking for someone to support his mission to find a new way to India, but no one wanted to help him. In fact, most of the kings and queens of

Europe made fun of him and told him it was too dangerous to try to sail around the world.

But Columbus didn't give up. He traveled to Spain looking for support. The Spanish king, Ferdinand, and his queen, Isabella, wanted to prove that Spain could be just as powerful and successful as its neighbor, Portugal. So in August 1492, they granted Christopher Columbus the supplies, men, and ships that he needed for his trip. The three ships the king and queen gave Columbus were named the *Niña*, the *Pinta*, and the *Santa Maria*.

INTERESTING!

One of the myths about Christopher Columbus (one you might even have read in one of your school textbooks) was that no one believed him when he said the world was round and not flat. But people living during Columbus's time—at least the people with some education—knew very well that the earth was round. A few centuries before the birth of Jesus, Greek scientists and philosophers already knew that the earth was round. In fact, around 200 BC, a Greek scholar named Eratosthenes of Cyrene had already figured out pretty accurately the distance around the world.

Time to Set Sail!

On August 3, 1492, Columbus and his men set sail from Palos, Spain. Columbus thought the journey would take only four weeks. But after more than two months at sea without spotting land, Columbus's men began to worry that they would be lost and would starve to death (and they had no idea where they were). On October 10, the other sailors began to turn against Columbus, so he made a deal with them: If they didn't find land within three days, they would turn around and head home.

It looked like Columbus's voyage might turn out to be a waste of time; but on October 12, 1492, one of the sailors spotted land. Columbus didn't know it at the time, but what he and his crew had discovered was an island in the Caribbean Sea.

Columbus named the newly discovered island San Salvador, but when he went ashore the next morning, he found that the people already living there called it Guanahani. Columbus met with some of the natives and traded with them. He stayed on the island for two days before setting sail again. He stopped at three other islands in the

WORTH REPEATING

"It was the Lord who put into my mind (I could feel His hand upon me) that fact that it would be possible to sail from here to the Indies. All who heard of my project rejected it with laughter, ridiculing me. There is no question that the inspiration was from the Holy Spirit, because He comforted me with rays of marvelous inspiration from the Holy Scriptures."
—Christopher Columbus

HISTORY MAKERS

Rodrigo de Triana (born 1469), also known as Juan Rodriguez, was a Spanish sailor who traveled on the sailing ship *Pinta* as part of Christopher Columbus's crew. Around two o'clock in the morning on October 12, 1492, de Triana became the first European since the Vikings to see any part of the North American continent. The land de Triana spotted was somewhere in the Bahamas in the Caribbean Sea.

INTERESTING!

When Columbus landed on Hispaniola, he was convinced he was in India. That's why he began calling the natives on the island *Indians*. Even after it was discovered that India was still half a world away, European explorers and settlers continued to refer to North American and South American natives as Indians.

Bahamas—which he named Santa Maria de la Concepción, Fernandina, and Isabella—before landing at Bariay Bay, Cuba, on October 28.

Columbus spent the last few days of October and all of November exploring the island of Cuba. While there, he looked for gold (he didn't find any) and for Chinese civilizations he had read about (he still didn't know he wasn't in Asia). On December 5, 1492, Columbus arrived at another island, which he named Hispaniola. Today, that island is where you'll find the nations of Haiti and the Dominican Republic.

On January 16, 1493, Columbus departed Hispaniola for the return trip to Spain. The *Niña* and the *Pinta* arrived in Palos, Spain, on March 15. Over the next several years, Columbus returned three more times to Cuba and Hispaniola, and he also visited places like modern-day Trinidad and Nicaragua.

It might sound funny now, but on Columbus's first voyage, he had no idea where he had landed. He had sailed almost all the way across the Atlantic Ocean, just as he had planned, but instead of reaching India, he landed in a place that no one from Europe knew existed. What's even more amazing is that Columbus never knew he hadn't reached India. In fact, by the time he died in 1506, he still didn't realize what he had discovered.

Columbus: A Man of Faith

You probably won't read about it in your school textbooks, but Christopher Columbus was a devout Christian who read his Bible and prayed regularly. Like any other European explorer during the pre-colonial period, Columbus had a desire to find new places and better ways to reach those places. But he also had a strong desire to tell people in other nations about Jesus. He especially wanted to take this message to people in eastern Asia.

After landing at the island he named San Salvador, Columbus wrote about his experiences with the natives who lived there: "As I saw that they were very friendly to us, and perceived that they could be much more easily converted to our holy faith by gentle means than by force, I presented them with some red caps, and strings of beads to wear upon the neck, and many other trifles of small value, wherewith they were much delighted and became wonderfully attached to us. I am of opinion that they would very readily become Christians, as they appear to have no religion."

John Cabot: North America's Real Discoverer

Before the beginning of the sixteenth century (the 1500s), Spain and Portugal did most of the exploring of the New World. But in 1497, King Henry VII of England sent an Italian explorer named John Cabot (Giovanni Caboto in Italian) to check out what Columbus had recently found.

Cabot explored what is now Newfoundland and Nova Scotia in Canada, as well as the area now known as New England in the United States. Even though another century would pass before England established a permanent colony in the New World, Cabot claimed those lands for England. Historians believe Cabot was the first European explorer to travel to the continent of North America since the early eleventh century.

How America Became "America"

Not long after Christopher Columbus died in 1506, people began to realize that what he had discovered was not a new route to India, but a completely different part of the world. The first person to make that suggestion was an Italian explorer named Amerigo Vespucci (1454–1512). Vespucci grew up in Florence, Italy. He enjoyed reading and collected a lot of books and maps. As a young man, he began working for bankers in Florence, and in 1492 he traveled to Spain to take care of business for his employer. While he was in Spain, he began working on ships. In 1499, he sailed with a crew to South America and saw the mouth of the Amazon River.

Vespucci made at least one more trip (probably two) across the Atlantic Ocean before he died of malaria (a disease often carried by mosquitoes) on February 22, 1512. He is remembered as the man who realized that the land that would later be known as America was not part of eastern Asia, as Columbus had believed, but a newly discovered continent. Vespucci is also remembered as the man this new continent was named after.

That happened around 1507, when a German preacher and mapmaker named Martin Wardseemüller printed a map of the known world with the name "America" printed across the South American continent. Wardseemüller had read of Amerigo Vespucci's travels to the New World, and he wanted to honor the Italian explorer by naming the newly discovered continent after him.

A few years later, Wardseemüller changed his mind about the name of Vespucci's New World discovery. But by then it was too late. He had already printed thousands of copies of his map and sold them to people all across Europe. Wardseemüller couldn't change the fact that everyone in Europe called the New World "America."

In 1538 a European mapmaker named Gerardus Mercator developed the first world map to include the continents of North America and South America. So even though Amerigo Vespucci wasn't one of the most important explorers to see the New World, his name became famous.

This turret is a much-photographed part of Puerto Rico's Morro Castle, begun about 30 years after Ponce de León became governor of the island.

Ponce de León: Picking up Where Columbus Left Off

Juan Ponce de León was a sailor who accompanied Christopher Columbus on his voyage to the New World in 1493. When Columbus returned to Europe, Ponce de León decided to stay in Hispaniola.

In 1508 Spain appointed Ponce de León governor of a nearby island called Boriquien (modern-day Puerto Rico). Legend has it that while Ponce de León was in Boriquien, he heard the natives' stories about a magical source of water called the Fountain of Youth. Supposedly, drinking water from the fountain made a person young again. According to legend, Ponce de León spent a few years trying to find out where the Fountain of Youth was. When he was told it was on an island called Bimini, he organized an expedition to go search for it.

Many historians doubt the accuracy of the Fountain of Youth story. But early in 1513, Ponce de León received permission from Spain to set sail from Boriquien. He loaded three ships—the *Santiago*, the *San Cristobal* and the *Santa Maria de la Consolacion*—with at least 200 men, and on March 4, 1513, they set sail.

Ponce de León's expedition sailed for several days and didn't find Bimini; but on March 27, they came within sight of what they thought was a large island (but was actually a long peninsula connected to North America). Sometime in early April 1513, Ponce de León became the first European known to have set foot on what is now the state of Florida. He named the area in honor of Spain's Easter celebration called *Pascua Florida*, which means "Feast of Flowers."

Ponce de León eventually returned to Boriquien, where he continued as governor, but in 1521 he began another voyage to Florida. This time, he was accompanied by about 200 people. They took with them about 50 horses, other livestock, and farming equipment, because they wanted to start a colony on the peninsula.

The expedition landed on the southwest coast of Florida and started to build a settlement. As the men worked to build houses, they were attacked by native tribesmen. Many of Ponce de León's men died in the attack, and he was wounded. The survivors boarded their ship and sailed to Cuba, where Ponce de León died of his wounds in July 1521.

Catching the Exploration Bug

The expeditions of Christopher Columbus, Juan Ponce de León, and John Cabot were just the beginning of European exploration of the New World. Before many more years had passed, explorers from several European nations boarded ships and headed west. Some of these explorers went looking for gold and other riches, while others just wanted to find out what these new lands might have to offer them and their people. By the one hundredth anniversary of Columbus's unintended voyage to the New World, dozens of other Europeans had embarked on explorations of their own.

Here is a list of some of those explorers and what they found:

- In 1519 a Spanish explorer and mapmaker named **Alonso de Pineda** (1494–1520) led several expeditions to map the western coastlines of the Gulf of Mexico. His map is believed to be the first document in the history of what later became the state of Texas. It is also the first map of the Gulf Coast region of the United States.

- In 1524 an Italian explorer named **Giovanni da Verrazano** (1485–1528), who was sailing for France, explored the east coast of North America, from Cape Fear (modern-day North Carolina) north to Nova Scotia. Along the way, he also discovered New York Harbor.

- In 1528 a Spanish explorer named **Alvar Cabeza de Vaca** (about 1488–about 1557) explored the territory that later became the states of Texas, Arizona, and New Mexico, as well as parts of northeastern Mexico.

- In 1534 a French explorer named **Jacques Cartier** (1491–1557) explored the Great Lakes area and the Saint Lawrence River. He was the first European to map the Gulf of Saint Lawrence and the shores of the Saint Lawrence River. Cartier claimed the area for France.

The Verrazano-Narrows Bridge, connecting the New York City boroughs of Staten Island and Brooklyn, was named for the Italian explorer who was the first European to sail into New York Harbor.

- On May 30, 1539, a Spanish explorer named **Hernando de Soto** (about 1500–1542) arrived on the west coast of Florida. He and his men were looking for gold and silver, and they explored much of southeastern North America. De Soto and his men camped for five months near what is now the city of

Tallahassee, Florida. De Soto died near the Mississippi River in 1542, but other members of his expedition eventually arrived in Mexico.

- In 1540 a Spanish conquistador (conqueror) named **Francisco Vásquez de Coronado** (1510–1554) explored southwestern North America, including what is now New Mexico. Coronado was looking for the mythical Seven Cities of Gold. Coronado also explored the Colorado River and what later became the state of Kansas.

WORTH REPEATING

"This land may be profitable to those that will adventure it."
—Henry Hudson, English explorer

- In 1540 a Spaniard named **Garcia López de Cárdenas** discovered the Grand Canyon.

- In 1542 a Portuguese explorer named **Juan Rodriguez Cabrillo** (about 1499–1543), who was sailing for Spain, explored the west coast of North America. Cabrillo is credited with discovering the coast of California.

- In 1559 a Spanish conquistador named **Tristán de Luna** (1519–1571) was sent on an expedition to conquer Florida. He established a short-lived colony in what is now Pensacola. It was one of the earliest European settlements in North America.

- In 1563 a Spanish explorer named **Francisco de Ibarra** (about 1539–1575) explored what is now New Mexico. He also founded the Mexican city of Durango.

- In 1577 an English sea captain named **Sir Francis Drake** (1544–1596) began his quest to sail completely around the world. He started from Plymouth, England, on December 13, 1577, and returned to the same place on September 26, 1580.

- In 1584 two Englishmen, **Philip Amadas** (1550–1618) and **Arthur Barlowe** (1550–1620), explored the coast of North Carolina. Both men were sailing on behalf of the English explorer Sir Walter Raleigh (about 1554–1618).

WORTH REPEATING

"There must be a beginning of anything great, but continuing to the end until it is thoroughly finished yields the true glory."
—Sir Francis Drake

- In 1585 **Sir Walter Raleigh** received permission from the king of England to explore and settle in North America. In June of that year, Raleigh established a short-lived colony on Roanoke Island (North Carolina).

- In 1598 a Spaniard named **Juan de Archuleta** explored what is now Colorado.

- In 1609 an English explorer named **Henry Hudson** (about 1565–about 1611), sailing on behalf of the Netherlands, discovered the area that would later become Delaware. Hudson's explorations led to the Dutch colonization of New York and Delaware.

North America's First European Settlement

In the next chapter, you will read how the colonies that eventually became the first 13 states at one time all belonged to Great Britain. But none of those colonies was the first permanent European settlement established in North America. That honor goes to a place called St. Augustine in northeast Florida.

Pedro Menéndez de Avilés established St. Augustine on orders from King Philip II of Spain, who told him to explore and colonize the territory and to destroy any other European settlements, including a French outpost called Fort Caroline. King Philip also told Menéndez to conquer (but not destroy) the Timucua, the native tribe that lived in the area.

Menéndez's fleet battled through Atlantic storms that claimed several of their ships, but on August 28, 1565, they first sighted land. On September 8—42 years before the first British settlement in North America was established— Menéndez (along with 500 soldiers, 200 sailors, and 100 passengers) established the settlement and named it in honor of St. Augustine of Hippo, a famous Christian writer who lived in the fourth and fifth centuries. Menéndez was also the first governor of Florida.

Jamestown— Where US History Really Began

By the beginning of the seventeenth century, European explorers had been traveling to North America for quite a long time. But in 1607, settlers from England built the first English settlement in North America, called Jamestown, in what is now Virginia. Even though the United States of America wouldn't be established for another 170 years, Jamestown in many ways was the real start of US history.

Florida has come a long way since Spanish adventurers first explored the area. Today, the state is a popular tourist destination—well known for sights such as rocket launches from Cape Canaveral.

HISTORY MAKERS

Pánfilo de Narváez (about 1470–1528) was a Spanish explorer and soldier best remembered for helping Spain conquer Cuba in 1511. He also led a Spanish expedition of about 300 men to North America in 1527. The explorers landed on the west coast of Florida (near what is now Tampa Bay) in April 1528. Many of the men died due to hurricanes and battles with the natives, and the rest were stranded when their ship's pilot sailed to Mexico without them. The abandoned men built five rafts and began sailing west toward Mexico. Only two of the rafts made it all the way to safety on Galveston Island (off the coast of Texas). Narváez died during the trip.

The year before the Jamestown settlers arrived, King James I of England (the same King James who authorized a translation of the Bible called the King James Version) gave a group of merchants representing the Virginia Company permission to settle in North America.

King James wanted to establish a settlement in the New World because he wanted to keep up with other European countries that already had colonies there. By that time, Spain had established colonies in South America, Central America, and parts of North America; and France had colonies in what is now eastern Canada.

On December 20, 1606, a party of men and boys boarded the ships *Susan Constant*, *Godspeed*, and *Discovery* and headed out from England. The passengers included carpenters, a blacksmith, a mason, a tailor, a goldsmith, a barber, and two doctors. Captain Christopher Newport was in charge of the expedition.

The Jamestown Landing

On May 14, 1607, 104 colonists landed on the coast of Virginia and began to set up camp. At first they lived in a tent camp, but within a month they completed construction of a large fort on the banks of the James River, which they named after King James I of England. By this time, seven leaders had been appointed: Christopher Newport, John Smith, John Ratcliffe, George Kendall, Edward Maria Wingfield, Bartholomew Gosnold, and John Martin. The council elected Wingfield as the colony's first president.

At first, things didn't go very well for the settlers. The water there made many of them sick, and some men died from their illnesses. They didn't have enough food to eat because many of the men didn't know how to farm or hunt. The summers were far hotter and the winters far colder than they were used to. And if all that wasn't enough, they had to deal with attacks from the Algonquian natives who lived in the area. Just eight months after the landing at Jamestown, only 38 of the original colonists were still alive.

King James I of England—in a painting from about 13 years after the Jamestown settlement was founded.

HISTORY MAKERS

John Ratcliffe was the captain of the *Discovery*, one of the three ships sent to settle the colony at Jamestown. Later, he became the second president of the colony. Ratcliffe died in December 1609 in an attack by Powhatan Indians.

INTERESTING!

Even though the Jamestown settlement was the first successful permanent English settlement in North America, it wasn't the first one attempted. In 1585 English settlers traveled to what is now Roanoke Island (near North Carolina). John White, the governor of the Roanoke colony, later returned to England for supplies, but when he returned in 1590, the settlers were gone. The settlement became known as The Lost Colony of Roanoke. To this day, no one knows what happened to the colonists.

Between January and October 1608, ships carrying several hundred more colonists from England arrived in Jamestown, and they found terrible conditions there. Not only that, a series of events made things even worse. On January 7, 1609, a fire broke out in the Jamestown fort, destroying many of the buildings, including the colony's first church. The fire also destroyed most of their provisions.

In September 1608, the Jamestown leaders elected John Smith as their new president, but Smith immediately had to deal with a bunch of very unhappy colonists. Many of them wanted to go back to England because they had to work so hard just to survive in the New World. Many others were disappointed that they couldn't find any gold in the area around the Jamestown colony.

Things got a lot worse for the Jamestown colonists during the winter of 1609–1610, which came to be known as Starving Time. Hostile natives surrounded the fort, which was already out of food. People who left the fort to try to find food died at the hands of the Native Americans, while the ones who stayed inside starved.

The mysterious word "Croatoan" was found carved in a post at the "Lost Colony" of Jamestown—but none of the more than 100 settlers were ever seen again.

When two ships, *Deliverance* and *Patience*, arrived, the people on board found only 60 starving survivors (out of about 500 colonists) in the ruins of the Jamestown fort.

On June 7 the survivors boarded the *Deliverance* and *Patience*—both of which had been built from the wreckage of a ship called *Sea Venture* that had run aground in a hurricane in Bermuda in July 1609—and got ready to head back to England. It looked like the end of the Jamestown settlement. But the two ships were stopped shortly after they left Jamestown and ordered to return and wait for Lord De La Warr, the newly appointed governor of Virginia, who was on his way with three ships filled with supplies. De La Warr arrived in Jamestown on June 10, 1610—just in time to save the remaining colonists' lives and persuade them not to give up and go home to England.

Jamestown's New "Cash Crop"

The arrival of the *Deliverance* and *Patience* came just at the right time. Not only did the ships carry food and other supplies the few survivors desperately needed, it also brought a man named John Rolfe, whose experiments with tobacco gave the settlement a crop that they could sell back to England and trade with the Native Americans.

Life remained very difficult in Jamestown after Rolfe's arrival. The people in the settlement had tried several ways to support themselves, but none of them had worked. Meanwhile, the Virginia Company kept sending more money and people to try to help.

Rolfe began growing tobacco in Virginia in 1612. The natives had already been growing tobacco there, but the colonists didn't like it. Rolfe planted a variety he had discovered in Bermuda and had sold in large quantities to English merchants.

Around the time Rolfe began growing tobacco in Virginia, he also met Pocahontas, the daughter of Powhatan, the Indian chief who had led his people to attack the colonists. Rolfe first met Pocahontas after some colonists kidnapped her and offered to trade her for English prisoners

HISTORY MAKERS

Alexander Whitaker (1585–1616) was a Christian minister who became known as The Apostle of Virginia. In 1611 Whitaker arrived at the Virginia Colony, where he established the first Presbyterian congregation. He also taught the Indian tribes in the area about Jesus and brought many of the natives to the Christian faith. His most famous convert was Pocahontas, who was baptized and given the English name Rebecca. By 1616 there were enough Native American Christians that the Virginia Company built Henrico College, which taught the Indians to read the Bible.

Freshly planted tobacco grows in modern-day Kentucky.

held by Powhatan. But the trade never happened. Instead, Pocahontas was taken to an English settlement, where she learned English and became a Christian. Rolfe married Pocahontas in the spring of 1614.

Rolfe's experiments with tobacco gave the colonists the cash crop they needed to survive, and that resulted in the growth and expansion of the Virginia Colony. Rolfe's marriage to Pocahontas led to peace between the Indians and colonists, which allowed the settlement to grow. Between 1618 and 1623, thousands of new settlers, hoping to get rich growing and selling tobacco, migrated to Virginia. During that time, the population of the Jamestown settlement grew to about 4,500 people. ✖

THE WEDDING OF POCAHONTAS.
With John Rolf

CHAPTER 2

The Colonial Era

The Pilgrims, the Puritans,
and Other English Colonists

Between 1607 and 1733, England established 13 colonies on the Atlantic coast of North America. Those colonies were Connecticut, Delaware, Georgia, Maryland, Massachusetts Bay, New Hampshire, New Jersey, New York, North Carolina, Pennsylvania, Rhode Island, South Carolina, and Virginia.

Even though all of these colonies belonged to England, each developed its own government, economy, and way of life. As you'll see, life was difficult at first for the people who lived in these colonies. But they kept their faith in God, kept working hard, and eventually established the first 13 states of the United States of America.

Who Were the Pilgrims?

By the early seventeenth century, many Christians in England were unhappy with the Church of England. During a historic event in the sixteenth century called the Protestant Reformation, the Church of England had broken away from the Catholic Church and made a lot of changes.

For some Christians though, the changes in the Church of England, the country's official church at the time, didn't go far enough. One group of Christians who were most unhappy with the Church of England was the Pilgrims. (They were also called Separatists because they wanted to separate from the Church of England.)

Another group of Christians who were unhappy with the church were the Puritans. The Puritans wanted the Church of England to stop using some of the practices used by the Catholic Church and to start worshipping God the way they believed the Bible said to do it. They were called Puritans because they wanted to *purify* the Church of England from all the influences of the Catholic Church.

The Pilgrims were different from the Puritans because they didn't believe the Church of England would ever change. The Pilgrims gave up hope after King James I refused to allow them to conduct their worship services the

WHAT THE MAYFLOWER COMPACT SAID

In the name of God, Amen. We, whose names are under-written, the loyal subjects of our dread sovereign Lord, King James, by the grace of God, of Great Britain, France, and Ireland, King, Defender of the Faith, etc.

Having undertaken, for the glory of God, and advancement of the Christian faith, and honor of our King and Country, a voyage to plant the first colony in the northern parts of Virginia; do by these presents, solemnly and mutually in the presence of God and one of another, covenant and combine ourselves together into a civil body politic, for our better ordering and preservation, and furtherance of the ends aforesaid; And by virtue hereof to enact, constitute, and frame, such just and equal laws, ordinances, acts, constitutions and offices, from time to time, as shall be thought most meet and convenient for the general good of the Colony; unto which we promise all due submission and obedience.

In witness whereof we have hereunto subscribed our names at Cape Cod the eleventh of November, in the reign of our sovereign Lord, King James, of England, France, and Ireland, the eighteenth, and of Scotland the fifty-fourth. Anno Domini, 1620.

way they believed the Bible instructed them. Not only that, but King James said that all church congregations—including the Puritans—must run their services the way the Church of England told them to (or it would lead to the death penalty). The Pilgrims decided that their only choice was to leave England.

Off to the New World... But First...

At first, a group of Separatists left England and traveled to Holland, where they stayed for several years. But soon they decided to leave Holland because they wanted their children to grow up English, not Dutch. They knew England had claimed territories in North America, so they made plans to sail across the Atlantic Ocean and start a colony.

After a difficult time of negotiations with the Virginia Company of London, the Pilgrims were given some land in North America. On September 6, 1620, a group of about 100 Pilgrims boarded the *Mayflower,* a 180-ton sailing ship, and set sail from Plymouth, England. About two months later, they landed near what is now Cape Cod, Massachusetts. The people on the *Mayflower* had intended to sail to the mouth of the Hudson River, but the leaders of the voyage decided to land farther north.

Not all of the colonists traveling on the *Mayflower* were members of the congregation that was starting the new colony. When the *Mayflower* landed in Massachusetts instead of New York, the agreed-upon landing spot, some of the people declared that no one on the ship could tell them what to do. In response to this minor rebellion, the leaders on the *Mayflower* wrote a now-famous document called the

Mayflower Compact, which said that everyone would agree to cooperate and do what was best for the new colony. On November 11, 1620, with the *Mayflower* anchored in the harbor at Cape Cod, 41 of the ship's passengers—all men— signed the Mayflower Compact, which established the laws that everyone in the new colony had to follow.

That same day, the *Mayflower* finally landed at Plymouth, where they would soon face a terrible first winter as colonists in the New World. A man named John Carver, who had worked to charter the *Mayflower*, and who was one of the most respected members of the group, was chosen the first governor of the Plymouth Colony.

The Pilgrims' first year at Plymouth was very difficult. Nearly half the settlers died of disease. But life slowly and steadily began to improve for the people who survived. The Pilgrims were able to make peace with the Indian tribes around them, which allowed them to begin making a living through farming, fishing, and trading with other people. No one got rich farming or fishing, but those pursuits allowed the people to take care of themselves without help from England after only five years.

HISTORY MAKERS

William Bradford (1590–1657), who was born in Yorkshire, England, and traveled to New England on the *Mayflower,* was the second governor of Plymouth Colony. He took that position after the death of John Carver in 1621 and served most of the rest of his life. He wrote the well-known *History of Plimoth Plantation*, which contains important historic accounts of the Plymouth Colony.

The Massachusetts Bay Colony

In 1630, about 10 years after the Pilgrims left Holland to form the Plymouth Colony, another group—the Puritans— left England to start a new colony in North America. They also came to what is now the state of Massachusetts, and they started a settlement called the Massachusetts Bay Colony.

Like the Pilgrims, the Puritans wanted to be able to worship God without interference from the Church of England. At first, the Puritans wanted to "purify" the Church of England from within. The English government didn't want the church to change, so it treated many Puritans very

WORTH REPEATING

"For we must consider that we shall be as a city upon a hill. The eyes of all people are upon us."
—From a sermon by John Winthrop to fellow Puritans on their way to Massachusetts

HISTORIC HAPPENINGS

Life was not easy for the Puritans living in Massachusetts during the colonial period. Probably the worst calamity the colonists faced was King Philip's War, which has also been called Metacom's Rebellion. It was a conflict between American Indians and inhabitants of the southern part of the New England colonies. It was named after Metacomet, the Native American leader, whom the English called King Philip. In April 1678, nearly two years after Metacomet died in battle, the war ended with the signing of a treaty at Casco Bay. Nearly half of the area's towns were destroyed, and its economy was nearly ruined. Many colonists died, including 10 percent of the men available to fight.

badly because of their beliefs and practices. Many Puritans died for what they believed in, and many more lost their businesses and homes.

One group of Puritans wanted to move away from England to live in a place where they could practice their religion without government interference or persecution. In 1629 England's new king, Charles I, issued a document called a charter, which gave the Puritans permission to move to North America and begin living and doing business there. This group of more than 1,000 Puritans was called the Massachusetts Bay Company, and its leader was John Winthrop.

In 1620 the Puritans of the Massachusetts Bay Company packed up their belongings and sailed for the New World. They landed near what is now Salem, Massachusetts, but they quickly moved to an area that is now part of Boston. The Puritans set up their own government and passed their own laws.

The first two years in the new settlement were difficult for the Puritans. About 400 people died during that time. But things started getting better, and more and more people moved to Massachusetts to join them. Ten years after the Puritans first landed, nearly 20,000 people lived in the colony. In time, the original settlement became several towns, including Newtown (now known as Cambridge), Lexington, Concord, Watertown, Charlestown, and many others.

As time went on, the settlers in the Massachusetts Bay Colony wanted more control over their own lives and less interference from England. King Charles II didn't want the colonists to be completely free to govern themselves, so in 1684 he canceled the Massachusetts Bay Company's charter. In 1691 England's King William III issued a new charter that unified the Massachusetts Bay Colony with the Plymouth Colony and other territories. The English government controlled the new colony, which was called the Province of Massachusetts Bay.

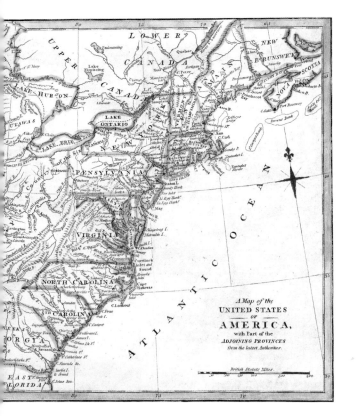

A Map of the
UNITED STATES
OF
AMERICA,
with Part of the
ADJOINING PROVINCES
from the latest Authorities

HISTORY MAKERS

John Wheelwright (1592–1679) was the brother-in-law of Anne Hutchinson, who was banished from the Massachusetts Bay Colony because she wanted people to be able to worship God the way they wanted. Wheelwright was also banished from Massachusetts because he spoke out to defend his sister-in-law. After he founded the Exeter settlement, the settlers there signed the Exeter Compact, which was a lot like the Mayflower Compact.

INTERESTING!

Maryland got its name when King Charles I of England instructed Lord Baltimore to name the colony after Queen Henrietta Maria (Queen Mary), King Charles's wife.

Two Down, 11 to Go!

Over the next 112 years after the founding of the Massachusetts Colony, 11 more colonies that would one day become states were founded. Here is a quick look at those 11 colonies:

New Hampshire: In 1623 a group of English settlers arrived in northern New England and started a fishing village near the mouth of the Piscataqua River. In 1638 a settler named John Wheelwright, who had been banished from the Massachusetts Bay Colony because he didn't want to follow their laws and rules, founded a settlement in New Hampshire called Exeter. Massachusetts controlled this new colony until it became a colony of England in 1679.

Maryland: In 1632 King Charles I of England gave Lord Baltimore (his real name was George Calvert) land where Catholics could live and worship as they wanted. Lord Baltimore put his son, Cecil Calvert, in charge of starting settlements in the new colony. In 1633 the first settlers left England and sailed to what became the Maryland Colony.

Connecticut: In the mid-1630s, colonists began moving to the Colony of Connecticut, established by Thomas Hooker, who had left the Massachusetts Bay Colony because he didn't like the strict rules there. In 1639 three settlements united to form a government in Connecticut. They also created a document called the Fundamental Orders of Connecticut, the first written constitution (or set of rules to live by) in American history. Many historians believe the Fundamental Orders became the basis of the United States Constitution. In 1662 King Charles II of England officially united Connecticut as a single colony.

Rhode Island: The Puritan leaders in the Massachusetts Bay Colony were very strict with the colonists who lived there. The people were required to worship God in the way these leaders thought was right. A young minister named Roger Williams (about 1603–about 1683) disagreed with the strict rules and spoke out against them. In 1636, a year after the Puritans forced Williams to leave the Massachusetts Bay Colony, he started a new settlement near modern-day Providence, Rhode Island. Two years later, Anne Hutchinson, who had also been expelled from Massachusetts, helped form a colony at Portsmouth. Later, the Rhode Island colony was formed from these and two other settlements.

Delaware: In 1631 Dutch traders attempted to settle in a coastal area east of Maryland, but they were killed in fights with the local natives. In 1638 a man named Peter Minuit led a group of Swedish settlers to the Delaware River area. They named the settlement New Sweden. In 1655 Holland captured the land from the Swedish, but in 1664 the British defeated the Dutch and took control of the area. Delaware was part of Pennsylvania from 1682 until 1701. The people of Delaware elected a state assembly in 1704.

North Carolina and South Carolina: In 1653, a group of Virginia colonists traveled south and settled in a new area. Ten years later, King Charles II of England gave eight men permission to settle the area south of Virginia. These men created Carolina, which included the area settled in 1653. But in 1729, due to arguments among the people settled in the area, England took over the colony and split it into North Carolina and South Carolina.

New Jersey: Not long after Henry Hudson explored the mid-Atlantic coastline of North America, Dutch and Swedish settlers started arriving there. The Dutch named their part of the territory New Netherland, and the Swedish named their part New Sweden. In 1664 the Dutch and Swedes surrendered control of the area to England. That same year, King Charles II of England granted control of the area to his brother James, the Duke of York. James gave land to two of his friends, Lord Berkeley and Sir George Carteret, and they founded a colony that, in 1702, became the New Jersey Colony.

New York: In 1664 Charles II granted the Dutch colony of New Netherland to his brother, the Duke of York. All the duke had to do was take control away from the Dutch. When the British fleet arrived, the Dutch colonists surrendered without a fight. The British renamed the area (as well as the city of New Amsterdam) New York in honor of the Duke of York.

Pennsylvania: This colony was named after its founder, William Penn, the leader of a group of Christians called the Religious Society of Friends, or Quakers. The Quakers, like the Puritans, had been persecuted by the English, and many of them wanted to start a colony in America. Penn, who was the son of a British Navy admiral, founded the colony in 1682, and it quickly grew into one of the largest British colonies in the New World.

Georgia: Fifty years after the founding of the Pennsylvania Colony, the last of the 13 British colonies was formed. In 1732 a British general and member of Parliament named James Oglethorpe received permission from King George II to create a new settlement between South Carolina and Florida. In 1733 Oglethorpe led a group of settlers in founding the city of Savannah in the colony he named in honor of the king. Georgia became a British colony in 1752.

HISTORY MAKERS

Jonathan Edwards (1703–1758) was an American preacher and Bible expert who also worked as a missionary to Native Americans. His preaching led to a spiritual awakening in the colonies. His most famous sermon was titled "Sinners in the Hands of an Angry God." Edwards was born in East Windsor, Connecticut. He entered Yale University in the fall of 1716, a month before his thirteenth birthday, and graduated in 1720 as the top student in his class.

Spiritual Revival in the Colonies

In the 1730s and 1740s, the powerful preaching of men such as Jonathan Edwards, George Whitefield, and many others led to a revival in the colonies. This revival—in which many people became interested in spiritual things—became known as the First Great Awakening. (There were three "great awakenings" in US history.)

The First Great Awakening started with the preaching of Edwards, who was a minister in Northampton, Massachusetts, and one of the best-known preachers of the time. Edwards preached about sin and the need for salvation through Jesus Christ. A lot of colonists came to hear Edwards preach, and many of them became Christians as a result.

Other preachers began to copy Edwards's style, and some traveled around the colonies to preach. It wasn't long before the Great Awakening affected people all the way from northern New England down to Georgia. People from all walks of life—rich and poor, educated and uneducated, free and slave—either converted to Christianity or began to take their faith more seriously.

WORTH REPEATING

"It was wonderful to see the change soon made in the manners of our inhabitants. From being thoughtless or indifferent about religion, it seemed as if all the world were growing religious, so that one could not walk through the town in an evening without hearing psalms sung in different families of every street."
—Benjamin Franklin, on the effect of George Whitefield's preaching on the colonies

In 1739 and 1740, George Whitefield, a young British preacher, traveled to North America and began touring the colonies, preaching and teaching. Whitefield's preaching style was very different from Jonathan Edwards's. While Edwards spoke slowly and in a serious tone, Whitefield spoke with more emotion and outward enthusiasm. His preaching attracted huge crowds everywhere he went, and countless people were converted to the Christian faith because of it.

The First Great Awakening was an important event in the history of the colonies that became the United States of America. It changed the way a lot of churches worshipped God, and it also brought Christianity to the African American slaves living and working in the colonies. It also led to what is called the evangelical movement, which emphasized the importance of spreading the message of the Gospel of Jesus Christ to people who hadn't heard it or didn't yet understand it.

Life in the Colonies

After reading about the founding of the 13 colonies, you might be wondering what life was like for the colonists. Well, a lot of that depended on which colony they lived in. The 13 colonies were established up and down

the east coast of North America, and each colony had its own churches, local government, and ways of making a living.

Many historians divide the colonies into three geographical areas: the New England colonies (New Hampshire, Massachusetts, Rhode Island, and Connecticut), the middle colonies (New York, New Jersey, Pennsylvania, and Delaware), and the southern colonies (Maryland, Virginia, North Carolina, South Carolina, and Georgia).

The New England colonies were located in the North, where there were lots of forests as well as animals whose skins were valuable for trade. There were also a lot of rivers and harbors in the region, making it easier to ship goods to and from other countries and other colonies. Many New England colonists made their living by fishing,

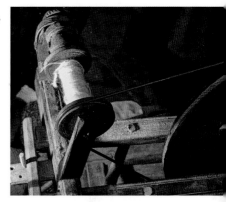

shipbuilding, harvesting trees for lumber, and fur trading. (The colonists often traded for furs with the Native Americans and shipped them overseas.) The soil in much of New England is rocky and therefore not very good for farming. For the most part, the farms in that area were big enough to provide for individual families, but too small to raise enough grain, vegetables, and fruit to trade with others.

The middle colonies enjoyed a good climate as well as good soil, and that allowed the colonists to make a living by farming. The farmers in the middle colonies planted and harvested grain and raised livestock for meat. The people of the middle colonies were known for making bread out of the grain the farmers harvested. There was a wide

variety of jobs in the middle colonies. People farmed or worked as tailors, glassblowers, silversmiths, and masons (stone and brick layers).

Of the three regions of colonies, the South was by far the best for farming. Those colonies were located on rich farmland that enjoyed excellent weather and long growing seasons. The people of the southern colonies grew most of their own food and also produced major cash crops such as tobacco, rice, and indigo (a plant that makes a bluish-purple dye)—none of which could be grown very well (if at all) in England. That is why the southern colonies did so much business with England. Most of these crops were grown on large farms called plantations, and the farmers usually used slaves to do the work. (You'll read more about slavery and how it divided the nation in Chapters 4 and 5).

Even though different colonies faced their own problems as they grew in size, one thing was true for all 13: Life was hard! The towns and villages weren't as well established as the ones in England that the people had come from; and just making it day to day was often a life-and-death struggle against the weather, disease, and hostile Native Americans.

But England was about to make things even worse for many of the colonists.

A Changing Relationship between England and Its Colonies

For the most part, the residents of the 13 colonies saw themselves as loyal subjects of the English king. But that was about to change, due mostly to the effects of the French and Indian War. Here's what happened:

INTERESTING!

The Liberty Bell, which was made in 1752 and is now on display at Independence Hall in Philadelphia, has long been a symbol of American independence. The bell was inscribed with part of a Bible verse from Leviticus 25:10: "Proclaim liberty throughout all the land unto all the inhabitants thereof." The Liberty Bell was originally used to call lawmakers to legislative sessions and to let citizens know about public meetings and proclamations.

During colonial times, England's main military rival was France. Eventually, England and France argued about ownership of the Ohio Territory and parts of Canada. When the dispute could not be settled by diplomacy (talks between national leaders), it was only a matter of time until war broke out between the British and the French.

It looked like the English would quickly and easily defeat the French. After all, they had a better-trained and better-equipped military. They also had the colonies, each of which had its own group of citizens who served in the army, known as the militia. However, the French had built a series of forts west of the Appalachian Mountains. One of those forts, Fort Duquesne, was located where Pittsburgh, Pennsylvania, is today.

In 1754 Lieutenant Colonel George Washington of the Virginia militia led a force of 150 soldiers in an effort to capture Fort Duquesne. Washington's men were badly outnumbered and were soon defeated by the French soldiers. Later, Washington was captured, but he was allowed to return to Virginia with a message telling the British that the Ohio Territory belonged to the French.

In early July 1755, the British sent General Edward Braddock, their commander-in-chief for North America, along with George Washington and many soldiers, to attack Fort Duquesne.

But the French, along with their Native American allies, won in a rout and General Braddock was killed in the battle. The French won because they fired from behind rocks and trees and other cover while the English troops marched in a straight line.

After the disastrous attack on Fort Duquesne, the British changed their strategy. They decided to fight the French in Canada instead. In 1763 after several years of fierce fighting in several big battles, Britain and France signed the Treaty of Paris, which stipulated that France would give up all claims to Canadian territories and the territory west of the colonies as far as the Mississippi River.

Who's Going to Pay for This War?

When the French and Indian War ended with England victorious, it was a relief to many people living in the 13 colonies. Great Britain's victory meant the British could keep Canada and several other territories in North America, and it also meant that the colonists didn't have to worry anymore about being taken over by the French.

But the colonists soon had another problem: To pay for the war effort, the British had gone into overwhelming debt. And because the war had been fought mostly to protect the American colonies, the British decided it was only right for the colonists, whom they still saw as their loyal subjects, to pay off that debt.

To help pay off its debt from the French and Indian War, the British government imposed sometimes steep taxes on the American colonies—and always without approval from the colonists.

Great Britain took in a lot of tax money from the colonists, who grew angrier and angrier because they were being taxed so heavily but couldn't do anything about it because they weren't represented in the British Parliament, which made the laws in England. They said it was "taxation without representation."

HISTORY MAKERS

James Otis Jr. (1725-1783) was a lawyer in colonial Massachusetts and a member of the Massachusetts Legislature. Otis strongly supported the political views that eventually led to the American Revolution. Even though others had used the phrase "taxation without representation" before Otis, he is remembered for saying, "Taxation without representation is tyranny." Tyranny is the mean and unfair treatment of a weaker person or country by a stronger one.

Here are some of those taxes (and other laws imposed by England) and how they affected the colonists:

Sugar Act: This 1764 law imposed a three-cent tax on foreign refined sugar and also increased taxes on coffee, indigo, and certain kinds of wine. It also banned the importation of rum and French wines into the colonies. These taxes didn't affect the general population in the colonies, but they were imposed without the colonists' consent.

Stamp Act: This was the first direct British tax on American colonists. Imposed in November 1765, it required every newspaper, pamphlet, and other public and legal document to carry a British seal or stamp, which cost money. The colonists protested the tax, and the British government repealed (or canceled) it in 1766. At the time of the repeal, though, the British passed another law, the Declaratory Act, which said that Great Britain was superior to, and held rule over, the American colonies.

HISTORY MAKERS

John Dickinson (1732–1808), a politician from Pennsylvania, became known as the "Penman of the Revolution" after his pamphlet *Letters from a Farmer in Pennsylvania*, which protested the Quartering Act, was printed and distributed throughout the colonies. Here are some words from that pamphlet:

If the British Parliament has a legal authority to issue an order that we shall furnish a single article for the troops here and compel obedience to that order, they have the same right to issue an order for us to supply those troops with arms, clothes, and every necessary, and to compel obedience to that order also; in short, to lay any burdens they please upon us. What is this but taxing us at a certain sum and leaving to us only the manner of raising it? How is this mode more tolerable than the Stamp Act?

Quartering Act: In March 1765, the British Parliament passed a law to address the needs of British soldiers who had been sent to the colonies to keep the peace. The law required each colonial assembly

to provide British soldiers housing (or "quarters"), bedding, and other necessities of life. Parliament expanded this to require the colonies to house soldiers in taverns and unoccupied houses. The colonists opposed this act because they were afraid of having the British army in all their towns and villages, and because they were having to pay to care for the British soldiers. Even though it wasn't a direct tax on the colonists, the Quartering Act cost the colonists a lot of money.

Townshend Acts: This was a series of 1767 laws, named for Charles Townshend, the British treasurer, that imposed new taxes on glass, lead, paints, paper, and tea. The colonists reacted to these new taxes the same way they did to the Sugar Act and Stamp Act. Eventually Britain repealed all the taxes except the tax on tea.

The British Parliament's new laws and new taxes on the 13 colonies served only to anger and frustrate the colonists as time went on. The final straw came on May 10, 1773, when Parliament passed the Tea Act. Even though the Tea Act didn't impose any new taxes on the colonists, it hurt colonial businessmen because it meant that more British tea would be shipped to the colonies and sold at lower prices.

HISTORIC HAPPENINGS

On March 5, 1770, five civilians died and several others were wounded when British soldiers opened fire on a gathering in Boston, Massachusetts. Both sides disputed the cause of the shootings, which came to be known as the Boston Massacre, but the violence helped spark a rebellion in some of the colonies and eventually led to the Revolutionary War.

The colonists had agreed not to buy things they had previously bought from English traders (an act called a boycott), including clothes, paper, and tea. But on December 16, 1773, a group of colonists, some dressed up as Native Americans, showed the British how serious they were about taxation without representation (and how much they disliked the Tea Act) when they boarded three English ships docked in Boston Harbor and threw their cargo of tea overboard.

This incident is known today as the Boston Tea Party, and it led to a series of new British laws that moved the colonists and the British military closer to war. ✖

CHAPTER 3

The Birth of the United States

The Revolutionary War through George Washington's Presidency

After the French and Indian War, the relationship between the 13 colonies and England began a fast downward spiral, as England continued to impose laws and levy taxes on the colonists without allowing them to be represented in Parliament.

The tension finally reached a boiling point after the Boston Tea Party. As one incident followed another, it began to appear that it was only a matter of time before military conflict broke out in North America.

In this chapter, you'll read about the last few events that led to the Revolutionary War—also known as the War for Independence. You'll also read about how the colonists won their independence in a David-and-Goliath-type war against a better-armed, more experienced British military. And you'll also read about how the newly formed United States, after some struggles, finally established its own government.

We're Not Gonna Take It Anymore!

The British government responded to the Boston Tea Party by passing several new laws meant to punish the colonists. One of those laws completely shut down Boston Harbor until the colonists had paid for the tea they had dumped into the water. Some of the new laws took away the colonists' freedom and required that they get permission from the British government before they held any public meetings. The British government also greatly limited the power of the individual colonies' legislatures (the groups that make laws).

The colonists referred to these new laws as "intolerable acts," and they became convinced they needed to take strong steps to protect themselves and their freedoms. To do that, 56 delegates representing the 13 colonies gathered in Philadelphia on September 5, 1774, for a meeting of the First Continental Congress. For the first time, the 13 colonies worked together to protect their individual freedoms and liberties.

WORTH REPEATING

"Is life so dear, or peace so sweet, as to be purchased at the price of chains and slavery? Forbid it, Almighty God! I know not what course others may take; but as for me, give me liberty or give me death!"
—Patrick Henry, a Virginia politician and Founding Father of the United States

HISTORY MAKERS

In 1750 a Virginia physician and explorer named Thomas Walker discovered the Cumberland Gap, a pass through the Appalachian Mountains long used by Native Americans. In 1775 as war between the colonies and England grew near, a Pennsylvanian-born frontiersman named Daniel Boone (1734–1820) was busy blazing his Wilderness Road along a trail through the Cumberland Gap. Boone and a team of 35 axmen widened the trail, making it possible for later pioneers to journey through the Appalachians from Virginia to Kentucky and Tennessee.

The First Continental Congress didn't waste much time before declaring at least some independence from England. It passed a resolution limiting the power of the British Parliament, including a declaration that Parliament would no longer be allowed to pass laws for the colonies. Parliament's right, as far as the colonies were concerned, would be only to regulate trade between the colonies and England. Finally, the Congress resolved that by December 1774, the colonies would no longer buy anything from Great Britain; and by September 1775, they would stop shipping goods to England.

Getting Ready for War

Many, if not most, of the colonists suffered because of what was happening between the 13 colonies and Great Britain, but the people in Boston had it far worse than others. After the English navy closed Boston Harbor, Boston merchants could no longer trade with other nations. Many colonists in Boston lost their jobs. Even worse, Great Britain sent huge numbers of soldiers to Boston, and the people there were expected to feed and house them.

By April 1775, tensions between the British and the colonists were very high, and some of the 13 colonies had already begun assembling volunteer armies to defend themselves if the British attacked.

Meanwhile, Great Britain ordered the Massachusetts governor to send troops to Boston to take away all the people's weapons and ammunition. Since the British military was the best trained and strongest in the world at that time, they expected little resistance when they marched into Boston.

What the British didn't know, however, was that the colonists were ready to fight. They had gathered a group of volunteer soldiers, called "minutemen" for their ability to assemble on a minute's notice. These farmers, shopkeepers, and common workers would immediately respond to any threat from the British.

The Battles of Lexington and Concord

On the night of April 18, 1775, about 700 British soldiers (also called Redcoats for the color of their uniforms), under the command of Lieutenant Colonel Francis Smith, marched from Boston toward Concord, where the colonists had hidden weapons and ammunition.

There were two things Smith and his men didn't know: First, weeks before the march, the militiamen had learned of the plan to capture their supplies and had moved them to other hiding places. Second, the militiamen knew about the planned attack, and they were able to mobilize quickly as the British troops drew near Concord.

Late that night, a silversmith named Paul Revere, and several other men on horseback, spotted the British soldiers as they marched toward Concord. The men rode out ahead of the advancing army to warn the militias, shouting, "The Redcoats are coming! The Redcoats are coming!" The warning gave the minutemen all the time they needed to prepare to stand up to the British soldiers.

The first shots of the Revolutionary War were fired near Lexington, Massachusetts, at sunrise on the morning of April 19, 1775. The minutemen

INTERESTING!

Even though Paul Revere became the most famous of the men who rode their horses through the countryside warning the colonists that the British were on their way, he actually never made it to Concord. Instead, he was captured by the Redcoats, who released him after he gave them a lot of false or misleading information. One of Revere's companions, a man named Samuel Prescott, avoided capture and got the message through to Concord. When the British arrived, the colonists were ready.

HISTORIC HAPPENINGS

Sometimes historians can point to a single moment as the start of an armed conflict. The American Revolution is an example. At dawn on April 19, 1775, in Lexington, Massachusetts, 77 minutemen stood face-to-face with more than 700 Redcoats. Just then, someone's musket—no one knows for sure whose it was—went off. Within seconds, eight colonists were dead and nine wounded. The rest retreated, joined up with other militiamen, and chased the British toward Concord, where the battle continued. Just like that, the Revolutionary War had begun!

HISTORIC HAPPENINGS

In January 1776, a writer named Thomas Paine wrote a pamphlet he titled *Common Sense*, which outlined the reasons it was time for the colonies to declare their independence from Great Britain and form their own nation. Many colonists read Paine's pamphlet, and thousands came to the same conclusion: It was time to break away from Great Britain. The pamphlet also changed the opinions of some colonial leaders who believed it was still possible for the colonies to settle their differences with Great Britain without going to war.

were heavily outnumbered and had to retreat at first, and the British troops continued their march toward Concord.

At the North Bridge in Concord, 500 minutemen attacked and defeated the British soldiers. Historians say this could have turned into a massacre had reinforcements not arrived as the British retreated and began heading back toward Lexington. About 1,700 British soldiers now began their march back to Boston, but they came under heavy fire from the militias. Eventually, the British troops made it to safety in Charlestown, Massachusetts.

Meanwhile, the militiamen surrounded Boston, preventing the British army from moving in and out of the city. After an 11-month period, called the Siege of Boston, the British were forced to withdraw from the town completely.

For the British, who believed their military was the finest in the world, the defeats in the battles of Lexington and Concord, as well as their retreat from Boston following the Siege of Boston, were embarrassing and humiliating. For the colonists, though, they were encouraging signs that they could stand up to the greatest military force in the world and come out victorious.

Extending an Olive Branch

Even though shots had been exchanged between the colonists and the British troops, and even though people on both sides had been wounded or killed, the two sides had not yet engaged in all-out war. In an effort to avoid war—and to prepare for it, if it was unavoidable—the Second Continental Congress began meeting in May 1775.

The Congress formed the American Continental Army, which coordinated the efforts of the militias of the 13 colonies. It also took additional steps to move the colonies toward independence from Great Britain. Though it had no formal authority, the Continental Congress acted as the national government of what would become the United States of America.

Some of the more radical members of the Second Continental Congress, led by John Adams, a representative from Massachusetts, believed it wasn't possible to avoid a full-blown war. But in July 1775, the Congress passed a resolution, written by John Dickinson of Pennsylvania and known as the Olive Branch Petition, which stated that the colonies did not want to go to war and were not seeking to become independent. They sent a written copy to King George III.

King George refused to even read the petition. Instead, he declared that the colonies had engaged in open rebellion against the king and against Great Britain.

King George III's refusal to even read the Olive Branch Petition pushed the colonies toward a choice between two options: They could either surrender unconditionally and remain subjects of Great Britain, or they could go to war to win their independence. Samuel Adams, a member of the Continental Congress, believed that King George had given the colonies an opportunity to make their push for independence from England.

There was still an opportunity for the colonies to avoid all-out war with Great Britain, but that opportunity ended in the summer of 1776, when the Continental Congress established a new nation called the United States of America.

WORTH REPEATING

"Believe me, dear sir: there is not in the British Empire a man who more cordially loves a union with Great Britain than I do. But, by the God that made me, I will cease to exist before I yield to a connection such terms as the British Parliament propose; and in this, I think I speak the sentiments of America."
—Thomas Jefferson, November 29, 1775

INTERESTING!

Although the Second Continental Congress approved the final wording of the Declaration of Independence on July 4, 1776, the actual date of its signing by the delegates from the 13 colonies isn't certain. Most historians believe the delegates signed it on August 2, 1776, a month after it was adopted.

The Declaration of Independence

Have you ever thought about what the July 4 holiday we celebrate every summer really means? If you're like a lot of Americans, you know it's a time when families and friends get together for picnics during the day and flashy, noisy fireworks displays after dark.

You probably know that the real name of the holiday is Independence Day. This is the day we celebrate and remember what some very courageous and motivated Americans did on July 4, 1776. On that day, the Second Continental Congress formally adopted the Declaration of Independence, which was a letter to King George III of England stating that the 13 colonies would no longer be part of the British Empire and also explaining why they had declared their independence.

The Continental Congress gave a highly educated Virginian named Thomas Jefferson the responsibility of writing a declaration of independence that would be sent to Great Britain once it was finished. After Jefferson finished writing the declaration, and after the Continental Congress officially approved it, a new, independent nation was born.

What's Really in the Declaration of Independence?

The Declaration of Independence begins by stating that sometimes it becomes necessary for one group of people to break away from another—in this case, the colonies broke away from Great Britain—to form their own nation, which is in keeping with the laws and the nature of God. It then explains that it is necessary to explain why they are splitting off to become an independent nation.

The declaration includes one of the best-known statements about human freedom of any document in history: "We hold these truths to be self-evident, that all men are created equal, that they are endowed by their Creator with certain unalienable rights, that among these are life, liberty, and the pursuit of happiness." The declaration says that when any human government gets in the way of those God-given rights, the people have the right to either make changes in the government or get rid of it completely.

The declaration presents a long list of the 13 colonies' complaints against King George III. Here are some highlights of that list, put in words that are easier to understand than the original:

The king won't allow us to pass laws that are for the good of everyone who lives here.

Even when the king allows us to pass laws, he won't allow us to put them into effect.

The king forces us to give up our rights to make the laws we need.

The king calls lawmakers to meet at the most inconvenient times, and in distant places, so that they can't show up to pass the laws.

The king takes away our rights by dissolving our representative bodies.

The king won't allow us to elect new representatives.

The king won't allow new settlers to come to America, or he puts difficult conditions on their immigration.

The king refuses to allow us to appoint our own judges, but instead appoints judges who always agree with him.

The king sends us new government officials we don't want, and he makes us pay them.

INTERESTING!

Most of the Founding Fathers of the United States were Christian men who believed the Bible. Almost half of the 56 men who signed the Declaration of Independence—24 to be exact—had earned degrees in Bible school or seminary.

IN CONGRESS, JULY 4, 1776.

The unanimous Declaration of the thirteen united States of America.

INTERESTING!

A total of 56 men signed the Declaration of Independence. These men, along with others who took part in the Revolutionary War or the drafting of the United States Constitution, are called the Founding Fathers of the United States of America. The most famous of those signatures was that of John Hancock, the president of the Continental Congress, because he was the first man to sign and he signed his name so big. Among the signers were two future presidents of the United States: John Adams (second president) and Thomas Jefferson (third president). Here is the complete list of the signers, by their home states:

Delaware: George Read, Caesar Rodney, Thomas McKean

Pennsylvania: George Clymer, Robert Morris, Benjamin Rush, James Smith, George Taylor, Benjamin Franklin, John Morton, George Ross, James Wilson

Massachusetts: John Adams, John Hancock, Elbridge Gerry, Samuel Adams, Robert Treat Paine

New Hampshire: Josiah Bartlett, William Whipple, Matthew Thornton

Rhode Island: Stephen Hopkins, William Ellery

New York: Lewis Morris, Francis Lewis, Philip Livingston, William Floyd

Georgia: Button Gwinnett, Lyman Hall, George Walton

Virginia: Richard Henry Lee, Carter Braxton, Thomas Jefferson, Thomas Nelson Jr., Francis Lightfoot Lee, Benjamin Harrison, George Wythe

North Carolina: William Hooper, John Penn, Joseph Hewes

South Carolina: Edward Rutledge, Arthur Middleton, Thomas Lynch Jr., Thomas Heyward Jr.

New Jersey: Abraham Clark, Francis Hopkinson, John Witherspoon, John Hart, Richard Stockton

Connecticut: Samuel Huntington, William Williams, Roger Sherman, Oliver Wolcott

Maryland: Charles Carroll, Thomas Stone, Samuel Chase, William Paca

Even in times of peace, the king sends British soldiers here without our permission, and those soldiers don't even have to obey our laws.

The king forces us to buy goods from England, even goods we can buy somewhere else.

The king imposes taxes on us without giving us any choice.

The king won't allow us to try accused criminals by jury, but instead sends people accused of pretend crimes back to England for their trials.

The king does everything he can to destroy our lives, including burning down our towns.

The king sends foreign soldiers to bring death, destruction, and tyranny.

The king takes our fellow Americans against their will and forces them to fight against their own friends and family.

The king tries to get our own people to revolt against our government and tries to get Native Americans to attack us.

When we complain about how the king has treated us, he only treats us worse.

The Declaration of Independence concludes by stating that the United States would be a new and independent nation made up of free and independent states that would no longer be under the authority of the British crown and that they would have the power and authority to wage war, to make alliances and treaties with other nations, to trade with any nation they wanted to, and do everything else an independent nation has the right to do.

Copies of this new document called the Declaration of Independence were soon distributed throughout the

You can read the original words of the Declaration of Independence in Appendix B (page 153).

colonies, which served to make the people more determined to break free of British rule.

The signers of the declaration knew the terrible, personal risks they took by signing the document. They also knew the declaration ensured that there would be no peaceful solution to the differences between the colonies and King George III.

A Revolutionary War

When King George III learned that the colonies had declared their independence from Great Britain, he sent many more soldiers to the colonies to fight. The colonists didn't look like much of a match for the British, who had the most powerful military force in the world at that time.

The colonial forces had become more organized by then, however. On June 14, 1775, the Continental Congress established the Continental Army to help coordinate the efforts of the 13 colonies in their rebellion against the rule of Great Britain. The Continental Congress appointed General George Washington as commander of the Continental Army.

The war was very hard on all the colonies, and many times it looked as if the British were going to win. But under Washington's courageous leadership, the American soldiers fought on.

Even though the Continental Army was fighting a powerful enemy, it had one key advantage. The colonial soldiers were defending their own homeland, while most of the British soldiers had been shipped over from England. Though the British at first had superior military forces, the Americans began winning important battles as the war went on.

WORTH REPEATING

"Resistance to tyranny becomes the Christian and social duty of each individual. . . . Continue steadfast and, with a proper sense of your dependence on God, nobly defend those rights which heaven gave, and no man ought to take from us."
—John Hancock, first signer of the Declaration of Independence

King George III

Help...from Great Britain's European Neighbors

Early on in the war, France, Spain, and the Dutch Republic (now known as the Netherlands) sent supplies, weapons, and ammunition to the colonies, but none of them wanted to get involved directly in the war.

HISTORY MAKERS

Benjamin Franklin (1706–1790) was one of the Founding Fathers of the United States and a great statesman and diplomat. He was also a writer, scientist, and inventor. Franklin invented the lightning rod, bifocals, the Franklin stove, an odometer for horse-drawn carriages, and a musical instrument called a "glass armonica." Franklin made many discoveries about electricity and also formed America's first public lending library and a fire department in Pennsylvania. After his death on April 17, 1790, approximately 20,000 people attended his funeral.

After some early British success, the war became a standoff, meaning neither side was winning or losing. The British navy was far superior to anything the colonists could muster, so the British controlled the American coastline. The American patriots, on the other hand, controlled the countryside, where 90 percent of the population lived.

In 1778 France became an ally of the Americans. Most historians agree this key development was necessary if the colonies were to win their independence.

Not long after the Continental Congress adopted the Declaration of Independence, they appointed Benjamin Franklin as minister to France. Franklin asked the French for help in the war, but at first they were reluctant to enter into another war with England. Eventually however, Franklin persuaded the French to openly enter the war (it also didn't hurt that the French saw that the colonies were having success in the war), and on February 6, 1778, the Treaty of Alliance with France was signed. As part of the treaty, France provided transportation to America for French officers, soldiers, and weapons.

Over the next two years, Spain and the Dutch Republic also went to war with Great Britain. Even in England, many Britons sided with the Americans.

With all that help, especially from French general Lafayette and other French soldiers, the United States won several big battles against the British. Finally in August 1788, after a French naval victory over the British in Chesapeake Bay, the English formally surrendered to George Washington at Yorktown, Pennsylvania.

Key Battles in the Revolutionary War

Earlier, you read how the battles of Lexington and Concord marked the beginning of the Revolutionary War. Here are some other important battles in that war:

The Battle of Bunker Hill (June 17, 1775): Just

days after the Continental Congress named General George Washington commander-in-chief of the Continental Army, the British started this battle (which was actually fought at Breed's Hill) when British general William Howe led 2,600 soldiers up into battle in Boston. British warships also fired on the patriots. The Americans fought bravely but had to retreat after a third charge by the British. Though the Americans withdrew, the Redcoats suffered heavy losses in this battle.

The Battle of Long Island (August 27, 1776): This

was the first major battle following the Declaration of Independence. The British had just lost Boston, so they were determined to take control of New York City, which they knew was important to the colonies because it was a key point of communication between the North and the South. In April 1776, General Washington, anticipating the arrival of the British, began positioning about 20,000 troops at the western end of Long Island. The British fleet arrived with 45,000 troops, and when they attacked, Washington was forced to cross the East River into Manhattan. After several more battles, the British drove the Continental Army completely out of New York City.

The Battle of Trenton (December 25, 1776):

After being forced to retreat from New York, General Washington knew his troops needed a victory to boost their morale. So on a snowy, icy evening on Christmas 1776, he led 2,500 soldiers across the Delaware River to Trenton, New Jersey, where the Americans attacked a group

HISTORIC HAPPENINGS

If you've ever wondered how much difficulty the soldiers from the Continental Army faced as they fought to win freedom for America—including *your* freedom—consider what some of them endured during the winter of 1777–1778. During a cold, snowy Pennsylvania winter, General George Washington's men camped at Valley Forge, living in tents until they were able to build some huts for shelter. Though they struggled just to survive—most of the men did not have warm clothing or adequate shoes—they emerged a stronger army as a result. Throughout the winter, they worked to improve their fighting skills. When spring finally came, they were more experienced and more disciplined, and ready to take on the British army.

of British soldiers. The Americans caught the British soldiers completely by surprise—most of them were sleeping—and killed more than 100 men and took 1,000 prisoners. Not a single American was killed, and the victory gave the Americans a big boost in morale.

The Battle of Princeton (January 3, 1777): Fresh off their victory at Trenton, General Washington's troops defeated the British at the Battle of Princeton.

The Battles of Saratoga (September 19 and October 7, 1777): This was a major victory for the American forces and a turning point in the Revolutionary War. The Americans fought British general John Burgoyne's army at Saratoga, New York. By the time the battles were over, the Americans had killed 440 British soldiers, wounded 695 more, and taken 6,222 captive. News of this American victory encouraged France to join the colonists against the British.

The Battle of Yorktown (September 28 to October 19, 1781): This battle didn't officially end the Revolutionary War, but it was the last major skirmish. General George Washington and French general Jean-Baptiste Ponton de Rochambeau led a combined force of American and French soldiers into battle against the forces of British lieutenant general Charles Cornwallis in the battle at Yorktown, Virginia. The combined French and American forces routed the British, and the battle ended when Cornwallis surrendered on October 19, 1781. This was the beginning of the end of the Revolutionary War.

Peace Breaks Out in America

On September 3, 1783, the Treaty of Paris was signed, officially ending the war. The Treaty of Paris recognized the United States as an independent nation and granted it control of the territories bounded on the east by the Atlantic Ocean, on the north by what is now Canada, on the south by Florida, and on the west by the Mississippi River.

The Americans had fought bravely—against their British enemies as well as against sometimes terrible weather—and had come out victorious against a military force that by all rights should have defeated them easily. But win they did, and now it was time to get down to the business of forming a government and beginning life as a new nation—the United States of America.

The Articles of Confederation

As the Revolutionary War raged on, the Continental Congress wrote a document called the Articles of Confederation, which was intended to provide the colonies some sort of unified government. On March 1, 1781, about three years after the Americans won their independence from the British, the 13 colonies ratified the Articles of Confederation, meaning it was now the law of the land in the United States.

The Articles of Confederation made the states and their legislatures supreme and gave each state the right to pass and enforce its own laws and collect taxes. The central government of the United States, however, was very weak and had very little authority to oversee interactions between the states. There was no executive branch (meaning a president and a cabinet, like we have today) and only limited judicial functions. The federal (national) government had no authority to collect taxes of any kind, and as a result, the nation went into debt that it couldn't repay.

It wasn't long before the leaders of the United States realized that having such a weak central government was not good for the states or for the unity of the new nation. Efforts to strengthen the central government failed, so in May 1787, a convention of representatives, or delegates, from 12 of the 13 states (Rhode Island refused to send representatives because it didn't want to lose the rights it had as a state) gathered to draft an entirely new constitution.

The Constitutional Convention

More than 50 delegates from the 12 participating states met in Philadelphia in May 1787 to begin drafting a new constitution. This was a gathering of some of the best-educated and most experienced men in the United States. They ranged in age from 40 to 81

HOW OUR GOVERNMENT WORKS

When the Founding Fathers met in Philadelphia to draft the United States Constitution, they wanted to prevent any one person, or group of people, from having too much power. But they didn't want a weak federal government with no power at all, like it had been under the Articles of Confederation. To protect the rights and liberties of all American citizens, the new government was divided between three separate but equal branches: the executive branch (the president and his cabinet), the legislative branch (the Congress, which passes laws), and the judicial branch (the courts, which interpret and apply the laws that the Congress passes).

Here is a quick look at the three branches of the federal government and the roles they play:

The Executive Branch: The president of the United States is the head of this branch of government. The president's power to create laws is limited to providing leadership and developing policies. The president can suggest new laws, but can't pass them without the approval of Congress.

The Legislative Branch: Each state is represented in the legislative branch, also known as Congress, by two senators and a number of members of the House of Representatives, based on the population of the state. The Senate and the House work together to make the nation's laws, but they also give more balance to the federal government, because a bill must pass both houses of Congress before it can become law. Once Congress passes a bill, the president can either sign it into law or veto it—which means to keep it from becoming law.

The Judicial Branch: This branch of the federal government examines the laws Congress passes to see if they meet with the standards of the Constitution and to make sure they don't violate the rights of citizens. The judicial branch has several levels, and the United States Supreme Court has the final say about whether a law is constitutional.

(Benjamin Franklin was the oldest). Some were wealthy landowners, while others were lawyers or judges. One thing they had in common was that they had held at least one public office.

As the convention began, the delegates discussed and debated the problems the Articles of Confederation had presented. But as the convention wore on, they decided that it made more sense to create a whole new constitution and a whole new central government than it did to rewrite the Articles of Confederation.

On September 17, 1787, after about four months of debate, arguing, and compromise, the delegates signed the Constitution of the United States, making it the law of the United States of America and creating a new federal government that had more power than the confederation of states that it replaced.

Our First President

The United States Constitution established that the new nation would be led by a president—one whose powers are limited by the balance among the three branches of government—and not by a monarch (a king or queen). It also held that the president would not be elected by a popular vote of the people but by the state legislatures, which were elected by the people. This type of government is called a republic.

At first, not everyone could vote for the electors like we can today. Only white men who owned property were allowed to vote. On January 7, 1789, American voters chose their first state electors, who cast their votes for the first president of the United States.

Most people expected that George Washington, who had become a national hero when he led the Continental Army so brilliantly during the Revolutionary War, would easily win the election, and that is exactly what happened. Washington won unanimously, taking every elector's vote, and was sworn into office on April 30, 1789. John Adams was elected the nation's first vice president.

Washington was again elected unanimously in 1792, and John Adams was again elected vice president. Washington would almost certainly have won a third term, but he refused to run because he believed no man should have that much power for that long.

George Washington's Legacy

By now you probably know that George Washington was the most important of the Founding Fathers. He led the Continental Army to victory over the British, played a key role in the forming of the US Constitution, and served two terms as president.

Washington's presidency was one of the most important in US history. In 1791, during his first term in office, 10 amendments—also known as the Bill of Rights—were made to the US Constitution.

About four years after the Constitution was signed into law, James Madison—a representative for the state of Virginia and later the fourth president of the United States—introduced 10 amendments to limit the power of the federal government and protect the freedom of individual American citizens from the government and from the whims of the majority.

The first United States Congress passed the Bill of Rights on September 25, 1789, and they officially became a part of the Constitution on December 15, 1791, after two-thirds of the states ratified (officially approved) them.

George Washington's cabinet (or group of close advisers) included Secretary of State Thomas Jefferson (who wrote the Declaration of Independence and eventually became the third president of the United States), Secretary of the Treasury Alexander Hamilton (who was instrumental in designing the United States Constitution), Secretary of War Henry Knox (a high-ranking officer during the Revolutionary War), and Attorney General Edmund Randolph (one of the 11 delegates from Virginia in the 1779 Continental Congress). Historians remember Washington as a president who relied heavily on his cabinet for advice in domestic and foreign affairs alike.

INTERESTING!

A lot of things have changed since that first United States presidential election in 1789. For one thing, *all* American citizens age 18 and older have the right to vote in presidential elections. One thing that hasn't changed much is the process we use to elect our presidents. Presidential elections are still decided by what is called the Electoral College system, meaning that individual voters vote in their states for electors, who in turn vote for president.

WORTH REPEATING

"I walk on untrodden ground. There is scarcely any part of my conduct that may not hereafter be drawn into precedent."
—George Washington, after being elected to his first term as US president

INTERESTING!

Most people believe that George Washington wore false teeth made of wood. While it's true he had lost his natural teeth and had to wear false ones, his fake choppers weren't made of wood but of hippopotamus ivory and gold. They were made by Dr. John Greenwood, who came to be known as the "father of modern dentistry."

HISTORY MAKERS

Eli Whitney (1765-1825) was an American inventor who is best known for inventing the cotton gin, a mechanical device that removes seeds from cotton. Before Whitney invented the cotton gin in 1793, people had to remove cotton seeds by hand, which went very slowly. The cotton gin helped make cotton an important cash crop in the South, which in turn led to the growth of slavery in that part of the country. (By the way, the word *gin* is short for "engine.")

Washington stopped the first serious challenge to federal authority when he sent troops to suppress the Whiskey Rebellion of 1794, in which Pennsylvania farmers refused to pay a tax. (The Constitution says that the federal government has the right to collect taxes.)

When it came to relationships with other nations, Washington believed strongly in neutrality, meaning he believed the United States should not take sides and should stay out of other nations' wars. He was criticized when he declared the Proclamation of Neutrality in 1793 because many people believed he owed more support to France, which had been so helpful during the Revolutionary War. Washington restated his belief in neutrality during his Farewell Address in 1796, when he warned the United States against becoming involved in foreign conflicts. His words helped shape American foreign policy for many decades to come.

THE FIRST TEN AMENDMENTS TO THE US CONSTITUTION (THE BILL OF RIGHTS)

First Amendment—Guarantees freedom of religion, speech, and the press, as well as the right to assemble and petition (or make requests to) the government.

Second Amendment—Guarantees the right to keep and bear arms (guns).

Third Amendment—Prohibits the forced housing of soldiers during times of peace.

Fourth Amendment—Prohibits unreasonable searches and seizures and spells out requirements for search warrants.

Fifth Amendment—Lays out rules for how a person accused of a crime can be put on trial, protects people on trial from having to testify against themselves, and protects people from being put on trial twice for the same crime. Also, this amendment keeps the government from taking somebody's private property for public use without paying a fair price for it.

Sixth Amendment—Guarantees the right to a fair and speedy trial by jury, the right to confront your accuser, the right to have witnesses at your trial, and the right to have a lawyer help you at the trial.

Seventh Amendment—Guarantees the right to a trial by jury in certain noncriminal (civil) cases.

Eighth Amendment—Prohibits excessive fines, excessive bail, and cruel and unusual punishment.

Ninth Amendment—Protects rights and liberties not specifically mentioned in the Constitution.

Tenth Amendment—Limits the powers of the federal government to those given to it by the United States Constitution.

CHAPTER 4

A Young Nation's Growing Pains

The Westward Expansion of the United States

Before the Revolutionary

War, not many colonists made their way west to explore and settle the land west of the Appalachian Mountains. That's mostly because the Appalachians were difficult to pass.

Three things changed that. First, Daniel Boone blazed his Wilderness Road through the Cumberland Gap, making it easier for explorers and settlers to negotiate the rugged Appalachian terrain. Second, Great Britain and the newly formed United States signed the 1783 Treaty of Paris, which ended the Revolutionary War and gave the United States all land east to the Mississippi River. Finally, in 1787, the Continental Congress passed the

Northwest Ordinance, which encouraged Americans to settle in the Northwest Territory, which the United States acquired after winning the Revolutionary War and which included land that became the states of Ohio, Indiana, Illinois, Michigan, and Wisconsin.

With the war over, a new pass cleared over the mountains, and a lot of new land to explore and settle, it wasn't long before Americans began moving west to explore and settle previously unknown places. By 1810, an estimated 200,000 to 300,000 people had traveled the Wilderness Trail on their way to Kentucky and the Ohio Valley.

In this chapter, you'll learn about the westward expansion of the United States and about the difficulties these people, called *pioneers*, faced as they explored and settled in new territory. You will also learn about how the United States acquired territories in the West that later became US states.

America's Biggest Bargain: The Louisiana Purchase

By the turn of the nineteenth century (another way of saying the beginning of the 1800s), three more territories had joined the original 13 colonies as states: Vermont in 1791, Kentucky in 1792, and Tennessee in 1796. The population of the United States was growing very quickly, and many people began looking for still more land where they could raise their families and make a living.

The US government also wanted more land. Thomas Jefferson, the third president of the United States, knew that the Louisiana Territory, which France owned at the time, had a lot of land—as much as or more than the United States already had. It also included the Mississippi River and the city of New Orleans, an important port city at the

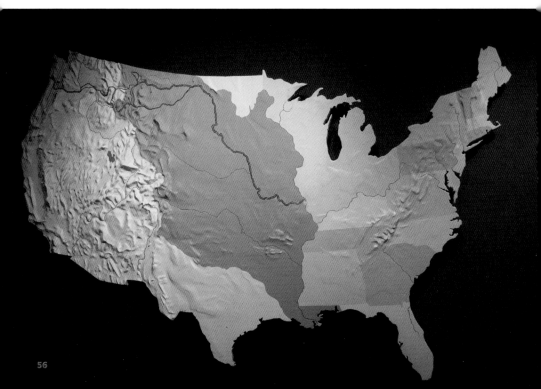

mouth of the Mississippi. Jefferson believed that making New Orleans part of the United States would make it easier to protect American shipping and settlements along the Mississippi.

Jefferson thought France might be willing to sell part of the Louisiana Territory. In 1802 he sent Robert Livingston, one of the Founding Fathers of the United States, to France with an offer to see if Emperor Napoleon Bonaparte would be willing to sell New Orleans and part of the banks of the Mississippi River. Livingston was authorized to offer $10 million for the land. At first, Napoleon refused the offer because he planned to expand his own empire into parts of North America. But Jefferson didn't want to give up on the idea, so he sent James Monroe, another Founding Father (who later became the fifth president of the United States), to France to see if Napoleon would reconsider America's offer.

Driving a Hard Bargain

The Americans had one big advantage in their goal of acquiring at least some of the Louisiana Territory: Napoleon was at war at the time, and it wasn't going well for him. He needed money to help his cause. Besides, he was so busy fighting his wars in Europe that it probably would have been impossible to pursue expansion in North America.

After Monroe traveled to France, Napoleon had a big change of heart. The French emperor offered to sell the United States *all* of the Louisiana Territory—828,000 square miles of land—and not just New Orleans and some of the banks of the Mississippi. Napoleon had just one condition for selling the Louisiana Territory to the Americans: They would have to kick in another $5 million.

The offer shocked both Livingston and Monroe. Even though they hadn't been authorized to spend $15 million, they accepted the offer before Napoleon had a chance to think it over. They obviously knew a great deal when they saw it! On April 30, 1803, the two Americans signed the Louisiana Purchase Treaty. After some debate, the US Congress ratified the treaty. The final transfer of funds to France came later that year, officially making the Louisiana Territory part of the United States.

WORTH REPEATING

"We have lived long, but this is the noblest work of our whole lives. . . . From this day the United States take their place among the powers of the first rank."
—Robert Livingston, after signing the Louisiana Purchase Treaty

The successful purchase of the Louisiana Territory was huge for America. Not only did it give the United States control of the Mississippi River—*all* of the Mississippi River!—and the port city of New Orleans, it also *doubled* the size of the United States. The purchase gave the United States territories that later became the states of Oklahoma, Nebraska, Kansas, Iowa, and Missouri, and parts of the land that became the states of Louisiana, Texas, Minnesota, Colorado, New Mexico, Wyoming, Montana, South Dakota, and North Dakota.

The Louisiana Purchase made it easier for American farmers to ship their crops to other countries and also peacefully eliminated a rival—France—that could have threatened the United States.

Checking Out the New Land

In the early 1800s, many people believed it was possible to cross the North American continent by sailing on a chain of rivers that stretched from the Mississippi River to the Pacific Ocean. If someone could find that chain, it would make travel from the eastern part of the continent to the west much easier.

President Jefferson wanted to find that network of rivers, which people back then called the Northwest Passage. Once the Louisiana Purchase was complete, he sent explorers named Meriwether Lewis (1774–1809) and William Clark (1770–1838) on an expedition to find the passage *and* to explore the new lands the United States had just bought from France.

Lewis and Clark, along with a crew of explorers, started their journey at the mouth of the Missouri River (where it flows into the Mississippi) on May 14, 1804. The expedition, called the Corps of Discovery, followed the Missouri River west.

HISTORIC HAPPENINGS

On March 1, 1803, Ohio became the seventeenth state in the union. After Congress passed the Northwest Ordinance, the first permanent settlement in Ohio was established in 1788, in Marietta, the capital of the Northwest Territory. In the 1790s, the settlers fought many violent battles with the Native Americans living in the area.

As they traveled, Clark carefully mapped the route while Lewis collected specimens of animals and plants to send back to Washington, DC. It was an extremely difficult trip. The men in Lewis and Clark's team rowed their three boats against the sometimes heavy Missouri River current and often had to get out of the boats to tow them from the riverbanks when the current became too treacherous. Even on a good day, the Corps of Discovery traveled only 13 or 14 miles.

Over the next several months, the party came in contact with several Indian tribes. All of the natives were friendly except the Lakota Sioux, who lived in what is now South Dakota.

In late August and early September, the party reached the Great Plains, a huge expanse of grasslands that covers parts of present-day Colorado, Kansas, Wyoming, Nebraska, New Mexico, North Dakota, South Dakota,

Texas, and Wyoming. Along the way, they saw amazing numbers of animals, including huge herds of wild buffalo.

In October 1804, Lewis and Clark decided to stop and build a fort—Fort Mandan—so they could spend the winter in what is now North Dakota. The following spring, they ordered a few of their men to head back down the river to take soil samples, minerals, plants, and some live animals (including some birds and a prairie dog) back to President Jefferson. The rest of the expedition continued up the Missouri River in canoes. When they reached what is now the state of Montana, they found the river too difficult to pass in canoes, so they bought some horses from the Shoshones and continued their journey on horseback.

HISTORY MAKERS

During the winter of 1804, Lewis and Clark hired a French-Canadian explorer and fur trader named Toussaint Charbonneau (1767–1843) and a Shoshone woman named Sacagawea (c. 1788–1812) to join their expedition. Sacagawea became a very important part of the expedition because she served as an interpreter between the party and the natives who lived near the headwaters of the Missouri River.

What Northwest Passage?

As they headed west from Montana, Lewis and Clark soon realized there was no Northwest Passage to discover. The Corps of Discovery carried maps showing the Missouri River and Columbia River systems separated only by a "ridge of hills" that would take a half a day to pass. What they found instead was a range of mountains—the Bitterroot Range, which is part of the Rocky Mountains—that took two weeks to cross.

It was September 1805 when the party reached the Bitterroots, but the mountains were already covered with snow. By the time the party crossed the mountains and reached present-day Weippe, Idaho, Lewis and Clark and their men hadn't eaten in days and were so weak they were barely able to walk. Fortunately, the Nez Percé Indians who lived in the area were very friendly to them. They welcomed them and fed them, helped them make

The Gateway Arch in St. Louis was built to honor America's westward expansion.

canoes for the next part of their journey, and agreed to take care of their horses until they returned on their way back east.

The expedition traveled downstream on the Clearwater, Snake, and Columbia Rivers in canoes. On November 15, 1805—a year and a half after they had started the journey—they reached the mouth of the Columbia River, where it flows into the Pacific Ocean. They built a fort on the south side of the river—near present-day Astoria, Oregon—and named it Fort Clatsop, after a nearby Indian tribe. They spent a cold, wet, windy winter in the fort before starting their trip back home.

Though Lewis and Clark didn't find a northwest passage to the Pacific (it simply didn't exist), their expedition wasn't a failure. They found the source of the Missouri River and had gathered a lot of information about the people, plants, animals, and geography of the places they saw. Lewis and Clark's discoveries helped make it possible for the United States of America to expand to the Pacific coast.

The War of 1812

The War of 1812, which lasted from 1812 to 1815, is sometimes called the Revolutionary War, Part II. That's because it was another war between the United States and Great Britain fought on the North American continent and because it ended with a victory for the Americans.

There were several reasons war broke out between the United States and Great Britain in 1812. First of all, the British had imposed a series of restrictions that hindered trade between the United States and France, which was also at war with the English at the time. Second, the English military practiced "impressment," which meant forcing American sailors to serve in the Royal Navy. Third, the British had been helping American Indian tribes that had been violently resisting the Americans' westward expansion.

President Jefferson wanted to keep American trade with overseas countries going, but he also wanted to keep America out of foreign wars. Jefferson tried to reason with the British, but when that didn't work, he and Congress passed the Embargo Act of 1807, which kept American ships from sailing not just to British and French ports, but to all foreign ports.

HISTORIC HAPPENINGS

On June 22, 1807, the crew of the British warship HMS *Leopard* attacked and boarded an American warship, the *Chesapeake*. The attack killed three aboard the *Chesapeake* and injured 18, including the ship's captain, James Barron. Even though this incident, the *Chesapeake-Leopard* Affair, didn't lead the United States directly into war with the British, many historians believe it was a factor in starting the War of 1812. That's because the American public was outraged by the incident and wanted something done about it.

Jefferson hoped the Embargo Act would hurt the British and French worse than it hurt the United States and that England would release its trade restrictions on France. But the Embargo Act wound up hurting American traders, whose goods sat in American ports. France and Britain, on the other hand, got along fine without receiving American goods.

In 1808 James Madison was elected as the fifth president of the United States. Before Thomas Jefferson left office, he signed a bill to repeal the Embargo Act. Meanwhile, the American public grew angrier and angrier because the British kept boarding American ships and forcing American sailors to serve in the British Royal Navy.

This Means War!

The people who wanted war with Great Britain at that time were called war hawks. Two of the most influential war hawks were Henry Clay, who had represented Kentucky in both the Senate and the House of Representatives, and John C. Calhoun, a politician from South Carolina. In 1812 they persuaded President Madison to

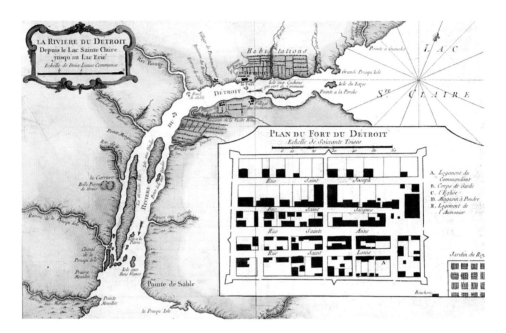

HISTORIC HAPPENINGS

Between 1812 and 1821, seven more states joined the union, bringing the total to 24. Louisiana became a state on April 30, 1812, followed by Indiana (December 11, 1816), Mississippi (December 10, 1817), Illinois (December 3, 1818), Alabama (December 14, 1819), Maine (March 15, 1820), and Missouri (August 10, 1821). After that, it would be 15 years before another state officially joined the union.

ask Congress for a declaration of war against Great Britain. Madison asked for the declaration and Congress gave it to him.

The United States lost the first "battle" of the War of 1812 without a shot being fired. Soldiers under the command of General William Hull crossed the border from Fort Detroit into Canada. At first, Hull knew he had the Canadian troops, who were serving under British commander Isaac Brock, badly outnumbered. But instead of attacking, Hull waited. After a while, he became convinced *he* was outnumbered and retreated to Fort Detroit then surrendered.

Despite the defeat at Fort Detroit, and despite the fact the British burned the White House, the Capitol, and other buildings in Washington, DC, in the Battle of Washington, the Americans defeated the British in the War of 1812. From September 12–15, 1814, the two sides met in the last official battle of the war, the Battle of Baltimore. Once that battle was finished, the British realized they didn't have enough soldiers left to keep fighting the

Americans and the French at the same time. On December 24, 1814, representatives from both sides met in Ghent (modern-day Belgium) and signed the Treaty of Ghent, which officially ended the War of 1812.

Unfortunately, the fighting didn't stop, even after the Treaty of Ghent was signed. In those days, communications traveled slowly and word of the treaty wouldn't reach the United States for weeks. On January 8, 1815, American troops fighting under General Andrew Jackson defeated the British at the Battle of New Orleans. That day, about 2,000 British troops died in a war that was already over.

The Indian Wars

Americans moving west faced all kinds of obstacles as they made their homes in new and unknown places. They had to navigate through sometimes rough terrain and bad weather to do it.

One of the biggest difficulties these pioneers faced was hostility from the people who already lived in the lands they wanted to settle—the American Indians, or Native Americans. Fighting between American settlers and

Native American tribes began as far back as the colonial days and lasted through the end of the 1800s. These battles have come to be known as the Indian Wars.

The natives who lived in North America before Europeans settled here lived in groups called tribes. There were many Indian tribes throughout North America, and each had its own culture, beliefs, and lifestyles. Throughout US history, starting in the colonial period, many Indian tribes fought with European settlers and with their descendants. Between the settlement of Jamestown in the early seventeenth century (the 1600s) and the end of the nineteenth century (the 1800s), there were literally dozens of Indian Wars.

From the early 1800s on, as Americans moved west in larger numbers, they encountered hostile natives who wanted to defend the lands they lived and hunted on. When Indian tribes came into contact with the American pioneers or with the US military, it often resulted in one of many Indian Wars fought during the nineteenth century. Here is a list of some of those wars and battles:

1832—The Black Hawk War in northern Illinois and southwestern Wisconsin

1849–1863—The Navajo conflicts in Arizona and New Mexico

1854–1890—The Sioux Wars in Wyoming, Minnesota, and South Dakota

1855–1856—The Rogue River War in southwestern Oregon

1861–1900—The Apache attacks in New Mexico, Arizona, Texas, and Mexico

1865–1868 and 1879—The Ute Wars in Utah

1872–1873—The Modoc War in northern California and southern Oregon

1874–1875—The Red River War in northwestern Texas

1876—Battle of Rosebud in Rosebud Creek in southern Montana

1876—Battle of the Little Bighorn in southern Montana

1877—The Nez Percé War in Oregon, Idaho, and Montana

1890—The Massacre at Wounded Knee in South Dakota

HISTORY MAKERS

Tashunka Witko (1842–1877), better known as Crazy Horse, was a Lakota Sioux chief remembered as a fierce warrior who earned the respect and fear of the United States Army during the Sioux Wars. Crazy Horse led a war party at the Battle of the Little Bighorn in June 1876. After Crazy Horse surrendered to US troops in 1877, he was fatally wounded by a military guard.

The longest and bloodiest of the Indian Wars was actually a series of wars between the Sioux Indians and the US military called the Sioux Wars. The Sioux lived on the Great Plains in the middle part of the United States, and they depended on buffalo for their food.

When large waves of settlers and prospectors crossed the Mississippi River and started passing through and settling in the plains, many started killing the huge herds of buffalo living there. Sioux warriors, including chiefs such as Sitting Bull and Crazy Horse, tried to protect their hunting grounds. That led to the Sioux Wars, which started in 1854 and ended in December 1890 with the Massacre at Wounded Knee.

The Texas Revolution

The story of how Texas became part of the United States starts in the early 1830s, when thousands of Americans began settling in Texas, a huge territory with a lot of farmland and other natural resources. By 1835 about 30,000 Americans and 8,000 Mexicans lived in Texas. The Americans living there wanted Texas to become part of the United States. The problem was that most of Texas at the time was part of Mexico.

The Alamo, San Antonio, Texas

In 1835 several battles broke out between the Texians (*Texian* was a term for American settlers in what was then northern Mexico) and Mexican soldiers. In December of that year, Texas formally declared itself independent from Mexico. The president of this new republic was a man named Sam Houston, and his secretary of state was Stephen F. Austin, one of the leaders of American settlements in the Texas territory.

Mexico's first major action following Texas's declaration of independence began on February 23, 1836, at the Alamo, a Texian-controlled fort near present-day San Antonio. The Texians fought bravely to defend the Alamo, but by the time the siege ended on March 6, 1836, a total of 189 had died—including famous Americans such as Jim Bowie and Davy Crockett. Mexico was victorious and now controlled the fort.

On March 20, 1836, the Mexican army, under the command of General José de Urrea, defeated Republic of Texas forces at the Battle of Coleto Creek. Following that battle, Mexican general Antonio López de Santa Anna ordered the massacre of 342 American prisoners, including their commander, Colonel

HISTORY MAKERS

David (Davy) Crockett (1786–1836) was a famous nineteenth-century frontiersman, politician, and soldier. Crockett served in the Tennessee state legislature starting in 1821, and in 1826 he was elected to represent Tennessee in the United States House of Representatives. He also served in the Texas Revolution.

James Fannin. This terrible event was called the Goliad Massacre.

A lot of Texians and other Americans were outraged at Santa Anna's cruelty in both of these battles, and many joined the Texian army to fight against Santa Anna's forces. On April 21, 1836, several hundred Texians defeated the much larger Mexican army at the Battle of San Jacinto, in present-day Harris County, Texas.

That battle ended the Texas Revolution. The Republic of Texas was now an independent nation, which extended in parts of present-day New Mexico, Oklahoma, Kansas, Colorado, and Wyoming. The Texas Republic remained independent until it joined the United States of America in 1845.

The Mexican-American War

Even though tensions between Texas and Mexico continued after the Texas Revolution, the two sides were mostly at peace for the next nine years. That changed in 1845, when the United States annexed Texas and it became the twenty-eighth state in the union.

HISTORIC HAPPENINGS

On March 3, 1845, before the outbreak of the Mexican-American War, Florida became the twenty-seventh state in the union. Spanish settlers had colonized Florida early on, but Spain lost control of the territory after the French and Indian War. Spain regained control of Florida after the Revolutionary War, but sold it to the United States in 1819.

After Texas became a part of the United States, border disputes with Mexico became a source of conflict. On April 25, 1846, a clash between Mexican and American soldiers became a war between the two countries. Battles in the Mexican-American War were fought in Texas, New Mexico, and California in the north, and in northern, central, and eastern Mexico, and in Mexico City in the south. When the US Army captured the Mexican capital, Mexico City, in September 1847, the war was all but over.

The Mexican-American War officially ended on February 2, 1848, when both sides signed the Treaty of Guadalupe Hidalgo. In the treaty, Mexico agreed to give up more than half of its territory in exchange for $15 million. The land Mexico gave up to the United States was called the Mexican Cession, and it included all of present-day California, Nevada, and Utah as well as parts of Arizona, Colorado, New Mexico, and Wyoming.

The United States gained nearly 30,000 more square miles of land from Mexico in 1853, when US ambassador to Mexico James Gadsden negotiated the purchase of land in what is now southern Arizona and southwestern New Mexico. This transaction is known as the Gadsden Purchase. Franklin Pierce, the fourteenth president of the United States, wanted the land because he thought it would be a good place to construct a southern transcontinental railway.

Westward Expansion: America's "Obvious Fate"

One of the United States' motivations for westward expansion in the 1830s and 1840s was a belief that came to be known as Manifest Destiny—which means "obvious fate." Many Americans believed that God had chosen the United States to expand "from sea to shining sea," including places such as Texas, California, and Oregon.

The term "manifest destiny" first appeared in an editorial in the July/August 1845 edition of the *United States Magazine and Democratic Review*. The article was published anonymously, but it has been attributed to editor John L. O'Sullivan. O'Sullivan wrote that it was America's "manifest destiny to overspread the continent allotted by Providence for the free development of our multiplying millions." O'Sullivan was referring specifically to the planned annexation of Texas, but he also stated that God had chosen America to become the superpower of that time and that this could be accomplished by expanding westward and establishing civilization in places that were occupied only by American Indian tribes.

Manifest Destiny caught on in America, and many newspapers and other media promoted the idea. It never became an official policy of the US government, but it greatly influenced many American politicians. One of the results was the Homestead Act of 1862, which encouraged Americans to move west and establish homes and colonies.

HISTORY MAKERS

Zachary Taylor (1784–1850) was the twelfth president of the United States (1849–1850) and an American military general who led American soldiers to victories over Mexican troops in the Battle of Palo Alto and the Battle of Monterrey in the Mexican-American War. Taylor, who had a 40-year military career, was known as Old Rough and Ready. On July 9, 1850, President Taylor died in office under mysterious circumstances.

HISTORIC HAPPENINGS

Between the beginning of the Texas Revolution and the end of the Mexican-American War, five more states were admitted to the union, bringing the total to 29. Arkansas became a state on June 15, 1836, followed by Michigan (January 26, 1837), Florida (March 3, 1845), Texas (December 29, 1845), and Iowa (December 28, 1846). Wisconsin became a state on May 29, 1848, bringing the total to 30.

Another Spiritual Awakening

As Americans moved west, a second big spiritual revival began to take place. In Chapter 2, you read about the First Great Awakening, which took place during colonial times. The movement known as the Second Great Awakening began early in the 1800s and lasted until the 1840s—though most of it took place during the 1820s and 1830s.

Where the preaching during the First Great Awakening focused mostly on people who were already in church, the work of many preachers and other spiritual leaders during the Second Great Awakening focused on people who didn't go to church. Preachers and teachers such as Charles G. Finney, Lyman Beecher, and Barton Stone spoke to large crowds at "revival meetings."

Even though some Christian leaders opposed what happened during the Second Great Awakening, it led to many thousands of conversions to Christianity and also to the growth of denominations such as the Methodists and Baptists.

As a result of the Second Great Awakening, many American Christians began to work to change their society. They became more aware of things that were wrong in America—such as slavery, the abuse of alcohol, and denying equal rights to women—and they believed it was their duty as Christians to fix as many of those wrongs as they could.

One of the wrongs many Christians, especially those living in the northeast states, wanted to fix was slavery. Many Christians already believed that slavery was wrong, but after the Second Great Awakening,

HISTORY MAKERS

Harriet Beecher Stowe (1811–1896) was an important American author and abolitionist and the daughter of antislavery preacher Lyman Beecher. In 1852, she wrote her best-known novel, *Uncle Tom's Cabin*, which described life for African Americans living under slavery. Millions of Americans read the novel or saw the play, and it motivated the antislavery movement in the North and angered proslavery people in the South. Stowe wrote more than 20 books, but *Uncle Tom's Cabin* is by far the best known and most influential.

more and more Christians began to see that owning other human beings against their will and forcing them to work for no pay was a terrible sin against God and against the enslaved people.

Not only did these Christians see that it was a sin to own slaves, they also believed that even *tolerating* slavery in their nation was a sin. That led to a growing "abolitionist movement," which called for the immediate elimination of slavery in the United States.

Hundreds of antislavery groups were formed during this time in American history. While the men in these groups gave speeches and wrote antislavery literature, the women worked to raise money and collect signatures to petition Congress to abolish slavery in the United States immediately. Many of the antislavery groups worked together, hoping to achieve their goal of abolishing slavery in every state of the union, not just in the North.

Compromises—Over Slavery

It might be hard to believe that there was a time when a lot of people in America actually *owned* slaves—when they bought and sold other human beings and forced them to work without pay on farms and in households—under sometimes terrible conditions.

Sadly, though, it's true. Slavery was a common practice in North America starting in the early colonial period. In fact, even some of the Founding Fathers owned slaves. But as time went on, people began to realize it was wrong for one human being to "own" another.

In 1780, just four years after the colonies declared their independence from Great Britain and formed the United States of America, Pennsylvania became the first state to pass laws that would eventually make slavery illegal. By 1850, very few people in the Northern states owned slaves. In the South, however, slavery continued to grow as a source of labor for jobs that required a lot of handwork—such as harvesting cotton and tobacco, two major crops in the South.

The issue of slavery deeply divided the Northern states from those in the South. That division only got worse when Missouri became a state in 1818. The settlers of Missouri wanted slavery to be legal in their state. However, members of Congress from the North didn't want another "slave state" admitted to the union.

This disagreement led to the Missouri Compromise, which Congress passed in 1820. The Missouri Compromise allowed Missouri to be a "slave state" and Maine to join the union as a "free state."

But the issue of slavery in the United States was far from settled. The Missouri Compromise meant that some states would still have legalized slavery while others would not, and that angered many people on both sides of the issue. The compromise also divided the United States with a line that ran across the country from the East Coast to the Pacific Ocean, with slave states to the south and free states to the north.

The deep division over the issue of slavery eventually led to another compromise.

The Compromise of 1850

HISTORIC HAPPENINGS

On January 24, 1848, James W. Marshall, a carpenter and sawmill operator, discovered gold in Northern California's American River, where he had gone to build a new sawmill for John Sutter. Marshall and Sutter tried to keep the discovery secret, but within months thousands of prospectors from all over the world made their way to California, all hoping to strike it rich. This was called the California Gold Rush. Many of the settlers arrived in 1849, so they were called forty-niners. Though a few people became wealthy and millions of dollars' worth of gold was found, few prospectors struck it rich. Some left California, but many began new lives in the state as farmers or business owners.

Thirty years after the Missouri Compromise, California asked to join the United States. The problem was that the Missouri Compromise would have divided California in half, with slavery legal in the south and illegal in the north. Making the problem even more complicated was that part of the territory held by Texas (a slave state) at the time was north of the line that separated slave states from free states.

These issues together created such division in the United States that many people feared a civil war would soon break out. But on January 29, 1850, a senator from Kentucky named Henry Clay offered a solution. Clay made these suggestions:

That Texas give up the land north of the line separating free states from slave states in exchange for $10 million, which it could use to pay off the remaining debt it owed Mexico following the Mexican-American War.

That California be admitted as a "free state."

That the territories of New Mexico (which included present-day Arizona at the time) and Utah be organized without mentioning slavery, meaning the people who lived there would decide the issue of slavery for themselves.

Adoption of the Fugitive Slave Act, which required all US citizens—North and South—to help in the return of runaway slaves.

The slave trade—but not slavery itself—would be made illegal in the District of Columbia, meaning slave owners there could keep their slaves.

At first, Clay's bills failed to pass Congress. And even if they had passed, President Zachary Taylor likely would have vetoed them. But in the fall of 1850, after Taylor died suddenly in office, Senator Stephen Douglas of Illinois helped push through the bills, which new president Millard Fillmore signed in September of that year.

Even though the Compromise of 1850 kept the nation from splitting in two, the issue of slavery continued to divide the country. Over the next decade, the division grew even wider. It was only a matter of time before they led to all-out war between the North and the South. ❌

CHAPTER 5

A Divided Nation

The Civil War and Reconstruction

Even though the Missouri Compromise and the Compromise of 1850 kept the nation from a war between the states—at least for a while—no one on either side of the slavery issue was satisfied. Those who favored legalized slavery didn't think it was right for the federal government to keep people from holding slaves, and those who opposed slavery saw the practice as sinful and unjust and wanted it outlawed in every state in the nation.

Looking back, we can see that a compromise on the issue of slavery was never going to work, because both sides were equally certain they were right. We

The bombardment of Fort Sumter, which touched off the fighting of the civil war.

can also see that it was only a matter of time before war broke out over the issue.

Finally, in 1861, the Civil War, or War Between the States, began. During four long years of fighting, more than 600,000 American soldiers died with more than 400,000 wounded. Some people believe that more than a million civilians died during the war. It has also been estimated that one in ten Northern men between the ages of 20 and 45 and three in ten Southern men between the ages of 18 and 40 died in the war.

Why the Civil War Happened

INTERESTING!

One issue that divided the North and South was taxes. Goods brought into the United States from foreign countries were subject to a tax called a tariff. Many people in the South believed the tariffs weren't fair, since the Southern states imported a lot more goods than the Northern states. Also, the way the Southerners saw it, the federal government was imposing taxes on goods produced in the South—such as cotton, sugar, and rice—but not on goods produced in the North.

If you were to ask most Americans why the Civil War happened, they would probably give you a simple answer: *slavery*. The North and the South went to war because the people in the South wanted to continue enslaving people to do their agricultural work, while people in the North believed slavery was wrong and immoral and that it shouldn't be allowed in a civilized country founded on the idea that God created all people equal.

In a sense, the issue of slavery was the "last straw" that led to the Civil War. But differences between the South and the North dated all the way back to the end of the Revolutionary War. Between 1787 and 1861, the North and the South had drifted apart in just about every way. Their politics were different, their economies were different, and their cultures were different.

One of the biggest issues between the North and the South in the years before the Civil War was what is called "states' rights." The South believed that state laws should carry more weight than federal laws, and when there was a disagreement between the two, states' rights should win out.

This issue of states' rights became even more important because, over the years, the populations of Northern and Midwestern states were growing far more rapidly than those in the South. That meant that the South lost a lot of its political power in Washington, DC, because areas with higher populations have more representation in Congress than those with lower populations.

In the years leading up to the Civil War, people started talking about the different "sections" of the United States. This is called *sectionalism*, and it led to a lot of anger and division within the United States. Before anyone knew it, the nation that had united itself to fight the British in the Revolutionary War had become a nation divided by sectional differences.

Why Did the South Still Want Slaves?

By the middle of the nineteenth century, the Northern states had pretty much ended the practice of slavery in their states. In the South, however, slavery had become a normal part of everyday life. But why did people in the South continue using slaves when people in the North had mostly stopped the practice? There are several reasons.

At first, the economy of the United States was built mostly on agriculture—the growing, harvesting, and buying and selling of goods produced on farms. But during the early 1800s, the North's economy changed and became more based on industry—making and selling things produced in factories—than on agriculture. In the South, however, the economy remained based almost completely on agriculture.

In the 1800s, most people in the South were farmers who made their money growing crops such as cotton, rice, sugarcane, and tobacco on big farms called plantations. To make their plantations more profitable, the owners needed cheap labor to do the work of planting, cultivating, and harvesting their crops.

The plantation owners relied on slaves to provide that labor. Some slaves worked in the fields, and some worked processing the crops for sale. Others did household chores in the plantation owners' homes.

Arguments over Slavery

Many Northerners didn't like the fact that slavery was growing and expanding in the South. They saw the practice as uncivilized and immoral. Some wanted slavery limited, while many others wanted to see it outlawed completely.

People in the Southern states argued that slavery had been a part of their way of life for more than two centuries and that it was protected by state and federal laws. They also argued that the US Constitution guaranteed their right to own property and be protected from the illegal seizure of that property. Since slaves were considered property in the South at that time, the Southerners argued that the federal government had no business telling them they couldn't practice slavery.

For decades, the South's distrust of the Northern states had been growing and getting worse. Southerners believed that no one in Congress would

HISTORY MAKERS

John Brown (1800–1859) was an American abolitionist whose radical (harsh and extreme) approach toward making slavery illegal led to his execution. While most abolitionists used peaceful tactics to help outlaw slavery, Brown believed in and practiced violence to get his antislavery views across. In 1856 he led the Pottawatomie Massacre, which resulted in the deaths of five men in Kansas. He also attempted an unsuccessful raid on a Virginia military armory in 1859. As a result, Brown was convicted of murder and treason against the state of Virginia and executed for his crimes.

listen to their concerns. Leaders in some Southern states talked openly of separating from the United States and forming their own government.

The Election of Abraham Lincoln

INTERESTING!

Even though the state of Virginia broke away from the United States and joined the Confederacy in 1861, people living in the western counties of Virginia didn't want to secede with the rest of the state. On June 20, 1863, this part of Virginia became a state of its own, called West Virginia.

In 1860 Abraham Lincoln's election as the sixteenth president of the United States only made the division between North and South worse. Southerners already believed that the federal government was interfering too much in their affairs, and they didn't think Lincoln would treat them fairly. That's because Lincoln was a member of the Republican Party, which many saw as friendly to abolitionists and Northern businessmen. Lincoln had also promised to keep the country united and to keep the new Western territories free of slavery.

For some of the Southern states, it was a simple choice: they would secede (break away) from the United States and form their own government. Lincoln thought their threats were a bluff and that the Southerners would never seriously consider leaving the union. But not long after Lincoln's election, Southern political leaders began calling for statewide votes to consider secession.

In December 1860, after Lincoln's election but before he took office, South Carolina became the first Southern state to secede from the United States. On February 4, 1861, Georgia, Florida, Alabama, Mississippi, and Louisiana joined South Carolina in a new nation called the Confederate States of America (the Confederacy for short), and Texas joined a month later. After the start of the Civil War, Virginia, Arkansas, North Carolina, and Tennessee also joined the Confederacy.

At the initial Confederate States Convention, Jefferson Davis, a Democratic senator from Mississippi and a champion of states' rights, was appointed as temporary president of the Confederacy. On November 6, 1861, Davis was formally elected after running unopposed.

Heading Toward a Civil War

President Lincoln had declared that he was willing to do whatever it took to keep the Southern states as part of the United States. Even after South Carolina led a parade of Southern states in seceding, there were Union forts in Confederate territory. The Confederates wanted the Union soldiers to leave the forts, and when Lincoln's predecessor, President James Buchanan, refused to surrender the forts, troops from the Southern states began taking them by force.

The Confederates warned Union soldiers to leave Fort Sumter, which sits at the entrance to the Charleston Harbor in South Carolina. When the Union troops refused to leave, on April 12, 1861, the Confederate States of America fired cannons at the fort. The attack lasted several hours. No one was killed or injured, but the fort was badly damaged. Rather than fight a battle he knew he couldn't win, Union Major Robert Anderson surrendered and allowed Confederate commanders to take control of the fort and its weapons.

> **INTERESTING!**
>
> Even though Delaware, Kentucky, Maryland, and Missouri were "slave states"—meaning states where slavery was still legal—they did not join the Confederacy. They were persuaded to stay in the union through a combination of political strategy and Union military pressure.

Up to this point, the war between the South and North was mostly a war of words. But with the attack on Fort Sumter, the Civil War had begun.

President Lincoln, who had done everything he could to avoid a war, responded to the attack on Fort Sumter by calling for volunteers from states still loyal to the union to help deal with this treasonous act on the part of the Confederacy. This led to the secession of the final four states to join the Confederacy: Virginia, Arkansas, North Carolina, and Tennessee.

This Shouldn't Take Too Long!

At the start of the Civil War, most people didn't believe it would last very long. Some even believed the war would last only a few months and that before long, Union soldiers would be welcomed home as conquering heroes.

The North had several advantages over the South at the beginning of the Civil War. They were far better off financially, producing about 75 percent of the nation's wealth, and they had a bigger army with much better weapons and supplies.

But the South had some advantages of its own, starting with the fact that most of the war would be fought on Southern territory. That meant the Confederate soldiers were defending their own land.

Both sides asked their states to raise companies of volunteer soldiers to fight. Tens of thousands of young men in both the North and the South enlisted. The men in the South wanted to protect their homes and their way of life, and the men in the North wanted to defeat the Southern states, bring the nation back together, and teach the rebellious South a lesson it wouldn't forget. Some of the Northern volunteer soldiers wanted to fight to abolish slavery.

Lincoln's New Goal

WORTH REPEATING

"There is no reason in the world why the negro is not entitled to all the natural rights enumerated in the Declaration of Independence, the right to life, liberty, and the pursuit of happiness. I hold that he is as much entitled to these as the white man."
—Abraham Lincoln, 1858

HISTORIC HAPPENINGS

Even though President Lincoln's Emancipation Proclamation freed most slaves living in the United States, the final abolition of slavery did not happen until 1865, when Congress passed the Thirteenth Amendment to the United States Constitution, which read, "Neither slavery nor involuntary servitude, except as a punishment for crime whereof the party shall have been duly convicted, shall exist within the United States, or any place subject to their jurisdiction." This amendment was ratified by the states on December 6, 1865.

Abraham Lincoln reads the Emancipation Proclamation to his advisors, called the "cabinet."

At the beginning of the Civil War, President Lincoln declared that the North was fighting the war to save the union, not to end slavery. But about a year after the war began, he changed his position. It was then that he wrote a document called the Emancipation Proclamation, which freed slaves in all the states that had left the union and joined the Confederacy.

On September 22, 1862, Lincoln issued a formal declaration of emancipation (which means freedom) of all slaves in the Confederate states that refused to return to the union by January 1, 1863. When none of the states returned, Lincoln formally issued the Emancipation Proclamation.

The Emancipation Proclamation had several effects. First, it granted freedom to all slaves in the Confederate states. Second, it made the abolition of slavery one of the main goals of the war. Third, it made it possible for

African American soldiers to serve in the Union Army and Navy. Finally, it made it impossible for England and France, European countries that were opposed to slavery, to help the Confederacy in its war effort.

How the Union Won the Civil War

The Union Army quickly took control of the border states— Delaware, Kentucky, Maryland, and Missouri—which were slave states that had not seceded from the Union before April 1861. The Union Navy also placed a naval blockade on coastal Confederate states. This kept them from exporting cotton, which they depended on for their wealth and for money to fight the war.

WORTH REPEATING

"I tremble for my country when I hear of confidence expressed in me. I know too well my weakness, that our only hope is in God."
—Robert E. Lee, Confederate general

In 1861 and 1862, neither side gained much ground from the other. The Confederacy stopped the Union from capturing its capital city of Richmond, Virginia. On June 13, 1863, Confederate General Robert E. Lee defeated Union forces in a battle at Winchester, Virginia, and then decided it was time to lead his men north into Pennsylvania.

After the victory at Winchester, the Confederates were confident they could defeat the Union Army by invading the North. Lee marched his men to Gettysburg, Pennsylvania, where they fought against the Union soldiers in a three-day battle called the Battle of Gettysburg.

HISTORIC HAPPENINGS

On November 19, 1863, President Lincoln gave one of the best—and most important—speeches in US history. He delivered the speech at Gettysburg, Pennsylvania, the place where the Battle of Gettysburg took place. Maybe you've heard the first line of Lincoln's famous speech: "Four score and seven years ago our fathers brought forth on this continent, a new nation, conceived in liberty, and dedicated to the proposition that all men are created equal." You can read President Lincoln's whole speech in Appendix C (page 153).

The Battle of Gettysburg, which was fought between July 1 and July 3, 1863, was one of the most important battles in the Civil War. It was also the bloodiest, with close to 51,000 casualties, including nearly 8,000 deaths.

On the first day of the battle, Lee's men outnumbered the Union soldiers, and the Union was forced to retreat from battle to the south side of the town of Gettysburg. General Lee wanted to finish the battle then and there, but his men delayed their attack, giving the Union time to set up its defenses and prepare to fight again the next day.

On the second day of fighting, both armies were at full strength. Lee attacked the Union Army, but they held their position. On the third day, Lee sent General George Pickett and 12,500 men to launch what he hoped would be the deciding attack in the battle—and in the war itself. In what has since been called Pickett's Charge, the general led his men on a direct attack against the Union Army. But more than half of Pickett's men were either killed or injured in the charge, forcing General Lee and the Confederate Army to retreat.

The Union Army, led by General George Meade, might have ended the war that day if he had pursued the retreating Confederate soldiers. But his men were exhausted by the fighting and did not pursue General Lee's troops. General Meade was later criticized, but he deserves credit for helping to save the Union.

The Battle of Gettysburg turned out to be a major turning point in the war for the Union. General Lee would never again attempt such a large offensive campaign against the Union. Even though the war continued for two more years, the Confederacy never recovered from its decisive defeat at Gettysburg.

The Beginning of the End for the Confederacy

On the morning of April 9, 1865, General Lee's Army of Northern Virginia met with General Ulysses S. Grant's Union Army for the final time in the war, in the Battle of Appomattox Court House. It was also one of the last battles of the Civil War.

Lee soon realized that his forces were outnumbered and that he had no choice but to surrender. That afternoon, he met with Grant at a house owned by Wilmer McLean, a grocer and former officer in the Virginia militia, to sign formal documents of surrender.

As Lee left McLean's house, mounted his horse, and rode away, Grant's men cheered in celebration. Grant, however, ordered them to stop their cheering. "The Confederates were now our countrymen," he later said, "and we did not want to exult over their downfall."

On April 12, the Army of Northern Virginia was disbanded and its officers and soldiers were given amnesty and allowed to return to their homes.

While some people celebrated the end of the war, General Grant knew there were still about 175,000 Confederate soldiers in the field. But as news of Lee's surrender spread, most of them laid down their weapons and stopped fighting. By the end of June, the last major Confederate armies had surrendered, ending the war.

The Civil War ended with the Union victorious, the country came back together (after a time, that is), and slavery ended in the United States. But the cost to both sides was staggering. In addition to the horrible loss of life, the South—where most of the war was fought—was devastated in nearly every way.

Now it was time to do the work of rebuilding the South, and of healing and reuniting a nation that had been at war with itself for four years.

Reconstructing the South

A terrible chapter in American history ended when the Union defeated the Confederacy in the Civil War. But that meant a new chapter was just beginning: bringing the nation back together as the United States of America. This part of American history is called the Reconstruction, and it started soon after the Civil War ended and lasted for 12 years, until 1877.

HISTORY MAKERS

Ulysses S. Grant (1822–1885) was the eighteenth president of the United States and a war hero who led the Union Army to victory over the Confederate States of America, which ended the Civil War and the Confederacy. Grant fought in the Mexican-American War, where he served under General Zachary Taylor. After the Civil War broke out, he joined the Union Army, and in 1864 he became the commanding general.

INTERESTING!

During the Civil War, Union and Confederate forces engaged in more than 50 major battles and more than 5,000 minor battles. Civil War battles took place in 23 states (Alabama, Arkansas, Florida, Georgia, Indiana, Kansas, Kentucky, Louisiana, Maine, Maryland, Minnesota, Mississippi, Missouri, New York, North Carolina, Ohio, Pennsylvania, South Carolina, Tennessee, Texas, Vermont, Virginia, and West Virginia) and in the District of Columbia, as well as in the Arizona Territory, the Colorado Territory, the Dakota Territory, the Indian Territory, the New Mexico Territory, and the Washington Territory.

HISTORY MAKERS

Thaddeus Stevens (1792–1868) was a powerful member of the United States House of Representatives during and after the Civil War. Stevens, along with a senator from Massachusetts named Charles Sumner (1811–1874), favored and pushed for Radical Reconstruction following the war.

Well before the Civil War ended, the members of Congress argued about the requirements for bringing the Southern states back into the union. Some favored a gentler approach to Reconstruction. They believed that the Union should not punish the South for seceding, but should instead take the steps necessary to heal and unite the nation as a whole. They also believed the federal government should play a limited role in changing the politics and social customs of the South.

Other members of Congress believed the US government should follow a course called Radical Reconstruction, which meant *punishing* the South for seceding and having the federal government more directly involved in the affairs of the Southern states. That included forcing political and social changes on the South that would make it more like the North. It also meant immediately granting the newly freed slaves (also called "freedmen") the same rights and liberties given to Southern white people. These members of Congress believed that if they didn't take that approach, the South would soon go right back to doing what it had done before.

Reconstruction. . .Lincoln Style

On December 8, 1863, about 16 months before the South surrendered to the North to end the Civil War, President Lincoln presented his vision for Reconstruction. Lincoln knew the Civil War would leave the nation, especially the South, devastated. He wanted to do everything he could to quickly heal the wounds the war had caused and put an end to the divisions between the North and the South.

WORTH REPEATING

"It is most cheering and encouraging for me to know that in the efforts which I have made, and am making, for the restoration of a righteous peace to our country, I am upheld and sustained by the good wishes and prayers of God's people."
—Abraham Lincoln

Lincoln's plan, called the Proclamation of Amnesty and Reconstruction, called for the federal government to appoint governors for the states that had seceded from the union and for pardons for all Southerners who took an oath of support to the US Constitution and the United States of America. This general pardon did not apply to high-ranking Confederate officials, who could only be pardoned by a special order from President Lincoln. A Confederate state could rejoin the union only after 10 percent of its qualified voters took the oath of allegiance.

Lincoln's proclamation didn't help the situation. Some members of Congress believed he was being too soft on the South and that his plan would make it easier for the South to go back to the way it was before the Civil War.

In 1864 Congress passed the Wade-Davis Bill, which said that before a state could rejoin the union, more than half of the state's male voters must take an "ironclad" oath saying they had never voluntarily supported the Confederacy. The Wade-Davis bill also prohibited former Confederate officials from voting or holding office. Lincoln refused to sign the Wade-Davis Bill, meaning it did not become law. Instead, he put his own plan for Reconstruction into effect.

Lincoln's Assassination

On April 14, 1865, five days after Confederate General Robert E. Lee surrendered to Union General Ulysses S. Grant to end the Civil War, a well-known actor named John Wilkes Booth shot President Lincoln as the president watched the play *Our American Cousin* at Ford's Theatre in Washington, DC. Lincoln died the next morning.

Lincoln's assassination was part of a bigger plot by Booth and two other men to kill the president, Vice President Andrew Johnson, and Secretary of State William H. Seward. Booth and his fellow plotters believed that if they killed all three men (who were the top three leaders in the US government), they would rally the Confederate troops to keep fighting and would also throw the Union government into chaos. But the plot was only partly successful. Seward was wounded but survived, and the attack on Johnson never happened.

Ford's Theater, shortly after President Lincoln's death.

The box seat in Ford's Theater, where Abraham Lincoln was shot.

On the day Abraham Lincoln died, he and Congress were nowhere near an agreement over Reconstruction. And for many years after that, the nation remained in turmoil over how to reunify the states.

When Lincoln died, Andrew Johnson became president during the difficult time when the nation wrestled with how to bring all the states back together.

A New National Leader, the Same National Problem

On April 15, 1865, Andrew Johnson became the seventeenth president of the United States. Many people expected him to impose harsher policies toward the former Confederate states than Lincoln would have. But Johnson agreed with Lincoln that the government should not seek to punish the Southern states, but instead treat them with leniency and forgiveness, so he decided to follow Lincoln's plan for Reconstruction.

On May 29, 1865, President Johnson issued a proclamation forgiving all Southerners (with the exception of a few key Confederate leaders) who took an oath of allegiance to the US Constitution and government. He also appointed temporary governors for the Southern states that were rejoining the union. In time, he pardoned all but a few high-ranking, wealthy Confederates and allowed the state governors he had appointed to appoint former Confederates to office.

Like Lincoln, Johnson didn't believe it was up to the federal government to force states to give the freedmen equal rights, so he left that issue up to the individual state governments. One of Johnson's conditions for a state to rejoin the union was that the state must ratify the Thirteenth Amendment, which abolished (put an end to) slavery. But he refused to use the power of the federal government to enforce the rights of the freedmen.

By the end of 1865, every Southern state but Texas had ratified the Thirteenth Amendment, organized a government, and elected members to Congress. Great strides had been made, and President Johnson declared that the Reconstruction was finished.

But it wasn't.

Back to Radical Reconstruction

Many members of Congress thought Johnson's Reconstruction policies didn't go nearly far enough. They believed that his policies, even though they called for states to ratify the Thirteenth Amendment, led to laws that treated former slaves unequally and also to the election of former Confederates to public office—including to Congress.

Members of Congress who favored Radical Reconstruction wanted to see more social and political change in the South, and they believed the only way for that to happen was for the federal government to command it. Instead of trying to make changes to Johnson's Reconstruction plans, the Congress enacted its own plan.

In early April 1866, Congress passed the Civil Rights Act of 1866, which protected freedmen from laws being passed in many Southern states to keep them from enjoying the same rights as white people. This act declared that

INTERESTING!

President Andrew Johnson's refusal to use federal power to guarantee equal rights for freed slaves meant that African Americans living in the South would not be treated as equal to their white neighbors. In fact, many Southern states established laws called "black codes," which limited the rights of the freedmen.

HISTORY MAKERS

During the time of Reconstruction, many in the United States Congress objected to the elections of former high-ranking officers of the Confederacy to the House of Representatives or Senate. One of those officers was a man named Alexander Stephens (1812–1883), who had been awaiting trial for treason when Georgia elected him to a seat in the US Senate. Congress barred Stephens (and others with backgrounds like his) from taking his seat, citing a clause in the US Constitution that states, "Each house [the House of Representatives and the Senate] shall be the judge of the qualifications of its own members."

HISTORIC HAPPENINGS

In 1867 the United States purchased Alaska from Russia for $7.2 million. The US government made the transaction on advice from Secretary of State William Seward. Many people thought the purchase was a big mistake, and they began calling it Seward's Folly. It turned out that Alaska was rich with natural resources, including abundant supplies of gold and oil. The purchase also gave the United States more land and removed Russian influence from the North American continent.

HISTORIC HAPPENINGS

In 1868 the US House of Representatives voted to impeach (charge with a crime) President Andrew Johnson for dismissing Secretary of War Edwin M. Stanton. Johnson acted in spite of the Tenure of Office Act, passed in 1867, which limited the power of the president to remove people from office without the approval of the Senate. Johnson became the first president to be impeached. When the House of Representatives impeaches a president, the Senate must then vote to decide whether the president should be removed from office. The Senate voted against removing Johnson by only one vote.

every person born in the United States "of every race and color" was now a citizen with the same rights as everyone else.

President Johnson vetoed the Civil Rights Act of 1866 because he thought it gave the federal government too much power. Many people were angry at Johnson for vetoing the bill, and Congress quickly voted to override the veto (Congress can set aside a presidential veto with a two-thirds vote of the membership), making it now the law in the United States. It was the first time in US history that Congress had overridden a presidential veto of a bill.

About two years later, on July 9, 1868, Congress ensured that the civil rights bill was enforced when it approved the Fourteenth Amendment, which guaranteed full citizenship rights to the freedmen. Congress also made ratification of this amendment a condition for rejoining the union.

In June 1868, Tennessee and six other Southern states formally rejoined the union. That same year, Congress prepared the Fifteenth Amendment—which prohibited states from denying any American the right to vote based on "race, color, or previous condition of servitude"—and made it a condition for the remaining states to rejoin the union. The rest of the former Confederate states were admitted by the end of 1870. Georgia was the last to be readmitted.

A Big Change at the Top

In 1869 Civil War hero Ulysses S. Grant was elected as the eighteenth president of the United States. Grant supported Congress' Radical Reconstruction plans. Grant was also reelected in 1873. Unfortunately, his presidency did not bring an end to the nation's turmoil over Reconstruction.

By 1870 the Radical Reconstructionists in Congress accomplished several of their goals. On February 3 enough states had ratified the Fifteenth Amendment for it to become law, which gave black people the right to vote. As a result, two African Americans won election to Congress: Senator Hiram Rhodes Revels (from Mississippi) and Representative Joseph Rainey (from South Carolina). In July Georgia became the last former Confederate state to be readmitted to the Union.

The Reconstruction era ended in 1877, the year after Republican Rutherford B. Hayes won a disputed election over Samuel Tilden to become the nineteenth president of the United States. Tilden won the popular vote (meaning more people cast a ballot for him than for Hayes) but lost in the electoral vote. Southern Democrats agreed to support Hayes's election if he would pull all federal troops out of South Carolina, Florida, and Louisiana, where they had helped keep Republicans in control.

This is called the Compromise of 1877, but it has also been called the Corrupt Bargain. Before Hayes took office, President Grant removed the soldiers from Florida, and Hayes removed them from South Carolina and Louisiana. Once the troops left, the Reconstruction era was officially over.

Sadly, the end of Reconstruction meant that many of the gains made by and for the freedmen since the end of the Civil War were reversed. Slavery remained illegal throughout the United States, including in the South, but in many states, former slaves and their children lost a lot of their rights as citizens. The Fifteenth Amendment may have given African Americans, who were the majority in states like Mississippi, Louisiana, and Alabama, the right to vote; but white supremacist groups

HISTORY MAKERS

Hiram Rhodes Revels (1827–1901) was an African American minister who became the first black man to serve in the United States Senate and the United States Congress. Revels represented Mississippi in 1870 and 1871, during Reconstruction. Earlier, Revels had served as a minister in the African Methodist Episcopal Church and as a chaplain for the US Army. He also helped organize two black Union regiments during the Civil War and took part in the Battle of Vicksburg in Mississippi.

GRANT

engaged in intimidation, violence, and sometimes murder to keep blacks from voting. That led to the election to Congress of Southern Democrats—also called Redeemer Democrats—who had opposed the gains the freedman made over the previous few decades.

Starting in 1876 (and lasting until the 1960s), Southern states began passing laws which led to separate public facilities—schools, transportation, restrooms, even drinking fountains—for whites and blacks. The South became more and more segregated, and anger and conflict between whites and blacks grew as a result.

CHAPTER 6

Immigration, Industry, and a Really Big War

The United States after the Civil War

Once the Civil War was over, the United States was again ready to begin growing as a global economic power. And grow it did! After the Civil War, American business and industry grew and expanded so fast that by the end of the nineteenth century, the United States' economy had replaced Great Britain's as the world's largest.

A lot of factors helped make possible America's rapid rise to the top. Those factors included a big increase in the number of people living in the United States, better transportation, and a lot of really cool inventions. (Okay, maybe some of them won't seem so cool to you now, but back then they were a really big deal.)

In this chapter, you'll read about how the United States of America had its own "population explosion" following the Civil War, and how all those new people helped American industry grow throughout the second half of the nineteenth century and the early part of the twentieth century.

You'll also read about how the United States became involved in the first global war in world history: World War I.

Immigration Heats Up in the United States

INTERESTING!

In Ireland a disease that killed potato crops led to a terrible time now called the Great Famine or the Irish Potato Famine. Between 1845 and 1852, the population of Ireland dropped by 2 million people. About half died from starvation and other disease, while the other half left the country to find a better life. Many of those people emigrated to the United States.

The United States of America has often been called a nation of immigrants, and history shows that is true. By the 1820s, every American who wasn't from one of the many Indian tribes throughout the land was either an immigrant or a descendant of immigrants.

Historians estimate that fewer than a million Europeans emigrated to North America during the seventeenth and eighteenth centuries. Immigration to the United States was slow after the Revolutionary War, but the number of people moving to America from other countries gradually increased around the 1820s. Starting in the 1840s, a huge wave of immigrants from Ireland and Germany began arriving on the shores of the United States.

These new immigrants were fleeing their homelands in Europe due to crop failures that led to famines and due to unrest in their native countries. Some historians estimate that between 1847 and 1854, an average of 335,000 people—almost half of them from Ireland—moved to the United States each year.

During the Civil War, immigration from Europe slowed down (after all, who wanted to move to a country being torn apart by war?). But once the Civil War ended, the number of people moving to the United States increased again. Between 1865 and 1873, more than 325,000 Europeans—from Great Britain, Germany, Ireland, and other countries—came to the United States every year.

For the most part, immigration to the United States increased every year after the Civil War. Before the Civil War, immigrants had to travel over the Atlantic Ocean on sailing ships. Many people died during the voyages. But after the war, the introduction of steamships—which were much faster than sailing ships—helped reduce the number of deaths. It also lowered the cost of migrating to North America.

Between 1836 and 1914, more than 30 million Europeans crossed the Atlantic Ocean to come to the United States. In 1907 alone, almost 1.3 million Europeans entered the country. By 1910, 13.5 million out of the 92.4 million people living in the United States were immigrants.

Some of the immigrants came to the United States only to work and make money before they returned home, but many others came to establish new homes in a place where they could make a better life for themselves and their families. While these new immigrants weren't always welcomed with open arms, they helped establish growing industries in the United States such as steel, coal, textiles, garment production, and automobiles. These new workers helped make the United States one of the world's most important countries economically.

INTERESTING!

The construction of the Transcontinental Railroad came after many years of politicking. In 1845 an American businessman named Asa Whitney (1797–1872) approached the US Congress with a plan calling for the federal government to help pay for the construction of a railroad from the Mississippi River to the Pacific coast. In 1853 Congress funded the surveying of potential routes for a railroad to the West Coast. On July 1, 1862—during the Civil War—Congress passed laws providing funds for a transcontinental line. This legislation called for two companies to build the railroad, with each receiving federal land grants and government loans for each mile of track built.

Chinese Immigrants' Big Contribution

In the 1850s, many young men from China left their homeland and migrated to North America to find work. These immigrants were fleeing a country where they couldn't find work and where the government was very unstable. Many ended up in Northern California, which was being settled at that time by people coming west for the gold rush. Most of these Chinese immigrants landed in the port city of San Francisco and then moved to the gold fields in the foothills of the Sierra Nevada mountains. Historians estimate that by the late 1850s, around 15,000 Chinese immigrants worked in California gold mines.

HISTORY MAKERS

Charles Crocker (1822–1888) was a founder of the Central Pacific Railroad and the man most responsible for recruiting immigrants from China to construct a large part of the first Transcontinental Railroad. Many of Crocker's business partners didn't think Chinese workers were big enough or strong enough for the backbreaking work, but Crocker hired them anyway, and they became known as Crocker's Pets. Unfortunately, Crocker treated the Chinese laborers terribly. He worked them to the point of exhaustion and paid them a lot less than his other workers. He also didn't pay for their food or housing.

When the California Gold Rush began to wind down, many of the Chinese immigrants who had worked in the mines started working on one of the most important (maybe *the* most important) construction projects of the 1800s: the first transcontinental railroad, which would provide a railway link between the East Coast and the Pacific.

Two railroad companies, the Union Pacific Railroad and the Central Pacific Railroad, began construction on the Transcontinental Railroad in 1863. The Union Pacific Railroad started in Omaha, Nebraska, and the Central Pacific Railroad started in Sacramento, California. On May 10, 1869, the two sections of railroad finally met at Promontory Summit, Utah. To celebrate the completion of the railroad, a ceremonial golden spike was driven into the final wooden tie by Leland Stanford, president of the Central Pacific Railroad.

Chinese immigrants did most of the work building the Central Pacific part of the first Transcontinental Railroad. These men worked in sometimes terrible conditions and for lower pay than other workers. They worked in the heat of the summer and in the extreme cold of the winter, and many of them died. They had to lay track on flat land, but they also had to build bridges over canyons and rivers and construct tunnels through the Sierra Nevada and Rocky Mountains. They used dynamite to bore the tunnels, and many workers were killed in the explosions.

Over the next few decades, more railroad lines were built. Three were completed in 1883: The Northern Pacific Railroad, which stretched from Lake Superior to Portland, Oregon; the Santa Fe Railroad, which traveled between Atchison, Kansas, and Los Angeles, California; and the Southern Pacific Railroad, which connected Los Angeles with New Orleans, Louisiana. In 1893 the Great Northern Railway was completed.

How important were these new railroads? Well, before they were completed, people had to travel west in wagon trains, on horseback, or on foot. Americans were traveling west and settling there, but the new railroads made it possible for people to travel west faster and more safely. A trip that once took months and was filled with all sorts of dangers now could be completed safely in a week or less.

Not only that, but people could now transport goods by train, which helped speed up economic expansion in the west and in the east. Before the railroad, trade between the eastern half of the United States and the western half was extremely difficult, if not impossible. But within ten years of the completion of the first Transcontinental Railroad, more than $50 million worth of goods were being shipped from one side of the continent to the other every year.

HISTORY MAKERS

John Pierpont (J. P.) Morgan (1837–1913) was the most important US banker during the rise of American industry in the late 1800s and early 1900s. Morgan supplied huge amounts of money that American businesses needed for expansion. By the early 1900s, he and his business partners had invested in many large corporations in the United States. In 1892 Morgan formed General Electric when he arranged the merger of Edison General Electric and Thomson-Houston Electric Company. He also formed the United States Steel Corporation in 1901.

The Rise of American Industry

In Europe and North America during the 1700s and 1800s, big changes took place in farming, manufacturing, mining, technology, and transportation. These changes were part of what is often called the Industrial Revolution, which transformed the way people produced goods and the way they were sold.

During colonial times, the American economy was based mostly on agriculture. But in the early 1800s, industry began to grow in the United States. That growth continued all the way through the Civil War. But manufacturing was far different back then than it is today. Most manufacturing was done in small shops using hand labor. Most of those businesses served small, local markets.

But once the Civil War was over, American industry began to change very quickly. As more Americans moved west of the Appalachians, they settled in places with a wide variety of natural resources, including trees for lumber; important minerals like iron ore and coal, both of which would play a huge role in manufacturing; and valuable minerals such as copper, silver, and gold.

The rise in American industry was also fueled by a huge increase in the number of people living here following the Civil War. As millions of people immigrated to the United States, a lot of babies were born here as well, and the population jumped from about 40 million people living in the United States in 1870 to almost 102 million in 1916. (If you're good at math, you might have already figured out that the US population increased more than 150 percent in less than 50 years!)

Having all those new people in the United States meant there were more people who wanted and needed the goods American businesses produced, and there were a lot more people available to do the work needed to *produce* those goods.

Another important reason for the expansion of American industry during this time was the development of machines that could do work that once had been done by hand. Mechanized production meant that all those new workers could produce goods much faster, allowing American businesses to produce and sell more products at a lower price. Now many more people could afford to buy the products produced by American industry.

Improvements in transportation—especially the growth of railroads—also helped the US economy to grow. In 1850 there were 9,000 miles of railroad lines operating in the United States; by 1900, that number had increased to nearly 200,000 miles of track. This made it possible for companies to ship their finished and unfinished goods *from* anywhere in the nation *to* anywhere in the nation.

As manufacturing grew in the United States, more and more companies needed money—also called *capital*—to expand their businesses. They got it from two sources: investors and banks. People eager to make money from the new manufacturing boom invested in the companies, which gave these businesses the money they needed to expand. Also, new banks opened all over the country, offering growing businesses low-interest loans to help them expand.

A Time of Invention

American inventors had developed newer and better products throughout the country's history. But the late 1860s was a time when inventors from both the United States and Europe developed amazing numbers of products the American people wanted to buy. Here are just a few products introduced between 1867 and 1879.

1867: Christopher Latham Sholes invented the first practical mechanical typewriter. On June 23, 1868, Sholes's invention was granted a patent (meaning that other people were prohibited from copying and selling their own version of Sholes's device, at least for a certain amount of time). Patents are an important way to protect inventors who invest a lot of time and money developing new products.

1874: Joseph F. Glidden improved an older type of fencing and received a patent for barbed wire.

1876: An inventor named Alexander Graham Bell received a patent for the telephone. Another inventor, Elisha Gray, is also credited with inventing the telephone, but Bell now receives credit for the invention because he patented his phone first.

1877: American inventor Thomas Alva Edison completed his first phonograph, a device used to record and play sounds. Edison's invention used paper—and later metal—cylinders for recording. Subsequent phonographs used vinyl discs, which remained popular until they were replaced by compact digital discs (CDs).

1879: Thomas Edison developed an improved electric light bulb. Edison wasn't the first inventor to introduce electric lighting, but his development made it practical and safe to use electric lighting in homes.

HISTORY MAKERS

Brothers Orville (1871-1948) and Wilbur Wright (1867-1912) were two Americans credited with inventing and building the world's first successful airplane. Other people had built "flying machines" before, but the Wrights' aircraft, called the Wright Flyer, was the first with controls that made fixed-wing powered flight possible. On December 17, 1903, the Wrights flew the Wright Flyer four times near Kill Devil Hills, about four miles south of Kitty Hawk, North Carolina.

How Cars Changed American Life and Industry

INTERESTING!

On January 6, 1912, New Mexico was admitted as the forty-seventh state. Just a little more than a month later, on February 14, 1912, Arizona became the forty-eighth state of the union. New Mexico and Arizona were the last two of the "lower 48" states admitted to the Union. Alaska and Hawaii would not be admitted until 1959.

HISTORY MAKERS

Henry Ford (1863–1947) was the founder of Ford Motor Company. He is credited with developing a manufacturing process called the assembly line, which involved setting up a "line" of workers who each added a part to the product as it moved down the line. For example, one worker would install the car's headlights, and the next worker would install the turn signals, and so on. In 1908 Ford introduced the Model T, the first car affordable to many working-class Americans. Between 1908 and 1927, Ford produced more than 15 million Model T's.

In 1885 a German inventor named Karl Benz produced the first gasoline-powered automobile. In 1891 an American named John W. Lambert produced the first gasoline-powered car in the United States.

Probably no invention changed the US economy more than the automobile. Before 1900 only the very well-to-do could afford to buy a car. That began to change in 1902, when Ransom Olds, founder of the Olds Motor Vehicle Company in Lansing, Michigan, began using a manufacturing process called assembly-line production at his company. This form of mass production made Olds's Curved Dash Oldsmobile the first low-priced car in American history.

Starting in 1914, Henry Ford, the founder of Ford Motor Company, added improvements to the assembly-line way of making cars. The results changed not only the automobile industry but other manufacturing around the world as well. Ford's cars came off the assembly line at amazing speed, and the number of injuries at his factories dropped compared to other car makers. That's mostly because his workers stayed in one place on the assembly line all day, rather than moving from place to place.

It wasn't long before most major industries in the United States began copying Ford's assembly-line production techniques. That led to higher productivity and lower production costs in American companies—and to lower prices for the people who bought their goods. Many companies that didn't use assembly-line production, including many car companies, went out of business because they couldn't compete. Those that adapted were able to prosper and grow.

The automobile industry, where mass production using assembly manufacturing got its start, expanded as more and more Americans could afford to buy cars. In 1900 Americans owned a total of only 8,000 cars. By 1916 that number had increased to 3.5 million.

How American Industry Changed America

The rapid growth of manufacturing in the United States affected the nation in many important ways. By 1890 America had become the world's leader in industrial production, passing up longtime leader Great Britain. By the turn of the twentieth century, the United States by far led the world in per capita (per person) income.

These changes in the US economy also changed the way a lot of people lived—and *where* they lived. Most new businesses in the United States during this period were located in cities—especially cities in the northern part of the country. (The South was still recovering from the Civil War and wouldn't catch up to the North for many years.) The kind of business you'd find depended on where you looked. Some areas of the country saw increases in coal mining, while others saw big jumps in the manufacture of clothing, automobiles, goods made of steel, and industrial machinery.

As these new businesses grew, they provided many job opportunities. People who had grown tired of trying to scratch out a living as farmers left the rural parts of the nation and moved to the cities, which grew very rapidly as a result. Many new cities were started during this time.

America's industrial production grew at an astonishing rate between the Civil War and the first two decades of the twentieth century. But while many Americans became very rich during this time, many more still lived in miserable poverty. They may have had jobs and a fairly steady income, but most made barely enough to survive.

Many workers were unhappy with their pay and with their working conditions. That led to the formation of labor unions in the United States,

HISTORY MAKERS

Samuel Gompers (1850-1924) was an important figure in the history of American labor unions, groups of workers who band together to demand better pay and job conditions from their employers. Gompers, who was born in England, founded the American Federation of Labor (AFL), a collection of labor unions in the United States. He served as the AFL's president from 1886 until 1894 and from 1895 until his death in 1924.

starting in 1869. Unions were formed when all the workers in a factory joined together to bargain with the business owners for higher pay and better working conditions. At first, the growth of this new labor movement was slow, but after the turn of the century, more and more workers joined labor unions.

Even though there were many problems to overcome—including some serious slowdowns in the US economy— America enjoyed a time of rapid economic expansion during the nineteenth and early twentieth centuries. The nation grew not only as an economic force but also as a military power. During the second decade of the twentieth century, that would prove to be very important, not only to the United States but to the rest of the world as well.

The World Goes to War

World history is filled with all kinds of wars between individual nations. But World War I was the first war fought between countries from all around the globe. World War I started in 1914 in Europe, but the United States didn't get involved until 1917.

World War I started over the assassination of two people: Austria's Archduke Franz Ferdinand and his wife, Sophie. On June 28, 1914, a Serbian man named Gavrilo Princip shot and killed the archduke and duchess while they visited the city of Sarajevo in the Austro-Hungarian province of Bosnia-Herzegovina.

Archduke Ferdinand was the nephew of Austria's emperor and was in line to become emperor after his uncle, but he was not very well liked in his country. At that time, Austria-Hungary (a union between Austria and Hungary that began in 1867) had been having problems with Serbia, and Ferdinand's assassination gave Austria-Hungary a good reason to attack.

Before attacking, though, Austria-Hungary made sure it had the backing of Germany, which had a treaty with Austria-Hungary. In the time between Archduke Ferdinand's assassination and the actual attack, Serbia gained the support of Russia, with whom the Serbians had a treaty. Russia also had treaties with France and Britain, which brought them both into the conflict.

Austria-Hungary officially declared war on Serbia on July 28, 1914. On August 1, Germany declared war on Russia, and two days later also declared war on France. On August 4, Britain declared war on Germany after the Germans invaded Belgium. Then, on August 6, Austria-Hungary declared war on Russia and Serbia declared war on Germany.

So at the start of World War I, three nations—France, Great Britain, and Russia—formed what was called the Entente Powers (or the Allies). Later, several other countries joined the Allies' fight against the Central Powers of Germany and Austria-Hungary.

The United States Enters World War I

The Entente Powers wanted the United States to join the war against the Central Powers. By 1917, after two years of fighting under terrible conditions, the Allies were running out of young men and supplies to fight the war. They knew America had a lot of soldiers, weapons, and supplies, and they did everything they could to persuade the United States to help them.

INTERESTING!

Before the interception of the Zimmermann Telegram, most Americans wanted to avoid going to war in Europe. At first, a lot of Americans believed the telegram was a forgery by the British to bring the United States into the war. In March 1917, Zimmermann himself confirmed that the telegram was not a forgery when he twice said, "I cannot deny it. It is true."

At that time, however, US foreign policy was based on "isolationism," which meant America would not get involved in other countries' wars. Many American leaders and citizens believed that the United States should not fight in a war that was so far away and didn't directly affect America.

But two major international events involving Germany and the United States helped bring the United States into World War I. First, on May 7, 1915, a German U-boat (submarine) fired torpedoes at the British ocean liner RMS *Lusitania*. The ship sank in 18 minutes, and 1,198 of the 1,959 people aboard died—including 159 Americans. The sinking of the *Lusitania* made most Americans very angry, and it soon became a symbol used in military recruiting campaigns.

The second incident was an intercepted message between Germany and Mexico early in 1917, called the Zimmermann Telegram. In the telegram, German foreign secretary Arthur Zimmermann promised Mexico help in reclaiming territories it had lost in the Mexican-American War if the United States entered World War I and sided with the Allies. The Germans hoped that a war between the United States and Mexico would keep the Americans occupied with fighting on their own soil. The British intercepted the message and warned the United States of its contents.

RMS *Lusitania* in New York Harbor.

When the press revealed the contents of the Zimmermann Telegram, the American public became angry at the Germans. This time, they were ready to go to war because the Germans had attempted to stir up a war between the United States and Mexico.

On April 2, 1917, President Woodrow Wilson asked Congress for a formal declaration of war against Germany. Congress granted the request four days later, meaning that the United States was now officially at war with Germany. General John J. Pershing was put in command of US forces in Europe. On June 26, 1917, the first American troops landed in St. Nazaire, France.

Russia Gets Out

As the United States entered World War I, internal conflict in Russia was about to lead to that nation's withdrawal from the war. In 1917 Czar Nicholas II was removed from power largely because he had led Russia into World War I, which led to the deaths of millions of Russians and left the nation in ruins. The new Russian government wanted out of the war so it could focus on rebuilding. On March 3, 1918, Russia signed the Brest-Litovsk Treaty with Germany, which ended Russia's involvement in World War I.

Russia's withdrawal from the war meant Germany could move troops that had been fighting on the eastern front in Russia back to the west, where they could face the American soldiers. Millions of soldiers and civilians died during the following year, but the Americans' entry into the war began turning the war in the Allies' favor.

European troops had been fighting and dying for more than three years, and the ones who remained were exhausted. The American soldiers were fresher and ready to continue the fight. It wasn't long before the Allies began advancing against the Central Powers.

On November 11, 1918, Germany surrendered and signed an agreement, called the Armistice, at Compiègne, France. The Armistice called for the fighting to end at the eleventh hour of the eleventh day of the eleventh month—11:00 in the morning on November 11. World War I was finally over—and not a moment too soon for many European nations. By the time the fighting stopped, about 10 million soldiers had died—an average of 6,500 for every day of the war—in addition to millions of civilians.

The Treaty of Versailles

On January 18, 1919, diplomats from several of the countries involved in World War I met at a peace conference in Versailles, France, to draft an agreement (or treaty) that would result in the official end of World War I. That agreement was called the Treaty of Versailles, which representatives from Germany and the Allied Powers signed on June 28, 1919.

The Treaty of Versailles was meant not just to end the war in Europe but to punish Germany for its part in the conflict. The treaty stated that the Germans would

1. take full responsibility for the damage caused during World War I (this is known as the "war guilt" clause)
2. give up much of its land (including its overseas colonies)
3. have its army limited to 100,000 soldiers
4. pay large amounts of money to the Allied Powers.

INTERESTING!

The three most important and influential men at the Paris Peace Conference in 1919 were British Prime Minister David Lloyd George, French Prime Minister Georges Clemenceau, and US President Woodrow Wilson. Germany was not represented at the conference.

On May 7, 1919, the Treaty of Versailles—which the Germans were told to sign within three weeks, or else!—was sent to the Germans. Because the treaty was so harsh on the Germans, they sent back a list of complaints about the agreement. The Allies ignored most of those complaints.

Rather than sign the Treaty of Versailles, German chancellor Philipp Scheidemann resigned. But the Germans had no military power to resist, so they had no choice but to sign the treaty. On June 28, 1919—five years to the day after the assassination of Archduke Franz Ferdinand—German representatives Hermann Müller and Johannes Bell signed the Versailles Treaty.

World War I had ended, but that was not the last time Germany would play a major role in starting a worldwide war. Many historians believe that the terms and conditions of the Treaty of Versailles punished the Germans so harshly that it helped create the conditions for the rise of the Nazis in Germany and the outbreak of World War II. ✖

CHAPTER 7

America Becomes a World Power

World War II through the Korean War

From the 1860s through the end of World War I, the United States enjoyed an amazing time of prosperity. Sure, there were some downturns along the way, but for the most part, nearly all parts of the American economy—especially manufacturing—boomed during this period.

After its success in World War I, the US military had a reputation as a strong power. After the war ended, the United States enjoyed a decade of economic growth and peace that are now called the Roaring Twenties.

Many people thought the peace and prosperity of the 1920s would never end. But starting in 1929, the United States (and the rest of the world) went through the difficult times you'll read about in this chapter: the Great Depression and World War II.

In this chapter, you'll also read about how world politics and military power changed by the end of World War II. You'll see how the United States and the Soviet Union, or USSR, became the two world military powers and how they entered into a decades-long rivalry that would change the world even more.

The Great Depression

During the 1930s, the United States went through a very difficult time called the Great Depression. This period in United States history began in September 1929, when the US stock market fell very quickly, causing many people to lose money they had invested in companies and corporations. Then on October 29, a day that came to be known as Black Tuesday, the stock markets suffered a second straight day of huge losses, costing thousands of investors many millions of dollars. Some people lost everything they had! The stock market crash scared many Americans and caused them to start saving their money rather than spending it. Because people stopped spending,

INTERESTING!

During the Great Depression, many people lost their jobs and their homes. Needing someplace to live, they built shacks or set up tents in areas near soup kitchens run by private charities. These "communities" of temporary housing were called Hoovervilles, after Herbert Hoover, who was president of the United States when the Great Depression started.

countless banks, businesses, and factories went out of business, which caused millions of people to lose their jobs and the money they had saved. Many of those people ended up homeless and penniless.

During the worst part of the Great Depression, the unemployment rate in the United States—meaning the percentage of people who wanted to work but couldn't find a job—was over 25 percent. Many of these people had to depend on the government or on private charities just to have a place to stay and enough food to eat.

The Great Depression didn't affect just the United States. It hurt almost every country in the world, and many nations had it worse than the United States. During the Great Depression, international trade dropped by about 50 percent. That's partly because countries raised tariffs (taxes on imported and exported goods) in an effort to protect their own businesses and industries. In some countries, the unemployment rate reached as high as 33 percent—one out of every three people was out of work.

FDR's "New Deal"

Herbert Hoover was president of the United States at the start of the Great Depression. After the October 1929 stock market crash, the US economy got worse almost every day. More and more people lost their jobs and their homes.

In 1932 Franklin Roosevelt was elected president, and almost immediately he began taking steps that he—and the rest of the nation—hoped would bring the country out of the Great Depression. Together, these steps were called the New Deal.

President Roosevelt's "New Deal" of 1934–1936 included many government programs that gave jobs to people who were out of work. For example, the Civilian Conservation Corps (CCC) put many young men to work in national forests. Also the Works Progress Administration (WPA) created many different types of jobs, including jobs in road, public school, and airport construction. Probably the best-known New Deal project was the Tennessee Valley Authority (TVA), which resulted in the construction of dams and electrical power plants along the Tennessee River.

The New Deal was also the beginning of Social Security, which is a government-run system that provides income for retired workers or those who can no longer work because they are sick or injured.

The New Deal included government programs that were meant to keep people from losing all their money if their bank went out of business. One of those programs created the Federal Deposit Insurance Corporation (FDIC), which replaces people's lost money when a bank either loses money or has to close its doors. Having the FDIC in place to insure against the loss of cash helped people begin to trust banks again.

A Slow and Painful Recovery

Different countries started to recover from the Great Depression at different times. For most, the recovery started in 1933. The United States' recovery began in the spring of 1933, but it was slow going for several more years. By 1940 the unemployment rate in the United States was down to 15 percent—better than the 25 percent during the worst part of the Depression, but still very high.

Over the past several decades, historians and economists (people who specialize in the study of the world's economies) have argued about what brought about the end of the Great Depression. Some believe the end came as a result of President Roosevelt's New Deal, while others believe military spending on World War II played a much more important role in bringing the United States out of its worst-ever economic downturn. Many others believe it was a combination of both.

WORTH REPEATING

"The only thing we have to fear is fear itself."
—President Franklin Roosevelt, during his first inaugural address in 1933

DID YOU KNOW?

The New Deal described in this chapter was actually President Roosevelt's second recovery plan. The first, which was put into effect in 1933–1934, set price and wage controls in all industries and also cut farm production to raise prices of goods produced on farms. This first New Deal ended in March 1935, when the US Supreme Court declared it unconstitutional.

THE ALLIED NATIONS VS. THE AXIS POWERS

Allied Nations
The British Empire
The Soviet Union (Russia)
The United States
France
Poland
China
Australia
Belgium
Brazil
Canada
Czechoslovakia
Ethiopia
Greece
Mexico
The Netherlands
New Zealand
Norway
Union of South Africa
Yugoslavia

Axis Nations
Germany
Japan
Italy
Hungary
Romania
Bulgaria
Finland*
Iraq*
Thailand*
San Marino*
Yugoslavia*
India*
*Nations that did not sign an official pact with the Axis nations but were allied with them during World War II.

There is no question, though, that the Great Depression ended at about the same time nations of the world began spending massive amounts of money on war materials at the start of World War II. It's also true that this increased spending provided jobs for people who had been unemployed.

World War II: How It All Started

World War II began in 1939 and ended in 1945. It was the most widespread military conflict in human history. Almost every nation in the world was involved, and eventually two opposing sides developed: the Allies, which included the United States, Great Britain, and the Soviet Union (Russia), also known as The Big Three; and the Axis, which included Germany, Italy, and Japan.

Even though World War II started in 1939, the United States didn't get involved until 1941. The American military fought World War II on two different fronts or "theaters"—one in the Pacific Ocean against Japan, and the other against the Axis powers in Europe. Before the war ended in 1945, more than 400,000 Americans lost their lives. A total of more than 72 million people—mostly civilians—died in World War II.

In some very important ways, the effects of the Great Depression led the world into World War II. Many of the nations worst affected by the Great Depression changed their leaders and their forms of government during that time. That included Germany, where Adolf Hitler's Nazi party rose to power and took control in January 1933.

The war in the Pacific started on July 7, 1937, when Japan invaded China. Earlier, the Japanese had invaded Manchuria, where they began developing industries and mining, believing it would stimulate economic growth and help bring Japan out of the Great Depression.

The European war began on September 1, 1939, when the Nazis began their invasion of Poland. Hitler wanted to expand his empire throughout Europe, including what was then the Soviet Union. He thought the best way to do that was to first invade Poland, which had been given some German territory after World War I.

War Spreads through Europe

After Germany invaded Poland, Britain and France quickly declared war on the Nazis. Germany easily overran Poland, and then in the spring of 1940, the Germans conquered Norway and Denmark. They followed those conquests by taking the Netherlands (also known as Holland), Belgium, and then France.

By then Germany controlled all of western Europe except for Great Britain. Hitler wanted to take Britain, too, so he started bombing the nation for weeks at a time in hopes the British people would be weakened enough for another easy German invasion.

The Germans bombed Britain all through the summer of 1940. The British fought back valiantly, shooting down large numbers of German planes. In October 1940, Hitler abandoned his plans to invade Britain and turned his attention to the Soviet Union, which he invaded in June 1941.

The United States supported Great Britain during this time, sending money, weapons, and ships. The United States had declared neutrality in the war, meaning the Americans would stay out of the conflict. But after German submarines sank several American ships, the United States moved closer to war with the Axis powers.

INTERESTING!

One of the reasons Nazi Germany was so successful early in World War II—at least until the United States joined the Allies—was a military strategy called blitzkrieg, which means "lightning war." This strategy called for tanks, planes, and soldiers to attack all at the same time. Using this strategy, Germany overwhelmed the smaller armies of its neighbors.

December 7, 1941: When World War II Became America's War

During the first few years of World War II, the American public was reluctant to get involved in the conflict. World War I was still fresh in most Americans' minds, and they didn't want to enter another war that could cost many thousands of American lives. That changed on December 7, 1941. At 7:55 that morning, the first wave of Japanese planes attacked the American naval base at Pearl Harbor in Oahu, Hawaii.

With little chance to prepare, American ships and sailors were nearly defenseless as the first wave of 183 Japanese warplanes attacked, followed by a second wave of 167 planes an hour later. The Americans tried to fight back, but by the time the attack was over, 21 of the 96 ships anchored in Pearl Harbor had been sunk, and others had been badly

HISTORIC HAPPENINGS

Eight US Navy battleships, three destroyers, and four other smaller ships were damaged in the December 7, 1941, attack on Pearl Harbor. Among the battleship casualties:

USS *Arizona*, which sank nine minutes after being struck by a torpedo, killing 1,177 aboard.

USS *Oklahoma*, which rolled on its side and pinned many of its crew underwater inside the ship. Of the Oklahoma's crew of 1,301, 429 died.

USS *West Virginia* sank after being struck numerous times by both torpedoes and bombs.

USS *Nevada*, after being struck several times by torpedoes and bombs during the first attack wave, the *Nevada* tried to get out to sea through the narrow channel leading into the harbor. Planes in the second wave attempted to sink the *Nevada* and block the channel, but the *Nevada*'s crew chose to run the ship aground instead.

WORTH REPEATING

"I fear that we have awakened a sleeping giant and filled him with a terrible resolve."
—Japanese Admiral Isoroku Yamamoto, after the attack on Pearl Harbor

damaged. The Japanese also attacked Hickam, Wheeler, and Bellows airfields, destroying 188 planes and damaging 159 more. A total of 2,403 people, including 68 civilians, died in the attack, and 1,178 more were wounded.

The day after the attack, President Roosevelt asked the United States Congress to declare war on Japan. Not only did Congress answer with an overwhelming "Yes!" but the American public was now united in a common goal: Make the Japanese pay for their attack on Pearl Harbor.

But the United States wouldn't be going to war only with Japan. On December 11, 1941, Germany and Italy declared war on the United States, which meant American forces would be fighting in the European theater of World War II and not just in the Pacific.

The Turning Point in the Pacific War

Within a week of the Pearl Harbor attack, Japan invaded the Philippines, Burma, and Hong Kong. Later, the Japanese also took Borneo, Java, and Sumatra. It was starting to look as if the Japanese had an overwhelming advantage against the United States. But things began to turn against Japan at the Battle of Midway, which took place June 4–7, 1942 (about six months after Pearl Harbor) at Midway Atoll—about one-third of the way across the Pacific Ocean between Honolulu, Hawaii, and Tokyo, Japan.

By the time the Battle of Midway was over, more than 3,000 Japanese had died and four Japanese aircraft carriers had been destroyed. This was the turning point in the Pacific War. The Allies now had the upper hand, and they used it to launch a huge counteroffensive (a time of fighting back) against the Japanese.

The US Navy, under the command of Admiral Chester Nimitz, launched the first stage of the counteroffensive. US Marines landed on the southwest Pacific island of Guadalcanal and other nearby islands in the Solomon Islands. Meanwhile, the US Army, under the command of General Douglas MacArthur and with help from Australian allies, took New Guinea's Papuan peninsula.

Over the next several months, Allied forces, under the command of Nimitz and MacArthur, so weakened the enemy's capabilities that it was only a matter of time before Japan would be completely defeated. In late November 1944, the Allies began strategically bombing the islands of Japan.

Even though there were two major campaigns left in the Pacific War—on Luzon in the Philippines and at Okinawa, Japan—the Japanese naval forces had been beaten down to the point that they were defenseless. Japan's air force had also been virtually destroyed. Not only that, Japanese cities were being bombed almost daily.

Victory in Europe

At first, the war in Europe didn't go very well for the United States and the rest of the Allied forces. Germany and the Axis won decisive victories everywhere they went. All through 1942, Germany continued bombing British cities. That summer, the Germans marched through southern Russia toward a huge city called Stalingrad (now Volgograd). The Nazis also had control of North Africa.

But the war began to turn the Allies' way in 1943. The Battle of Stalingrad raged on between August 1942 and early February 1943. On February 2, after an estimated two million military and civilian deaths, the Nazis and their allies were forced to surrender. Like the Battle of Midway in the Pacific War, the Battle of Stalingrad proved to be a turning point in the European theater.

INTERESTING!

The attack on the US base at Pearl Harbor was a devastating blow to America's ability to fight from the sea, but it wasn't the crippling attack Japanese Admiral Isoroku Yamamoto, who had planned the attack, had hoped it would be. For one thing, the American aircraft carriers normally moored at Pearl Harbor were not in port that day but were out to sea. History shows that the aircraft carrier was the US Navy's dominant ship and that by failing to sink the American carriers, the Japanese left the American fleet ready for war. Also, of the 21 ships the Japanese attack sank on December 7, 1941, all but three were raised, repaired, and sailed during the war.

WORTH REPEATING

"Build me a son, O Lord, who will be strong enough to know when he is weak, and brave enough to face himself when he is afraid, one who will be proud and unbending in honest defeat, and humble and gentle in victory."
—Douglas MacArthur

HISTORY MAKERS

George Smith Patton III (1885–1945) was a US Army officer who is best remembered for his leadership as a commander during World War II. As a US Army general, Patton played a key role in the Allied invasion and victory in North Africa in November 1942. He also led advances across France and Germany in 1944–1945, which led to the end of World War II.

WORTH REPEATING

"You will bring about the destruction of the German war machine, the elimination of Nazi tyranny over the oppressed peoples of Europe, and security for ourselves in a free world. . . . I have full confidence in your courage, devotion to duty, and skill in battle. We will accept nothing less than full victory. Good luck, and let us all beseech the blessings of Almighty God upon this great and noble undertaking."
—General Dwight D. Eisenhower, giving the D-day order on June 6, 1944

Later that year, British and American troops took North Africa from the Nazis. Once the Allies had control of North Africa, they turned their attention to Italy. In September 1943, Italian troops officially surrendered to the Allies. Meanwhile, the Soviets were driving the Germans out of one Soviet city after another.

Even though the Allies were making advances all over Europe, Germany wasn't ready to give up the fight. The Nazis fought to keep control of Italy, but Allied forces held on and continued making gains there.

On June 6, 1944, American, British, and Canadian troops landed on the beaches of Normandy, France. This was called D-day. The Americans suffered many casualties, but the massive invasion ended with the Allies in control of the French beaches, and it was the beginning of the end for Hitler's control of France. Two months later, Paris was liberated. After that, the Allies made steady progress against the Axis powers all over Europe as German troops began retreating toward Berlin, the German capital.

In December 1944, the Germans began one last counterattack against the Allies. It was called the Battle of the Bulge, and it took place in parts of Belgium, Luxembourg, and France. At first, the German army was successful, but in January 1945, Hitler had to withdraw his troops.

The Allies were victorious over the Nazis in the Battle of the Bulge, and it was only a matter of months before the Allied victory was complete. In the spring of 1945, Soviet troops attacked Berlin while American and British troops

strengthened their hold on Italy. In April 1945, Adolf Hitler killed himself, and in early May the Germans surrendered. The European part of World War II was over.

In the final days of the war, the Allies made a terrible discovery inside Nazi Germany. As the Soviets marched through Eastern Europe and into Germany, they found many concentration camps where the Nazis imprisoned Jews, political prisoners, gypsies, and other people they didn't like. Some of the camps were prisons where people were treated terribly and made to perform slave labor. But some camps were death camps, where people were sent to be murdered. The Nazis murdered millions of people in these camps. This terrible part of human history is called the Holocaust.

INTERESTING!

The Soviet Union was formed in 1922, after the Russian Revolution of 1917, when Russia joined with the Ukraine, Belorussia (now Belarus), the Trancaucasian Federation (Armenia, Azerbaijan, and Georgia) to form the Union of Soviet Socialist Republics (the USSR). By 1940 nine more republics joined the USSR for a total of fifteen. The Soviet Union was dissolved in 1991.

Japan's Final Surrender

On August 6, 1945, a Boeing B-29 bomber called the *Enola Gay* flew over the Japanese city of Hiroshima and dropped the first atomic bomb ever used during wartime. The bomb, which was code-named Little Boy, caused massive destruction and the deaths of tens of thousands of people. Three days later, a second atomic bomb fell—this one code-named Fat Man—this time on the city of Nagasaki.

Some important military figures from the United States were sure that dropping two atomic bombs on Japan— only a few days apart—would quickly cause the Japanese to surrender. That is exactly what happened.

Over the decades since the United States dropped two atomic bombs on Japan, ending the war in the Pacific, people have argued and debated whether or not it was the right thing to do. People who believe it was right say that dropping the bombs meant Allied forces would not have to invade mainland Japan, meaning many Allied lives would be saved. But people who oppose the use of the atomic weapons argue that the United States was going to win the war anyway, so there was no reason to use weapons that caused such terrible death and destruction.

On August 15, 1945, Japanese Emperor Hirohito announced his country's surrender and ordered his soldiers to stop fighting. On September 2, officials from the Japanese government boarded the USS *Missouri* and signed the Japanese surrender. The war in Europe had already ended by this time, meaning that September 2, 1945 (now known as V-J Day—for "Victory over Japan") marked the end of the biggest, bloodiest war in human history.

A New Kind of War—The Cold War

When World War II ended, the world looked very different from how it had been before the war. Most important, Germany, Japan, and Italy were no longer the military powers they had once been. Now, only two world

powers—the United States and the Soviet Union—were left.

The United States and the Soviet Union had been allies against Nazi Germany and the rest of the Axis countries during World War II, but not long after the war ended, the two countries entered into a long period of mutual distrust—and ill will—toward each other. This period of history is known as the Cold War.

During the Cold War, which began in about 1947 and ended in 1991, the United States and the USSR engaged in political conflict, military threats, and proxy wars (meaning wars fought by or for countries allied with either the United States or the USSR) between what was called the "Communist world" (the Soviet Union and its allies) and the "Western world" (the United States and its allies).

During the Cold War, the United States and the USSR never entered into any direct major military conflict with each other. But the two countries were fierce rivals in just about every other way imaginable. Both nations placed military forces in strategic parts of the world, and each spied on the other and spread propaganda. They both spent billions of dollars on an "arms race," with both countries stockpiling nuclear and conventional weapons.

America's First Real "Cold War" War

The Korean War, which started on June 25, 1950, and ended on July 27, 1953, was the first major armed conflict between the Communist world and the non-Communist world. It started when Communist North Korea invaded non-Communist South Korea. Although the Soviet Union stayed out of the war for the most part, armed forces from the United States and China fought in the war.

Japan ruled the Korean Peninsula starting in 1910 and ending with its defeat in World War II. Following Japan's surrender in 1945, the peninsula was divided along the Thirty-eighth Parallel (a line going all the way around the earth 38 degrees north of the equator). After World War II, troops from the United States occupied the southern part

of the peninsula and troops from the Soviet Union occupied the North. In 1948 the South and the North established separate governments. The Communist North was called the Democratic People's Republic of Korea, and the South was called the Republic of Korea.

There had been minor battles and raids between the two sides in the months leading up to the invasion, but all-out war started between North Korea and South Korea on June 25, 1950, when the North Korean army crossed the Thirty-eighth Parallel—the border between the two countries—and invaded its neighbor to the south.

After the invasion, US President Harry Truman felt a lot of public pressure to do something about it. This was during the Cold War, and most people in the United States saw Communism as the world's biggest threat. Truman met with his advisers, who recommended that the US military conduct air strikes against North Korean targets. Truman ordered the air strikes and also ordered the US Navy's Seventh Fleet to move into position to protect the island of Formosa (now Taiwan).

Going to War...But Not Alone

HISTORY MAKERS

Douglas MacArthur (1880–1964) not only served as the UN's supreme commander during the first part of the Korean War, he also served as supreme commander of the Allied war effort in the Pacific during World War II. MacArthur also directed the Allies' postwar occupation of Japan. Early in the Korean War, he planned the landing at Inchon, which helped South Korea take back territory North Korea had taken when it invaded in 1950. MacArthur retired from military service as the most decorated serviceman in American history.

On June 25, 1950, the United Nations Security Council unanimously passed Resolution 82, which condemned the invasion of South Korea. The Soviet Union, which had veto power over UN Security Council resolutions, boycotted the meeting. Two days later, the Security Council published Resolution 83, which recommended that member nations offer military assistance to South Korea.

North Korea had a lot more soldiers than South Korea, though the South's troops were better trained and had better equipment. Not only that, the suddenness of the attack surprised the South. North Korea would likely have overrun South Korea had it not been for help from the United States and the UN.

At first, the Korean War didn't go very well for the United States and its allies. Early on, North Korean soldiers overwhelmed the UN forces and drove them into a small area around the city of Pusan, which is located in the southeastern corner of the Korean Peninsula. The forces desperately held their position along what was called the Pusan Perimeter.

President Harry S. Truman

US general Douglas MacArthur, the UN supreme commander in Korea, knew something had to be done before it was too late. He wanted to order an invasion far behind the North Korean troops at Inchon, which was on the peninsula's west coast. After receiving approval for the attack, MacArthur ordered the invasion. On September 15, 1950, the first UN troops stormed the beach at Inchon.

The attack caught North Korea completely by surprise. The UN forces quickly took Inchon and then marched toward Seoul, the capital city of South Korea, which the North Koreans had captured earlier. On September 25, after days of terrible fighting, the UN forces retook Seoul. Meanwhile, forces that had been trapped at the Pusan Perimeter were able to break out and push the enemy toward the north.

After the landing at Inchon and the breakout from the Pusan Perimeter, the North Koreans were in full retreat. UN forces quickly retook all of South Korea and continued north, into North Korea. It looked like the war was almost over.

A Whole New Problem in Korea

After UN troops reached the Yalu River on the border of North Korea and Communist China, the Chinese feared that they were about to be invaded. In late November 1950, Chinese soldiers poured into North Korea. Now the UN and South Korea were fighting two enemies: North Korea and China.

China's attack pushed the UN troops back to the Thirty-eighth Parallel, the original border between North and South Korea. The key battle in China's offensive was called the Battle of Chosin Reservoir, which resulted in a major loss for the UN forces. The United States First Marine Division suffered the heaviest losses in the battle.

General MacArthur urged President Truman to declare war on China, and even wanted the United States to use atomic weapons against the Chinese. When he openly criticized President Truman in 1951, he was relieved of his command.

WORTH REPEATING

"We have now gained a truce in Korea. We do not greet it with wild rejoicing. We know how dear its cost has been in life and treasure."
—President Dwight D. Eisenhower

The Korean War continued on into 1953, with neither side taking much territory from the other. When Dwight D. Eisenhower became the thirty-fourth president of the United States, he decided to end the war, which he called a "stalemate," meaning neither side could win. That made the Korean War the first war the United States fought in and did not win.

During much of the war, officials from both sides took part in talks to bring peace back to the Korean Peninsula. That peace came on July 27, 1953, when representatives from North Korea, China, and the UN signed a cease-fire called the Korean Armistice Agreement. The agreement established a demilitarized zone (DMZ) around the Thirty-eighth Parallel. To this day, troops from North Korea on one side and South Korea and the United States on the other defend the DMZ.

Even though more than four million people died in the Korean War, including more than 50,000 Americans, the Korean War isn't as well remembered as either World War II or the Vietnam War. That is why the Korean War is often called "America's Forgotten War." ✖

CHAPTER 8

Four Decades of Big Change

The 1960s through Y2K

One thing you've probably noticed as you've read through this book is that US history is filled with all kinds of changes—changes in how people live, think, and do business with one another.

But in the period of American history between the end of the 1950s through the close of the twentieth century, it seemed as if everything that *could* change *did* change. The world underwent huge changes in technology and business, and the culture in the United States was almost completely transformed.

Even though good things happened during the 1960s (for example, the US government passed civil rights legislation that gave African Americans the same rights as everyone else), the United States went through sometimes painful social change, due in large part to the Vietnam War.

During this era, the United States also became the world's only military superpower when the Soviet Union broke apart in the early 1990s. That event changed the already large role the United States played throughout the world.

This chapter will give you a quick look at the events that took place between 1960 and the end of the millennium. After you've read it, you'll understand how different the world became in just 40 years.

When the "Cold War" Heated Up

One of the most important—and scary—Cold War events was what is now called the Cuban Missile Crisis, which took place in 1962. The Cuban Missile Crisis is regarded as the closest the world has ever come to widespread nuclear war.

The Cuban Missile Crisis involved three countries: the United States, the Soviet Union, and of course, Cuba. The crisis came to national attention on October 14, 1962, when a US Air Force U-2 spy plane captured pictures proving that the Soviet Union was constructing missile bases in Cuba, which is located only 90 miles from the Florida coast.

HISTORIC HAPPENINGS

On April 16, 1961, less than three months after John F. Kennedy was sworn in as president of the United States, a military force made up of Cuban exiles who had been trained by the Central Intelligence Agency (CIA) attempted to overthrow the government of Cuban dictator Fidel Castro when they launched what is now known as the Bay of Pigs Invasion. The exiles, who had the support and encouragement of the US government, were defeated in less than three days by Cuban armed forces, which had been trained and equipped by the Soviet Union.

WORTH REPEATING

"We will not prematurely or unnecessarily risk the costs of worldwide nuclear war in which even the fruits of victory would be ashes in our mouth—but neither will we shrink from that risk at any time it must be faced."
—President John F. Kennedy, in an October 22, 1962, speech to the nation

The Bay of Pigs today.

Cuba and the Soviet Union began construction of the bases, which would have housed missiles with the ability to strike most of the continental United States, after unsuccessful attempts by the United States to overthrow Fidel Castro's Cuban regime in 1961. Also, in 1958 the United States had installed nuclear-tipped missiles in Italy and Turkey, and the Soviets wanted to have their own weapons closer to North America.

When President Kennedy announced the situation to the American public, he said the United States had demanded that the Soviets dismantle the missile bases under construction in Cuba and remove all their offensive weapons. He also announced that the United States would impose a blockade around Cuba, not allowing any ships to sail to Cuba. The United States also considered military attack on Cuba.

Kennedy's administration didn't believe the Soviets would agree to his demands, but thought they were prepared for a military conflict with the

United States. In a letter to President Kennedy, Soviet leader Nikita Khrushchev said that the announced blockade of Cuba was "an act of aggression propelling humankind into the abyss of a world nuclear-missile war."

The confrontation ended peacefully—and quickly. On October 28, 1962, President Kennedy and the United Nations secretary-general reached an agreement with the Soviet Union. The Soviets agreed they would close their weapons bases in Cuba in exchange for an American promise never to invade Cuba again. In a secret agreement, the United States also agreed to remove some of its weapons systems from Europe and Turkey.

Entering the Vietnam War... One Step at a Time

The second of the United States' wars fought during the Cold War period was the Vietnam War. Vietnam is a small country in Southeast Asia. The Vietnam War, which began in 1957 and ended in 1975, was fought between Communist North Vietnam and non-Communist South Vietnam.

During the Vietnam War, the Soviet Union, China, and North Korea supported North Vietnam, while the United States—along with allies Thailand, Australia, New Zealand, and the Philippines—supported South Vietnam. The Soviet Union never sent fighting troops to the Vietnam War, but the United States did.

HISTORIC HAPPENINGS

On August 28, 1963, between 200,000 and 300,000 Americans gathered in Washington, DC, for the Great March on Washington. The march was in support of civil rights for African Americans. That day at the Lincoln Memorial, the great civil rights leader Martin Luther King Jr. delivered his famous "I Have a Dream" speech, calling for harmony between the races. The march is credited with moving Congress to pass the 1964 Civil Rights Act and the 1965 Voting Rights Act. You can read Dr. King's whole speech in Appendix D (page 154).

The war happened because North Vietnam wanted to reunite North and South into a single nation. The two countries were separated in 1954, after France was defeated in a conflict called the First Indochina War. For many years before that, the country was called French Indochina.

After the First Indochina War, the plan was for French Indochina to temporarily split into two countries until closely supervised free elections could be held in 1956. The elections were never held, so the two remained split—into the Democratic Republic of Vietnam (the North) and the State of Vietnam (the South).

Starting around 1957, a group called the Vietcong, which called itself the National Liberation Front (NLF), began assassinating important people in South Vietnam. The Vietcong were actually South Vietnamese rebels who agreed with North Vietnam's goal of uniting the North and South into one country.

Before sending troops to fight in Vietnam, the United States backed the anti-Communist government in South Vietnam. That included sending military advisers to help train the South Vietnamese army. In 1959 North

Vietnam started giving more and more military assistance to the Vietcong, which used that assistance in attacks on South Vietnamese military units. The United States responded to these attacks by sending even more help to South Vietnam, including soldiers who served as military advisers.

A Terrible Day for the United States

As the 1964 presidential election approached, President Kennedy was confident he would easily defeat his Republican opponent, Arizona Senator Barry Goldwater. Kennedy believed a big win would mean he had the support of the American people for the changes he wanted to make in the country. But he also knew there would still be some roadblocks to his plan. In Texas, Vice President Lyndon Johnson's home state, a disagreement between Governor John Connally and Senator Ralph Yarborough prompted President Kennedy to tour the state of Texas with both men to give the public a show of unity in the party.

HISTORY MAKERS

Barry Goldwater (1909–1998) was a conservative politician who represented the state of Arizona for five terms in the US Senate. Goldwater was the Republican Party's nominee for president in the 1964 election, but he lost to Democrat Lyndon Johnson. Goldwater was known as "Mr. Conservative" because he helped lead a resurgence of the conservative movement in the United States in the 1960s.

HISTORIC HAPPENINGS

On July 2, 1964, President Lyndon Johnson signed the Civil Rights Act of 1964, which outlawed many forms of discrimination against African Americans and women. This legislation, which passed Congress despite objections from many Southern Democrats, was intended to address some of the problems that arose after Reconstruction. It ended voter registration requirements designed to keep blacks from voting, as well as racial segregation in schools, at the workplace, and at facilities that served the general public.

On Friday, November 22, 1963, President Kennedy and his wife, Jacqueline, were riding in an open limousine traveling in a motorcade through downtown Dallas. Governor Connally was riding with them, and the three waved at crowds gathered on the streets to see the president.

At 12:30 in the afternoon, shots rang out, and the president was struck in the neck and head. Though he was rushed to the hospital, President Kennedy died a few hours later. Governor Connally was also seriously wounded in the attack, but he survived. Vice President Lyndon Johnson took the oath of office as president just minutes after the announcement that Kennedy had died.

Investigators quickly discovered that the shots that killed President Kennedy had come from a sixth-floor window of the Texas School Book Depository building. Lee Harvey Oswald, an employee in the building, was seen leaving the building right after the shots were fired. It wasn't long before police arrested Oswald in a movie theater.

Police questioned Oswald for two days. Oswald claimed he was innocent, but it was discovered that he had purchased the rifle used in the shooting for $12.78 through a mail-order business. Also, his palm prints were found on the rifle.

Once the police were done questioning Oswald, they led him from the Dallas city jail to the county jail. As Oswald was being led out, Jack Ruby, a Dallas nightclub owner with connections to organized crime, shot and killed the accused assassin. Ruby was arrested on the spot and was later convicted of murder for killing Oswald. On January 3, 1967, he died of lung cancer—while awaiting a second trial in the killing of Oswald.

On November 25, 1963, President Kennedy's body was buried at Arlington National Cemetery in Virginia. Representatives from more than 90 nations, including the Soviet Union, attended the funeral. Jacqueline Kennedy lit an "eternal flame," which still burns over President Kennedy's grave.

HISTORIC HAPPENINGS

On April 4, 1968, an escapee from the Missouri State Penitentiary named James Earl Ray shot the great civil rights leader Martin Luther King Jr. as he stood on a second-floor balcony of the Lorraine Motel in Memphis, Tennessee. King later died of his wounds. Many of the people who worked with King called for a peaceful response to the murder, but riots broke out in many US cities.

A New President, a New Policy in Vietnam

Under President Kennedy, US involvement in the Vietnam War was limited to aid and advice to the South Vietnamese military. That changed under President Johnson, who, in 1965, began sending hundreds of thousands of combat troops to Vietnam. By 1968 around a half million US soldiers were serving there.

Starting on January 31, 1968, North Vietnamese soldiers, along with the Vietcong, began a military campaign against South Vietnam and the United States called the Tet Offensive. They attacked military and civilian targets throughout South Vietnam in hopes of winning the war with a massive and focused assault that would lead to the fall of the South Vietnamese government in Saigon.

Up to that point, the Tet Offensive was the largest military operation by either side in the Vietnam War. At first the US and South Vietnamese armies were surprised by the scope of the

attack, but they quickly regained control of the areas under attack and inflicted heavy casualties on the Vietcong and North Vietnamese forces.

Although the Tet Offensive resulted in a military victory for South Vietnam and the United States, it was a psychological victory for the Vietcong and caused President Johnson's administration all kinds of trouble at home. The American people, who had been led to believe that the United States and South Vietnam were winning the war, were shocked by the size of the Communist attack. More and more Americans began telling the US government to bring the American troops home from Vietnam and let the South Vietnamese fight for themselves.

The End of the Vietnam War

INTERESTING!

As the Vietnam War dragged on, President Johnson's popularity as president declined steadily. He had won the election in 1964, and he was eligible to run again. But on March 31, 1968, Johnson concluded a nationally televised speech with this announcement: "I shall not seek, and I will not accept, the nomination of my party for another term as your president."

Though President Johnson knew that South Vietnam and the United States had defeated the Vietcong in the Tet Offensive, the Vietcong won the battle of public opinion. Making things worse for President Johnson was a report in 1968 that US forces had suffered the worst week for casualties in the entire war. During 1968 more than 16,500 American soldiers died in the Vietnam War.

After the Tet Offensive, the United States began to slowly withdraw many of its soldiers from the country while training and equipping the South Vietnamese to continue fighting. This policy was called Vietnamization.

In 1973 the United States pulled almost all its troops out of Vietnam. In January of that year, North and South Vietnam signed a peace treaty in Paris, and the last American ground troops left Vietnam two months later,

leaving only a few as military advisers. Even though the cease-fire had been called, fighting between North and South Vietnam started up again soon after the US soldiers left. Without the United States there to defend South Vietnam, North Vietnam attacked, and on April 30, 1975, the war ended when South Vietnam surrendered to North Vietnam. After that, Vietnam was again a united country.

A Man on the Moon

Before we move on to what happened in the United States after the Vietnam War, let's rewind a bit, back to 1961. On May 25 of that year, President Kennedy addressed Congress and proposed a wild idea: that the United States speed up its space program and set a goal of sending astronauts to the moon by the end of the 1960s.

Kennedy's goal of sending a man to the moon before 1970 was part of what is called the Space Race, which was yet another part of the Cold War. By 1961 the Soviet Union had pulled ahead of the United States in the Space Race. In October 1957, the Soviets sent a satellite called *Sputnik* into orbit, and a month later they sent the first animal (a dog named Laika) into space. Then in April 1961, the Soviets sent the first human—Yuri Gagarin—into space.

The United States had some catching up to do, and President Kennedy knew it. His goal became reality on the morning of July 16, 1969, when a Saturn V rocket carrying the Apollo 11 mission and its crew of astronauts Neil Armstrong, Edwin "Buzz" Aldrin, and Michael Collins launched from Florida's Kennedy Space Center. Apollo 11 included a command module called *Columbia* and a lunar lander (the vehicle that would actually land on the moon's surface) called the *Eagle*.

Three and a half days after blastoff, Apollo 11 reached the moon's orbit. On July 20, astronauts Armstrong and Aldrin landed the *Eagle* on an area of the moon's surface called the Sea of Tranquillity while Collins stayed behind in the command module taking photographs and conducting scientific experiments. About six and a half hours later, with hundreds of millions of people watching on television worldwide, Armstrong became the first human to set foot on the moon's surface when he stepped out of the *Eagle* and put his left foot down.

Aldrin and Armstrong spent three hours on the moon's surface that day, collecting soil and rock samples and setting up instruments. They also planted an American flag and left a commemorative plaque. Armstrong also spoke the famous words, "That's one small step for man, one giant leap for mankind."

Armstrong and Aldrin spent a total of 21 hours on the moon before lifting off in the *Eagle* to return to the spaceship *Columbia* and the voyage back home. The three-man crew splashed down in the Pacific Ocean on July 24, 1969—eight days after liftoff from the moon.

Over the next few years, American astronauts made five more successful moon landings. The last one took place on December 11, 1972. Another mission to the moon, Apollo 13, launched on April 11, 1970, but the astronauts had to return to earth after an oxygen tank exploded, causing severe damage to the spacecraft's electrical system. All three astronauts—James Lovell, John Swigert, and Fred Haise—returned safely.

What's a Watergate?

President Richard S. Nixon

During the Vietnam War, there were many disagreements among the American public about whether the United States should be fighting in such a faraway place. Once the war was over, Americans hoped that their country could start moving in a better direction. But people's optimism started to fade after what is called the Watergate scandal—which began on June 17, 1972, when Washington, DC, police arrested five men for breaking in to the Democratic National Committee headquarters at the Watergate building in Washington.

At first, President Nixon denied any involvement in the burglary. But over a span of several months, more and more evidence mounted against some of Nixon's staff members. Some of the people who had worked for Nixon revealed that the president had recorded several conversations about the break-in, including the fact that he had tried to cover up the scandal.

President Nixon tried to keep the recordings from going public, and after several months of legal battles, the United States Supreme Court ruled that he had to hand over the recordings. President Nixon knew he had two choices: stay in office and face impeachment by the House of Representatives or resign. On August 9, 1974, President Nixon, the thirty-seventh president of the United States, became the first and only president to resign from the highest office in America.

After Nixon's resignation, his vice president, Gerald Ford, took office as the thirty-eighth president of the United States. President Ford later pardoned Nixon, meaning the former president wouldn't have to face criminal charges for his part in the Watergate scandal.

A Tough Four Years

On November 2, 1976, Jimmy Carter, the former governor of Georgia, defeated Gerald Ford to become the thirty-ninth president of the United States. The American people wanted more than anything to put the Watergate scandal behind them, and many hoped that would happen after Carter defeated Ford.

Unfortunately, Carter's presidency was a tough four years for the nation. The national economy suffered due to high inflation, high interest rates, high unemployment, and a severe shortage of oil due to lower sales by oil-producing nations.

But things got a lot worse for President Carter on November 4, 1979, when students in the Middle Eastern nation of Iran stormed the US Embassy in Tehran, the capital city, and took 66 Americans hostage. The students did that in support of what is called the Iranian Revolution (or the Islamic Revolution), which led to the replacement of Iran's monarchy (a system of government with a king) with an Islamic Republic under the rule of Ayatollah Ruholla Khomeini, who led the revolution.

A crowd of about 500 students rushed the embassy after learning that Shah Mohammad Reza Pahlavi, their former national leader (*shah* was an Iranian title for a king), had been admitted to an American hospital for medical treatment. The militants took 66 Americans captive. Of those, 13 were released on November 19 and 20, 1979, and another was released on July 11, 1980. The remaining 52 remained in Iranian captivity.

This incident is called the Iran Hostage Crisis, and it lasted for a total of 444 days. President Carter, who already faced a very difficult reelection campaign because the United States was in the middle of a deep recession, tried everything he could to get the hostages released, but nothing he tried worked.

In 1980 two things happened that helped end the hostage crisis. First, the Shah died in Egypt. Second, Iraq invaded Iran, starting the long and bloody Iran-Iraq War. Now, the Iranians were open to ways to end the hostage crisis. After Ronald Reagan defeated Jimmy Carter in the 1980 presidential election, negotiations for the hostages' release began. Iran released the 52 hostages on January 20, 1981, just as Reagan was completing his inaugural address after being sworn in as the fortieth president of the United States.

HISTORIC HAPPENINGS

Sports fans—and even those who weren't sports fans—from the United States took great pride and satisfaction in a Cold War-era victory over the Soviet Union's hockey team in the 1980 Winter Olympic games in Lake Placid, New York. The Soviets were thought to be unbeatable, but Team USA pulled off one of the greatest upsets in sports history with a 4–3 win. Team USA went on to win the gold medal with a win over Finland in the championship game.

INTERESTING!

In 1980 the United States didn't send athletes to the Summer Olympics, which were held in Moscow, the capital of the Soviet Union. President Carter decided to boycott the Olympics after the Soviet Union invaded Afghanistan in 1979. It was the only time since the modern Olympics began in 1896 that the United States has not participated in an Olympic competition.

The "Reagan Revolution" and the End of the Cold War

Ronald Reagan served as the president of the United States from 1981 until 1989. During that time, he worked to bring the American economy out of a deep recession, to strengthen the US military, and to oppose the Soviet Union wherever he could. The changes President Reagan made are often called the Reagan Revolution.

By the time President Reagan took office in 1981, the Cold War had been going on for more than three decades and had cost the United States *trillions* of dollars and more than 100,000 lives in the Korea and Vietnam wars.

HISTORIC HAPPENINGS

On April 24, 1980, the United States military attempted to rescue the 52 American hostages being held in Iran, in Operation Eagle Claw. The mission failed, largely because of a sandstorm in the desert, and it resulted in the loss of two US military aircraft as well as the deaths of eight American servicemen and an Iranian civilian. US Secretary of State Cyrus Vance, who had opposed the mission, resigned after its failure.

HISTORIC HAPPENINGS

On March 30, 1981, just 69 days into his presidency, Ronald Reagan was badly wounded by gunfire from a man named John Hinckley Jr. Reagan's press secretary, James Brady, a Washington police officer named Thomas Delahanty, and a Secret Service agent named Timothy McCarthy were also wounded in the attack, which took place outside the Washington Hilton Hotel. Reagan recovered from his wounds and was released from the hospital on April 11. Reagan became the first US president to survive being shot in an assassination attempt. Reagan later said he believed God spared his life so that he could go on to fulfill a greater purpose.

HISTORIC HAPPENINGS

On Tuesday, January 28, 1986, the people of the United States— including hundreds of thousands viewing on television—were shocked and saddened at the news that the space shuttle *Challenger* exploded 73 seconds after liftoff, killing all seven of its crew members: Michael J. Smith, Dick Scobee, Ronald McNair, Ellison Onizuka, Christa McAuliffe, Gregory Jarvis, and Judith Resnik.

WORTH REPEATING

"Mr. Gorbachev, open this gate. Mr. Gorbachev, tear down this wall!" —President Ronald Reagan, on June 12, 1987, challenging Soviet leader Mikhail Gorbachev to destroy the Berlin Wall

The president saw the Soviet Union as a constant threat to freedom around the world, so he put into action what became known as the Reagan Doctrine. Under the Reagan Doctrine, the United States provided aid to anti-Communist movements in African, Asian, and Latin American countries that were supported by the Soviet Union.

Some historians give President Reagan a lot of credit for helping bring an end to the Cold War, but others believe the Soviet Union would have eventually collapsed on its own, which would have ended the Cold War. Others believe that both Reagan and Soviet leader Mikhail Gorbachev, who came to power in 1985, both helped end the Cold War.

There were many reasons for the end of the Soviet Union and the Cold War. In December 1991, more than two years after Ronald Reagan left office and was replaced by George H.W. Bush, the Soviet Union broke up into 15 separate countries. Americans—and people from around the world— celebrated the end of the Soviet Union and saw it as a victory for freedom.

The Cold War was now history, and the world—and America's place in it—had changed. Now there were no longer two military superpowers but just one: the United States. The world was still an uncertain, dangerous place, but the United States would no longer have to deal with its rival from the end of World War II.

The First Gulf War

Just before the end of the Cold War—and after the Soviet Union had stopped being a world military power—the United States found itself in a position where leadership was required during an international conflict.

The Persian Gulf War started on August 2, 1990, when Iraqi president Saddam Hussein ordered his forces to invade Kuwait and take control of the small, defenseless nation. Saddam ordered the invasion because he believed

Kuwait was actually part of Iraq. He also believed that Kuwait's oil rigs near the border between the two countries had been siphoning off some of Iraq's oil supplies.

Saddam Hussein believed that the United States and other nations wouldn't come to Kuwait's defense, but he was wrong. Within days of the Iraqi invasion, the United States, as well as other members of the United Nations, demanded that Iraq immediately leave Kuwait. Not long after that, the United States and other UN

HISTORY MAKERS

H. Norman Schwarzkopf (born 1934), who is also known as "Stormin' Norman" and "The Bear," served as a US Army general and as commander of the Coalition Forces in the Persian Gulf War of 1991. Schwarzkopf had previously served in Vietnam and was promoted to the rank of general in 1988.

HISTORY MAKERS

Henry Ross Perot (born 1930) is a very successful American businessman who is best remembered for running for president of the United States in 1992 and 1996. In 1992, Perot ran against President George H. W. Bush and Democratic challenger Bill Clinton. Perot won almost 19 percent of the popular vote that year, and many people believe his candidacy helped Bill Clinton win the election by taking votes away from President Bush.

member nations sent troops to Saudi Arabia and other areas of the Persian Gulf region. This part of the war was called Operation Desert Shield.

On January 16, 1991—after Iraq refused to withdraw from Kuwait—a US-led coalition of UN nations began bombing Iraq and its forces in Kuwait. This part of the effort to liberate Kuwait was called Operation Desert Storm.

Saddam Hussein responded to the bombing by launching missiles (developed by the Soviet Union and known by the name Scud) at Israel

and Saudi Arabia. Saddam hoped that firing missiles at Israel would bring that nation into the war and cause other Arab nations to come to Iraq's defense. Just as Israel was set to retaliate against Iraq, President George H. W. Bush promised to protect Israel from the Scuds using US Patriot missiles, which shot down the Scuds.

By the time the Allied armies launched the ground war, the Iraqi forces in Kuwait were already beaten because the intense bombing campaign had cut off their supplies. Thousands of Iraqi soldiers in Kuwait, knowing the cause was hopeless, surrendered without a fight. Even when Iraq's Republican Guard, which was better trained and better equipped than other Iraqi forces, chose to fight, the Allies used better-quality American, British, and French equipment to quickly defeat them.

By February 26, 1991, the Allies had taken control of Kuwait City. Meanwhile, Allied forces chased the Iraqi army back toward the Iraq-Kuwait border. In southern Iraq, Allied forces gathered at the Euphrates River near Basra in southern Iraq, while rebellions against Saddam Hussein's government began. President Bush ordered a cease-fire on February 27, and the remaining Iraqi troops were allowed to return home. The fighting ended on March 3, 1991, when Iraq accepted the terms of the cease-fire.

President George H. W. Bush.

The Close of the Twentieth Century

Though President George H. W. Bush led the Allies to victory over Iraq in the Persian Gulf War, the United States was going through an economic downturn during the last year of his term in office. That helped open the door to the election of the forty-second president of the United States, William Jefferson Clinton.

President Clinton won reelection in 1996 despite several scandals during his first term. That made him the first Democrat to serve two full terms as president since Franklin Delano Roosevelt more than 50 years earlier.

HISTORIC HAPPENINGS

On December 19, 1998, the US House of Representatives voted to impeach President Bill Clinton on charges of perjury and obstruction of justice. Clinton was accused of lying about a relationship he'd had with a young woman. But when the US Senate failed to reach the two-thirds majority vote needed to remove an impeached president from office, President Clinton remained in office. He was the second US president in history to be impeached by the House of Representatives.

President Bill Clinton

During Clinton's eight years in office, the United States enjoyed strong economic growth. In 1993 he signed the Family and Medical Leave Act, which required businesses who employed a large number of people to allow their employees unpaid leave when they had family or medical emergencies. Also, he worked with Republicans, who took control of the House of Representatives and the Senate in 1994, to reduce the nation's budget deficit. In 1999 the government ran on a balanced budget (meaning it didn't spend more than it took in through taxes) for the first time since 1969. ✖

CHAPTER 9

History Still in the Making

The Start of the Twenty-first Century

The 1990s were a relatively peaceful and prosperous time for most Americans (though there were a few international conflicts along the way). But as 1999 turned to 2000, things quickly became more uncertain.

The first two-plus decades of the new millennium featured some unique historic events for the United States: a presidential election that wasn't decided for weeks after the vote was taken, a horrible terrorist attack on our home soil, two long wars, the election of our first African American president, the election of a man who had never held public office, and a devastating pandemic.

Much of the history that took place during these years is still being written as scholars debate the importance and meaning of these events. In this chapter, you'll read about the people and events that made the most recent decades in US history so memorable.

An Unforgettable Presidential Election

The US presidential election of 2000 pitted Democrat Al Gore, the vice president of the United States and a former senator from Tennessee, against Republican George W. Bush, governor of Texas and the son of former president George H. W. Bush.

This election made history for a lot of reasons. First of all, it was the closest one since 1876: Bush won the election with 271 electoral votes to Gore's 266. Second, it was only the fourth presidential election in which a candidate won the electoral vote but not the popular vote (Gore received 543,895 more votes than Bush nationwide).

Al Gore

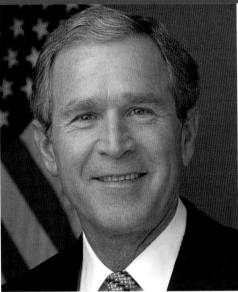

George W. Bus

Historically, most close elections are followed by accusations of fraud and disputes over vote counts. The 2000 presidential election was no exception. In fact, it was one of the most bitterly disputed elections in US history.

What Happened on November 7, 2000...and Beyond

The presidential election of 2000 was close throughout, so close that it came down to one state—Florida—and a few hundred votes separating the candidates. Early in the evening of that Election Day, the Associated Press, based on several factors, declared Vice President Gore the winner in Florida. But just a few hours after that declaration, the vote count in Florida tightened, and networks started describing the election as "too close to call."

Justices of the US Supreme Court were drawn into the battle between George W. Bush and Al Gore in the 2000 presidential election.

Eventually, after five weeks of legal challenges and lawsuits—some going all the way to the US Supreme Court—Gore went on national television to tell the American people that he had accepted Bush's victory. On January 20, George Bush was sworn in as the 43rd president of the United States. He was reelected in 2004 and served eight years.

September 11: A Dark Day in American History

When people mention certain dates, you know which event they're talking about. September 11, 2001, is one of those dates. When people say "September 11" or "9/11," you know they're talking about one of the worst days in American history.

Early that morning, nineteen members of the terrorist group al-Qaeda hijacked four commercial airliners and began using them as weapons against targets inside the United States. At 8:46 a.m. Eastern Time, one of those groups of hijackers crashed American Airlines Flight 11 into the World Trade Center's North Tower in New York City. Less than 20 minutes later, United Airlines flight 175 hit the South Tower. Both buildings collapsed less than two hours later.

At 9:37 a.m., another group of hijackers flew American Airlines Flight 77 into the Pentagon, the headquarters for the United States Department of Defense, which is located in Arlington, Virginia. At 10:03 a.m., the fourth

HISTORIC HAPPENINGS

September 11, 2001, was not the first time militants attempted to destroy the World Trade Center. On February 26, 1993, a man named Ramzi Yousef planted 1,500 pounds of explosives in the underground garage of the North Tower. The explosion killed six people and damaged the North Tower. Yousef fled to Pakistan after the bombing but was later arrested and brought back to the United States to stand trial for the attack.

flight, United Airlines Flight 93, crashed in a field near Shanksville, Pennsylvania, after passengers on board learned of the other attacks through telephone calls and fought back against the hijackers.

A Strong Response

In the days following the September 11 attacks, the United States worked to find out who was responsible. Once the United States and international intelligence were certain that al-Qaeda had carried out the attacks, the US began an anti-terrorism campaign against the Taliban, the Afghanistan government which had allowed terrorist leader Osama bin Laden and al-Qaeda to live and train there.

On October 7, 2001, the United States military, along with British armed forces, launched Operation Enduring Freedom—a campaign to find Osama bin Laden, end al-Qaeda's use of Afghanistan as a base for worldwide terrorist operations, remove the Taliban from power, and help the Afghan people create a new government.

Within three months after September 11, all of the major Taliban-controlled cities had fallen to the United States and its allies. Bin Laden and other top al-Qaeda leaders fled the country. The United States continued to search for him until May 1, 2011, when a team of Navy Seals stormed a compound in Abbottabad, Pakistan, and shot and killed him.

Most of the Taliban's top leaders left Afghanistan and fled to neighboring Pakistan. The Islamic Republic of Afghanistan was established with a temporary government under the leadership of Hamid Karzai. In 2004 the Afghan people voted to keep Karzai's government in power.

In 2003, Taliban forces, which were stationed in Pakistan, attempted to fight back against Karzai's government and against international troops in Afghanistan. When the US war in Afghanistan began, many people thought it wouldn't last long; however, it ended up surpassing the Vietnam War of the 1960s and 1970s as America's longest war.

The Second War with Iraq

In 2003, the United States went to war with Iraq again. President Bush and British Prime Minister Tony Blair believed Iraq was making "weapons of mass destruction" (or WMD) and was in league with al-Qaeda. To prevent WMDs from ending up in the hands of terrorists, American planes and the US Navy began bombing and firing missiles at key targets in and near the Iraqi capital city of Baghdad early in the morning on March 19, 2003. This launched the Iraq War, which is also called the Second Gulf War or Operation Iraqi Freedom.

After a few weeks of intense raids, the US-led coalition finally extended its control over the city of Baghdad.

US Army soldiers and local leaders walk down a mountain path in Afghanistan.

Mission Accomplished?

On May 1, 2003, President Bush boarded the aircraft carrier USS *Abraham Lincoln* and delivered the now-infamous "Mission Accomplished" speech, declaring that major combat in Iraq had ended.

But even though the United States and its allies had thoroughly defeated Iraq's military forces, the war was far from over.

That July, troops from the US 101st Airborne Division killed Uday and Qusay Hussein, the sons of Saddam Hussein. Then, on December 13, Saddam himself was captured, and he was later executed by the Iraqi government for war crimes. However, the United States military remained in Iraq for several more years, battling different groups that wanted the Americans to leave.

After President Bush's "Mission Accomplished" speech, forces from the United States and its allies saw an increase in attacks in different regions of Iraq. As US casualties from various attacks mounted, the American public stopped supporting the war—especially after no weapons of mass destruction were found in Iraq—and President Bush's popularity began to decline.

HISTORY MAKERS

Colin Powell (1937–2021) was a retired US Army general who served as the 65th secretary of state under President George W. Bush. Powell was the first African American to serve as secretary of state. During his military career, Powell served in several very important positions, including Chairman of the Joint Chiefs of Staff (the highest-ranked position in the US military) during the Gulf War of 1991.

Colin Powell (left) discussing the Gulf War with General Normal Schwarzkopf, commander of the coalition forces.

HISTORIC HAPPENINGS

On the morning of August 29, 2005, Hurricane Katrina, one of the strongest hurricanes in recorded history, slammed into the Gulf Coast area of the United States. At least 1,836 people died, making Katrina the deadliest hurricane to hit the United States since 1928. The storm also did $81 billion in damage. New Orleans, Louisiana, suffered the highest number of deaths as 80 percent of the city was flooded.

A National Change of Course

In the 2006 elections (which were called "midterm elections" because the next presidential election wasn't until 2008), President Bush's political party, the Republicans, lost badly to the Democrats, who took a 233–202 advantage in the House of Representatives and forged a tie in the United States Senate.

After the 2006 elections, the war in Iraq continued, and many people believe the war played a part in the outcome of the 2008 presidential election.

Another Historic Election

On February 10, 2007, Barack Obama, then serving as a senator from the state of Illinois, announced that he would run for president of the United States. On August 27, 2008, after a long season of campaigning against other Democrats, Obama was declared the Democratic Party's nominee, making him the first African American in history to run for president on a major party ticket.

As George W. Bush's second term as president neared its end, things weren't looking good for his party, the Republicans. The US military was mired in two wars and the national economy wasn't performing well. Even worse for the Republicans, the American economy in 2008 slid into the deepest recession since the Great Depression.

Historically, when the United States economy is in trouble, it spells doom for the political party in charge. Even though George W. Bush would be leaving office, people still associated the nation's economic problems with his party.

On November 4, 2008, Barack Obama defeated Republican John McCain in the presidential election, making Obama the first African American to win election as president of the United States.

A Big Change at the Top...and Other Places

After Barack Obama was sworn into office as the 44th president of the United States in January 2009, many of his supporters hoped he would move the country in a completely different direction than Bush had. Adding to that hope was the fact that the Democrat party now had a 257–178 advantage in the House and a smaller majority in the Senate.

Illinois senator Barack Obama, a Democrat, speaks at the 2008 Democratic National Convention. He would go on to defeat Republican John McCain to become the 44th president.

Many believed the country should immediately withdraw from the wars in Afghanistan and Iraq, that the Patriot Act should not be renewed, that the government should provide all people with health insurance, that wealthy Americans should pay more of their income in taxes, and that the government should do a lot more to protect the environment.

In late February 2009, President Obama announced that he wanted to withdraw US combat troops from Iraq within eighteen months, but that he would leave about 50,000 troops in the country "to advise and train Iraqi security forces and to provide intelligence and surveillance."

When President Obama first took office, people who agreed with his positions on those and other issues hoped he would take advantage of the Democrats' big advantage in Congress to pass laws they liked. On the other side, though, some thought President Obama wanted to do too much and make the government too big. They feared the Democratic advantage in Congress would make it too easy for Obama to pass controversial laws.

President Obama's Big Victory

In March 2010, President Obama used his advantage in Congress to help pass the Patient Protection and Affordable Care Act and the Health Care and Education Reconciliation Act of 2010. Together, these two bills made up what is called "health care reform."

Polls showed that both bills were very unpopular, yet they passed in Congress—the Senate in December 2009 and the House of Representatives in March 2010—without a single yes vote from the Republican side. In the final House vote, 178 Republicans and 34 Democrats voted against the bill.

After the bill's passage, it was challenged legally on the basis that some parts of the law—especially the part that requires all US citizens to have health insurance—were unconstitutional. Supporters said it would help lower health insurance costs, but critics said it would violate individual Americans' personal liberties.

On November 6, 2012, Obama and Vice President Joe Biden defeated former Massachusetts governor Mitt Romney and his running mate Paul Ryan to win a second term as president and vice president of the United States. Obama won the popular vote (51.1 percent to 47.2 percent) as well as the electoral college by a count of 332 to 206.

HISTORY MAKERS

Edward "Ted" Kennedy (1932–2009) was a United States Senator from Massachusetts who served nearly 47 years in the Senate, making him one of the longest-serving senator in US history. Edward Kennedy was the youngest brother of President John F. Kennedy and Senator Robert F. Kennedy, who were both assassinated in the 1960s. Edward Kennedy first entered the Senate after a 1962 special election to replace his brother John. He was elected to a full six-year term in 1964 and was reelected seven more times before his death on August 25, 2009.

2016: A Shocking Election Night Surprise

Barack Obama wasn't eligible to run for a third term as President of the United States. That meant that two new candidates—Democrat Hillary Clinton and Republican Donald Trump—would face off in the 2016 election to become the 45th president of the United States.

Clinton was an experienced politician who had served as the First Lady of the United States, as a US senator, and as the US Secretary of State for the Obama administration. Trump, however, was a political "outsider" who had never held political office but was well known as a businessman and reality television show host.

Nearly every pre-election poll had Clinton rolling to an easy win. But on Election Day of 2016 (November 8), Trump won in what many publications called "the most stunning upset in American history." Trump lost the popular vote by more than 2.8 million votes but won 30 states and 304 electoral votes to Clinton's 227.

Trump's Legacy

The first three years of the Trump presidency were a boom time for the American economy. The overall unemployment rate dropped to 3.5 percent, the lowest in 50 years. Unemployment rates for nearly all ethnic groups fell to record lows, and the rate for women fell to its lowest level in almost 70 years.

In addition, Trump appointed three United States Supreme Court justices—Neil Gorsuch to replace Antonin Scalia, Brett Kavanaugh to replace Anthony Kennedy, and Amy Coney Barrett to replace Ruth Bader Ginsburg. This gave conservatives a 6–3 majority in the nation's highest court.

Though many Americans strongly disagreed with Trump's policies and found his communication style abrasive, it looked after almost three years like he had a good chance of being reelected in 2020. But that all changed when a deadly microscopic enemy arrived on the shores of the United States.

New York businessman Donald Trump campaigns in Arizona. He defeated his Democrat opponent Hillary Clinton in his first run for public office.

The COVID-19 Pandemic

On December 31, 2019, the Chinese government reported an outbreak of pneumonia in Wuhan, China. Later, the cause of the outbreak was identified as SARS-CoV-2, which causes the highly contagious disease called COVID-19. Very quickly, the disease spread in Wuhan and then throughout the rest of the world, including the United States.

On January 21, 2020, officials in Washington state announced the first confirmed case of COVID-19 on US soil, and on January 30, 2020, the World Health Organization (WHO) declared the COVID-19 outbreak a "Public Health Emergency of International Concern." A few days later, the first US death from the disease was reported in California.

On March 11, the WHO declared the virus a "pandemic" (an outbreak of a disease that spreads across countries or continents). Two days later, the Trump administration declared a nationwide emergency, issuing a travel ban on non-US citizens traveling from 26 European countries due to the virus.

By late April of 2020, one million cases of COVID-19 had been reported in the US. About a month later, Johns Hopkins University claimed that 100,000 Americans had died from it.

Over the next several months, officials from most of the 50 US states issued stay-at-home orders in an effort to slow the spread of COVID-19. That meant businesses, schools, and even churches were closed down. But by the middle of June 2020, more than two million Americans had become infected. Even President Trump and First Lady Melania Trump tested positive on October 2.

COVID-19 also had a terrible effect on the US economy. In the spring of 2020, the unemployment rate in the US reached 14.7 percent—the worst since the Great Depression.

As of August 2023, there had been more than 100 million cases of COVID-19 diagnosed in America with more than a million deaths...though there has been some debate as to how accurate the figures are. Some question whether the deaths were all "from" the virus or in some cases "with" it—meaning a person had the virus in their body but actually died from a different cause.

Eventually, America began to emerge from the pandemic, and life started returning to normal. On May 5, 2023, the WHO declared an end to the global Public Health Emergency for COVID-19. The disease is no longer a pandemic but is still in what is called an "endemic" stage, meaning SARS-CoV-2 will stay with us humans from now on.

HISTORY MAKERS

Dr. Anthony Stephen Fauci (born December 24, 1940) is an American scientist and immunologist (someone who studies certain diseases). He was director of the National Institute of Allergy and Infectious Diseases (NIAID) from 1984 to 2022 and the chief medical advisor to the president from 2021 to 2022. During the COVID-19 pandemic, he served under President Trump as one of the lead members of the White House Coronavirus Task Force, even though Trump and Fauci often disagreed over COVID-19 policy. Fauci later served as a member of the White House COVID-19 Response Team under President Biden.

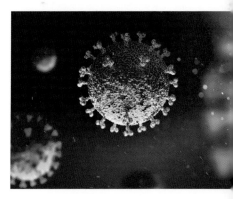

Another Change at the Top

Heading into Election

Day 2020, Donald Trump faced pressing problems in his bid for reelection. The COVID-19 pandemic and the severe economic downturn it caused—as well as unrest following the death of George Floyd at the hands of Minneapolis, Minnesota police officers—made the boom times of Trump's first three years seem like a distant memory for many voters.

Though Trump and many of his supporters disputed the final vote and electoral college totals, former vice president Joe Biden and his running mate Kamala Harris (one of California's two senators) took office in January of 2021. Biden ultimately received 306 electoral votes to Trump's 232.

Joe Biden began his tenure as the 46th president of the United States on January 20, 2021. At age 78, he began his term as the oldest president in American history. Biden immediately began reversing many of Trump's policies regarding the economy, energy policy, and border security.

HISTORIC HAPPENINGS

On January 6, 2021, following Joe Biden's electoral victory over Donald Trump, a mob stormed the US Capitol Building in Washington, D.C. Many people had gathered in the city to protest what they saw as a questionable election. A small percentage of people broke into the building. Each side accuses the other of creating the conditions that led to the unfortunate incident.

CHAPTER 10

Where Do We Go from Here?

Though this book is almost complete, history continues.

As this book was being produced, the 2024 presidential election was a picture of uncertainty. Would Joe Biden run for reelection? Could Republican front-runner Donald Trump overcome numerous Democrat-led legal challenges as he sought his party's nomination?

The US was not officially at war, as the last US troops were pulled out of Afghanistan in 2021, though the federal government was strongly supporting Ukraine in its conflict with Russia. COVID-19 was no longer a pandemic, though the virus still lingered. The national economy continued to struggle as politicians argued over inflation, taxes, and government spending.

Maybe all this uncertainty makes you uncomfortable. Maybe some important people in your life are out of work or worried about what big event will happen next—and what it will mean to all of us as Americans.

Where do we go from here? Only God knows. But never forget that He's in control!

Appendix A: The Presidents of the United States of America

George Washington, 1789–1797

John Adams, 1797–1801

Thomas Jefferson, 1801–1809

James Madison, 1809–1817

James Monroe, 1817–1825

John Quincy Adams, 1825–1829

Andrew Jackson, 1829–1837

Martin Van Buren, 1837–1841

William Henry Harrison, 1841

John Tyler, 1841–1845

James K. Polk, 1845–1849

Zachary Taylor, 1849–1850

Millard Fillmore, 1850–1853

Franklin Pierce, 1853–1857

James Buchanan, 1857–1861

Abraham Lincoln, 1861–1865

Andrew Johnson, 1865–1869

Ulysses S. Grant, 1869–1877

Rutherford B. Hayes, 1877–1881

James A. Garfield, 1881

Chester A. Arthur, 1881–1885

Grover Cleveland, 1885–1889

Benjamin Harrison, 1889–1893

Grover Cleveland, 1893–1897

William McKinley, 1897–1901

Theodore Roosevelt, 1901–1909

William Howard Taft, 1909–1913

Woodrow Wilson, 1913–1921

Warren G. Harding, 1921–1923

Calvin Coolidge, 1923–1929

Herbert Hoover, 1929–1933

Franklin D. Roosevelt, 1933–1945

Harry S Truman, 1945–1953

Dwight D. Eisenhower, 1953–1961

John F. Kennedy, 1961–1963

Lyndon B. Johnson, 1963–1969

Richard M. Nixon, 1969–1974

Gerald R. Ford, 1974–1977

James E. "Jimmy" Carter, 1977–1981

Ronald Reagan, 1981–1989

George H. W. Bush, 1989–1993

William J. Clinton, 1993–2001

George W. Bush, 2001–2009

Barack Obama, 2009–2017

Donald Trump 2017–2021

Joe Biden 2021–

Appendix B: The Declaration of Independence

IN CONGRESS, July 4, 1776.

The Unanimous Declaration of the Thirteen United States of America

When in the course of human events, it becomes necessary for one people to dissolve the political bands which have connected them with another, and to assume among the powers of the earth, the separate and equal station to which the Laws of Nature and of Nature's God entitle them, a decent respect to the opinions of mankind requires that they should declare the causes which impel them to the separation.

We hold these truths to be self-evident, that all men are created equal, that they are endowed by their Creator with certain unalienable Rights, that among these are Life, Liberty and the pursuit of Happiness.

That to secure these rights, Governments are instituted among Men, deriving their just powers from the consent of the governed.

That whenever any Form of Government becomes destructive of these ends, it is the Right of the People to alter or to abolish it, and to institute new Government, laying its foundation on such principles and organizing its powers in such form, as to them shall seem most likely to effect their Safety and Happiness. Prudence, indeed, will dictate that Governments long established should not be changed for light and transient causes; and accordingly all experience hath shewn that mankind are more disposed to suffer, while evils are sufferable, than to right themselves by abolishing the forms to which they are accustomed. But when a long train of abuses and usurpations, pursuing invariably the same Object evinces a design to reduce them under absolute Despotism, it is their right, it is their duty, to throw off such Government, and to provide new Guards for their future security.

Such has been the patient sufferance of these Colonies; and such is now the necessity which constrains them to alter their former Systems of Government. The history of the present King of Great Britain is a history of repeated injuries and usurpations, all having in direct object the establishment of an absolute Tyranny over these States. To prove this, let Facts be submitted to a candid world.

He has refused his Assent to Laws, the most wholesome and necessary for the public good.

He has forbidden his Governors to pass Laws of immediate and pressing importance, unless suspended in their operation till his Assent should be obtained; and when so suspended, he has utterly neglected to attend to them.

He has refused to pass other Laws for the accommodation of large districts of people, unless those people would relinquish the right of Representation in the Legislature, a right inestimable to them and formidable to tyrants only.

He has called together legislative bodies at places unusual, uncomfortable, and distant from the depository of their public Records, for the sole purpose of fatiguing them into compliance with his measures.

He has dissolved Representative Houses repeatedly, for opposing with manly firmness his invasions on the rights of the people.

He has refused for a long time, after such dissolutions, to cause others to be elected; whereby the Legislative powers, incapable of Annihilation, have returned to the People at large for their exercise; the State remaining in the meantime exposed to all the dangers of invasion from without, and convulsions within.

He has endeavored to prevent the population of these States; for that purpose obstructing the Laws for Naturalization of Foreigners; refusing to pass others to encourage their migrations hither, and raising the conditions of new Appropriations of Lands.

He has obstructed the Administration of Justice, by refusing his Assent to Laws for establishing Judiciary powers.

He has made Judges dependent on his Will alone, for the tenure of their offices, and the amount and payment of their salaries.

He has erected a multitude of New Offices, and sent hither swarms of Officers to harass our people, and eat out their substance.

He has kept among us, in times of peace, Standing Armies without the Consent of our legislatures.

He has affected to render the Military independent of and superior to the Civil power.

He has combined with others to subject us to a jurisdiction foreign to our constitution, and unacknowledged by our laws; giving his Assent to their Acts of pretended Legislation:

For Quartering large bodies of armed troops among us:

For protecting them, by a mock Trial, from punishment for any Murders which they should commit on the Inhabitants of these States:

For cutting off our Trade with all parts of the world:

For imposing Taxes on us without our Consent:

For depriving us in many cases, of the benefits of Trial by Jury:

For transporting us beyond Seas to be tried for pretended offences:

For abolishing the free System of English Laws in a neighboring Province, establishing therein an Arbitrary government, and enlarging its Boundaries so as to render it at once an example and fit instrument for introducing the same absolute rule into these Colonies:

For taking away our Charters, abolishing our most valuable Laws, and altering fundamentally the Forms of our Governments:

For suspending our own Legislatures, and declaring themselves invested with power to legislate for us in all cases whatsoever.

He has abdicated Government here, by declaring us out of his Protection and waging War against us.

He has plundered our seas, ravaged our Coasts, burnt our towns, and destroyed the lives of our people.

He is at this time transporting large Armies of foreign Mercenaries to complete the works of death, desolation and tyranny, already begun with circumstances of Cruelty & perfidy scarcely paralleled in the most barbarous ages, and totally unworthy the Head of a civilized nation.

He has constrained our fellow Citizens taken Captive on the high Seas to bear Arms against their Country, to become the executioners of their friends and Brethren, or to fall themselves by their Hands.

He has excited domestic insurrections amongst us, and has endeavored to bring on the inhabitants of our frontiers, the merciless Indian Savages, whose known rule of warfare, is an undistinguished destruction of all ages, sexes and conditions.

In every stage of these Oppressions We have Petitioned for Redress in the most humble terms: Our repeated Petitions have been answered only by repeated injury. A Prince whose character is thus marked by every act which may define a Tyrant, is unfit to be the ruler of a free people.

Nor have We been wanting in attentions to our British brethren. We have warned them from time to time of attempts by their legislature to extend an unwarrantable jurisdiction over us. We have reminded them of the circumstances of our emigration and settlement here. We have appealed to their native justice and magnanimity, and we have conjured them by the ties of our common kindred to disavow these usurpations, which would inevitably interrupt our connections and correspondence. They too have been deaf to the voice of justice and of consanguinity. We must, therefore, acquiesce in the necessity, which denounces our Separation, and hold them, as we hold the rest of mankind, Enemies in War, in Peace Friends.

We, therefore, the Representatives of the United States of America, in General Congress, Assembled, appealing to the Supreme Judge of the world for the rectitude of our intentions, do, in the Name, and by Authority of the good People of these Colonies, solemnly publish and declare, That these United Colonies are, and of Right ought to be Free and Independent States; that they are Absolved from all Allegiance to the British Crown, and that all political connection between them and the State of Great Britain, is and ought to be totally dissolved; and that as Free and Independent States, they have full Power to levy War, conclude Peace, contract Alliances, establish Commerce, and to do all other Acts and Things which Independent States may of right do. And for the support of this Declaration, with a firm reliance on the protection of divine Providence, we mutually pledge to each other our Lives, our Fortunes and our sacred Honor. ✖

Appendix C: Abraham Lincoln's Gettysburg Address

Fourscore and seven years ago our fathers brought forth on this continent a new nation, conceived in liberty and dedicated to the proposition that all men are created equal.

Now we are engaged in a great civil war, testing whether that nation, or any nation so conceived and so dedicated, can long endure. We are met on a great battlefield of that war. We have come to dedicate a portion of that field as a final resting place for those who here gave their lives that that nation might live. It is altogether fitting and proper that we should do this. But, in a larger sense, we cannot dedicate, we cannot consecrate, we cannot hallow this ground. The brave men, living and dead, who struggled here have consecrated it far above our poor power to add or detract. The world will little note, nor long remember what we say here, but it can never forget what they did here. It is for us the living, rather, to be dedicated here to the unfinished work which they who fought here have thus far so nobly advanced. It is rather for us to be here dedicated to the great task remaining before us—that from these honored dead we take increased devotion to that cause for which they gave the last full measure of devotion—that we here highly resolve that these dead shall not have died in vain—that this nation shall have a new birth of freedom and that government of the people, by the people, for the people, shall not perish from the earth.

Appendix D: Martin Luther King Jr.'s "I Have a Dream" Speech

I am happy to join with you today in what will go down in history as the greatest demonstration for freedom in the history of our nation.

Five score years ago, a great American, in whose symbolic shadow we stand today, signed the Emancipation Proclamation. This momentous decree came as a great beacon light of hope to millions of Negro slaves who had been seared in the flames of withering injustice. It came as a joyous daybreak to end the long night of their captivity.

But one hundred years later, the Negro still is not free. One hundred years later, the life of the Negro is still sadly crippled by the manacles of segregation and the chains of discrimination. One hundred years later, the Negro lives on a lonely island of poverty in the midst of a vast ocean of material prosperity. One hundred years later, the Negro is still languishing in the corners of American society and finds himself an exile in his own land. So we have come here today to dramatize a shameful condition.

In a sense we have come to our nation's capital to cash a check. When the architects of our republic wrote the magnificent words of the Constitution and the Declaration of Independence, they were signing a promissory note to which every American was to fall heir. This note was a promise that all men, yes, black men as well as white men, would be guaranteed the unalienable rights of life, liberty, and the pursuit of happiness.

It is obvious today that America has defaulted on this promissory note insofar as her citizens of color are concerned. Instead of honoring this sacred obligation, America has given the Negro people a bad check, a check which has come back marked "insufficient funds." But we refuse to believe that the bank of justice is bankrupt. We refuse to believe that there are insufficient funds in the great vaults of opportunity of this nation. So we have come to cash this check—a check that will give us upon demand the riches of freedom and the security of justice. We have also come to this hallowed spot to remind America of the fierce urgency of now. This is no time to engage in the luxury of cooling off or to take the tranquilizing drug of gradualism.

Now is the time to make real the promises of democracy. Now is the time to rise from the dark and desolate valley of segregation to the sunlit path of racial justice. Now is the time to lift our nation from the quick sands of racial injustice to the solid rock of brotherhood. Now is the time to make justice a reality for all of God's children.

It would be fatal for the nation to overlook the urgency of the moment. This sweltering summer of the Negro's legitimate discontent will not pass until there is an invigorating autumn of freedom and equality. Nineteen sixty-three is not an end, but a beginning. Those who hope that the Negro needed to blow off steam and will now be content will have a rude awakening if the nation returns to business as usual. There will be neither rest nor tranquility in America until the Negro is granted his citizenship rights. The whirlwinds of revolt will continue to shake the foundations of our nation until the bright day of justice emerges.

But there is something that I must say to my people who stand on the warm threshold which leads into the palace of justice. In the process of gaining our rightful place we must not be guilty of wrongful deeds. Let us not seek to satisfy our thirst for freedom by drinking from the cup of bitterness and hatred.

We must forever conduct our struggle on the high plane of dignity and discipline. We must not allow our creative protest to degenerate into physical violence. Again and again we must rise to the majestic heights of meeting physical force with soul force. The marvelous new militancy which has engulfed the Negro community must not lead us to a distrust of all white people, for many of our white brothers, as evidenced by their presence here today, have come to realize that their destiny is tied up with our destiny. They have come to realize that their freedom is inextricably bound to our freedom. We cannot walk alone.

As we walk, we must make the pledge that we shall always march ahead. We cannot turn back. There are those who are asking the devotees of civil rights, "When will you be satisfied?" We can never be satisfied as long as the Negro is the victim of the unspeakable horrors of police brutality. We can never be satisfied, as long as our bodies, heavy with the fatigue of travel, cannot gain lodging in the motels of the highways and the hotels of the cities. We cannot be satisfied as long as the Negro's basic mobility is from a smaller ghetto to a larger one. We can never be satisfied as long as our children are stripped of their selfhood and robbed of their dignity by signs stating "For Whites Only". We cannot be satisfied as long as a Negro in Mississippi cannot vote and a Negro in New York believes he has nothing for which to vote. No, no, we are not satisfied, and we will not be satisfied until justice rolls down like waters and righteousness like a mighty stream.

I am not unmindful that some of you have come here out of great trials and tribulations. Some of you have come fresh from narrow jail cells. Some of you have come from areas where your quest for freedom left you battered by the storms of persecution and staggered by the winds of police brutality. You have been the veterans of creative suffering. Continue to work with the faith that unearned suffering is redemptive.

Go back to Mississippi, go back to Alabama, go back to South Carolina, go back to Georgia, go back to Louisiana, go back to the slums and ghettos of our northern cities, knowing that somehow this situation can and will be changed. Let us not wallow in the valley of despair.

I say to you today, my friends, so even though we face the difficulties of today and tomorrow, I still have a dream. It is a dream deeply rooted in the American dream.

I have a dream that one day this nation will rise up and live out the true meaning of its creed: "We hold these truths to be self evident: that all men are created equal."

I have a dream that one day on the red hills of Georgia the sons of former slaves and the sons of former slave owners will be able to sit down together at the table of brotherhood.

I have a dream that one day even the state of Mississippi, a state sweltering with the heat of injustice, sweltering with the heat of oppression, will be transformed into an oasis of freedom and justice.

I have a dream that my four little children will one day live in a nation where they will not be judged by the color of their skin but by the content of their character.

I have a dream today.

I have a dream that one day, down in Alabama, with its vicious racists, with its governor having his lips dripping with the words of interposition and nullification; one day right there in Alabama, little black boys and black girls will be able to join hands with little white boys and white girls as sisters and brothers.

I have a dream today.

I have a dream that one day every valley shall be exalted, every hill and mountain shall be made low, the rough places will be made plain, and the crooked places will be made straight, and the glory of the Lord shall be revealed, and all flesh shall see it together.

This is our hope. This is the faith that I go back to the South with. With this faith we will be able to hew out of the mountain of despair a stone of hope. With this faith we will be able to transform the jangling discords of our nation into a beautiful symphony of brotherhood. With this faith we will be able to work together, to pray together, to struggle together, to go to jail together, to stand up for freedom together, knowing that we will be free one day.

This will be the day when all of God's children will be able to sing with a new meaning, "My country, 'tis of thee, sweet land of liberty, of thee I sing. Land where my fathers died, land of the pilgrim's pride, from every mountainside, let freedom ring."

And if America is to be a great nation this must become true. So let freedom ring from the prodigious hilltops of New Hampshire. Let freedom ring from the mighty mountains of New York. Let freedom ring from the heightening Alleghenies of Pennsylvania!

Let freedom ring from the snowcapped Rockies of Colorado!

Let freedom ring from the curvaceous slopes of California!

But not only that; let freedom ring from Stone Mountain of Georgia!

Let freedom ring from Lookout Mountain of Tennessee!

Let freedom ring from every hill and molehill of Mississippi. From every mountainside, let freedom ring.

And when this happens, when we allow freedom to ring, when we let it ring from every village and every hamlet, from every state and every city, we will be able to speed up that day when all of God's children, black men and white men, Jews and Gentiles, Protestants and Catholics, will be able to join hands and sing in the words of the old Negro spiritual, "Free at last! free at last! thank God Almighty, we are free at last!"

9 Dja65/SS; 11 (top) Evgeniy Kazantsev/SS; (bottom) Nickolay Khoroshkov/SS; 12 DaLiu/SS; 13 Yangchao/SS; 14–15 Charles Plant/SS; 16 eskystudio/SS; 17 LesPalenik/SS; 18 Mihai_Andritoiu/SS; 20 Jose Antonio Perez/SS; 21 WM; 22 State Archives of North Carolina/WM; 23 Alexey Stiop/SS; 24 Library of Congress/WM; 25 Israel Mckee/SS; 26–27 YZm/SS; 28–29 I. Pilon/SS; 31 Everett Collection/SS; 32 Danny Xu/SS; 33 (top) ChiccoDodiFC/SS; (bottom) nayef hammouri/SS; 34 L F File/SS; 34–35 Chris Light/WM; 36 British Library/WM;Plateresca/SS; 44 Voinakh/SS; 45 Susan Law Cain/SS; 47 Ntguilty/SS; 48 John LeBlanc/SS; 52 (top) US Capitol/WM; (bottom) Kovalchuk Oleksandr/SS; 55 (top) Castleski/SS; (bottom) Jwwaddles/SS; 56 Jose Gil/SS; 57 vkilikov/SS; 59 Everett Collection/SS; 60 Rudy Balasko/SS; 62 WM; 63 Google Art Project/WM; 64 Maroonbeard/WM; 65 Dean Fikar/SS; 66 University of Texas at Arlington Libraries/WM; 68 Steve Broer/SS; 71 (top) Zoran Milic/SS; (bottom) Library of Congress/WM; 73 Morphart Creation/SS; 74–75 MidoSemsem/SS; 76 Everett Collection/SS; 77 Jason Bolinger/SS; 78 Adam Parent/SS; 80 zulufoto/SS; 81 Everett Collection/SS; 82 Kathleen Cole/WM; 84–85 Kovalchuk Oleksandr/SS; 86 Victor Moussa/SS; 87 (top) palasha/SS; (bottom) Library of Congress/WM; 88 Everett Collection/SS; 89 Marzolino/SS; 90–91 Perfect Gui/SS; 92 lynea/SS; 93 (top) Library of Congress/WM; (bottom left) James Steidl/SS; (bottom center) Mega Pixel/SS; (bottom right) Pressmaster/SS; 94 Westermak/SS; 96 Everett Collection/SS; 97 Vtldtlm/SS; 98 Everett Collection/SS; 99 Prachaya Roekdeethaweesab/SS; 101 FAawRay/SS; 102 Everett Collection/SS; 103 FDR Presidential Library & Museum/WM; 105 Red_Baron/SS; 106–107 ranchorunner/SS; 108 National Portrait Gallery/WM; 109 (top) WM; (bottom) Everett Collection/SS; 110 VectorPlotnikoff/SS; 111 Wollertz/SS; 112 Everett Collection/SS; 113 National Archives and Records Administration/WM; 115 Nerthuz/SS; 116 Radomir Rezny/SS; 117 Naval History and Heritage Command/WM; 118 (top) National Archives and Records Administration/WM; (bottom) Sidhe/SS; 119 Springfield Daily News/WM; 120–121 Michael Barera/WM; 121 Bubba73/WM; 122 LBJ Museum & Library/WM; 123 NASA/WM; 124 NASA/WM; 125 (top) National Archives and Records Administration/WM; (bottom) Vsevolod33/SS; 127 WM; 128 Edward Valachovic/WM; 129 (top) Prachaya Roekdeethaweesab/SS; (bottom) Everett Collection/SS; 130 Everett Collection/SS; 131 WM; 132 National Archives and Records Administration/WM; 133 Joseph Sohm/SS; 134 (top, left and right) WM; (bottom) davidsmith520/SS; 135 US National Archives/WM; 136 US Navy/WM; 137 US Army/WM; 138 (top) Den4is/SS; (bottom) US Army/WM; 139 NOAA/WM; 140 Library of Congress/WM; 142 Gage Skidmore/WM; 143 Andrii Vodolazhskyi/SS; 144 Christopher Michel/WM; 145 Lightspring/SS; 146–151 all WM; 165 Cheda/SS; 167 (top) Cheda/SS; (bottom) Baka Sobaka/SS; 168 US Air Force/WM; 169 Patriots711/WM; 170 Cheda/SS; 171 (left) f11photo/SS; (right) Vlad G/SS; 172 WM; 173 Cheda/SS; 174 (top left) ESB Professional/SS; (bottom left) Paul Brady Photography/SS; (right) Victorian Traditions/SS; 175 Everett Collection/SS; 176 Cheda/SS; 177 (left) Garrick Gillette/SS; (right) Sean Pavone/SS; 178 (both) Library of Congress/WM; 179 Cheda/SS; 180 (left) Aubrey Gough/SS; (right) Sean Pavone/SS; 181 Everett Collection/SS; 182 Cheda/SS; 183 Sergii Figurnyi/SS; 184 (top) cdrin/SS; (bottom) Mark R/SS; 185 Cheda/SS; 186 (left) Sean Pavone/SS; (right) National Museum of the US Navy/WM; 187 Library of Congress/WM; 188 Cheda/SS; 189 (both) Sean Pavone/SS; 190 Hans Peters/WM; 191 Cheda/SS; 192 ND700/SS; 193 NASA/WM; 194 Cheda/SS; 195 Sean Pavone/SS; 196 (left) Everett Collection/SS; (right) MidoSemsem/SS; 197 Cheda/SS; 198 (left) Sergii Figurnyi/SS; Kidfly182/WM; 200 Cheda/SS; 201 (left) Kevin Ruck/SS; (right) David Ross/SS; 202 Roland Gerrits/WM; 203 Cheda/SS; 204 (left) ESB Professional/SS; (right) Nina B/SS; 206 K.L. Kohn/SS; 207 (left) Sean Pavone/SS; (right) Sneaky Buddy/SS; 208 Everett Collection/SS; 209 Cheda/SS; 210 (left) f11photo/SS; (top right)

Barry Fowler/SS; (bottom right) Zack Frank/SS; 212 Cheda/SS; 213 (left) ESB Professional/SS; (right) Zack Frank/SS; 214 Library of Congress/WM; 215 Cheda/SS; 216 (top) AevanStock/SS; (bottom) arthurgphotography/SS; 217 MDart10/SS; 218 Cheda/SS; 219 (top) Clare Bonthrone/SS; (bottom) pisaphotography/SS; 221 Cheda/SS; 222 (left) f11photo/SS; (right) PhotosByLarissaB/SS; 223 Los Angeles Times Photographic Collection/WM; 224 Cheda/SS; 225 (left) Sean Pavone/SS; (right) Shannon/WM; 226 Library of Congress/WM; 227 Cheda/SS; 228 JaySi/SS; 229 (top) Skipper Pappy D/SS; (bottom) Library of Congress/WM; 230 Cheda/SS; 231 ESB Professional/SS; 232 (left) George Dodd III/SS; (right) National Archives and Records Administration/WM; 233 Cheda/SS; 234 (top left) Wangkun Jia/SS; (bottom left) Hank Shiffman/SS; (right) Sara Winter/SS; 236 Cheda/SS; 237 Sean Pavone/SS; 238 (left) Everett Collection; (right) National Archives and Records Administration/WM; 239 Cheda/SS; 240 (left) mnapoli/SS; (right) DaFoos/WM; 241 Naval Historical Center/WM; 242 Cheda/SS; 243 f11photo/SS; 244 Richard from USA/WM; 245 Cheda/SS; 246 (left) NASA/WM; (right) Virginia Blount/SS; 247 Songquan Deng/SS; 248 Cheda/SS; 249 Brandon Seidel/SS; 251 Cheda/SS; 252 (left) Henryk Sadura/SS; (right) Rexjaymes/SS; 253 WM; 254 Cheda/SS; 255 (left) Outtherestudio/SS; (top right) Nancy Gill/SS; (bottom right) Bryan Neuswanger/SS; 257 Cheda/SS; 258 logoboom/SS; 258 Los Paseos from Earth/WM; 260 Cheda/SS; 261 f11photo/SS; 262 Library of Congress/WM; 263 Cheda/SS; 264 (top) Jess Kraft/SS; (bottom) Matthew Connolly/SS; 265 WM; 266 Cheda/SS; 267 (left) Ian Ferg/SS; (right) TommyBrison/SS; 268 NASA/WM; 269 Cheda/SS; 270 (left) Joseph Sohm/SS; (right) Jon Bilous/SS; 272 Cheda/SS; 273 (top) Virrage Images/SS; (bottom) Christopher Moswitzer/SS; 275 Cheda/SS; 276 (top) Esme/SS; (bottom) Zack Frank/SS; 278 Cheda/SS; 279 (left) Wicker Imaging/SS; (right) Snehit Photo/SS; 280 Chris Owen/WM; 281 Cheda/SS; 282 (left) Real Window Creative/SS; (right) gavinreece/SS; 284 Cheda/SS; 284 (left) traveling_okie/SS; (right) critterbiz/SS; 286 Benjamin F Sullivan/SS; 287 Cheda/SS; 288 (left) Mihai_Andritoiu/SS; (right) Jason Maehl/SS; 289 Jack A./SS; 290 Cheda/SS; 291 (left) mahaloshine/SS; (right) Serge Yatunin/SS; 292 US Geological Survey/WM; 293 Cheda/SS; 294 (top) Charles Knowles/SS; (bottom) Karl Eggleston/SS; 295 J.J. Gouin/SS; 296 Cheda/SS; 297 (left) Spark Dust/SS; (right) Anthony Heflin/SS; 298 Jeffrey B. Banke/SS; 299 Cheda/SS; 300 (top) Joe Guetzloff/SS; (bottom left) Tomas Nevesely/SS; (bottom right) YegoroV/SS; 302 Cheda/SS; 303 (top) Sean Pavone/SS; (bottom) John A Davis/SS; 305 Cheda/SS; 306 (left) LizCoughlan/SS; (right) DBrower/SS; 307 Danita Delimont/SS; 308 Cheda/SS; 309 (top left) Dreamframer/SS; (right) iacomino FRiMAGES/SS; (bottom) Png Studio Photography/SS; 311 Cheda/SS; 312 (top) Real Window Creative/SS; (bottom) TripWalkers/SS; 313 Adam Van Spronsen/SS; 314 Cheda/SS; 315 (top) SCStock/SS; (bottom) Norbert Turi/SS; 316 Alexey Kamenskiy/SS; 317 MH Anderson Photography/SS; 318 South North Photography/SS

SS=Shutterstock / WM=Wikimedia

THE
AMERICAN
ADVENTURE!

A Conservative Christian
Kids' Guide to US History

WHAT'S IN THIS BOOK

What You'll Be Reading

You probably already know that the United States of America is a nation made up of 50 individual states, each with their own governments, economies, and ways of life. But what would you say if your friend were to ask how each of the 50 states came to be?

The 50 states weren't started when someone took a map of our country and just drew boundary lines through rivers, mountain ranges, and other landmarks. Actually, the story of how our 50 states became states is a lot more interesting than that—and a lot more fun to read about, too.

It all started early in the 1600s, when European settlers started arriving in what is now the eastern US and began establishing settlements called "colonies." By 1770, more than 2 million immigrants made their homes in 13 British colonies. For many years, most of the colonists remained loyal to England. But after a time, issues regarding taxation and a lack of representation in the British government convinced more and more colonists that they needed to make a break with their Mother Country.

In 1776 the Continental Congress formally adopted the Declaration of Independence, a document written mostly by Thomas Jefferson that was an official declaration to Great Britain that the colonists would no longer be English subjects but citizens of a newly formed, independent nation. American colonists had been fighting the British for several years, but the Declaration of Independence led to all-out war in a conflict called the American Revolutionary War.

After a long and bitter war between the British and the colonists, America emerged as an independent nation in 1783. In 1787 the United States Constitution was adopted at the Constitutional Convention in Philadelphia. Over the next several months, nine states ratified the Constitution, putting it into full effect on March 4, 1789. By this time 11 former colonies had become states, and over the next 170 years, another 39 states were welcomed into the Union for a total of 50.

This book is about those 50 states. It's about how they were first explored and settled, how they became states, and what they became once they became a part of the Union—also known as the United States of America.

As you read this book, you'll find some fun and informative facts about each of the 50 states, starting with Delaware (the first official state of the US) and ending with Hawaii (the 50th state). As you make your way through the pages, you'll be reading the following:

> an overview of each state, including fun information like its nickname, its official state bird and flower, its state song and motto, how it ranks among the 50 in area and population, and its counties (as well as some funny-sounding names of towns)

> how each state's constitution acknowledges faith in God

> some important historical dates, people, and facts

> details about important cities, natural features, and people

> each state's weird or unusual attractions

> some Christian history or facts about each state

As you dig into this book, there is something you should keep in mind: it won't teach you everything there is to know about each state. We could give you a book of this size about *each* state, and it still wouldn't give us enough space to tell the whole story of its history, the people who live there, each state's heritage of faith, or the natural features you can see if you visit there.

What we hope this book will do is give you a basic overview of what's important about each of the 50 united states—including their legacies of faith in God. We hope it will help you to understand how different the states are from one another, yet how united they are as one nation under God. ★

★★★ ONE ★★★

DELAWARE

The First State

BECAME A STATE ON: December 12, 1787	
NICKNAMES: The First State, The Diamond State, Blue Hen State, Small Wonder	
STATE BIRD: blue hen of Delaware	
STATE FLOWER: peach blossom	
STATE SONG: "Our Delaware"	
STATE MOTTO: Liberty and Independence	
POPULATION/RANK: 897,934/45	
TOTAL AREA/RANK: 2,489.27 square miles/49	
LIST OF COUNTIES: Kent, New Castle, Sussex	
FUNNY TOWN NAMES: Black Hog Landing, Locustville, Sheep Pen Landing	

DECEMBER 7, 1787

DE

SOME IMPORTANT DELAWARE HISTORY

> In 1609, Henry Hudson, exploring on behalf of the Dutch and looking for a northwest passage to China and Japan, discovers what would become known as Delaware Bay. A year later, English sea captain Samuel Argall names the bay and the river that flows into it after Lord De La Warr (Thomas West), the governor of the Virginia colony at the time.

> In 1631 Dutch traders attempt to settle in a coastal area east of Maryland, but they were killed in fights with the local natives.

> In 1638 a man named Peter Minuit leads a group of Swedish settlers to the Delaware River area. They name the new settlement New Sweden.

> In 1655 Holland captures the settlement from the Swedish, but in 1664 the British defeated the Dutch and took control of the area.

> On July 1, 1776 Caesar Rodney, a member of the Continental Congress, rides 70 miles through a terrible heat wave and thunderstorms to Philadelphia to cast a decisive vote in favor of American independence.

> On December 7, 1787, Delaware becomes the first of three other states to ratify the new United States Constitution that month, thereby becoming the first of the 50 United States.

Delaware's capital is full of historic buildings. . .and also home to Dover International Speedway, where NASCAR races are held several times a year.

IMPORTANT CITIES IN DELAWARE

Delaware's capital is full of historic buildings. . .and also home to Dover International Speedway, where NASCAR races are held several times a year.

DOVER: Dover is the second largest city and the state capital of Delaware. It is also the county seat of Kent County. It is located on the St. Jones River in the Delaware River coastal plain. William Penn named the city after a town by the same name in the county of Kent, England. In 1777, the capital of Delaware was moved from Newcastle, which was located on the Delaware River, to Dover.

WILMINGTON: Located where the Christina River and Brandywine Creek meet, Wilmington is the largest city in Delaware. Thomas Penn named the city after his friend Spencer Compton, Earl of Wilmington.

RIVERS, MOUNTAINS, AND OTHER NATURAL STUFF

DELAWARE RIVER/DELAWARE BAY: The Delaware River is a major river that flows through parts of five U.S. states—New York, New Jersey, Pennsylvania, Maryland, and Delaware. The Delaware River flows into Delaware Bay in an area bordered by New Jersey and Delaware. As European settlers began arriving in the area, it was inhabited by the Lenape Indians, who called the bay Poutaxat and the River Lenape Wihittuck, which means "the rapid stream of the Lenape."

NANTICOKE RIVER: The Nanticoke River is an important tributary of the Chesapeake Bay. It is 64.3 miles long and starts in Kent County in Delaware and forms the boundary between Dorchester and Wicomico counties in Maryland. The most notable Delaware community located on the banks of the Nanticoke River is Seaford.

WEIRDNESS IN DELAWARE

THE OLD LIBRARY MUSEUM: If you ever find yourself in New Castle, Delaware, you might have a chance to visit the Old Library Museum. It's quite a sight—the building is a hexagonal (six-sided) structure built in 1892 by the New Castle Library Society. It's not certain who designed the building, but many people believe Philadelphia architect Frank Furness was responsible.

SOME DELAWARE VIPS

ANNIE JUMP CANNON (1863–1941): The daughter of Delaware shipbuilder Wilson Lee Cannon, Annie Jump Cannon was an astronomer who grew up in Dover, Delaware. She was an important player in the development of the modern method of classifying stars and worked with Edward C. Pickering in creating what is called the Harvard Classification Scheme, which was the first serious attempt to classify stars based on their temperatures.

"SUGAR" RAY LEONARD (BORN 1956): Delaware's best-known athlete is probably Sugar Ray Leonard, who was born in Wilmington. At the 1976 Summer Olympics in Montreal, Canada, Leonard won the Gold Medal in the light heavyweight division.

As a professional boxer, he won world championships in five weight divisions, beating fellow future International Boxing Hall of Fame inductees Wilfred Benítez, Thomas Hearns, Roberto Durán, and Marvin Hagler.

Vice President Joe Biden

JOE BIDEN JR. (BORN 1942): Joe Biden became the 45th president of the United States following the November 2020 election. A former U.S. senator from Delaware and vice president under Barack Obama (2009–2017), Biden was born in Scranton, Pennsylvania, but moved to Delaware with his family in the early 1950s. He was elected to the U.S. Senate six times, the first time in 1972, before he resigned to serve as Obama's running mate. They were elected twice, in 2008 and 2012.

DELAWARE'S CHRISTIAN CONNECTION

On February 15, 1643, a Swedish Lutheran clergyman named John Campanius (1601–83), also known as John Campanius Holm, arrived at what was then called New Sweden. He traveled from Sweden to serve as chaplain for the first Swedish settlers to Fort Christina, near present-day Wilmington, Delaware, and to serve as a missionary to the Lenape Indians. ★

GOD IN DELAWARE'S CONSTITUTION (PREAMBLE)

Through Divine goodness, all men have by nature the rights of worshiping and serving their Creator according to the dictates of their consciences, of enjoying and defending life and liberty, of acquiring and protecting reputation and property, and in general of obtaining objects suitable to their condition, without injury by one to another; and as these rights are essential to their welfare, for due exercise thereof, power is inherent in them; and therefore all just authority in the institutions of political society is derived from the people, and established with their consent, to advance their happiness; and they may for this end, as circumstances require, from time to time, alter their Constitution of government.

TWO

PENNSYLVANIA

Birthplace of the United States

PA

SOME IMPORTANT PENNSYLVANIA HISTORY

> In 1609 Henry Hudson claims land for the Dutch that would become Pennsylvania.

> In 1643 Swedes establish first permanent settlement in Pennsylvania.

> In 1655 the Dutch seize Swedish settlements.

> In 1664 British capture Dutch colonies in name of Duke of York.

> In 1681 King Charles II grants William Penn Pennsylvania.

> In 1682 William Penn arrives in Pennsylvania and establishes Philadelphia.

> In 1688 Germantown Quakers adopt America's first anti-slavery resolution.

> In 1767 the boundary between Maryland and Pennsylvania is established and named the Mason-Dixon Line.

> In 1774 the First Continental Congress meets secretly in Philadelphia.

> In 1775 the Second Continental Congress meets; George Washington is named supreme commander.

BECAME A STATE ON: December 12, 1787	
NICKNAMES: Keystone State, Coal State, Oil State, Quaker State, State of Independence	
STATE BIRD: ruffed grouse	
STATE FLOWER: mountain laurel	
STATE SONG: "Pennsylvania"	
STATE MOTTO: Virtue, Liberty, and Independence	
POPULATION/RANK: 12,763,536/6	
TOTAL AREA/RANK: 46,055.24 square miles/33	
LIST OF COUNTIES: Adams, Allegheny, Armstrong, Beaver, Bedford, Berks, Blair, Bradford, Bucks, Butler, Cambria, Cameron, Carbon, Centre, Chester, Clarion, Clearfield, Clinton, Columbia, Crawford, Cumberland, Dauphin, Delaware, Elk, Erie, Fayette, Forest, Franklin, Fulton, Greene, Huntingdon, Indiana, Jefferson, Juniata, Lackawanna, Lancaster, Lawrence, Lebanon, Lehigh, Luzerne, Lycoming, McKean, Mercer, Mifflin, Monroe, Montgomery, Montour, Northampton, Northumberland, Perry, Philadelphia, Pike, Potter, Schuylkill, Snyder, Somerset, State Level Sites, Sullivan, Susquehanna, Tioga, Union, Venango, Warren, Washington, Wayne, Westmoreland, Wyoming, York	
FUNNY TOWN NAMES: Bird-in-Hand, Fairchance, Schwenksville	

The nighttime skyline of downtown Philadelphia, Pennsylvania.

Independence Hall is part of Independence National Historical Park in Philadelphia. It is located on Chestnut Street between 5th and 6th Streets.

> In 1776 the "Committee of Five" of the Second Continental Congress (John Adams, Benjamin Franklin, Thomas Jefferson, Robert R. Livingston, and Roger Sherman) is formed to draft a declaration of independence from Britain. The resulting document is signed in Philadelphia. Pennsylvania is established as a commonwealth.

> From 1777 to 1778 British troops occupy Philadelphia; General George Washington (America's first president) and his Continental Army spend the winter at Valley Forge, Pennsylvania.

> In 1777 the Congress of the United States is moved from Philadelphia to New York.

> In 1780 Pennsylvania becomes first state to abolish slavery.

> In 1787 Pennsylvania becomes second state to ratify US Constitution.

> From 1790 to 1800 Philadelphia is capital of US.

> In 1812 Harrisburg becomes state capital.

IMPORTANT CITIES IN PENNSYLVANIA

PHILADELPHIA: The largest city in Pennsylvania, Philadelphia is located in the southeastern part of the commonwealth. It is also the second largest city on the East Coast of the US. The city was founded in 1682 by William Penn, who intended for it to serve as the capital of the Pennsylvania Colony. Philadelphia is a major city in US history. It is where the Founding Fathers of the United States met and signed the Declaration of Independence in 1776 and the United States Constitution in 1787. It served as the nation's capital during the Revolutionary War and while Washington, DC, was being constructed.

PITTSBURGH: The second largest city in Pennsylvania, Pittsburgh is located in southwestern Pennsylvania. Pittsburgh is called "the Steel City" because it is home to more than 300 steel-related businesses, and "the Bridge City" for its 446 bridges.

HARRISBURG: The ninth largest city in Pennsylvania, Harrisburg is the state's capital. It is located on the east bank of the Susquehanna River. Harrisburg was incorporated as a city and was established as the state capital in 1812.

RIVERS, MOUNTAINS, AND OTHER NATURAL STUFF

SUSQUEHANNA RIVER: The sixteenth largest river in the US by water volume and the longest in the East Coast region that drains directly into the Atlantic Ocean, the Susquehanna River is 464 miles long. It is an important river in Pennsylvania because it drains almost half of the state's land area. Dozens of Pennsylvania cities and towns are located along the Susquehanna.

MOUNT DAVIS: At 3,213 feet above sea level, Mount Davis is the highest point in the Commonwealth of Pennsylvania. It is located in the Forbes State For-

GOD IN PENNSYLVANIA'S CONSTITUTION (PREAMBLE)

We, the people of the Commonwealth of Pennsylvania, grateful to Almighty God for the blessings of civil and religious liberty, and humbly invoking His guidance, do ordain and establish this Constitution.

est near the southern border of the state. Visitors can reach the Mount Davis summit by car or by the several hiking trails on the mountain.

PINE CREEK GORGE: Sometimes called the Grand Canyon of Pennsylvania (in miniature, of course!), the Pine Creek Gorge is a 47-mile-long canyon carved out by Pine Creek in the Tioga State Forest in Pennsylvania. Its deepest point is about 1,450 feet at the southern end, near Waterville.

WEIRDNESS IN PENNSYLVANIA

THE MÜTTER MUSEUM: The Mütter Museum is a medical museum located in Philadelphia. It is a strange attraction but educational at the same time. It is home to a collection of medical oddities, anatomical specimens, wax models, and medical equipment. In 1958 Dr. Thomas Dent Mütter donated the collection, hoping to further medical research and education. Today, however, the museum is open to the public. The museum features the famous Hyrtle Skull Collection, the tallest human skeleton on display in North America, slides of Albert Einstein's brain, and many even weirder displays.

SOME PENNSYLVANIA VIPS

WILLIAM PENN (1644–1718): William Penn was born in London, England, and was the founder of the British province of Pennsylvania, which would one day become the American Commonwealth of Pennsylvania. He was also a leader in the development of the city of Philadelphia. Penn was a devout Christian who believed strongly in religious freedom and in pacifism (avoiding war).

BENJAMIN FRANKLIN (1706–1790): Benjamin Franklin was born in Boston, Massachusetts, but later moved to Philadelphia. He was one of America's

Founding father, politician, inventor, writer, and publisher Benjamin Franklin.

Founding Fathers, a writer, a printer, a politician, a scientist, a musician, and a diplomat (among many other things). Franklin is sometimes called "the First American." He was elected to the Second Continental Congress and worked on a committee of five men who helped draft the Declaration of Independence. Franklin signed the Declaration in 1776.

REGGIE JACKSON (BORN 1946): Born in Wyncote, Pennsylvania, Reggie Jackson was a Major League Baseball outfielder who is best remembered for hitting three home runs in three consecutive at-bats in game 7 of the New York Yankees' World Series–clinching win over the Oakland A's in 1977. Jackson was named to 14 All-Star teams and won five World Series. He was inducted into the Baseball Hall of Fame in 1993.

PENNSYLVANIA'S CHRISTIAN CONNECTION

PENNSYLVANIA: THE BIRTHPLACE OF AMERICAN RELIGIOUS FREEDOM. In 1682, almost a full century before the American colonists declared their independence from England, William Penn (the founder of the British province of Pennsylvania) gave voice to what was then a radical idea: that people should be free to worship God according to their own consciences. Penn worked to make Pennsylvania a place of religious freedom and not a place where everybody had to attend the same church. He called this the "Holy Experiment," and it influenced the American Founding Fathers to include religious freedom as part of the United States Constitution. ★

★★★ THREE ★★★

NEW JERSEY

Land of Liberty and Prosperity

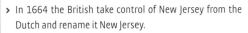

NJ

BECAME A STATE ON: December 18, 1787	
NICKNAME: the Garden State	
STATE BIRD: American goldfinch	
STATE FLOWER: common blue violet	
STATE SONG: "I'm from New Jersey"	
STATE MOTTO: Liberty and Prosperity	
POPULATION/RANK: 8,864,590/11	
TOTAL AREA/RANK: 8,721.30 square miles/47	
LIST OF COUNTIES: Atlantic, Bergen, Burlington, Camden, Cape May, Cumberland, Essex, Gloucester, Hudson, Hunterdon, Mercer, Middlesex, Monmouth, Morris, Ocean, Passaic, Salem, Somerset, State Level Sites, Sussex, Union, Warren	
FUNNY TOWN NAMES: Ho-ho-kus, Hopatcong, Timbuctoo	

SOME IMPORTANT NEW JERSEY HISTORY

> In 1524 Giovanni de Verrazano explores coastline.

> In 1609 Henry Hudson sails into Newark Bay, claims the land for the Dutch, and names it New Netherlands.

> In 1638 a Swedish colony is established along lower Delaware River.

> In 1664 the British take control of New Jersey from the Dutch and rename it New Jersey.

> In 1736 New Jersey forms its own government.

> In 1776 New Jersey adopts first state constitution; George Washington crosses Delaware River from Pennsylvania in surprise attack on British. Washington defeats British at Battle of Trenton.

> In 1783 Princeton serves as US capital, followed by Trenton in 1784.

> On December 18, 1787, New Jersey becomes third US state.

> In 1790 Trenton is declared state capital; New Jersey is first state to sign Bill of Rights.

> In 1846 the first baseball game is played at Hoboken.

IMPORTANT CITIES IN NEW JERSEY

NEWARK: Newark, which is located in northeastern New Jersey, is the largest city in the state. Newark was founded in 1666 and was formed as a township in 1693. It's located by the Atlantic Ocean on Newark Bay and is a major air, shipping, and rail hub of the United States.

Steel Pier amusement park rides in Atlantic City, New Jersey. The Steel Pier park opened in 1898.

JERSEY CITY: Jersey City is the second largest city in New Jersey. It is located in northeastern New Jersey. Like Newark, Jersey City is an important port city.

TRENTON: Trenton is New Jersey's 10th largest city and the state's capital. The area that would become Trenton was first settled in 1679 by Quakers who left Great Britain to avoid persecution and to practice their faith freely. Trenton was the site of George Washington's first military victory of the American Revolutionary War, the Battle of Trenton. Trenton became the New Jersey state capital in 1790.

The New Jersey capitol building in Trenton.

RIVERS, MOUNTAINS, AND OTHER NATURAL STUFF

DELAWARE RIVER: The Delaware River serves as the natural boundary between Pennsylvania and New York, between New Jersey and Pennsylvania, and most of the boundary between Delaware and New Jersey. Historically, the Delaware River is best remembered for George Washington's crossing on the night of December 25–26, 1776. Washington and his army crossed the river for a successful surprise attack on Hessian troops occupying Trenton, New Jersey, on behalf of the British during the American Revolutionary War.

An artist's depiction of General George Washington's historic crossing of the Delaware River near Trenton, New Jersey.

HIGH POINT: At 1,803 feet above sea level, the highest point in New Jersey is called. . .well, High Point. High Point is part of the Kittatinny Mountains, which are actually a long ridge of hills in northwestern New Jersey. At the peak of High Point is a 222-foot-tall pillar built in 1930 to honor those who have died in war. You can see three states—New Jersey, New York, and Pennsylvania—from the top of High Point.

THE NEW JERSEY PALISADES: Also called simply the Palisades or Hudson Palisades, the New Jersey Palisades are a row of steep cliffs located along the west side of the Hudson River in northeastern New Jersey and southern New York. The Palisades begin at Jersey City and stretch north about 20 miles to near Nyack,

New York. The cliffs rise almost vertically from near the edge of the river, reaching 300 to 540 feet, depending on the exact location.

WEIRDNESS IN NEW JERSEY

THE WORLD'S LARGEST LIGHT BULB: There's nothing all that weird about a museum that honors the work of the great American inventor Thomas Edison. Built in 1938, the Thomas Edison Memorial Tower and Menlo Park Museum in Edison, New Jersey, do just that. But the museum features a 118-foot-tall tower topped with the World's Largest Light Bulb. The bulb, which commemorates one of Edison's great inventions, stands 14 feet tall and weighs eight tons. The light bulb is illuminated at night. The museum was remodeled and reopened in 2012.

SOME NEW JERSEY VIPS

GROVER CLEVELAND (1837–1908): Grover Cleveland was the only US president to serve two nonconsecutive terms. He served from 1885 to 1889 and from 1893 to 1897, making him the 22nd and 24th presidents of the United States. Cleveland was born in Caldwell, New Jersey.

DAVE THOMAS (1932–2002): Dave Thomas is an American businessman who is best known as the founder and CEO of the fast-food chain Wendy's. He was born in Atlantic City, New Jersey. He opened his first Wendy's restaurant in Columbus, Ohio, in 1969.

SHAQUILLE O'NEAL (BORN 1972): Born in Newark, New Jersey, Shaquille O'Neal was one of the best centers ever to play in the National Basketball Association. O'Neal played college basketball at Louisiana State University before being drafted

U.S. President Grover Cleveland, who was born in New Jersey and served two non-consecutive terms as president.

by the Orlando Magic with the first pick of the 1992 NBA Draft. He played 19 years in the NBA, winning Rookie of the Year in 1992–1993 and NBA Most Valuable Player in 1999–2000. He was selected to the NBA All-Star game 15 times, led the league in scoring twice, and was named all-NBA 14 times. He teamed with Kobe Bryant to lead the Los Angeles Lakers to three straight NBA championships, in 2000, 2001, and 2002. He joined the Miami Heat in 2007 and won his fourth NBA championship in 2006.

NEW JERSEY'S CHRISTIAN CONNECTION

OCEAN GROVE is a small New Jersey community whose founding is rooted in the efforts of two ministers—William B. Osborn and Ellwood H. Stokes—and other clergymen. Osborn, Stokes, and the others founded the Ocean Grove Camp Meeting Association in 1869 so they could develop a Christian summer camp meeting site on New Jersey's seashore. By the early 1900s, the meeting ground had become known as "the Queen of Religious Resorts." The Ocean Grove Camp Meeting Association still owns the land and leases it to homeowners and businesses. The land is located within Neptune Township in New Jersey. ★

★★ FOUR ★★

GEORGIA

A Peach of a State

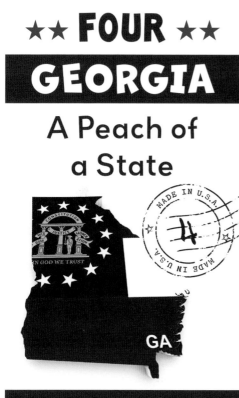

GA

SOME IMPORTANT GEORGIA HISTORY

> In 1540 Spanish explorer Hernando de Soto explores Georgia.

> On February 12, 1733, James Oglethorpe of England founds the British colony of Georgia, the last of the 13 original colonies.

> In 1787 Georgia becomes the fourth state to ratify US Constitution.

> In 1787 Georgia becomes the fourth state of the US.

> In early 1861, Georgia joins the Confederacy, 11 Southern states that seceded from the Union in 1860 and 1861.

> On April 12, 1861, the United States Civil War begins when Confederate ships fire upon Union soldiers at Fort Sumter, a key Union fort in South Carolina.

> In 1864 many Civil War battles take place in Georgia.

BECAME A STATE ON: January 2, 1788	
NICKNAME: the Peach State	
STATE BIRD: brown thrasher	
STATE FLOWER: Cherokee rose	
STATE SONG: "Georgia on My Mind"	
STATE MOTTO: Wisdom, Justice, Moderation	
POPULATION/RANK: 9,687,653/9	
TOTAL AREA/RANK: 59,425 square miles/24	

LIST OF COUNTIES: Appling, Atkinson, Bacon, Baker, Baldwin, Banks, Barrow, Bartow, Ben Hill, Berrien, Bibb, Bleckley, Brantley, Brooks, Bryan, Bulloch, Burke, Butts, Calhoun, Camden, Candler, Carroll, Catoosa, Charlton, Chatham, Chattahoochee, Chattooga, Cherokee, Clarke, Clay, Clayton, Clinch, Cobb, Coffee, Colquitt, Columbia, Cook, Coweta, Crawford, Crisp, Dade, Dawson, De Kalb, Decatur, Dodge, Dooly, Dougherty, Douglas, Early, Echols, Effingham, Elbert, Emanuel, Evans, Fannin, Fayette, Floyd, Forsyth, Franklin, Fulton, Gilmer, Glascock, Glynn, Gordon, Grady, Greene, Gwinnett, Habersham, Hall, Hancock, Haralson, Harris, Hart, Heard, Henry, Houston, Irwin, Jackson, Jasper, Jeff Davis, Jefferson, Jenkins, Johnson, Jones, Lamar, Lanier, Laurens, Lee, Liberty, Lincoln, Long, Lowndes, Lumpkin, Macon, Madison, Marion, McDuffie, McIntosh, Meriwether, Miller, Mitchell, Monroe, Montgomery, Morgan, Murray, Muscogee, Newton, Oconee, Oglethorpe, Paulding, Peach, Pickens, Pierce, Pike, Polk, Pulaski, Putnam, Quitman, Rabun, Randolph, Richmond, Rockdale, Schley, Screven, Seminole, Spalding, Stephens, Stewart, Sumter, Talbot, Taliaferro, Tattnall, Taylor, Telfair, Terrell, Thomas, Tift, Toombs, Towns, Treutlen, Troup, Turner, Twiggs, Union, Upson, Walker, Walton, Ware, Warren, Washington, Wayne, Webster, Wheeler, White, Whitfield, Wilcox, Wilkes, Wilkinson, Worth

FUNNY TOWN NAMES: Enigma, Hopeulikit, Jot Em Down Store

> In the spring of 1865, the US Civil War ends when Robert E. Lee surrenders to Ulysses S. Grant at Appomattox Courthouse in Virginia.

> In 1868 Atlanta becomes Georgia's state capital.

> In 1870 Georgia is readmitted to the Union.

IMPORTANT CITIES IN GEORGIA

Every state is known for something, and Georgia is known for its delicious peaches.

ATLANTA: Atlanta is the most populous city in Georgia and the state capital. It was established in 1837. In 1864 the Union Army burned most of Atlanta to the ground, sparing just the churches and hospitals. Atlanta was gradually rebuilt following the American Civil War and in time became a center of American commerce.

AUGUSTA: Augusta is Georgia's third most populous city. It was founded in 1735 by Englishman James Oglethorpe, the founder of the British Georgia Colony. Augusta is well known in the world of sports as the host city of the the Masters Golf Tournament.

SAVANNAH: Established in 1733, Savannah is the oldest city in Georgia and currently the state's fifth largest city. Savannah was Georgia's first state capital and was an important port city during the American Revolutionary War and Civil War. It is still an important Atlantic seaport.

RIVERS, MOUNTAINS, AND OTHER NATURAL STUFF

PROVIDENCE CANYON: Sometimes called "Georgia's Little Grand Canyon," Providence Canyon is actually a network of gorges located in Stewart County. Providence Canyon includes several plateaus, cliffs, and peaks. Sediment-stained minerals have turned different areas of Providence Canyon amazing shades of red, pink, purple, black, brown, and yellow.

ALTAMAHA RIVER: Another of Georgia's natural marvels is the Altamaha River. Sometimes called Georgia's "Little Amazon," it is Georgia's largest river but not its longest.

BRASSTOWN BALD: At 4,784 feet above sea level at its summit, Brasstown Bald is the highest natural point in Georgia.

An autumn view from Brasstown Bald, the highest natural point in Georgia.

WEIRDNESS IN GEORGIA

TANK TOWN, USA: If you've ever wondered what it would be like to drive a 15-ton armored military vehicle over a junk car (and who hasn't?), then a visit to Tank Town in Morganton, Georgia, might be for you. The place's name might be a little misleading, since there are no tanks to be found. Instead, visitors can pay to drive a British FV432 and crush an old car to smithereens.

GOD IN GEORGIA'S CONSTITUTION (PREAMBLE)

To perpetuate the principles of free government. . .we the people of Georgia, relying upon the protection and guidance of Almighty God, do ordain and establish this Constitution.

SOME GEORGIA VIPS

JACKIE ROBINSON (1919–1972): Born in Cairo, Georgia, Jackie Robinson was the first African American to play in Major League Baseball in what is

called the "Modern Era." Robinson not only broke the "color barrier" that had been in place for six decades, but he also had an outstanding career. In 10 seasons for the Dodgers, he played in six World Series and was selected to six All-Star games.

Jackie Robinson, the first African American to play major league baseball in the modern era, was commemorated on a postage stamp in 1999.

He was named Rookie of the Year in 1947 and was the first black player named National League Most Valuable Player (1949). He was inducted into the Baseball Hall of Fame in 1962.

JIMMY CARTER (BORN 1924): Jimmy Carter, who was born in Plains, Georgia, served as the 39th president of the United States (1977–1981). Before he became president, he served his country as an officer in the US Navy before becoming a peanut farmer. He also served two terms as a Georgia state senator and one as governor of his home state.

MARTIN LUTHER KING JR. (1929–1968): Martin Luther King Jr., who was born in Atlanta, was a great civil rights leader who worked for racial equality and civil rights in the United States. After graduating from college, Dr. King became a minister and moved with his wife to Alabama. He won the Nobel Peace Prize in 1964. Dr. King was assassinated on April 4, 1968, in Memphis, Tennessee.

The great civil rights leader Martin Luther King Jr. was born in Atlanta, Georgia.

GEORGIA'S CHRISTIAN CONNECTION

On February 8, 1736, John and Charles Wesley came to the Georgia colony from their home in England at the request of James Oglethorpe, who had founded the colony just a few years earlier. Oglethorpe wanted John to be the minster at the Savannah Parish and Charles to serve as his secretary. John Wesley also saw his time in Savannah as an opportunity to bring the Christian message of salvation through Jesus Christ to the natives in the area. The two brothers returned to England after a few years, but both experienced their own spiritual renewals, and they wanted others to experience what they had. John became a powerful traveling preacher, and Charles went on to write dozens of well-known Christian hymns. ★

★★★ FIVE ★★★
CONNECTICUT
The Nutmeg State

BECAME A STATE ON: January 9, 1788	
NICKNAMES: the Nutmeg State, the Land of Steady Habits, the Constitution State, the Provisions State	
STATE BIRD: American robin	
STATE FLOWER: mountain laurel	
STATE SONG: "Yankee Doodle"	
STATE MOTTO: *Qui transtulit sustinet* ("He who is transplanted still sustains")	
POPULATION/RANK: 3,590,347/29	
TOTAL AREA/RANK: 5,543.33 square miles/48	
LIST OF COUNTIES: Fairfield, Hartford, Litchfield, Middlesex, New Haven, New London, State Level Sites, Tolland, Windham	
FUNNY TOWN NAMES: Bedlam Corner, Happyland, Hassunadchuauck	

SOME IMPORTANT CONNECTICUT HISTORY

> In 1614 Dutch trader Adriaen Block sails up the Connecticut River and lands near present-day Hartford.

> In 1633 the Dutch establish a permanent settlement in the area.

> 1635 the first English settlers arrive in what is now Windsor.

> In 1636 Massachusetts colonists found Hartford.

> In 1637 settlers and Pequot Indians are at war; Captain John Mason leads colonists to victory.

> In 1638 New Haven is founded.

> In 1675–1676 Connecticut participates in King Philip's War.

> In 1730s and 1740s the first Great Awakening takes place in the colonies.

> In 1774 Connecticut sends representatives to meeting of First Continental Congress in Philadelphia.

> In 1787 the Connecticut Compromise is enacted at the Philadelphia Constitutional Convention, allowing equal representation in Senate and House of Representatives by population.

> On January 9, 1788, Connecticut approves Federal Constitution and becomes fifth US state.

The HMS *Bounty,* docked at Captain's Cove in Bridgeport, Connecticut.

The city of Hartford sits along the banks of the Connecticut River.

IMPORTANT CITIES IN CONNECTICUT

BRIDGEPORT: Located in southwestern Connecticut, Bridgeport is the largest city in the state. The first English settlement of the area that became Bridgeport was established between 1639 and 1665 and was called Pequonnock. The village was later called Newfield and still later, Stratfield. In 1800 it was chartered as the borough of Bridgeport then as a city in 1836.

NEW HAVEN: New Haven is located in the central part of southern Connecticut and is the second largest city in the state. English Puritans founded New Haven in 1638. Today, New Haven is the home of the Ivy League school Yale University.

HARTFORD: Hartford is the state's fourth largest city and its state capital. At almost 400 years old, it is one of the oldest cities in the United States. Today it bears the nickname the "Insurance Capital of the World" because it is home to many insurance companies' headquarters.

RIVERS, MOUNTAINS, AND OTHER NATURAL STUFF

THE CONNECTICUT RIVER: The longest river in New England, the Connecticut River flows 410 miles through four US states, including Connecticut. It starts at the US border with the Canadian province of Canada and empties into Long Island Sound, providing about 70 percent of the sound's fresh water.

MOUNT FRISSELL: Standing at 2,380 feet above sea level at the peak of its south slope, Mount Frissell is the highest natural point in the state of Connecticut.

LONG ISLAND SOUND: Long Island Sound is an Atlantic Ocean estuary located between Long Island, New York, to the south and Connecticut to the north. The Connecticut River empties into the sound at Old Saybrook, Connecticut. Several major cities are situated along Long Island Sound, and more than 8 million people live within its watershed.

WEIRDNESS IN CONNECTICUT

JOSEPH STEWARD MUSEUM OF NATURAL AND OTHER CURIOSITIES: Located in Hartford, Connecticut, in a building called the Old State House is a strange exhibit called the Museum of Natural and Other Curiosities. The museum is a re-creation of Joseph Steward's 1798 collection of natural history displays and natural curiosities. Steward was a minister and well-known portrait painter who wanted more people to come and see his paintings, so he collected and displayed several "natural and artificial curiosities." Today, the collection includes an 18-foot-long Egyptian crocodile, a calf with two complete heads, several stuffed animals and animal heads, and what is called the "horn of a unicorn."

NATHAN HALE (1755–1776): A soldier for the Continental Army during the American Revolutionary War, Nathan Hale is best remembered for his final words before being hanged by British soldiers: "I regret that I have but one life to give for my country." Born in Coventry, Connecticut, he earned the reputation as an American hero and in 1885 was named the official state hero of Connecticut.

Harriet Beecher Stowe motivated the anti-slavery movement in the United States with her novel *Uncle Tom's Cabin*.

HARRIET BEECHER STOWE (1811–1896): Born in Litchfield, Connecticut, Harriett Beecher Stowe was a Christian woman who is best known for her 1852 novel *Uncle Tom's Cabin*, which told the story of life under slavery for African Americans living at the time. It was an important book because it reached millions and helped further motivate anti-slavery forces in the northern US. *Uncle Tom's Cabin* was so influential that when President Abraham Lincoln met Harriet in 1863, during the American Civil War, he is reported to have said, "So, you're the little woman who wrote the book that made this great war."

GOD IN CONNECTICUT'S CONSTITUTION (PREAMBLE)

The people of Connecticut acknowledging with gratitude, the good providence of God, in having permitted them to enjoy a free government; do. . .ordain and establish the following constitution and form of civil government.

WALTER CAMP (1859–1925): Born in New Britain, Connecticut, Walter Camp was a football player and coach who came to be known as the "Father of American Football" because he designed many of the game's rules. Camp played college football at Yale from 1876 to 1882 and served as the college's head football coach from 1888 through 1892. He also coached at Stanford University in California. He was inducted into the College Football Hall of Fame as a coach in 1951.

Jonathan Edwards (1703–1758) was an important—and famous—preacher and theologian who was born in what is now South Windsor, Connecticut. An important figure in the First Great Awakening, a spiritual revival that took place in the American colonies in the 1730s and 1740s, Edwards served as pastor of a church in Northampton, Massachusetts. He is probably best remembered for his classic sermon "Sinners in the Hands of an Angry God." ★

SIX

MASSACHUSETTS

The Bay State

MA

BECAME A STATE ON: February 6, 1788
NICKNAME: the Bay State
STATE BIRD: black-capped chickadee
STATE FLOWER: mayflower
STATE SONG: "All Hail to Massachusetts"
STATE MOTTO: By the sword we seek peace, but peace only under liberty
POPULATION/RANK: 6,547,629/14
TOTAL AREA/RANK: 10,555 square miles/44
LIST OF COUNTIES: Barnstable, Berkshire, Bristol, Dukes, Essex, Franklin, Hampden, Hampshire, Middlesex, Nantucket, Norfolk, Plymouth, State Level Sites, Suffolk, Worcester
FUNNY TOWN NAMES: The X, Tree of Knowledge Corner

SOME IMPORTANT MASSACHUSETTS HISTORY

> In 1602 English explorer Bartholomew Gosnold explores coast of Massachusetts.

> In 1620 pilgrims sailing on the *Mayflower* arrive at Cape Cod and establish a settlement named Plymouth Plantation.

> In 1621 Pilgrims sign a treaty with the Wampanoag Indians and celebrate first Thanksgiving.

> In 1629 the Massachusetts Bay Company is chartered.

> In 1630 the city of Boston is founded.

> In 1675 settlers are attacked by Indians during King Philip's War.

> On December 16, 1773, colonists disguised as Native Americans storm ships moored in Boston Harbor and throw their cargo—tea—into the harbor. The event is known as the Boston Tea Party, and it was in protest of high taxes on tea.

> On April 19, 1775, the first battle of the American Revolution is fought at Lexington and Concord, as well as other towns.

> In 1776 the colonial troops gain the first major victory of the American Revolution when they force British soldiers to evacuate Boston.

> On February 6, 1788, Massachusetts becomes the sixth US state.

> In 1820 Massachusetts and Maine are separated.

An aerial view of historic Boston, Massachusetts.

IMPORTANT CITIES IN MASSACHUSETTS

BOSTON: Boston is the Massachusetts state capital, the largest city in the state, and the largest in New England. Boston is also one of the oldest cities in the United States. In 1630 Puritan colonists from England founded Boston. It was the site of several important events of the American Revolution, including the Boston Massacre, the Boston Tea Party, the Battle of Bunker Hill, and the Siege of Boston.

LOWELL: The fourth most populous city in Massachusetts, Lowell was founded in the 1820s as a manufacturing center. It is known as the cradle of the Industrial Revolution.

CAMBRIDGE: Cambridge is the fifth most populous city in Massachusetts. It is located north of Boston, directly across the Charles River. The city is home to two of the most prestigious universities in the United States—Harvard and Massachusetts Institute of Technology. Cambridge officially became a city in 1846.

RIVERS, MOUNTAINS, AND OTHER NATURAL STUFF

MASSACHUSETTS BAY: Massachusetts Bay is an Atlantic Ocean bay that forms part of the coastline of Massachusetts. The bay extends about 42 miles, from Cape Cod in the north to Plymouth Harbor in the south. The westernmost point of Massachusetts Bay is the city of Boston. Massachusetts Bay is one of several bays on the state's coast that give it the nickname "the Bay State."

BOSTON HARBOR: Discovered in 1614 by English soldier/explorer John Smith, Boston Harbor is a natural harbor that is part of Massachusetts Bay. The city of Boston sits on the shore of Boston Harbor, which is the site of several historic events, including the Boston Tea Party in 1773. By the mid to late 1600s, nearly all imports coming into Boston and the rest of New England came by way of Boston Harbor. The harbor covers about 50 square miles and is home to 34 islands.

GOD IN MASSACHUSETTS'S CONSTITUTION (PREAMBLE)

We, therefore, the people of Massachusetts, acknowledging, with grateful hearts, the goodness of the great Legislator of the universe. . .do agree upon, ordain, and establish the following declaration of rights and frame of government as the constitution of the commonwealth of Massachusetts.

THE CHARLES RIVER: The Charles River, which is 80 miles long, is an important river in eastern Massachusetts. It starts at Echo Lake Hopkinton and flows through 23 cities and towns before it empties into the Atlantic Ocean at Boston Harbor. At its mouth, the Charles River forms the border between downtown Boston and Cambridge and Charlestown.

Harvard University's bridge spans the Charles River between Cambridge and Boston.

WEIRDNESS IN MASSACHUSETTS

If you're ever in the mood to see some plumbing fixtures (toilets, sinks, and others) and you happen to be in Massachusetts, then stop by the **PLUMBING MUSEUM IN WATERTOWN** (no kidding!), Massachusetts. Actually, you'll need to make an appointment to visit this attraction, which is open Monday through Thursday each week.

SOME MASSACHUSETTS VIPS

JOHN HANCOCK (1737–1793): John Hancock was the president of the Second Continental Congress and was one of the first men to sign the Declaration of Independence. His signature on that document was so large and stylish that the term "John Hancock" has come to mean the same thing as the word *signature*. John Hancock was born in Braintree, Massachusetts.

John Hancock's name on the Declaration of Independence is probably the most famous signature in the world.

JOHN F. KENNEDY (1917–1963): Kennedy was the 35th president of the United States, serving from January 1961 until he was assassinated in Dallas, Texas, on November 22, 1963. In addition to serving as a commander during World War II, he served as a congressional representative of Massachusetts (1947–1953) and in the US Senate (1953–1960). Kennedy was born in Brookline, Massachusetts.

GEORGE HERBERT WALKER BUSH (BORN 1924): After serving as vice president of the United States under President Ronald Reagan, George H. W. Bush was elected 41st US president (1989–1993). Bush had served as a congressman, an ambassador, and director of the CIA. He is the last former president who is a veteran of World War II. Bush was born in Milton, Massachusetts.

MASSACHUSETTS'S CHRISTIAN CONNECTION

South Hamilton, Massachusetts, is home to Gordon-Conwell Theological Seminary, one of the largest evangelical Christian seminaries in the world—and also one of the most influential. Gordon-Conwell was founded in 1969 when two Christian institutions founded in the late 1880s—Gordon Divinity School and Conwell School of Theology—merged to form the seminary. A. J. Gordon and Russell Conwell were both Baptist ministers, but the seminary they founded is now nondenominational. ★

★★★ SEVEN ★★★

MARYLAND

The Old Line State

BECAME A STATE ON: April 28, 1788	
NICKNAMES: Old Line State, Little America, Free State	
STATE BIRD: Baltimore oriole	
STATE FLOWER: black-eyed Susan	
STATE SONG: "Maryland My Maryland"	
STATE MOTTO: *Fatti maschil, Parole femine* (Manly Deeds, Womanly Words)	
POPULATION/RANK: 5,884,563/19	
TOTAL AREA/RANK: 12,406.68 square miles/42	
LIST OF COUNTIES: Allegany, Anne Arundel, Baltimore, Baltimore City, Calvert, Caroline, Carroll, Cecil, Charles, Dorchester, Frederick, Garrett, Harford, Howard, Kent, Montgomery, Prince George's, Queen Anne's, Somerset, St. Mary's, State Level Sites, Talbot, Washington, Wicomico, Worcester	
FUNNY TOWN NAMES: Accident, Point of Rocks	

SOME IMPORTANT MARYLAND HISTORY

> In 1498 Italian explorer John Cabot sails along eastern shore near present-day Worcester County, Maryland.

> In 1572 Spaniard Pedro Menendez de Aviles explores Chesapeake Bay.

> In 1608 British explorer Captain John Smith explores Chesapeake Bay.

> In 1632 King Charles I of England grants Maryland Charter to Cecilius Calvert; the colony is named Maryland after Queen Henrietta Maria of France.

> In 1634 English settlers land at St. Clement's Island.

> In 1649 all Maryland Christians are granted religious freedom by Act of Religious Toleration.

> In 1692 Maryland is declared a British royal colony.

> In 1695 Annapolis becomes capital of Maryland.

> In 1729 Baltimore is founded.

> In 1763–1767 Englishmen Charles Mason and Jeremiah Dixon survey boundary line with Pennsylvania; Mason-Dixon Line is established as Maryland's northern boundary.

> In 1774 Maryland chooses delegates to the Continental Congress.

> In 1776 four Marylanders sign Declaration of Independence; Maryland adopts Declaration of Rights and first state constitution.

> In 1777 Thomas Johnson becomes first governor of Maryland.

> In 1783 Annapolis is named US capital.

> On April 28, 1788, Maryland became seventh US state.
> In 1791 Maryland donates land for new capital in Washington, DC.
> In 1814 Francis Scott Key writes "The Star-Spangled Banner" during British attack of Fort McHenry.
> In 1845 the US Naval Academy is founded at Annapolis.
> In 1865 John Wilkes Booth of Maryland assassinates President Abraham Lincoln.

IMPORTANT CITIES IN MARYLAND

Annapolis, Maryland, is home to the United States Naval Academy.

The beautiful nighttime skyline of Baltimore, Maryland.

BALTIMORE: Located in central Maryland, Baltimore is the largest city in the state. It was founded in 1729. It was the site of key events associated with the American Revolution. For example, the Second Continental Congress met in Baltimore from December 1776 to February 1777, which made the city the capital of the United States during those few months. The Battle of Baltimore during the War of 1812 took place in Baltimore in 1814.

FREDERICK: Frederick is the second largest incorporated city in Maryland. It was founded in 1745 by a man named Daniel Dulany and settled by a party of German immigrants not long after that. Today, Frederick is home to Fort Detrick, a military installation.

ANNAPOLIS: Annapolis, the seventh largest city in Maryland, is the state's capital. After the signing of the Treaty of Paris, which ended the Revolutionary War with Great Britain, Annapolis temporarily served as the capital of the United States. Annapolis is home to the US Naval Academy.

RIVERS, MOUNTAINS, AND OTHER NATURAL STUFF

POTOMAC RIVER: The Potomac River, which is about 405 miles long, is the fourth largest river in the Atlantic coast region of the US and the 21st largest in the entire nation. Most of the lower Potomac is located in Maryland.

DEEP CREEK LAKE: Maryland holds the distinction of being the only US state with no natural lakes, but it is home to several manmade bodies of water. The largest of those is Deep Creek Lake, which covers about 3,900 acres and has 69 miles of shoreline. Deep Creek Lake is the result of Deep Creek Dam, a hydroelectric project on Deep Creek in the 1920s. The lake is a popular fishing destination.

BACKBONE MOUNTAIN: Actually a ridge of the Allegheny Mountains, which are part of the central Appalachian Mountain Range, Backbone Mountain stretches about 39 miles southwest to southeast in West Virginia and Maryland. Backbone Mountain includes a spot called Hoye-Crest, which at 3,360 feet above sea level is the highest point in the state of Maryland.

GOD IN MARYLAND'S CONSTITUTION (PREAMBLE)

We, the people of the State of Maryland, grateful to Almighty God for our civil and religious liberty. . .

WEIRDNESS IN MARYLAND

STAR WARS TOYS MUSEUM

Thomas G. Atkinson of Linthicum Heights, Maryland, was just 13 years old when he first saw the original *Star Wars*. Since then, he's been absolutely nutty about everything having to do with the *Star Wars* movies, so nutty that his own house is a real home to the *Star Wars* Toys Museum, which features just about every piece of *Star Wars* memorabilia ever made—toys, action figures, plates, cups, cookie jars, posters, games, and so on.

SOME MARYLAND VIPS

FRANCIS SCOTT KEY (1779–1843): Born in what is now Carroll County, Maryland, Francis Scott Key was an American lawyer, author, and poet who is best known for writing the lyrics to the US national anthem, "The Star-Spangled Banner." Key wrote the poem after witnessing the bombardment of American forces at Fort McHenry during the Battle of Baltimore on the night of September 13–14, 1814.

HARRIET TUBMAN (1820–1913): Harriet Tubman was born into slavery in Dorchester County in Maryland and was severely beaten by slave masters as a child. She escaped slavery in 1849 and then courageously made more than 19 missions to free more than 300 slaves. She was helped in her missions by a string of fellow abolitionists and safe houses that came to be known as the "Underground Railroad." Tubman worked for the Union Army during the American Civil War, serving as a cook, a nurse, and later as an armed scout and spy.

GEORGE HERMAN "BABE" RUTH JR. (1895–1948): The man who is probably Maryland's greatest athlete of all time is also one of the best ever (some say *the* best ever) to play baseball in the major leagues. Ruth played 22 seasons (1914–1935) and set many Big League batting records, including most home runs in a season (60 in 1927) and most career home runs (714). Both of those records have since been broken. Ruth, who was born in Baltimore, began his career as a left-handed pitcher for the Boston Red Sox before being sent to the New York Yankees, where he made his mark as a hard-hitting outfielder.

A 1930 photo of one of the greatest baseball players of all time, Maryland's own Babe Ruth.

MARYLAND'S CHRISTIAN CONNECTION

Antietam Bible College, which is located in Hagerstown, Maryland, was founded in 1976. Its programs and courses are designed to prepare students to be pastors, missionaries, and teachers—as well as church secretaries and administrators. Antietam Bible College's stated mission is to "biblically and academically train and equip born-again believers with skills to rightly divide the Word of God, to effectively communicate the gospel of Jesus Christ, and to make Christ-honoring life applications." ★

★★★ EIGHT ★★★

SOUTH CAROLINA

The Palmetto State

BECAME A STATE ON: May 23, 1788	
NICKNAME: the Palmetto State	
STATE BIRDS: wild turkey, Carolina wren	
STATE FLOWER: yellow jessamine	
STATE SONG: "Carolina"	
STATE MOTTO: *Dum spiro spero* (While I breathe, I hope)	
POPULATION/RANK: 4,723,723/24	
TOTAL AREA/RANK: 32,020.20 square miles/17	
LIST OF COUNTIES: 96 District, Abbeville, Aiken, Allendale, Anderson, Ashe, Bamberg, Barnwell, Beaufort, Berkeley, Calhoun, Charleston, Cherokee, Chester, Chesterfield, Claremont, Clarendon, Colleton, Darlington, Dillon, Dorchester, Edgefield, Fairfield, Florence, Georgetown, Greenville, Greenwood, Hampton, Horry, Jasper, Kershaw, Lancaster, Laurens, Lee, Lexington, Lowcountry, Marion, Marlboro, McCormick, Newberry, Oconee, Orangeburg, Pendleton, Pickens, Richland, Saluda, Spartanburg, State Level Sites, Sumter, The Piedmont, Union, Williamsburg, York	
FUNNY TOWN NAMES: Coosawhatchie, Ketchuptown, Polecat Landing	

SOME IMPORTANT SOUTH CAROLINA HISTORY

> In 1521 the first recorded Spanish expedition reaches Carolina coast.

> In 1670 first permanent English settlements and the capital city, Charles Town (Charleston), are founded.

> In 1706 French and Spanish attack Charles Town during Queen Anne's War.

> In 1712 the territory of Carolina is divided into North and South; each has its own governor.

> In 1774 South Carolina sends five delegates to First Continental Congress.

> In 1783 Charles Town is renamed Charleston.

> In 1786 South Carolina capital is moved from Charleston to Columbia.

> On May 23, 1788, South Carolina becomes eighth US state.

> In 1860 South Carolina becomes first state to secede from the Union prior to the Civil War.

> In 1861 the first shots of the Civil War are fired by Confederate forces upon Fort Sumter.

> 1865 Union General William Sherman's troops reach Middleton Place Plantation and leave it in ruins, then burn the city of Columbia to the ground; the Civil War ends.

> In 1868 South Carolina is readmitted to the Union.

> In 1963 Rivers High School in Charleston becomes first racially integrated high school in South Carolina.

IMPORTANT CITIES IN SOUTH CAROLINA

A view of downtown Columbia, South Carolina, from Finlay Park.

COLUMBIA: Columbia is the largest city in South Carolina and the state's capital. It is located in the central part of the state, which is why it was chosen as the state capital in 1786. It was established as a city in 1854. Columbia was the site of the South Carolina Secession Convention, which directly led to South Carolina being the first state to secede from the Union before the American Civil War.

CHARLESTON: Located in southeastern South Carolina, Charleston is the second largest city—and the oldest—in the state. Charleston was founded in 1670 and was named "Charles Towne" after King Charles II of England. The city was first called Charleston in 1783.

NORTH CHARLESTON: As its name implies, North Charleston is located just north of Charleston on the central South Carolina coast. It is the third largest city in the state. From late in the 17th century through the American Civil War, North Charleston was home to many plantations and was a major producer of rice. To-

day, North Charleston is one of South Carolina's major industrial centers. It was incorporated as a city in 1972.

RIVERS, MOUNTAINS, AND OTHER NATURAL STUFF

SANTEE RIVER: At 143 miles long, the Santee River is the largest river in South Carolina. It forms in central South Carolina, near the city of Columbia. From there, it flows about five miles in a southeasterly direction before entering Lake Marion, a reservoir formed by the Santee Dam that was built during the Great Depression. The Santee Dam is a hydroelectric dam that provides electricity for the state. English settlers

Dusk at Table Rock State Park in in the Blue Ridge Mountains of South Carolina.

named the river after the Santee Indian tribe, but before that Spanish explorers called it the Jordan.

JOHNS ISLAND: Also known as "John's Island," this is South Carolina's largest island. It is also the fourth largest island on the East Coast of the US. It covers 84 square miles and is home to about 14,000 people.

SASSAFRAS MOUNTAIN: At 3,560 feet, Sassafras Mountain is the highest point in South Carolina. It is part of the Blue Ridge Mountains, which are part of the Appalachians.

THE BUTTON KING MUSEUM

If you really like buttons (the kind you find on your clothes, that is), then the Button King Museum in Bishopville, South Carolina, should be on your can't-miss list of attractions if you're ever in the Palmetto State. The museum is the creation of a man named Dalton Stevens, whose obsession with buttons dates back more than 30 years. It includes a button-covered outhouse and toilet, a 1983 Chevrolet Chevette covered in 150,000 buttons, and a hearse covered in 600,000 more.

SOME SOUTH CAROLINA VIPS

PIERCE BUTLER (1744–1822): Pierce Butler was a statesman and a Founding Father who represented South Carolina in the Continental Congress and at the 1787 Constitutional Convention. Butler was also one of the first US senators to represent South Carolina.

JOHN C. CALHOUN (1782–1850): Born near Abbeville, South Carolina, John C. Calhoun was an American statesman who served in the South Carolina state legislature and later as a US congressman, secretary of war and secretary of state, US senator, and the seventh vice president of the United States (under President John Quincy Adams).

A reporter approaches boxer Joe Frazier in an airport.

GOD IN SOUTH CAROLINA'S CONSTITUTION (PREAMBLE)

We, the people of the State of South Carolina, in convention assembled, grateful to God for our liberties, do ordain and establish this Constitution for the preservation and perpetuation of the same.

JOE FRAZIER (BORN 1944): Joe Frazier was a heavyweight boxer who held the world heavyweight championship from 1970 to 1973 and who won a gold medal in the 1964 Olympics in Tokyo, Japan. Frazier fought Muhammad Ali for the world championship three times, including a fight in 1971 in which he beat Ali to become the undisputed world heavyweight champion. Frazier, who was born in Beaufort, South Carolina, is one of the state's greatest athletes of all time.

SOUTH CAROLINA'S CHRISTIAN CONNECTION

During the period between the late 1850s and the early 1900s, the US went through a period of spiritual revival that historians call the Third Great Awakening. A minister in South Carolina named John L. Girardeau (1825–1899) was a key figure in a revival that took place in the city of Charleston among slaves who lived in that city. Despite opposition, Girardeau began preaching and praying at the mostly black Anson Street Presbyterian Church. Every night for about eight weeks, Girardeau preached to crowds of up to 2,000 people on "sin and repentance, faith and justification, and regeneration." Hundreds of people—black and white alike—became Christians, and churches around the city began growing. ★

★★★ NINE ★★★

NEW HAMPSHIRE

The Granite State

BECAME A STATE ON: June 21, 1788	
NICKNAME: the Granite State	
STATE BIRD: purple finch	
STATE FLOWER: purple lilac	
STATE SONG: "Old New Hampshire"	
STATE MOTTO: Live Free or Die	
POPULATION/RANK: 1,320,718/42	
TOTAL AREA/RANK: 9,349.94 square miles/46	
LIST OF COUNTIES: Belknap, Carroll, Cheshire, Coos, Grafton, Hillsborough, Merrimack, Rockingham, State Level Sites, Strafford, Sullivan	
FUNNY TOWN NAMES: Beans, Cowbell Corners, Dummer	

SOME IMPORTANT NEW HAMPSHIRE HISTORY

> In 1623 the Dover settlement is founded.

> In 1629 English colonizer John Mason receives land grant and names the new settlement New Hampshire.

> In 1641 the Massachusetts Colony gains control of New Hampshire settlements.

> In 1691 New Hampshire permanently separates from Massachusetts and becomes the royal province (colony) of New Hampshire.

> In 1774 New Hampshire declares independence from England.

> In 1778 New Hampshire is first state to hold constitutional convention.

> In 1783 New Hampshire refers the US Constitution to citizens for approval.

> On June 21, 1788, New Hampshire ratifies US Constitution and becomes ninth US state.

> In 1808 the New Hampshire state capital is established in Concord.

> In 1833 the first US public library is founded in Peterborough.

> In 1853 Franklin Pierce of New Hampshire becomes 14th US president.

IMPORTANT CITIES IN NEW HAMPSHIRE

MANCHESTER: New Hampshire's largest city, Manchester is located in the central-southern part of the state. The area that would become Manchester was first settled by Europeans in the early 1700s. Before it was called Manchester, the city had several other names, including Nutfield, Tyng's Town, Harrytown, and Derryfield. It received the name "Manchester" in 1810 and was incorporated as a city in 1846.

NASHUA: Nashua, New Hampshire's second largest city, is located in the central part of southern New Hampshire. What is now Nashua was originally part of Dunstable, Massachusetts, the earliest settlement in what is now southern New Hampshire. The settlement was part of Massachusetts until the border between Massachusetts and New Hampshire was settled in 1741. The town of Dunstable was incorporated in 1746. The name was changed to Nashua in 1836.

CONCORD: New Hampshire's third largest city and the state capital, Concord is located in southern-central New Hampshire. The area that would become Concord was first settled in 1725 by people from Haverhill, Massachusetts. The town was first incorporated in 1734 and called "Rumford." It was renamed Concord in 1765.

RIVERS, MOUNTAINS, AND OTHER NATURAL STUFF

MERRIMACK RIVER: The Merrimack River is a 117-mile-long river that starts in Franklin, New Hampshire, where the Pemigewasset and Winnipesaukee Rivers meet. From there, it flows to the south into Massachusetts before turning northeast and emptying into the Atlantic Ocean in Newburyport. The central-southern part of New Hampshire and most of northeastern Massachusetts are known as the Merrimack Valley.

LAKE WINNIPESAUKEE: The largest lake in New Hampshire, Lake Winnipesaukee is a natural body of water that measures about 21 miles in length by 1 to 9 miles in width. The lake's surface area is 69 square miles—71 square miles including Paugus Bay. It is the third largest lake in New England. The lake is home to at least 253 islands (some less than a quarter-acre in size) and several peninsulas.

MOUNT WASHINGTON: Standing 6,288 feet above sea level, Mount Washington is the highest peak not just in New Hampshire but in the entire northeastern United States. It is located in the Presidential Range of the White Mountains. Mount Washington is well known for its dangerous weather—on April 12, 1934,

The summit of Mount Washington is the highest natural point in the northeastern United States.

> ## GOD IN NEW HAMPSHIRE'S CONSTITUTION (PART I, ARTICLE 5)
>
> Every individual has a natural and unalienable right to worship God according to the dictates of his own conscience and reason; and no subject shall be hurt, molested, or restrained, in his person, liberty, or estate, for worshiping God in the manner and season most agreeable to the dictates of his own conscience. . . .

a gust of wind measuring 231 miles an hour was recorded at the summit.

WEIRDNESS IN NEW HAMPSHIRE

You probably know that Stonehenge is a mysterious, manmade grouping of rocks in England. (If you don't, then look it up. It's actually pretty cool!) But what you might not know is that the United States has its own Stonehenge-like collection of rock formations. Located in Salem, New Hampshire, about 40 miles north of Boston, Massachusetts, is about 30 acres of cave-like dwellings, manmade (apparently) rock formations, and other mysterious structures. No one knows for sure who is responsible for what you can see at what was once known as Mystery Hills Caves but is now simply called "America's Stonehenge."

SOME NEW HAMPSHIRE VIPS

FRANKLIN PIERCE (1804–1869): Franklin Pierce was the 14th president of the United States (1853–1857) and the only president born in New Hampshire (Hillsborough). Pierce also served in the US House of Representatives and the US Senate. He was a veteran of the Mexican-American War and served as a brigadier general in the US Army.

EARL SILAS TUPPER (1907–1983): Best known as the inventor of Tupperware, Earl Silas Tupper was an American businessman and inventor. He was born in Berlin, New Hampshire. He founded the Tupperware Plastics Company in 1938 and began introducing Tupper Plastics to hardware and department stores about 10 years later. In the early 1950s he stopped selling his products through retail stores and began selling at "Tupperware parties" in private homes.

ALAN SHEPARD (1923–1998): The American astronaut Alan Shepard was born in Derry, New Hampshire. Shepard worked as a naval aviator and test pilot before becoming a NASA astronaut. In 1961 he became the second person—and first American—to travel into space. Ten years later, he commanded the Apollo 14 mission and became the fifth person to walk on the moon. Shepard retired from the US Navy and NASA in 1974 and became a very successful businessman.

A closeup of astronaut Alan Shepard, a New Hampshire native, in the Mercury capsule.

NEW HAMPSHIRE'S CHRISTIAN CONNECTION

Before the American Revolution, the five major denominations in New Hampshire (and in most of the rest of the colonies) were Congregational, Baptist, Quaker (Society of Friends), Presbyterian, and Church of England (Anglican). That changed in 1819, when the New Hampshire legislature passed the Toleration Act, which ended public support and recognition of any one denomination. Since then, no single church has received public support and all of them are supported by the people in the congregation. ★

★★★ TEN ★★★

VIRGINIA

The Mother of All States

BECAME A STATE ON: June 25, 1788	**TOTAL AREA/RANK:** 59,424.77/24
NICKNAMES: the Old Dominion State, Mother of Presidents, Mother of States	**LIST OF COUNTIES:** Accomack, Albemarle, Alleghany, Amelia, Amherst, Appomattox, Arlington, Augusta,
STATE BIRD: cardinal	Bath, Bedford, Bland, Botetourt, Brunswick, Buchanan,
STATE FLOWER: American dogwood	Buckingham, Campbell, Caroline, Carroll, Charles
STATE SONG: "Carry Me Back to Old Virginny"	City, Charlotte, Chesterfield, Clarke, Craig, Culpeper,
STATE MOTTO: *Sic semper tyrannis* (Thus always to tyrants)	Cumberland, Dickenson, Dinwiddie, Essex, Fairfax, Fauquier, Floyd, Fluvanna, Franklin, Frederick, Giles,
POPULATION/RANK: 9,992,167/8	Gloucester, Goochland, Grayson, Greene, Greensville,
FUNNY TOWN NAMES: Croaker, Dumfries, Frogtown	Halifax, Hanover, Henrico, Henry, Highland, Isle of

LIST OF COUNTIES (continued): Wight, James City, King and Queen, King George, King William, Lancaster, Lee, Loudoun, Louisa, Lunenburg, Madison, Mathews, Mecklenburg, Middlesex, Montgomery, Nelson, New Kent, Northampton, Northumberland, Nottoway, Orange, Page, Patrick, Pittsylvania, Powhatan, Prince Edward, Prince George, Prince William, Pulaski, Rappahannock, Richmond, Roanoke, Rockbridge, Rockingham, Russell, Scott, Shenandoah, Smyth, Southampton, Spotsylvania, Stafford, Surry, Sussex, Tazewell, Warren, Washington, Westmoreland, Wise, Wythe, York

SOME IMPORTANT VIRGINIA HISTORY

> In 1607 Jamestown, the first permanent English settlement, is established.

> In 1611 settler John Rolfe begins cultivation of tobacco, the major cash crop at that time.

> In 1622 347 colonists die in an Indian massacre.

> In 1624 King James of England makes Virginia a royal colony.

> In 1699 the town of Williamsburg is established and named Virginia's capital.

> In 1774 the First Continental Congress meeting is held, with Virginians George Washington and Patrick Henry in attendance.

> In 1775 Patrick Henry gives his famous speech ending with "Give me liberty or give me death."

> In 1776 Virginian Thomas Jefferson writes the Declaration of Independence.

> In 1779 the Virginia capital is moved from Williamsburg to Richmond.

> In 1781 at Yorktown, British forces surrender to French and American forces serving under General George Washington.

> In 1786 Virginia passes the Statute of Religious Freedom, giving Virginians the right to choose their religion and church.

> On June 25, 1788, Virginia becomes the 10th US state.

> In 1789 George Washington is elected first US president.

> In 1801 Thomas Jefferson is elected third US president.

> In 1809 James Madison, who is known as the "Father of the Constitution," is elected fourth US president.

> In 1809 James Monroe is elected fifth US president.

> In 1861 Virginia secedes from the Union and joins the Confederacy as the American Civil War begins.

> In 1863 West Virginia is formed from 50 western Virginia counties.

> In 1865 Confederate General Robert E. Lee surrenders to Union General U. S. Grant at Appomattox; the Civil War ends.

> In 1870 Virginia is readmitted to the Union.

> In 1913 Virginian Woodrow Wilson is elected 28th US president.

IMPORTANT CITIES IN VIRGINIA

VIRGINIA BEACH: A resort city located on the Atlantic Ocean at the mouth of Chesapeake Bay, Virginia Beach is the largest city in Virginia. The first English settlers who came to America landed at Cape Henry in what would become Virginia Beach in 1607. The first permanent settlement in what would become Virginia Beach was established at Lynnhaven Bay in 1621.

NORFOLK: Norfolk is Virginia's second largest city. It is located in southeastern Virginia and is named for a large harbor located at the mouth of Chesapeake Bay. Norfolk is home to the largest navy base in the world, Naval Station Norfolk.

RICHMOND: Richmond, which is located in the southeastern part of central Virginia, is the capital of the commonwealth and its fifth largest city. Richmond was founded in 1737, and it became Virginia's capital in 1780. It was at Richmond's St. John's Church that Patrick Henry delivered his "Give me liberty or give me death" speech. During the American Civil War, Richmond was the capital of the Confederacy.

RIVERS, MOUNTAINS, AND OTHER NATURAL STUFF

Richmond, Virginia's capital city, sits on the banks of the James River.

CHESAPEAKE BAY: Chesapeake Bay is the largest estuary in the US. It stretches about 200 miles from the Susquehanna River to the Atlantic Ocean. The Chesapeake Bay Watershed, the area of land that drains into the bay, covers 64,000 miles and includes part of six states (Delaware, Maryland, New York, Pennsylvania, Virginia, and West Virginia), as well as Washington, DC. More than 150 rivers and streams flow into the watershed. It is 2.8 miles wide at its narrowest and 30 miles wide at its widest. Chesapeake Bay is well known for its production of seafood.

THE JAMES RIVER: At 348 miles long, the James River has the distinction of being the 12th longest US river that flows in only one state. The James River headwaters are in the Appalachian Mountains. It flows into the Chesapeake Bay at Hampton Roads, Virginia. Jamestown, the first English settlement in the Americas, was located along the banks of the James River.

WEIRDNESS IN VIRGINIA

In Petersburg, Virginia, is a two-story house made not of concrete and wood but of 2,200 old tombstones. A man named Oswald Young built the house in 1934 out of tombstones from the graves of Union soldiers who died in the 1864–1865 siege of Petersburg during the American Civil War.

SOME VIRGINIA VIPS

GEORGE WASHINGTON (1732–1799): George Washington, who was born in Westmoreland County, Virginia, was one of the most important figures

in American history—maybe *the* most important. He was one of the Founding Fathers of the United States and served as a general and the commander-in-chief of the colonial armies during the American Revolution and as the first president of the United States, serving from 1789 to 1797. He presided over the convention that drafted the US Constitution.

Virginia native George Washington was a hero in the Revolutionary War—and the first president of the United States.

THOMAS JEFFERSON (1743–1826): Born in Shadwell, Virginia, Thomas Jefferson was a Founding Father who earned the nickname "the Father of the Declaration of Independence" for his role in drafting that important document. He represented Virginia at the Continental Congress and was a leading figure in America's fight for independence from Great Britain. After the Revolutionary War, Jefferson served as governor of Virginia, as the first secretary of state, and as vice president under John Adams. He was the third president of the United States (1801–1809).

Founding Father—and third president of the United States—Thomas Jefferson.

WOODROW WILSON (1856–1924): Woodrow Wilson was born in Staunton, Virginia. He was the 28th president of the United States (1913–1921). Wilson was president during World War I. He is remembered for starting the Federal Reserve System, which helps regulate the US economy by controlling the money supply, and for changing the income tax system so that people who made more money are taxed at a higher rate than others.

GOD IN VIRGINIA'S CONSTITUTION (BILL OF RIGHTS, XVI)

Religion, or the Duty which we owe our Creator. . .can be directed only by Reason. . .and that it is the mutual duty of all to practice Christian Forbearance, Love and Charity towards each other.

VIRGINIA'S CHRISTIAN CONNECTION

In 1971 the Reverend Jerry Falwell, pastor of Thomas Road Baptist Church in Lynchburg, Virginia, founded Lynchburg Baptist College, a Christian school that would later become Liberty University, now the world's biggest evangelical Christian university. Liberty boasts a total enrollment—on campus and online—of well over 100,000 students. Its sports teams, the Flames, play in the NCAA's large-school Division I. ★

★★★ ELEVEN ★★★

NEW YORK

The Empire State

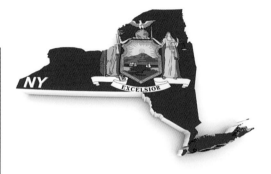

BECAME A STATE ON: July 26, 1788	
NICKNAME: the Empire State	
STATE BIRD: eastern bluebird	
STATE FLOWER: rose	
STATE SONG: "I Love New York"	
STATE MOTTO: *Excelsior* (Ever Upward)	
POPULATION/RANK: 19,570,261/3	
TOTAL AREA/RANK: 54,556.00 square miles/27	
LIST OF COUNTIES: Albany, Allegany, Bronx, Broome, Cattaraugus, Cayuga, Charlotte, Chautauqua, Chemung, Chenango, Clinton, Columbia, Cortland, Delaware, Dutchess, Erie, Essex, Franklin, Fulton, Genesee, Greene, Hamilton, Herkimer, Jefferson, Kings (Brooklyn), Lewis, Livingston, Madison, Monroe, Montgomery, Nassau (Long Island), New York City, Niagara, Oneida, Onondaga, Ontario, Orange, Orleans, Oswego, Otsego, Putnam, Queens (Long Island), Rensselaer, Richmond (Staten Island), Rockland, Saratoga, Schenectady, Schoharie, Schuyler, Seneca, St. Lawrence, State Level Sites, Steuben, Suffolk (Long Island), Sullivan, Tioga, Tompkins, Tryon, Ulster, Warren, Washington, Wayne, Westchester, Wyoming, Yates	
FUNNY TOWN NAMES: Fishkill, Yonkers	

SOME IMPORTANT NEW YORK HISTORY

> In 1524 explorer Giovanni da Varrazano, sailing on behalf of France, sails into New York Harbor.

> In 1609 Henry Hudson explores Hudson River; Samuel de Champlain explores northeastern New York.

> In 1626 the Dutch purchase Manhattan Island from local Indians.

> In 1664 England conquers New Netherlands and changes name to New York.

> In 1673 the Dutch capture New Amsterdam; the English take it back the following year.

> In 1674 New Amsterdam is renamed New York City.

> In 1776 New York declares independence from England.

> In 1777 New York adopts its first state constitution.

> In 1785 New York City is named the nation's capital.

> On July 26, 1788, New York becomes 11th US state.

197

> In 1789 George Washington is inaugurated as first US president in New York City.
> In 1797 Albany is named state capital.
> In 1825 the Erie Canal is completed.
> In 1827 slavery is abolished in New York.
> In 1886 the Statue of Liberty is dedicated.
> In 1901 President William McKinley is assassinated in Buffalo; Theodore Roosevelt is elected president of US.
> In 1952 the United Nations Headquarters are completed in New York City.
> On September 11, 2001, terrorists hijack commercial airliners and fly them into the World Trade Center, collapsing both towers.

IMPORTANT CITIES IN NEW YORK

The Statue of Liberty stands in New York Harbor, welcoming visitors and immigrants alike.

NEW YORK CITY: With a population of about 8.4 million, New York City is the largest city in the United States and the 20th largest in the world. Located on one of the world's largest natural harbors, New York is a major center of world commerce and finance. It is also a major center for media, art, and entertainment. It got its start in 1624, when it was founded as a trading post by Dutch colonists. The area came under British control in 1664. New York City served as the US capital from 1785 until 1790.

BUFFALO: Located in western New York on the eastern shores of Lake Erie, Buffalo is the second largest

> ### GOD IN NEW YORK'S CONSTITUTION (PREAMBLE)
>
> We the people of the State of New York, grateful to Almighty God for our freedom, in order to secure its blessings, do establish this constitution.

city in New York. The area that would become Buffalo was first settled around 1789 near Buffalo Creek. After the opening of the Erie Canal in 1825, Buffalo grew very quickly and was incorporated as a city in 1832.

ALBANY: The sixth largest city in New York, Albany is the state's capital. It sits on the west bank of the Hudson River. Albany was first settled by Europeans in 1614 and was officially chartered as a city in 1686. It became the capital of New York in 1797. It is considered one of the oldest surviving settlements from the original 13 colonies.

The famous Wonder Wheel Ferris Wheel in Coney Island was built in 1920.

RIVERS, MOUNTAINS, AND OTHER NATURAL STUFF

LONG ISLAND: The largest island in the 48 adjoining US states, Long Island is almost the most populous in the US with almost 7.2 million residents. At 1,401 square miles, it is the 10th largest island in the 50 United States (the first nine are located in Hawaii and Alaska) and the 148th largest in the world. Long Island stretches 118 miles northeast from New York Harbor into the Atlantic Ocean, is home to four counties, and has a maximum width (north to south) of 23 miles.

HUDSON RIVER: The Hudson River is a 315-mile-long river that flows through eastern New York. It begins at Henderson Lake in Newcomb, New York, then flows south past the state capital of Albany before forming a natural boundary between New York City and the state of New Jersey. It empties into the Upper New York Bay. The Hudson River is named after Englishman Henry Hudson, who explored it in 1609.

MOUNT MARCY: At 5,344 feet above sea level, Mount Marcy is the highest point in the state of New York. It is located in the Adirondack Mountains and is popular with hikers.

WEIRDNESS IN NEW YORK

THE WORLD'S SMALLEST CHURCH

Oneida, New York, is home to the Cross Island Chapel, the smallest church in the United States. The chapel is only 51 by 81 inches in size, and it can accommodate only two people—three if they remain standing. The church was built in 1989.

SOME NEW YORK VIPS

THEODORE ROOSEVELT (1858–1919): Theodore Roosevelt, who was born in New York City, was the 26th president of the United States (1901–1909). He was sworn in as president at the age of 42, making him the youngest person ever to serve in the office. He was President McKinley's vice president but became president in 1901 when McKinley was assassinated. He won the presidential election in 1904.

LOU GEHRIG (1903–1941): Also known as "the Iron Horse," Lou Gehrig played 17 seasons in Major League Baseball (1923–1939) for the New York Yankees. Gehrig, who was born in New York City, was a great hitter. He won six World Series championships with the Yankees and was selected to the All-Star game seven times. He was the first major league player to have his number retired and was elected to the Baseball Hall of Fame in 1939. Gehrig set the record for consecutive games played (2,130), a record that stood until Cal Ripken, Jr., broke it in 1995. Gehrig's streak ended in 1939 after he was diagnosed with amyotrophic lateral sclerosis (ALS), which is now often called Lou Gehrig's disease.

JONAS SALK (1914–1995): Up until the late 1950s, polio was one of the most feared diseases in the world. That changed after Jonas Salk, who was born in New York City, developed the first successful vaccine for the disease. Salk attended the New York University School of Medicine, but he never wanted to be a practicing physician. Instead, he focused on medical research. Salk's polio vaccine was introduced in 1957.

NEW YORK'S CHRISTIAN CONNECTION

The New York Theological Seminary (NYTS) is a nondenominational institution located in Manhattan in New York City. One of the best-known NYTS alumni is Eugene H. Peterson (1932-2018), who has written more than 32 books and who developed *The Message: The Bible in Contemporary Language*. ★

★★★ TWELVE ★★★

NORTH CAROLINA

The Old North State

BECAME A STATE ON: November 21, 1789	
NICKNAMES: Tar Heel State, Old North State	
STATE BIRD: cardinal	
STATE FLOWER: American dogwood	
STATE SONG: "The Old North State"	
STATE MOTTO: *Esse quam videri* (To be, rather than to seem)	
POPULATION/RANK: 9,752,073/10	
FUNNY TOWN NAMES: Frogsboro, Lizard Lick, Whynot	

TOTAL AREA/RANK: 53,818.51 square miles/28

LIST OF COUNTIES: Alamance, Albemarle, Alexander, Alleghany, Anson, Archdale, Ashe, Avery, Bath, Beaufort, Bertie, Bladen, Brunswick, Buncombe, Burke, Bute, Cabarrus, Caldwell, Camden, Carteret, Caswell, Catawba, Chatham, Cherokee, Cherokee Reservation (Qualla Boundary), Chowan, Clay, Cleveland, Columbus, Craven, Cumberland, Currituck, Dare, Davidson, Davie, Dobbs, Duplin, Durham, Edgecombe, Forsyth, Franklin, Gaston, Gates, Glasgow, Graham, Granville, Greene, Guilford, Halifax, Harnett, Haywood, Henderson, Hertford, Hoke, Hyde, Iredell, Jackson, Johnston, Jones, Lee, Lenoir, Lincoln, Macon, Madison, Martin, McDowell, Mecklenburg, Mitchell, Montgomery, Moore, Nash, New Hanover, Northampton, Onslow, Orange, Pamlico, Pasquotank, Pender, Perquimans, Person, Pitt, Polk, Randolph, Richmond, Robeson, Rockingham, Rowan, Rutherford, Sampson, Scotland, Stanly, State Level Sites, Stokes, Surry, Swain, Transylvania, Tryon, Tyrrell, Union, Vance, Wake, Warren, Washington, Watauga, Wayne, Wilkes, Wilson, Yadkin, Yancey

SOME IMPORTANT NORTH CAROLINA HISTORY

> In 1524 explorer Giovanni da Verrazano explores coastal areas of North Carolina for France.

> In 1540 Spanish explorer Hernando de Soto explores southwestern part of North Carolina in search of gold.

> In 1584–1585 Sir Walter Raleigh sends colonists to establish English settlement on Roanoke Island.

> In 1587 John White establishes second English colony at Roanoke.

> In 1729 North Carolina becomes a royal English colony.

> In 1776 North Carolina becomes first state to vote for independence.

> On November 21, 1789, North Carolina becomes 12th US state.

> In 1794 North Carolina capital is moved from New Bern to Raleigh.

> In 1828 North Carolina native Andrew Jackson becomes seventh US president.

> In 1845 North Carolina native James Polk becomes 11th US president.

> In 1861 North Carolina leaves the Union; American Civil War (1861–1865) begins.

> In 1868 North Carolina is readmitted to Union.

> In 1903 the Wright brothers make man's first successful flight at Kitty Hawk.

GOD IN NORTH CAROLINA'S CONSTITUTION (PREAMBLE)

We, the people of the State of North Carolina, grateful to Almighty God. . .do, for the more certain security thereof and for the better government of this State, ordain and establish this Constitution. . . .

A memorial to Orville and Wilber Wright's historic flight near Kill Devil Hill in North Carolina.

IMPORTANT CITIES IN NORTH CAROLINA

An autumn view of the Charlotte, North Carolina, skyline.

CHARLOTTE: Nicknamed the "Queen City," Charlotte is located in southwestern North Carolina. It is the largest city in the state and the 23rd largest in the United States. The area was first settled in 1755, and Charlotte was established as a town in 1768.

RALEIGH: Raleigh, which is located in central North Carolina, is the capital of North Carolina and the second largest city in the state. It is called the "City of Oaks" because there are so many oak trees there. Raleigh is named after Sir Walter Raleigh, the Englishman who established the lost Roanoke Colony on Roanoke Island.

GREENSBORO: Greensboro is located in the central part of northern North Carolina. It is the third largest city in the state. The city is named after Major General Nathanael Green, the commander of the American forces at the March 15, 1781, Battle of Guilford Courthouse.

RIVERS, MOUNTAINS, AND OTHER NATURAL STUFF

MOUNT MITCHELL: At 6,684 feet, Mount Mitchell is not only the highest point in North Carolina but also the highest peak in the Appalachian Mountains and in the eastern United States. It is located near Burnsville, North Carolina, and is part of the Black Mountains, which are part of the Appalachians.

CAPE FEAR RIVER: The Cape Fear River flows 202 miles from around Haywood, North Carolina, in a southeastern direction until it empties into the Atlantic Ocean at Cape Fear. It was an important waterway during the colonial period of US history because it provided the primary route of transportation from the Atlantic Ocean to the interior of North Carolina.

LAKE WACCAMAW: In 1929 Lake Waccamaw, a freshwater lake in Columbus County, was named the state lake of North Carolina. It is an oval-shaped lake that measures about 5.2 miles long by 3.5 miles wide and has a surface area of 8,938 acres.

WEIRDNESS IN NEW NORTH CAROLINA

BELHAVEN MEMORIAL MUSEUM

The Belhaven Memorial Museum in Belhaven, North Carolina, features the strange collections of an eccentric character named Eva Blount Way, who didn't seem to find anything too strange (or sometimes disgusting) to keep in her home. Three years after Mrs. Way's death in 1962 at the age of 92, all her collections were moved from her home to the museum. There you can see a two-headed kitten, a hair-lipped dog, mummified squirrels, large pickled tumors collected from a local hospital, a flea bride and groom decked out in wedding attire, and. . .well, the list goes on and on.

SOME NORTH CAROLINA VIPS

ANDREW JACKSON (1767–1845): Andrew Jackson was the seventh president of the United States (1829–1837). Jackson was born in either North Carolina, South Carolina, or near the border between the two states. As a US Army general, Jackson defeated the Creek Indians at the 1814 Battle of Horseshoe Bend and British forces at the Battle of New Orleans in 1815. Jackson's toughness as an officer earned him the nickname Old Hickory.

DALE EARNHARDT SR. (1951–2001): Dale Earnhardt Sr. was one of the greatest NASCAR drivers of all time. He won a total of 76 races and earned seven NASCAR Winston Cup Championships, tying him with Richard Petty for the most of all time. Earnhardt, who was born in Kannapolis, North Carolina, was called "The Intimidator" for his aggressive driving style. He died after an accident on the last lap of the 2001 Daytona 500. He is a member of the NASCAR Hall of Fame.

MICHAEL JORDAN (BORN 1963): Michael Jordan was born in Brooklyn, New York. He is considered perhaps the greatest professional basketball player of all time. Jordan played college basketball for three seasons at the University of North Carolina and was a member of the Tar Heels national championship team in 1982.

NORTH CAROLINA'S CHRISTIAN CONNECTION

Billy Graham has preached the gospel of Jesus Christ to more people than anyone else in history.

BILLY GRAHAM (1918–2018) was the best-known and most-admired Christian evangelist of the 20th and early 21st centuries. He grew up on a diary farm near Charlotte, North Carolina. From the beginning of his ministry in the early 1940s, Graham preached the gospel to hundreds of millions of people throughout the world, far more than anyone in history. In 1950 he founded the Billy Graham Evangelistic Association in Minneapolis, Minnesota. The ministry's headquarters relocated to his hometown of Charlotte in 2003. Graham was a spiritual adviser to several US presidents and expanded his ministry to include radio broadcasts, televised crusades, and *Decision* magazine, the official BGEA publication. He died just eight months short of age 100. ★

★★★ THIRTEEN ★★★

RHODE ISLAND

America's Little Rhody

BECAME A STATE ON: May 29, 1790	
NICKNAMES: the Plantation State, the Ocean State, Little Rhody	
STATE BIRD: Rhode Island red	
STATE FLOWER: common blue violet	
STATE SONG: "Rhode Island's It for Me"	
STATE MOTTO: Hope	
POPULATION/RANK: 1,050,292/43	
TOTAL AREA/RANK: 1,545.05 square miles/50	
LIST OF COUNTIES: Bristol, Kent, Newport, Providence, State Level Sites, Washington	
FUNNY TOWN NAMES: Annawomscutt, Hog Island, Woonsocket	

SOME IMPORTANT RHODE ISLAND HISTORY

> In 1524 Florentine Giovanni de Verrazano explores Narragansett Bay and Rhode Island coastline.

> In 1614 Dutch trader Adriaen Block discovers island now named for him.

> In 1635 William Blackstone becomes first settler of what would become Rhode Island.

> In 1636 Roger Williams founds Providence on land he acquired from Indians.

> In 1637 Anne Hutchison founds Portsmouth after being banished from Massachusetts for heresy.

> In 1647 Rhode Island is united with Providence, forming single government.

> In 1663 King Charles II grants charter for Rhode Island settlement.

> From 1675 to 1676 King Philip's War between Narragansett Tribe and colonists results in several thousand Indian deaths and the deaths of hundreds of colonists.

> In 1774 Connecticut and Rhode Island prohibit importing of slaves.

> In 1776 Rhode Island Colony declares independence from Great Britain.

> In 1776 Stephen Hopkins, governor of Rhode Island, signs Declaration of Independence.

> In 1777–1778 British forces occupy Newport and colonial forces flee to Bristol.
> In 1778 Battle of Rhode Island results in partial colonial victory.
> In 1779 British forces evacuate Rhode Island.
> On May 29, 1790, Rhode Island becomes 13th US state.
> In 1812 Rhode Island refuses to take part in the War of 1812.

IMPORTANT CITIES IN RHODE ISLAND

An evening view of Providence, capital of Rhode Island.

PROVIDENCE: Located in eastern Rhode Island, Providence is the state's largest city (and the third largest in the New England region) and its capital. It was founded in 1636, making it one of the oldest cities in the United States.

WARWICK: Located in central Rhode Island, Warwick is the second largest city in the state. It was founded in 1642 by a man named Samuel Gorton, who purchased the land from Narragansett Indian chief Sachem Miantonomi.

PAWTUCKET: Located in northeastern Rhode Island and bordering Providence, Pawtucket is the fourth largest city in the state. Pawtucket was a major producer of processed cotton during the American Industrial Revolution.

RIVERS, MOUNTAINS, AND OTHER NATURAL STUFF

JERIMOTH HILL: At 812 feet above sea level, Jerimoth Hill is the highest natural point in Rhode Island. It is located in the Providence County town of Foster, near Rhode Island's border with Connecticut. The hill was donated to Brown University in the 1900s, and the college still uses it as an astronomy observatory.

NARRAGANSETT BAY: Located on the northern side of Rhode Island Sound, Narragansett Bay is an important bay and estuary in Rhode Island. The bay's surface area is 147 square miles, making it New England's biggest estuary. Small parts of the bay extend

The Clairborne Pell Bridge crosses Narragansett Bay and connects Jamestown and Newport, Rhode Island.

into Massachusetts. There are more than 30 islands in the bay, the three largest of which are Aquidneck Island, Conanicut Island, and Prudence Island.

AQUIDNECK ISLAND: With a land area of just under 40 square miles, Aquidneck Island is the largest island in Rhode Island's Narragansett Bay. Its official name is "Rhode Island," but it is called "Aquidneck Island" to help distinguish the island from the state.

WEIRDNESS IN RHODE ISLAND

At 9 feet tall and 58 feet long, **NIBBLES WOODAWAY** is billed as the world's largest bug. Nibbles is the fiberglass mascot of a pest-control company called Big Blue Bug Solutions, and he's perched atop the company's building in Providence, Rhode Island.

SOME RHODE ISLAND VIPS

ROGER WILLIAMS (1603–1683): The cofounder of the Rhode Island Colony, Roger Williams was an English minister who acted on his belief that people should be free to worship God as their consciences led them to. In 1635 he was expelled from the Massachusetts Bay Colony for speaking out against the strict rules of the colony's Puritan leaders, so he started a new colony near modern-day Providence, Rhode Island, called the Providence Plantation. There he founded the first Baptist church in America, the First Baptist Church of Providence. Williams organized the first attempt to prohibit slavery in any of the original 13 colonies.

A statue of Rhode Island cofounder Roger Williams in Providence.

ANNE HUTCHINSON (1591–1643): Anne Hutchinson, who was born in England, is considered one of the most important women in American colonial history. Like Roger Williams, Hutchinson was banished from the Massachusetts Bay Colony for advocating for more religious freedom among the people. She was banished from the colony around 1737 and then moved on to form a new colony at Portsmouth, Rhode Island. The colony of Rhode Island was later formed out of the settlements at Providence and Portsmouth, as well as others.

GOD IN RHODE ISLAND'S CONSTITUTION (PREAMBLE)

We, the people of the State of Rhode Island and Providence Plantations, grateful to Almighty God for the civil and religious liberty which He hath so long permitted us to enjoy. . .do ordain and establish this Constitution of government.

NATHANAEL GREENE (1742–1786): Born in Warwick, Rhode Island, Nathanael Green was a hero of the American Revolutionary War. He was considered General George Washington's most dependable and accomplished officer. Among his many other military accomplishments, Greene commanded the Revolutionary War's Southern Campaign, and he and his men forced British general Charles Cornwallis to flee the Carolinas.

RHODE ISLAND'S CHRISTIAN CONNECTION

When Roger Williams, an English minister and the cofounder of the Rhode Island Colony, first arrived in the area that is now Providence, Rhode Island, he sensed that God had a purpose for his being there. That is why he named the new colony "Providence." In the biblical sense, the word *providence* refers to God's presence and plan for everything the Christian does and experiences. Williams, who left the Massachusetts Bay Colony because he wanted to create a colony where people were free to worship God in ways they believed pleased Him, named the area in honor of what he called "God's merciful Providence." ★

★★★ FOURTEEN ★★★

VERMONT

The State of Freedom and Unity

BECAME A STATE ON: March 4, 1791	
NICKNAME: the Green Mountain State	
STATE BIRD: hermit thrush	
STATE FLOWER: red clover	
STATE SONG: "These Green Mountains"	
STATE MOTTO: Freedom and Unity	
POPULATION/RANK: 626,011/49	
TOTAL AREA/RANK: 9,614.26/45	
LIST OF COUNTIES: Addison, Bennington, Caledonia, Chittenden, Essex, Franklin, Grand Isle, Lamoille, Orange, Orleans, Rutland, State Level Sites, Washington, Windham, Windsor	
FUNNY TOWN NAMES: Beanville, Dummerston Center, Mosquitoville	

OME IMPORTANT VERMONT HISTORY

> In 1535 French explorer Jacques Cartier is the first European to explore Vermont.

> In 1609 French explorer Samuel de Champlain claims region that would become Vermont region for France.

> In 1666 Fort St. Anne, the first European settlement in Vermont, is built at Isle La Motte.

> In 1724 the British establish Fort Drummer, the first permanent European settlement in Vermont.

> In 1764 Vermont becomes part of New York.

> In 1777 the Battle of Hubbardton, the only battle of the Revolutionary War fought in what is now Vermont, is waged; Vermont declares independence from Great Britain.

> On March 4, 1791, Vermont becomes 14th US state.

> In 1805 Montpelier is named Vermont's state capital.

> In 1814 US forces gain control of Lake Champlain, stopping British invasion.

> In 1823 the Champlain Canal opens, creating water route between Vermont and New York City.

> In 1881 Vermont native Chester Arthur becomes 21st president of the United States.

GOD IN VERMONT'S CONSTITUTION (CHAPTER I, ARTICLE 3)

That all men have a natural and unalienable right to worship Almighty God, according to the dictates of their own consciences and understanding, regulated by the word of God. . .

IMPORTANT CITIES IN VERMONT

BURLINGTON: Located in northwestern Vermont, Burlington is the most populous city in the state. It was incorporated as a city in 1865. The ice cream company Ben & Jerry's makes its headquarters in Burlington.

ESSEX: Located in northwestern Vermont, Essex is a small town of about 19,000 residents, but it is the second largest municipality in the state. It was incorporated as a town in 1763.

MONTPELIER: Montpelier, the 13th largest city in Vermont, is the smallest state capital in the US. The first permanent settlement of the area began in 1787 and was named after the French city of Montpelier. It became Vermont's state capital in 1805.

The small town of Montpelier, Vermont's capital, is almost hidden among the trees and hills.

RIVERS, MOUNTAINS, AND OTHER NATURAL STUFF

OTTER CREEK: At about 112 miles in length, it's the longest river entirely in the state of Vermont. It flows out of the Valley of Vermont before flowing through the communities of Wallingford, Rutland, Brandon, Middlebury, and Vergennes and emptying into Lake Champlain at the town of Ferrisburg.

Lake Champlain, photographed from Burlington, Vermont.

LAKE CHAMPLAIN: Lake Champlain is a large lake located mostly in New York and Vermont (some of it is located in Quebec, Canada). It measures up to 125 miles long and 14 miles wide and has a surface area of 490 square miles. The Champlain Valley, the region around Lake Champlain in Vermont and New York, is the most populous area of Vermont. Burlington, the state's largest city, is located on the lake.

MOUNT MANSFIELD: With a summit that peaks at 4,393 feet above sea level, Mount Mansfield is the highest mountain in Vermont. The mountain's summit is located in the Chittenden County town of Underhill, while the ridgeline extends into the town of Stowe. Weird fact about Mount Mansfield: when you look at it from the east or west, it looks like an elongated human profile—complete with a forehead, nose, lips, chin, and Adam's apple.

WEIRDNESS IN VERMONT

PHINEAS GAGE MEMORIAL: The tiny town of Cavendish and a 19th-century resident named Phineas Gage have a strange claim to fame. In 1843, when Gage was 25 years old, he was working at a construction site in the town when a premature explosion shot a 3.5-foot iron bar through the air—and through Gage's skull. Amazingly, Gage recovered from the accident with a bad eye and some scarring, but also changes to his personality. Today, a small park in the middle of Cavendish is home to a memorial to the incident. On a boulder at the site is a large bronze plate telling Gage's story—with both words and an image of what the iron bar did to his skull.

SOME VERMONT VIPS

SAMUEL DE CHAMPLAIN (C. 1574–1635): In 1609 French navigator/explorer Samuel de Champlain—known as "the Father of New France"—claimed what would later become the 14th US state for his home country of France and discovered Lake Champlain. He named the lake after himself. The year before, he had founded New France and Quebec City. He also drew up the first accurate map of the east coast of what would become Canada.

CALVIN COOLIDGE (1872–1933): Born in the tiny Vermont town of Plymouth, Calvin Coolidge was the 30th president of the United States (1923–1929). Coolidge became involved in Massachusetts politics and eventually served as governor of the state. He was elected the 29th vice president of the United States in 1920 and became president after the sudden death of Warren G. Harding

Calvin Coolidge, thirtieth president of the United States, was born in Vermont.

in 1923. Coolidge won the election in 1924 and served until 1929.

JOHN DEERE (1804–1886): Born in Rutland, Vermont, John Deere was a manufacturer and blacksmith who invented the first commercially successful steel plow and who founded Deere & Company, one of the world's largest manufacturers of agricultural and construction equipment. Deere moved to Illinois, where he invented his steel plow in 1838. By 1855, his factory made and sold more than 10,000 plows. His invention came to be known as "the Plow That Broke the Plains."

VERMONT'S CHRISTIAN CONNECTION

In 2006 the First Congregational Church of Bennington (also known as the Old First Church), located in Bennington, Vermont, celebrated its 200th birthday. The original congregation of the Old First Church first gathered on December 3, 1762. Its current meeting place was completed in 1805. Today, the church calls itself the "first church built in Vermont that reflects the separation of church and state." That meant that the government would not play any part in the church's ministry or in the maintenance of its building. ★

★★★ FIFTEEN ★★★

KENTUCKY

Where the Grass Is Blue

BECAME A STATE ON: June 1, 1792	
NICKNAME: Bluegrass State	
STATE BIRD: cardinal	
STATE FLOWER: goldenrod	
STATE SONG: "My Old Kentucky Home"	
STATE MOTTO: United we stand, divided we fall	
POPULATION/RANK: 4,380,415/26	
TOTAL AREA/RANK: 40,409.02 square miles/37	
FUNNY TOWN NAMES: Bugtussle, Chicken Bristle, Monkey's Eyebrow	

LIST OF COUNTIES: Adair, Allen, Anderson, Ballard, Barren, Bath, Bell, Boone, Bourbon, Boyd, Boyle, Bracken, Breathitt, Breckinridge, Bullitt, Butler, Caldwell, Calloway, Campbell, Carlisle, Carroll, Carter, Casey, Christian, Clark, Clay, Clinton, Crittenden, Cumberland, Daviess, Edmonson, Elliott, Estill, Fayette, Fleming, Floyd, Franklin, Fulton, Gallatin, Garrard, Grant, Graves, Grayson, Green, Greenup, Hancock, Hardin, Harlan, Harrison, Hart, Henderson, Henry, Hickman, Hopkins, Jackson, Jackson Purchase, Jefferson, Jessamine, Johnson, Kenton, Knott, Knox, LaRue, Laurel, Lawrence, Lee, Leslie, Letcher, Lewis, Lincoln, Livingston, Logan, Lyon, Madison, Magoffin, Marion, Marshall, Martin, Mason, McCracken, McCreary, McLean, Meade, Menifee, Mercer, Metcalfe, Monroe, Montgomery, Morgan, Muhlenberg, Nelson, Nicholas, Ohio, Oldham, Owen, Owsley, Pendleton, Perry, Pike, Powell, Pulaski, Robertson, Rockcastle, Rowan, Russell, Scott, Shelby, Simpson, Spencer, State Level Sites, Taylor, Todd, Trigg, Trimble, Union, Warren, Washington, Wayne, Webster, Whitley, Wolfe, Woodford

SOME IMPORTANT KENTUCKY HISTORY

> In 1654 Virginian Colonel Abram Wood surveys area that would become Kentucky.

> In the 1720s France claims most of the land.

> In 1767 frontiersmen Daniel Boone and John Findley travel into Kentucky through Cumberland Gap.

> In 1774 James Harrod constructs first permanent Kentucky settlement at Fort Harrod.

> In 1780 Virginia divides Kentucky County into three separate counties: Fayette, Jefferson, and Lincoln.

> In 1782 the last battle of American Revolution is fought at Blue Licks.

> On June 1, 1792, Kentucky becomes 15th US state.

> In 1796 the Wilderness Road, a route for settlers to reach Kentucky from the east, opens for wagons.

> In 1818 President Andrew Jackson purchases the western portion of Kentucky from the Chickasaw Indians (Jackson Purchase).

> In 1861 Kentucky declares neutrality in Civil War and issues proclamation asking both sides to stay off Kentucky soil; Kentucky becomes 13th Confederate state.

> In 1862 the first battle of the American Civil War on Kentucky soil is fought near Prestonsburg.

> In 1875 the first Kentucky Derby is run at Churchill Downs.

Horses relaxing at one of Kentucky's many horse farms.

along the Kentucky River. After Kentucky became a US state in early 1792, a committee of five prominent men was appointed to choose the capital city of Kentucky. Several communities competed, but Frankfort was chosen.

IMPORTANT CITIES IN KENTUCKY

An evening view of the skyline of Louisville, Kentucky's largest city.

LOUISVILLE: The largest city in Kentucky, Louisville is located in the central part of the commonwealth. It is one of the oldest cities west of the Appalachian Mountains. The settlement that would become the city of Louisville was founded in 1778. Louisville is known as the host city of the Kentucky Derby.

LEXINGTON: Located in north-central Kentucky, Lexington is the second largest city in the state. It was founded in 1775. Lexington is located in Kentucky's Bluegrass Region and is known as "the Horse Capital of the World."

FRANKFORT: Frankfort is the capital city of Kentucky and the fifth smallest state capital in the United States. It is located on the north-central part of the state

RIVERS, MOUNTAINS, AND OTHER NATURAL STUFF

MAMMOTH CAVE: With about 400 miles of surveyed passageways, Mammoth Cave is the longest known cave system in the world. This system of caves, which is located in central Kentucky, is officially named the Mammoth-Flint Ridge Cave System.

The historic entrance to Kentucky's Mammoth Cave.

KENTUCKY RIVER: The Kentucky River is an important river in Kentucky because it supplies drinking water to about one-sixth of the state's population. It

GOD IN KENTUCKY'S CONSTITUTION (PREAMBLE)

We, the people of the Commonwealth of Kentucky, grateful to Almighty God for the civil, political, and religious liberties we enjoy, and invoking the continuance of these blessings, do ordain and establish this Constitution.

starts in eastern Kentucky at Beattyville then flows 260 miles—mostly northward—before it empties into the Ohio River at Carrollton, Kentucky.

BLACK MOUNTAIN: Located in southeastern Kentucky, Black Mountain is the highest peak in the Commonwealth of Kentucky. Black Mountain's summit, which is found in Harlan County, is 4,145 feet above sea level.

WEIRDNESS IN KENTUCKY

VENT HAVEN MUSEUM: The New Haven Museum in Fort Mitchell, Kentucky, is the world's only museum dedicated to ventriloquism. It's also the site of an annual ventriloquist convention. The museum features more than 700 dolls and other objects related to ventriloquism—including dolls that belonged to famous ventriloquist Edgar Bergen.

SOME KENTUCKY VIPS

JEFFERSON DAVIS (1808–1889): Born in Fairview, Kentucky, Jefferson Davis was the president of the Confederate States of America during the American Civil War (1861–1865). Davis was raised on plantations in Mississippi and Louisiana before graduating from the US Military Academy at West Point. He served the United States as a colonel in the Mexican-American War (1846–1848) and as the US secretary of war under President Franklin Pierce.

ABRAHAM LINCOLN (1809–1865): Illinois is known as "the Land of Lincoln," but Abraham Lincoln, the 16th president of the United States, was actually born in a log cabin in Hodgenville, Kentucky. He served as president from March 4, 1861, until April 15, 1865. During Lincoln's presidency, the country's southern states seceded from the Union because Lincoln and the northern states wanted to make slavery illegal in the US. The American Civil War started six weeks after he became president. The war lasted from 1861 until 1865, with the Union (the North) defeating the Confederacy (the South). Lincoln had a plan to reunite the country, but he never had a chance to put it into effect because he was shot at Ford's Theater in Washington, DC, on April 14, 1865, and died the next day.

MUHAMMAD ALI (1942–2016): Considered one of the top athletes in Kentucky history, Muhammad Ali (born Cassius Marcellus Clay Jr.) was a heavyweight boxer who won the Olympic gold medal at the Rome Olympics in 1960 before winning the World Heavyweight Championship three different times.

KENTUCKY'S CHRISTIAN CONNECTION

Located in Grayson, Kentucky, Kentucky Christian University (KCU) is a Christian university founded in 1919. When it was founded, it was called "Christian Normal Institute," and it included a high school, a junior college, and a training program for schoolteachers. In the 1920s the institute began focusing on training students for Christian ministry. Kentucky Christian University calls itself the "the Great Commission University." ★

SIXTEEN

TENNESSEE

The Volunteer State

BECAME A STATE ON: June 1, 1796	
NICKNAME: the Volunteer State	
STATE BIRD: northern mockingbird, northern bobwhite	
STATE FLOWER: iris	
STATE SONG: "Tennessee"	
STATE MOTTO: Agriculture and Commerce	
POPULATION/RANK: 6,456,243/17	
TOTAL AREA/RANK: 42,143.27 square miles/36	
LIST OF COUNTIES: Anderson, Bedford, Benton, Bledsoe, Blount, Bradley, Campbell, Cannon, Carroll, Carter, Cheatham, Chester, Claiborne, Clay, Cocke, Coffee, Crockett, Cumberland, Davidson, Decatur, DeKalb, Dickson, Dyer, Fayette, Fentress, Franklin, Gibson, Giles, Grainger, Greene, Grundy, Hamblen, Hamilton, Hancock, Hardeman, Hardin, Hawkins, Haywood, Henderson, Henry, Hickman, Houston, Humphreys, Jackson, James, Jefferson, Johnson, Knox, Lake, Lauderdale, Lawrence, Lewis, Lincoln, Loudon, Macon, Madison, Marion, Marshall, Maury, McMinn, McNairy, Meigs, Monroe, Montgomery, Moore, Morgan, Obion, Overton, Perry, Pickett, Polk, Putnam, Rhea, Roane, Robertson, Rutherford, Scott, Sequatchie, Sevier, Shelby, Smith, State Level Sites, Stewart, Sullivan, Sumner, Tipton, Trousdale, Unicoi, Union, Van Buren, Warren, Washington, Wayne, Weakley, White, Williamson, Wilson	
FUNNY TOWN NAMES: Bugscuffle, Nankipoo, Nolichucky	

SOME IMPORTANT TENNESSEE HISTORY

> In 1541 Spanish explorer Hernando de Soto claims it for Spain.

> In 1566 Spaniards build fort near present-day Chattanooga.

> In 1673 Englishmen James Needham and Gabriel Arthur explore Tennessee River Valley.

> In 1750 Dr. Thomas Walker leads group of Virginians into Tennessee, reaching Cumberland River and Cumberland Mountains.

> In 1757 South Carolinians build Fort Loudon on the Little Tennessee River.

> In 1760 Cherokee Indians capture Fort Loudon.

> In 1763 the French and Indian Wars end, and France surrenders claims to lands east of Mississippi River in Treaty of Paris.

> In 1768 Iroquois Indians give up Tennessee land claims to English.

> In 1775 Daniel Boone blazes trail from Virginia across mountain at Cumberland Gap to open land for settlement.

> In 1779 Jonesboro becomes first chartered town and oldest permanent settlement in Tennessee.

> On June 1, 1796, Tennessee becomes 16th US state.

> In 1815 Andrew Jackson leads Tennessee troops in victory over British at Battle of New Orleans in final battle of War of 1812.

> In 1818 the western boundary of Tennessee is extended to Mississippi River.

> In 1826 Nashville becomes state capital.

> In 1861 Tennessee becomes last state to secede from Union.

> In 1866 Tennessee is the first former Confederate state readmitted to Union.

IMPORTANT CITIES IN TENNESSEE

MEMPHIS: The largest city in Tennessee, Memphis is located in the southwestern corner of the state. It is the largest city on the Mississippi River. Tennessee became the 16th state in the US in 1796, but Memphis didn't officially become a city until more than two decades later.

An evening view of downtown Nashville and its waterfront.

NASHVILLE: Located in north-central Tennessee along the Cumberland River, Nashville is the state's capital and its second largest city. The town of Nashville was founded in 1779 and was named after Francis Nash, a hero from the American Revolutionary War. Nashville was incorporated as a city in 1806 and named the permanent state capital of Tennessee in 1843. It is a hub of the music industry, giving it the nickname "Music City."

KNOXVILLE: Knoxville, which is Tennessee's third largest city, is located in the central-eastern part of the state. It was first settled in 1786 and served as Tennessee's first capital. During the American Civil War, Knoxville was occupied at different times by both Confederate and Union armies.

RIVERS, MOUNTAINS, AND OTHER NATURAL STUFF

The Tennessee River Gorge, viewed from Lookout Mountain.

TENNESSEE RIVER: The largest tributary of the Ohio River, the Tennessee River flows 652 miles from its start near Knoxville. From Knoxville, it flows southwest through eastern Tennessee before it crosses into Alabama. It forms a loop in northern Alabama before flowing back into Tennessee. It empties into the Ohio River near Paducah, Kentucky.

CLINGMANS DOME: At 6,643 feet above sea level, Clingmans Dome is the highest peak in Tennessee and the third-highest peak east of the Mississippi River. It is part of the Great Smoky Mountains of Tennessee and North Carolina. Clingmans Dome has two other peaks called "subpeaks": the 6,560-foot Mount Buckley to the west and the 6,400-foot Mount Love to the east.

BLUE SPRING CAVE: Located in White County in central Tennessee, Blue Spring Cave is the longest cave in the state and the ninth longest in the United States. Up until 1989, only 500 feet of Blue Spring Cave had been explored. That year, cave explorers discovered a larger passage that they named Johnson Avenue. As of 2012, the surveyed length of Blue Spring Cave is 38.4 miles.

WEIRDNESS IN TENNESSEE

MUSEUM OF SALT AND PEPPER SHAKERS

Gatlinburg, Tennessee, is home to the Museum of Salt and Pepper Shakers, which has on display more than 20,000 pairs of shakers from all over the world—as well as a pretty good-sized collection of pepper mills.

SOME TENNESSEE VIPS

DAVY CROCKETT (1786–1836): Born in Greene County, Tennessee, Davy Crockett was a 19th-century frontiersman, politician, and soldier. He is often called "King of the Wild Frontier." Crocket grew up in east Tennessee and later served as a colonel in the Lawrence County militia. In 1825 he was elected to represent the Volunteer State in the US House of Representatives. After running for election again in 1835, he left for Texas, where he took part in the Texas Revolution in early 1836. He died at the Battle of the Alamo on March 6, 1836.

ALVIN C. YORK (1887–1964): Better known simply as "Sergeant York," Alvin C. York was the greatest American hero of World War I. York, who was born in Pall Mall, Tennessee, was a Christian man who struggled with the idea of going to war and killing. But he was awarded the Medal of Honor for leading an October 8, 1918, attack on a German machine-gun nest, killing 32 German

Sgt. Alvin York

soldiers and capturing 132 others, and knocking out 35 German machine guns.

WILMA RUDOLPH (1940–1994): One of Tennessee's greatest athletes, Wilma Rudolph established a reputation as the fastest woman in the world after her performance in the 1956 and 1960 Olympic Games. At the 1960 Summer Olympics in Rome, she became the first American woman to win three gold medals in track and field in a single Olympic Games. She was born in Saint Bethlehem, Tennessee, and competed in college at Tennessee State University.

TENNESSEE'S CHRISTIAN CONNECTION

BRYAN COLLEGE was founded in Dayton, Tennessee, in 1930 with the purpose of teaching students a Christian worldview. Bryan still requires students to achieve core competencies in subjects such as Christian worldview and spiritual formation, but it also offers a variety of ministry training and Bible majors, as well as minors in biblical languages, Bible, Christian leadership, Greek, missions, and philosophy. ★

> ## GOD IN TENNESSEE'S CONSTITUTION (ARTICLE I, SECTION 3)
>
> That all men have a natural and indefeasible right to worship Almighty God according to the dictates of their own conscience. . .that no human authority can, in any case whatever, control or interfere with the rights of conscience; and that no preference shall ever be given, by law, to any religious establishment or mode of worship.

★★★ SEVENTEEN ★★★

OHIO

The Mother of Presidents

OH

BECAME A STATE ON: March 1, 1803	

BECAME A STATE ON: March 1, 1803

NICKNAMES: the Buckeye State, Mother of Presidents, the Heart of It All, Birthplace of Aviation

STATE BIRD: cardinal

STATE FLOWER: scarlet carnation

STATE SONG: "Beautiful Ohio"

STATE MOTTO: With God, All Things Are Possible

POPULATION/RANK: 11,536,504/7

TOTAL AREA/RANK: 44,824.90 square miles/34

LIST OF COUNTIES: Adams, Allen, Ashland, Ashtabula, Athens, Auglaize, Belmont, Brown, Butler, Carroll, Champaign, Clark, Clermont, Clinton, Columbiana, Coshocton, Crawford, Cuyahoga, Darke, Defiance, Delaware, Erie, Fairfield, Fayette, Franklin, Fulton, Gallia, Geauga, Greene, Guernsey, Hamilton, Hancock, Hardin, Harrison, Henry, Highland, Hocking, Holmes, Huron, Jackson, Jefferson, Knox, Lake, Lawrence, Licking, Logan, Lorain, Lucas, Madison, Mahoning, Marion, Medina, Meigs, Mercer, Miami, Monroe, Montgomery, Morgan, Morrow, Muskingum, Noble, Ottawa, Paulding, Perry, Pickaway, Pike, Portage, Preble, Putnam, Richland, Ross, Sandusky, Scioto, Seneca, Shelby, Stark, Summit, Trumbull, Tuscarawas, Union, Van Wert, Vinton, Warren, Washington, Wayne, Williams, Wood, Wyandot

FUNNY TOWN NAMES: Businessburg, Chagrin Falls, Knockemstiff, Put-in-Bay

SOME IMPORTANT OHIO HISTORY

> In 1670 French explorer Robert Cavalier de LaSalle is the first European to "discover" the Ohio River.

> In 1763 the Treaty of Paris leads to France giving up all rights to territories in North America to Great Britain.

> In 1783 another Treaty of Paris ends the American Revolutionary War; England recognizes American independence and gives up all claims to lands in the Ohio country.

> In 1787 the US Congress enacts the Northwest Ordinance, which establishes the Northwest Territory, including lands that would become modern-day Ohio.

> In 1803 President Thomas Jefferson signs legislation making Ohio the 17th state.

A panoramic view of the skyline of Columbus, Ohio's capital city.

IMPORTANT CITIES IN OHIO

COLUMBUS: Columbus is Ohio's capital and the largest city in the state. It is located in the central part of Ohio. The city was founded in 1812 and was named after explorer Christopher Columbus. It was officially chartered as a city on March 3, 1834, even though it had functioned as the state capital since 1816.

CLEVELAND: The second largest city in Ohio, Cleveland is located in northeastern Ohio on the southern shore of Lake Erie. It was founded in 1769. Because it was located near important waterways, Cleveland quickly became a center for manufacturing and commerce.

CINCINNATI: Cincinnati, Ohio's third largest city, is located on the north bank of the Ohio River at the Ohio-Kentucky border, near Indiana. The area that would become Cincinnati was first settled in 1788. Cincinnati was the first major US city founded after the American Revolution.

RIVERS, MOUNTAINS, AND OTHER NATURAL STUFF

OHIO RIVER: The Ohio River is 981 miles long. It starts where the Allegheny and Monongahela Rivers meet in Pittsburgh, Pennsylvania, and ends where it flows into the Mississippi River at Cairo, Illinois. It flows through or borders the states of Illinois, Indiana, Kentucky, Ohio, Pennsylvania, and West Virginia. More than 10 percent of the US population lives in the Ohio River Basin.

CUYAHOGA RIVER: The Cuyahoga River flows through northeastern Ohio and feeds into Lake Erie. The Cuyahoga is an important river in US history but for a very weird reason: at one time, it was one of the most polluted rivers in the United States— so polluted that at least 13 fires had broken out on the river. The last time the river caught fire was in 1969, and that fire helped spark the environmental movement and several acts of Congress related to the environment.

LAKE ERIE: By surface area, Lake Erie is the fourth largest of the five Great Lakes of North America. It is the southernmost of the Great Lakes and is bounded

Rock House, a cave structure in Hocking Hills, Ohio.

by Ontario, Canada, to the north, Ohio and Pennsylvania to the south, and Michigan to the west. The major Ohio cities of Cleveland and Toledo are located on the shores of Lake Erie. Near Cleveland, the popular Huntington Beach, Edgewater Beach, and Headlands State Park are on the banks of Lake Erie.

WEIRDNESS IN OHIO

HOUSE OF TRASH: In the tiny southeastern Ohio village of Philo, at a place called Blue Rock Station, is a strange feature: a house made of garbage. That's right! Instead of new lumber, Sheetrock, concrete, and other materials most houses are made of, this home is made out of old tires, empty cans and bottles, recycled wood, and other materials you'd find in your local garbage disposal facility.

SOME OHIO VIPS

ULYSSES S. GRANT (1822–1885): After leading the Union Army to victory in the American Civil War, Ulysses S. Grant was elected as the 18th president of the United States. He served two four-year terms as president (1869–1877). Grant was born in Point Pleasant, Ohio.

A statue of General Ulysses S. Grant, the Civil War hero for the Union Army and the eighteenth president of the United States, in front of the U.S. Capitol Building in Washington, DC. Grant was one of seven presidents born in Ohio.

JAMES GARFIELD (1831–1881): The 20th president of the United States, James Garfield was elected to the nation's highest office after serving nine terms in a row in the US House of Representatives. His presidency started on March 4, 1881, but lasted just 200 days. On July 2, 1881, he was assassinated by Charles J. Guiteau. Garfield was born in a log cabin in what is now Moreland Hills, Ohio.

GOD IN OHIO'S CONSTITUTION (PREAMBLE)

We, the people of the State of Ohio, grateful to Almighty God for our freedom, to secure its blessings and promote our common welfare, do establish this Constitution.

NEIL ARMSTRONG (1930–2012): The first human to step foot on the moon, Neil Armstrong was born near Wapakoneta, Ohio. Armstrong was one of three crew members of Apollo 11, the space mission that landed the first humans on the moon. The landing took place on July 20, 1969, and Armstrong set foot on the moon's surface on July 21. Before becoming an astronaut, he was an officer in the United States Navy and served in the Korean War.

OHIO'S CHRISTIAN CONNECTIONS

By the late 1700s, many people in America no longer attended church services or spent much time or energy on their Christian faith. That began to change in the late 1700s through about the 1850s, with what historians call the "Second Great Awakening," a spiritual revival that was very strong in the Northeast and Midwest. One of the key preachers of the Second Great Awakening was a man named Charles Finney, who preached in western New York during the early 1820s. In 1835 Finney became a professor at Oberlin College, a Christian school in Oberlin, Ohio. Finney eventually served as Oberlin College's president. ★

★★★ EIGHTEEN ★★★
LOUISIANA
The Pelican State

MADE IN U.S.A.
DE IN U.S.A.

BECAME A STATE ON: April 30, 1812	
NICKNAMES: Sportsman's Paradise, Child of the Mississippi, Sugar State, Pelican State, Creole State, Bayou State	
STATE BIRD: brown pelican	
STATE FLOWER: magnolia	
STATE SONG: "Give Me Louisiana"	
STATE MOTTO: Union, Justice, and Confidence	
POPULATION/RANK: 4,601,893/25	
TOTAL AREA/RANK: 51,839.70 square miles/31	
LIST OF PARISHES: Acadia, Allen, Ascension, Assumption, Attakapas, Avoyelles, Baton Rouge, Beauregard, Bienville, Bossier, Caddo, Calcasieu, Caldwell, Cameron, Carroll, Catahoula, Claiborne, Concordia, De Soto, East Baton Rouge, East Carroll, East Feliciana, Evangeline, Feliciana, Franklin, Grant, Iberia, Iberville, Jackson, Jefferson, Jefferson Davis, Lafayette, Lafourche, LaSalle, Lincoln, Livingston, Madison, Morehouse, Natchitoches, Opelousas, Orleans, Ouachita, Plaquemines, Pointe Coupee, Rapides, Red River, Richland, Sabine, St. Bernard, St. Charles, St. Helena, St. James, St. John the Baptist, St. Landry, St. Martin, St. Mary, St. Tammany, State Level Sites, Tangipahoa, Tensas, Terrebonne, Union, Vermilion, Vernon, Washington, Webster, West Baton Rouge, West Carroll, West Feliciana, Winn	
FUNNY TOWN NAMES: Cranky Corner, Goober Hill, Kickapoo	

SOME IMPORTANT LOUISIANA HISTORY

> In 1519 Spanish explorer Alonso de Pineda reaches the mouth of Mississippi River.

> In 1541–1542 Hernando de Soto explores area.

> In 1682 Robert Cavalier claims Mississippi watershed for France and names area after King Louis XIV.

> In 1714 Juchereau de St. Denis founds first permanent settlement in Louisiana.

> In 1718 Jean Baptiste le Moyne founds New Orleans.

> In 1723 New Orleans becomes capital of Louisiana.

> In 1762 King Louis XV of France gives Charles II of Spain all land west of Mississippi.

> In 1800 Spain gives Louisiana back to France.

> In 1803 US purchases Louisiana Territory from France.

> On April 30, 1812, Louisiana becomes 18th US state.

- In 1849 Baton Rouge becomes capital of Louisiana.
- In 1861 Louisiana secedes from Union and joins the Confederacy.
- In 1868 Louisiana is readmitted to Union.
- In 1879 Louisiana adopts new state constitution.

IMPORTANT CITIES IN SOUTH CAROLINA

NEW ORLEANS: Located in southeastern Louisiana and straddling the Mississippi River, New Orleans is the largest city in Louisiana and a major port city. It is well known for its unique foods, music (it is considered the birthplace of American jazz), and its yearly celebrations and festivals. In terms of the amount of cargo handled, New Orleans is the largest port on the Gulf of Mexico, the second largest in the United States, and the third largest in the world.

BATON ROUGE: Located in the southeastern part of central Louisiana along the Mississippi River, Baton Rouge is the state's capital and second largest city. Baton Rouge got its name around 1699, when the party led by a French explorer named Sieur d'Iberville saw a red cypress pole covered with bloody animals in the area. They called the pole, and the area, le bâton rouge, which means "the red stick." European settlement of Baton Rouge started in 1719, when the French established it as a military post. Baton Rouge was incorporated as a city in 1817 and became Louisiana's capital in 1849.

SHREVEPORT: Shreveport, which is located in northwestern Louisiana on the banks of the Red River, is the third largest city in the state. It was founded in 1836 and established as a city three years later. Many locals call Shreveport "the Port City."

RIVERS, MOUNTAINS, AND OTHER NATURAL STUFF

DRISKILL MOUNTAIN: Located in north-central Louisiana near the city of Bryceland, Driskill Mountain (also known as Mount Driskill) is the highest natural summit in the state with an elevation of 535 feet above sea level.

A beautiful sunset over Louisiana's Lake Pontchartrain.

LAKE PONTCHARTRAIN: Lake Pontchartrain, which is located in southeastern Louisiana, near New Orleans, isn't technically a lake but an estuary that is connected to the Gulf of Mexico through the Rigolets strait. The lake is filled with brackish water (part salt water, part freshwater). It sits in six different Louisiana parishes and covers an area of 630 square miles. It stretches 40 miles east to west and 24 miles north to south.

A dramatic view of downtown New Orleans from across the Mississippi River.

GOD IN LOUISIANA'S CONSTITUTION (PREAMBLE)

We, the people of Louisiana, grateful to Almighty God for the civil, political, economic, and religious liberties we enjoy, and desiring to protect individual rights to life, liberty, and property. . .do ordain and establish this constitution.

MISSISSIPPI RIVER DELTA: Off Louisiana's southeastern coast, the Mississippi River Delta is a landform formed over time at the mouth of the Mississippi River. River deltas are formed when rivers carry sediment downstream to their mouths over long periods of time. The land making up the Mississippi River Delta looks like a tangled bird's claw. It is always changing but was changed radically in 2005 when hurricanes Katrina and Rita destroyed much of the delta. The Mississippi River Delta extends from the southern coast of Louisiana up to 50 miles.

WEIRDNESS IN LOUISIANA

THE ABITA MYSTERY HOUSE: Most people have this crazy notion that garbage belongs in a Dumpster and, later, a landfill or recycling center. Not so with artist/inventor John Preble of Abita Springs, Louisiana. He's the owner of the Abita Mystery House, which features various contraptions, miniaturized replicas of towns, tributes to Mardi Gras, Louisiana-themed sculptures, and many others—all made out of items more suited for a garbage can than a museum.

SOME LOUISIANA VIPS

JOHN WILLIS MENARD (1838–1893): Though he wasn't born in Louisiana, John Willis Menard is a historical figure in the state. In 1868 he became the first African American elected to the US House of Representatives. In the 1868 special election to replace James Mann, who had died in office, Menard was denied the congressional seat on the basis of a challenge by the election's loser, Caleb S. Hunt. On February 27, 1869, Menard became the first American black to address the US House.

MICHAEL ELLIS DEBAKEY (1908–2008): Born in Lake Charles, Louisiana, Michael DeBakey was a world-famous cardiac surgeon whose innovations forever changed the treatment of heart patients. DeBakey developed a medical device called a roller pump, which helped make open-heart surgery possible.

PEYTON MANNING (BORN 1976): Peyton Manning, who was born in New Orleans, Louisiana, is considered one of the greatest quarterbacks in NFL history. Manning played his first 14 pro seasons for the Indianapolis Colts before joining the Denver Broncos for the 2012 season. Manning is a four-time NFL Most Valuable Player who led the Colts to eight division championships, two American Football Conference championships, and one Super Bowl championship. With the Broncos, Manning set NFL records for passing yards (5,477) and touchdown passes (55) in one season. His Broncos won Super Bowl 50 in 2016. He was elected to the Pro Football Hall of Fame in 2021.

LOUISIANA'S CHRISTIAN CONNECTION

JIMMY GID THARPE, SR. (1930–2008) was a Baptist minister in Shreveport who made a big impression on his home state of Louisiana. In the early 1960s he established Baptist Christian College as well as Baptist Christian Academy. In 1973 he founded Louisiana Baptist University and Theological Seminary, which was originally called Baptist Christian University. He is also believed to have established about 75 churches in Louisiana and Texas, the last of which was Sibley Baptist Tabernacle in his hometown of Sibley, Louisiana. ★

★★★ NINETEEN ★★★

INDIANA

The Hoosier State

BECAME A STATE ON: December 11, 1816	
NICKNAME: Hoosier State	
STATE BIRD: cardinal	
STATE FLOWER: peony	
STATE SONG: "On the Banks of the Wabash, Far Away"	
STATE MOTTO: The Crossroads of America	
POPULATION/RANK: 6,483,802/15	
TOTAL AREA/RANK: 36,417.73 square miles/38	
LIST OF COUNTIES: Adams, Allen, Bartholomew, Benton, Blackford, Boone, Brown, Carroll, Cass, Clark, Clay, Clinton, Crawford, Daviess, Dearborn, Decatur, De Kalb, Delaware, Dubois, Elkhart, Fayette, Floyd, Fountain, Franklin, Fulton, Gibson, Grant, Greene, Hamilton, Hancock, Harrison, Hendricks, Henry, Howard, Huntington, Jackson, Jasper, Jay, Jefferson, Jennings, Johnson, Knox, Kosciusko, La Porte, Lagrange, Lake, Lawrence, Madison, Marion, Marshall, Martin, Miami, Monroe, Montgomery, Morgan, Newton, Noble, Ohio, Orange, Owen, Parke, Perry, Pike, Porter, Posey, Pulaski, Putnam, Randolph, Ripley, Rush, St. Joseph, Scott, Shelby, Spencer, Starke, Steuben, Sullivan, Switzerland, Tippecanoe, Tipton, Union, Vanderburgh, Vermillion, Vigo, Wabash, Warren, Warrick, Washington, Wayne, Wells, White, Whitley	
FUNNY TOWN NAMES: Floyd Knobs, French Lick, Knawbone, Possum Trot, Santa Claus	

SOME IMPORTANT INDIANA HISTORY

> Between 1700 and 1735, the French establish three outposts along the Wabash-Maumee trade route—one near present-day Fort Wayne, one near present-day Lafayette, and one at present-day Vincennes.

> In 1783 the Treaty of Paris gives land that would become Indiana to the United States. The following year, Clarksville becomes the first authorized American settlement in Indiana.

> Between 1787 and 1803 Indiana was part of what is known as the Northwest Territory, or the Territory Northwest of the River Ohio.

> In 1800 the Indiana Territory is established from Northwest Territory lands. The territory includes most of present-day Indiana, all of Illinois and Wisconsin, and parts of Minnesota, Michigan, and Ohio.

> In 1805 the Michigan Territory is separated from the Indiana Territory. Four years later, the Illinois Territory is created.

> On December 11, 1816, Indiana becomes the 19th US state. Jonathan Jennings is the state's first governor.

> In 1848 members of the Neil's Creek Abolitionist Church in Lancaster, Indiana, found the Eleutherian Institute, the first college in Indiana to admit students of all races and both genders.

IMPORTANT CITIES IN INDIANA

A view of the Indianapolis skyline at sunset.

INDIANAPOLIS: Indiana's capital city, Indianapolis, is the largest city by population in the state. It was selected as the state capital in 1820, replacing Corydon as Indiana's seat of government.

FORT WAYNE: The second largest city in Indiana, Fort Wayne is located in northeastern Indiana. It got its start when Anthony Wayne, a US Army officer during the American Revolutionary War, built an actual fort (one in a series he built) near a tribal village in 1794.

EVANSVILLE: Indiana's third largest city by population, Evansville is sometimes called "River City" because it is located on a bend in the Ohio River in southwestern Indiana. The area was first settled by Americans in 1812, and it was incorporated as a city in 1819.

RIVERS, MOUNTAINS, AND OTHER NATURAL STUFF

A view of Lake Michigan from the Indiana Dunes.

GREAT LAKES PLAINS: Forming most of the northern one-third of the state of Indiana, the Great Lakes Plains are also called the Northern Lake or Moraine region of the state. These plains start with sand dunes along the Lake Michigan shoreline. Farther inland are mostly flat plains with a few low hills, which are often called "moraines."

TILL PLAINS: If you traveled south of the Great Lakes Plains, you'd come to a wide area in central Indiana called the Till Plains. The Till Plains are part of what is called the Great Corn Belt of the Midwest, but farmers also grow soybeans and other grains in the area's fertile soil. Rolling hills and valleys are also found in this region, including Hoosier Hill, Indiana's highest point, which is located in the Till Plains near the Indiana-Ohio border.

WABASH RIVER: Indiana's state river, the Wabash is a 503-mile-long river that flows southwest from northwestern Ohio, across northern Indiana, and then to southern Illinois. It forms the Illinois-Indiana border before draining into the Ohio River.

GOD IN INDIANA'S CONSTITUTION (PREAMBLE)

To the end, that justice be established, public order maintained, and liberty perpetuated; we, the People of the State of Indiana, grateful to almighty God for the free exercise of the right to choose our own form of government, do ordain this Constitution.

WEIRDNESS IN INDIANA

THE WORLD'S LARGEST BALL OF PAINT: Tourists traveling through Alexandria, a small town in east-central Indiana, can be treated to a roadside attraction known simply as "the World's Largest Ball of Paint." Actually, the ball isn't all paint; it's really a baseball a man named Michael Carmichael has been applying layers of paint to since January 1, 1977. To date, the ball is covered with more than 20,000 layers of colored paint and weights more than 1,000 pounds.

SOME INDIANA VIPS

WILBUR WRIGHT (1867–1912): The older of the two famous Wright brothers, Wilbur Wright was born in Millville, Indiana. Wilbur and his brother Orville, who was born in Ohio, were credited with inventing and building the world's first successful airplane. Between 1905 and 1907, the Wright brothers developed technology that made fixed-wing, powered flight possible.

LARRY BIRD (BORN 1956): Larry Bird, who was born in West Baden, Indiana, and raised in nearby French Lick, was one of the greatest professional basketball players of all time. He played his entire NBA career (1979–1992) for the Boston Celtics, helping the team to three NBA championships.

JOHN WOODEN (1910–2010): As coach of the UCLA Bruins, John Wooden, who was born in Hall, Indiana, accomplished things no other coach has ever accomplished (or probably ever will). Nicknamed "the Wizard of Westwood," John Wooden coached UCLA to 10 NCAA championships in 12 seasons—including seven in a row from 1967 to 1973.

John Wooden earned his reputation as one of the greatest basketball coaches of all time at UCLA—but he was born in Hall, Indiana.

INDIANA'S CHRISTIAN CONNECTION

The city of Fort Wayne is often called the "City of Churches," a nickname dating back to the late 1800s, when the city was a regional headquarters for Lutheran, Episcopal, and Catholic denominations. Four major Christian denominations have their headquarters in the city today: the American Association of Lutheran Churches, the Fundamental Baptist Fellowship Association; Missionary Churches Inc., and the Fellowship of Evangelical Churches. The city is now home to about 360 churches. ★

★★★ TWENTY ★★★

MISSISSIPPI

A Hospitable Place

BECAME A STATE ON: December 10, 1817

NICKNAME: the Magnolia State, the Hospitality State

STATE BIRD: northern mockingbird, wood duck

STATE FLOWER: magnolia

STATE SONG: "Go, Mississippi"

STATE MOTTO: *Virtute et Armis* (By Valor and Arms)

POPULATION/RANK: 2,984,926/31

TOTAL AREA/RANK: 48,430.19/32

LIST OF COUNTIES: Adams, Alcorn, Amite, Attala, Benton, Bolivar, Calhoun, Carroll, Chickasaw, Choctaw, Claiborne, Clarke, Clay, Coahoma, Copiah, Covington, Desoto, Forrest, Franklin, George, Greene, Grenada, Hancock, Harrison, Hinds, Holmes, Humphreys, Issaquena, Itawamba, Jackson, Jasper, Jefferson, Jefferson Davis, Jones, Kemper, Lafayette, Lamar, Lauderdale, Lawrence, Leake, Lee, Leflore, Lincoln, Lowndes, Madison, Marion, Marshall, Monroe, Montgomery, Neshoba, Newton, Noxubee, Oktibbeha, Panola, Pearl River, Perry, Pike, Pontotoc, Prentiss, Quitman, Rankin, Scott, Sharkey, Simpson, Smith, State Level Sites, Stone, Sunflower, Tallahatchie, Tate, Tippah, Tishomingo, Tunica, Union, Walthall, Warren, Washington, Wayne, Webster, Wilkinson, Winston, Yalobusha, Yazoo

FUNNY TOWN NAMES: Chickenbone, Grin, Swampbottom

SOME IMPORTANT MISSISSIPPI HISTORY

> In 1540–1541 Spanish explorer Hernando de Soto enters Mississippi and discovers the Mississippi River.

> In 1673 French missionary Jacques Marquette and fur trapper Louis Jolliet explore Mississippi River.

> In 1699 French explorer Pierre Le Moyne and his teenage brother Jean Baptiste Le Moyne build Fort Maurepas, the first capital of the French colony in North America.

> In 1716 Fort Rosalie (now Natchez) is established.

> In 1763 the English take control of Mississippi after French and Indian War.

> Between 1781 and 1783 Spain controls the southern part of Mississippi while the US controls the northern part.

> In 1797 Spain yields control of Mississippi to the US.

> In 1798 Mississippi is organized as an American territory.

> In 1812 Mississippi takes control of the West Florida Territory.

> On December 10, 1817, Mississippi becomes 20th US state.

> In 1822 Jackson becomes the Mississippi state capital.

> In 1861 the American Civil War begins and Mississippi secedes from Union.

> In 1870 Mississippi is readmitted to Union.

> In 1962 James Meredith, the first black registrant at the University of Mississippi, enters UM.

> In 2005 Hurricane Katrina causes severe damage along the Mississippi coast.

IMPORTANT CITIES IN MISSISSIPPI

The Mississippi State capitol building in Jackson.

JACKSON: Jackson is the state capital of Mississippi and is located in the southwestern-central part of the state. It was founded in 1821 at the site of a trading post called Lefleur's Bluff. The area became the state capital after the Mississippi state legislature assigned three men to find a good place for a state capital. They picked the area that is now Jackson and named it after General Andrew Jackson—the future seventh president of the United States—in honor of his victory in the Battle of New Orleans in the War of 1812.

GULFPORT: Located in southern Mississippi along the coast, Gulfport is the second largest city in the state. Gulfport was incorporated as a city on July 28, 1898. Gulfport is now an important seaport and a popular tourist destination.

SOUTHAVEN: Southaven is the third largest city in Mississippi. It is located in the northwestern part of the state and is considered a suburb of Memphis. Southaven was incorporated as a city in 1981 and is one of the fastest growing cities in the nation.

RIVERS, MOUNTAINS, AND OTHER NATURAL STUFF

MISSISSIPPI RIVER: Flowing about 2,320 miles, the Mississippi River is the second longest river in the United States, after the Missouri River. It is the fourth longest river in the world, and it borders or flows through ten US states. At its widest point, the Mississippi measures over seven miles across. It starts in northern Minnesota and then flows south all the way to the Gulf of Mexico. It is an important river in US history and is still important because it provides water for irrigation and other uses and because it is an important waterway for the transport of goods and people.

A map of the Mississippi River and its major tributaries.

YAZOO RIVER: The Yazoo River flows 188 miles from Greenwood, Mississippi, before it empties into the Mississippi River just north of Vicksburg, Mississippi. The Yazoo River was an important waterway during the American Civil War. In fact, 29 ships sunk during the war are still beneath the river's surface.

GOD IN MISSISSIPPI'S CONSTITUTION (PREAMBLE)

We, the people of Mississippi in convention assembled, grateful to Almighty God, and involving His blessing on our work, do ordain and establish this Constitution.

WOODALL MOUNTAIN: Like other states in the gulf region, Mississippi isn't known for its mountains. In fact, the highest point in the state is the peak of Woodall Mountain (which is more a hill than a mountain), which stands 806 feet above sea level.

WEIRDNESS IN MISSISSIPPI

GRACELAND TOO: There's nothing weird—or really unusual—about liking Elvis Presley. Even though the King of Rock and Roll died in 1977, people of all ages still listen to his music. . .or at least know some of his songs. But Graceland Too, a museum in Holly Springs, Mississippi, dedicated to all things Elvis, takes it to a whole other level. Museum curator and creator Paul McLeod has created a wall-to-wall, floor-to-ceiling tribute to Elvis that is covered in every imaginable sort of Elvis memorabilia, as well as a collection of tens of thousands of recordings of Elvis's music.

ELVIS PRESLEY (1935–1977): Born in Tupelo, Mississippi, Elvis Presley was one of the most successful and popular entertainers in US history. Presley moved with his family to Memphis, Tennessee, when he was 13 years old. He began his music career in 1954, and his first No. 1 hit was his 1956 single "Heartbreak Hotel." Elvis went on to become the top-selling solo artist in the history of recorded music. His albums sold an estimated 600 million copies worldwide. Elvis appeared in his first movie—*Love Me Tender*—in 1956. Elvis is often called "the King of Rock and Roll."

JIM HENSON (1936–1990): Jim Henson, who was born in Greenville, Mississippi, was a puppeteer, artist, screenwriter, and director (among many other things) best known as the creator of the Muppets. Henson and his puppets performed on the television shows *Sesame Street* and *The Muppet Show*.

JAMES MEREDITH (BORN 1933): In 1962 James Meredith became the first African-American student admitted to the University of Mississippi, which had been a segregated (all-white) school. Meredith's decision to enroll at UM was an important event in the civil rights movement.

US marshals walk James Meredith to class at the University of Mississippi.

Born in Kosciusko, Mississippi, Meredith was motivated by President John F. Kennedy's inaugural address and hoped enrolling at UM would pressure Kennedy's administration to enforce civil rights for American blacks.

MISSISSIPPI'S CHRISTIAN CONNECTION

SOUTHEASTERN BAPTIST COLLEGE is a Baptist Bible college located in Laurel, Mississippi. The college was founded in 1948 and is nationally accredited by the Association for Biblical Higher Education. Students at Southeastern Baptist College can earn degrees in Bible, business, general education, and church ministries. All the non-Bible, non-ministry courses are taught from a Christian perspective. SBC's mission statement is to "glorify God by providing quality postsecondary education from a biblical worldview in a Christian atmosphere." ★

★★★ TWENTY-ONE ★★★

ILLINOIS

The Land of Lincoln

MADE IN U.S.A. 21 MADE IN U.S.A.

LIST OF COUNTIES: Adams, Alexander, Bond, Boone, Brown, Bureau, Calhoun, Carroll, Cass, Champaign, Christian, Clark, Clay, Clinton, Coles, Cook, Crawford, Cumberland, DeKalb, DeWitt, Douglas, DuPage, Edgar, Edwards, Effingham, Fayette, Ford, Franklin, Fulton, Gallatin, Greene, Grundy, Hamilton, Hancock, Hardin, Henderson, Henry, Iroquois, Jackson, Jasper, Jefferson, Jersey, Jo Daviess, Johnson, Kane, Kankakee, Kendall, Knox, Lake, LaSalle, Lawrence, Lee, Livingston, Logan, Macon, Macoupin, Madison, Marion, Marshall, Mason, Massac, McDonough, McHenry, McLean, Menard, Mercer, Monroe, Montgomery, Morgan, Moultrie, Ogle, Peoria, Perry, Piatt, Pike, Pope, Pulaski, Putnam, Randolph, Richland, Rock Island, Saline, Sangamon, Schuyler, Scott, Shelby, St. Clair, Stark, State Level Sites, Stephenson, Tazewell, Union, Vermilion, Wabash, Warren, Washington, Wayne, White, Whiteside, Will, Williamson, Winnebago, Woodford

BECAME A STATE ON: December 3, 1818

NICKNAME: the Prairie State, Land of Lincoln

STATE BIRD: northern cardinal

STATE FLOWER: viola

STATE SONG: "Illinois"

STATE MOTTO: State Sovereignty, National Union

POPULATION/RANK: 12,875,255/5

TOTAL AREA/RANK: 57,914.38/25

FUNNY TOWN NAMES: Goofy Ridge, Kickapoo, Roachtown

SOME IMPORTANT ILLINOIS HISTORY

> In 1673 French explorers Jacques Marquette and Louis Jolliet arrive in Illinois.

> In 1717 Illinois is part of French colony of Louisiana.

> In 1720 Fort de Chartres becomes seat of government in Illinois.

> In 1763 the Treaty of Paris gives Britain possession of Illinois.

> In 1787 Illinois becomes part of Northwest Territory.

> In 1800 Illinois is included in Indiana Territory.

> In 1809 the United States Congress creates Illinois Territory.

> On December 3, 1818, Illinois becomes 21st US state, and Kaskaskia is chosen as capital.

> In 1820 Vandalia becomes Illinois state capital.

> In 1830 Abraham Lincoln moves to Illinois.

> In 1837 Chicago is incorporated as city.

> In 1839 Springfield becomes state capital.

> In 1860 Illinois resident Abraham Lincoln is elected US president.

> In 1864 Lincoln is reelected US president.

> In 1865 Illinois becomes first state to ratify Thirteenth Amendment abolishing slavery. Lincoln is assassinated in Washington, DC.

> In 1871 Chicago fire destroys 18,000 downtown buildings.

> In 1893 the World's Fair is held in Chicago.

IMPORTANT CITIES IN ILLINOIS

The skyline of Chicago, Illinois, third largest city in the United States.

CHICAGO: Chicago is an international hub of transportation, finance, commerce, industry, and technology in northeastern Illinois. It is the largest city in the state and the third largest in the US. The city of Chicago was incorporated in 1837. Chicago has several nicknames, including "the Windy City," "Chi-Town," and "City of the Big Shoulders."

JOLIET: Joliet is the fourth largest city in Illinois. It is located about 40 miles southwest of Chicago. It is believed that the name "Joliet" comes from the name of French-Canadian explorer Louis Jolliet, who visited the area in 1673.

SPRINGFIELD: Springfield is the sixth largest city in Illinois and serves as the state capital. The area that would become Springfield was first settled in the late 1810s, around the time Illinois became a state. Springfield became the third capital of Illinois in 1839, replacing Vandalia (capital from 1819 to 1839), which replaced Kaskaskia (1818–1819). Springfield's most famous past resident is Abraham Lincoln, who lived there from 1837 until 1861.

RIVERS, MOUNTAINS, AND OTHER NATURAL STUFF

ILLINOIS RIVER: An important tributary of the Mississippi River, the Illinois River is about 273 miles long. It drains a large portion of central Illinois. Because it connected the Great Lakes to the Mississippi River, it was an important waterway among the natives who lived in the area and for early French traders. French colonial settlements along the river helped form the area known as the Illinois Country.

THE SHAWNEE HILLS: The Shawnee Hills is an area of southern Illinois that extends from Elizabethtown to the Illinois-Missouri border. The beauty of the Shawnee Hills and the Shawnee National Forest makes the area a popular tourist/sightseeing destination. In other parts of the Shawnee Hills, limestone and coal are mined.

CHARLES MOUND: At 1,235 feet above sea level, Charles Mound is the highest natural point in Illinois. The hill's summit is about a quarter mile from the Illinois-Wisconsin border. It is named after

Elijah Charles, who was one of the area's first permanent settlers.

WEIRDNESS IN ILLINOIS

OLNEY, ILLINOIS: HOME OF THE WHITE SQUIRRELS:
We all know what squirrels usually look like. The little critters are usually covered in a mixture of gray and brown fur, and they have long, fluffy tails. There are some squirrels, however, that don't fit the usual mold. White squirrels are covered in fur that is. . .well, white! And they don't always do well in nature because they

are so easy for predators to spot. With that in mind, the people of Olney, Illinois, have established their town as a safe haven for white squirrels and named it the "White Squirrel Capital of the World."

White squirrels are rare animals—except in Olney, Illinois, where they are protected and cared for.

SOME ILLINOIS VIPS

WALT DISNEY (1901–1966): Walt Disney, who was born in Chicago, was an American businessman, animator, cartoonist, screenwriter, and director who cofounded Walt Disney Productions, which would grow to become one of the best-known and most successful movie production companies in the world. Disney and his staff of artists and animators created some of the world's most famous characters, including Mickey Mouse.

Walt Disney in 1938.

DWYANE WADE (BORN 1982): Dwyane Wade is one of Chicago's greatest all-time athletes. He has won three NBA championships with the Miami Heat (2006, 2012, 2013), and was named an NBA All-Star 13 Times.

GOD IN ILLINOIS'S CONSTITUTION (PREAMBLE)

We, the people of the State of Illinois—grateful to Almighty God for the civil, political, and religious liberty which He has permitted us to enjoy and seeking His blessing upon our endeavors. . .do ordain and establish this Constitution for the State of Illinois.

Wade played college basketball at Marquette University in Milwaukee, Wisconsin, before the Heat selected him with the fifth pick in the 2003 NBA Draft. In 2023, he was inducted into the basketball hall of fame.

HILLARY RODHAM CLINTON (BORN 1947): Hillary Rodham Clinton is a lawyer and politician who was born in Chicago, Illinois. She was the First Lady to Bill Clinton when he served as governor of Arkansas and as president of the United States. She served as a US Senator from New York from 2001 to 2009. She ran for US president in 2008 but lost to eventual president Barack Obama in the race for the Democratic nomination.

ILLINOIS'S CHRISTIAN CONNECTION

MOODY BIBLE INSTITUTE: Dwight Lyman Moody (1837–1899) was a famous evangelist who was born in Northfield, Massachusetts, and who founded Moody Church, Northfield School, and Mount Hermon School in Massachusetts. But he also made a lasting impression on the city of Chicago, founding Moody Bible Institute, a Christian institution of higher learning in the Near North Side of Chicago in 1886. Moody also has campuses in Spokane, Washington, and Plymouth, Michigan. ★

★★★ TWENTY-TWO ★★★

ALABAMA

At the Heart of Dixie

BECAME A STATE ON: December 14, 1819

NICKNAMES: Yellowhammer State, Cotton State, Heart of Dixie

STATE BIRD: yellowhammer, wild turkey

STATE FLOWER: camellia

STATE SONG: "Alabama"

STATE MOTTO: *Audemus jura nostra defendere* ("We Defend Our Rights")

POPULATION/RANK: 4,822,023/23

TOTAL AREA/RANK: 52,419.02/30

LIST OF COUNTIES: Autauga, Baker (now Chilton County), Baldwin, Barbour, Benton (now Calhoun County), Bibb, Blount, Bullock, Butler, Calhoun, Chambers, Cherokee, Chilton, Choctaw, Clarke, Clay, Cleburne, Coffee, Colbert, Conecuh, Coosa, Covington, Crenshaw, Cullman, Dale, Dallas, Decatur (now Madison County and Jackson County), DeKalb, Elmore, Escambia, Etowah, Fayette, Franklin, Geneva, Greene, Hale, Hancock (now Winston County), Henry, Houston, Jackson, Jefferson, Lamar, Lauderdale, Lawrence, Lee, Limestone, Lowndes, Macon, Madison, Marengo, Marion, Marshall, Mobile, Monroe, Montgomery, Morgan, Perry, Pickens, Pike, Randolph, Russell, Sanford (now Lamar County), Shelby, St. Clair, State Level Sites, Sumter, Talladega, Tallapoosa, Tuscaloosa, Walker, Washington, Wilcox, Winston

FUNNY TOWN NAMES: Boar Tush, Gobblers Crossing, Possum Trot

SOME IMPORTANT ALABAMA HISTORY

> In 1519 Spanish explorer Alonzo Alvarez de Piñeda explores Gulf of Mexico, including Mobile Bay.

> In 1702 Le Moyne brothers establish Fort Louis de la Mobile and settlement on Mobile River.

> In 1712 La Moyne brothers move fort and settlement to present-day Mobile.

> In 1780 Spanish capture Mobile during American Revolution.

> In 1798 the Mississippi Territory is organized.

> In 1799 the US takes possession of Fort St. Stephens from Spanish.

> In 1802 Georgia formally cedes western claims at 31st parallel.

> In 1805–1806 white settlement of Indian lands begins.

> In 1813 the US captures Mobile from Spanish.

> In 1817 the Alabama Territory is created.

> In 1818 the first legislature of the Alabama Territory meets at St. Stephens; Cahaba is designated as state capital.

> On December 14, 1819, Alabama becomes 22nd US state.

> In 1826 Tuscaloosa becomes new Alabama state capital.

> In 1846 Montgomery is selected as new state capital.

> In 1849 fire destroys capitol in Montgomery.

> In 1852 Senator William Rufus King is elected US vice president but dies before taking office.

> In 1861 Alabama becomes fourth state to secede from Union.

> In 1868 Alabama is readmitted to Union.

GOD IN ALABAMA'S CONSTITUTION (PREAMBLE)

We, the people of the State of Alabama. . .invoking the favor and guidance of Almighty God, do ordain and establish the following constitution. . . .

IMPORTANT CITIES IN ALABAMA

A view of downtown Birmingham, the largest city in Alabama.

BIRMINGHAM: Birmingham is the largest city in the state of Alabama and is located in the north-central part of the state. It was founded in 1871 when three farm towns merged to create a much larger community. From the year it was founded through the end of the 1960s, Birmingham was an important center of industry in the American South.

MONTGOMERY: The capital city of Alabama, Montgomery is the second largest city in the state. It is located in the southeastern part of central Alabama, on the Alabama River. It was incorporated in 1819 when two smaller towns on the Alabama River merged. It became the state capital in 1846. In February of 1861, as the American Civil War was beginning, it was chosen as the first capital of the Confederate States of America. In May of that same year, the Confederacy's capital was moved to Richmond, Virginia. In the 1960s Montgomery was the site of major events in the civil rights movement.

MOBILE: Mobile is a city located on the Gulf Coast in southwest Alabama and is the third largest city in the state. Mobile is Alabama's only saltwater port. The Port of Mobile is the 12th largest port in the United States.

RIVERS, MOUNTAINS, AND OTHER NATURAL STUFF

ALABAMA RIVER: The Alabama River measures about 318 miles in length and is formed where the Tallapoosa and Coosa Rivers meet, about six miles north of Montgomery, Alabama. From there, the river flows west then southwest until it unites with the Tombigbee River to form the Mobile and Tensaw Rivers, which empty into Mobile Bay. The Alabama River's width is 50 to 200 yards, depending on location. During the 1800s, the Alabama River was a major waterway for the transportation of goods. It is still used for transportation of produce grown in the area.

MOBILE BAY: Mobile Bay is an important seaport in southern Alabama. It is an inlet for the Gulf of Mexico and is the fourth largest estuary in the United States. The mouth of Mobile Bay is formed by Fort Morgan Peninsula to the east and Dauphin Island to the west. The Mobile and Tensaw Rivers empty into the northern end of the bay. Dog River, Deer River, and Fowl River empty into the western side of the bay, and Fish River flows into the eastern side. Mobile Bay covers

A stunning sunset over Alabama's Mobile Bay.

413 square miles of surface area. It is 31 miles long and a maximum of 24 miles wide.

WETUMPKA IMPACT CRATER: The Wetumpka crater is the only confirmed impact crater in Alabama. An impact crater is a depression in the earth's surface created by the impact of an object from outer space, such as a meteorite. The Wetumpka crater is located in east-central Alabama, east of downtown Wetumpka in Elmore County. The crater is 4.7 miles wide and was discovered in 1969–1970. It was confirmed as an impact crater in 1998.

WEIRDNESS IN ALABAMA

PEST CONTROL MUSEUM: The Pest Control Museum in Decatur, Alabama, was originally set up by Cook's Pest Control to provide training for employees on insects and the damage they can do to homes, businesses, and other structures. The displays drew a lot of interest from customers, so over time the display grew into a full-blown museum that features some really big insect specimens, including roaches and beetles.

SOME ALABAMA VIPS

HELEN KELLER (1880–1968): Helen Keller, who was born in Tuscumbia, Alabama, is famous for overcoming blindness and deafness to become a prolific author, activist, and speaker. She was the first deaf-blind person ever to earn a bachelor of arts degree. Keller was inducted into the Alabama Women's Hall of Fame in 1971.

ROSA PARKS (1913–2005): Rosa Parks, who was born in Tuskegee, Alabama, was the civil rights leader who is best known for refusing to give up her seat to a white passenger during a bus ride on December 1, 1955. Parks's act of civil disobedience (she actually broke the law when she refused to give up her seat) became an important symbol in the civil rights movement in the 1950s and 1960s. Parks has been called the "First Lady of Civil Rights" and the "Mother of the Freedom Movement."

Rosa Parks was a key figure in the Civil Rights Movement of the 1950s and 1960s.

JESSE OWENS (1913–1980): Jesse Owens was a track and field athlete from Oakville, Alabama, who made history by winning four gold medals in the 1936 Olympics in Berlin, Germany. Owens's performance at the 1936 games was also significant because it took place in front of Germany's leader, Adolf Hitler, who wanted to use the games to demonstrate what he saw as the superiority of the white race.

ALABAMA'S CHRISTIAN CONNECTION

CAESAR BLACKWELL (1769–1845) was a famous preacher in the late 18th and early 19th centuries whose story is in some ways sad (he lived as a slave and died as a slave) but also very inspiring. Blackwell, who was born in Montgomery, Alabama, lived in a time when African Americans weren't often allowed to serve as pastors or church leaders. But he rose above his "station" in life and became such a popular, powerful preacher that white congregations often invited him to speak in their churches. ★

★★★ TWENTY-THREE ★★★

MAINE

The Pine Tree State

ME

BECAME A STATE ON: March 15, 1820

NICKNAME: the Pine Tree State

STATE BIRD: black-capped chickadee

STATE FLOWER: white pine cone

STATE SONG: "State of Maine Song"

STATE MOTTO: *Dirigo* ("I Direct")

POPULATION/RANK: 1,329,192/41

TOTAL AREA/RANK: 35,384.65 square miles/39

LIST OF COUNTIES: Androscoggin, Aroostook, Cumberland, Franklin, Hancock, Kennebec, Knox, Lincoln, Oxford, Penobscot, Piscataquis, Sagadahoc, Somerset, State Level Sites, Waldo, Washington, York

FUNNY TOWN NAMES: Bald Head, Ducktrap

SOME IMPORTANT MAINE HISTORY

> In 1497 Italian explorer John Cabot claims land near Cape Breton for King Henry VII of England.

> In 1524 explorer Giovanni de Verrazano is the first European to explore coast of Maine.

> In 1604 France establishes first European colony in Maine, at the mouth of St. Croix River.

> In 1604–1605 Frenchman Samuel de Champlain explores and maps the Maine coastline and the Penobscot River.

> In 1622 Englishmen Sir Ferdinando Gorges and John Mason are granted rights to lands of present-day Maine and New Hampshire; Gorges names territory "Maine."

> In 1652 Maine is annexed by Massachusetts.

> In 1675 King Philip's War, a conflict between Indians and the English and French, begins.

> On March 15, 1820, Maine becomes 23rd US state.

> In 1832 the Maine state capital is established in Augusta.

> In 1852 Harriet Beecher Stowe of Brunswick writes *Uncle Tom's Cabin*.

> In 1860 Maine native Hannibal Hamlin is named Abraham Lincoln's vice president.

IMPORTANT CITIES IN MAINE

PORTLAND: Located in southeastern Maine on the Maine coast, Portland is the largest city in the state.

An aerial view of downtown Portland, Maine.

Maine became a state in 1820, and Portland was named its capital. In 1832 the capital was moved to Augusta.

LEWISTON: Located in south-central Maine, along the Androscoggin River, Lewiston is the second largest city in the state. It is about 30 miles north of Portland and about 127 miles north of Boston, Massachusetts. Lewiston was incorporated as a town in 1795 and became a city in 1863.

AUGUSTA: Located on the Kennebec River, Augusta is the seventh most populous city in Maine and the state capital. Augusta is known as the third smallest US state capital (behind Montpelier, Vermont, and Pierre, South Dakota) and the easternmost of all state capitals. It became Maine's state capital in 1827.

RIVERS, MOUNTAINS, AND OTHER NATURAL STUFF

Near Rumford, Maine, is Pennacook Falls on the Androscoggin River.

Maine is known for its lighthouses. This one is in Portland and is one of more than 60 lighthouses on the coast of Maine.

ANDROSCOGGIN RIVER: The Androscoggin River flows 178 miles through the states of New Hampshire and Maine. It starts in Errol, New Hampshire, and flows mostly south before it takes an eastward turn into Maine and eventually empties into the Gulf of Maine. It is a very popular fishing stream.

MOUNT KATAHDIN: By far the highest peak in Maine, Mount Katahdin stands 5,268 feet above sea level. It is located in Baxter State Park, which is in north-central Maine in Piscataquis County.

MOUNT DESERT ISLAND: Located in Hancock County off the coast of Maine, Mount Desert Island is the second largest island on the US eastern seaboard (behind Long Island) and the sixth largest in the contiguous United States (also known as the "Lower 48"). It covers an area of 108 square miles. About 10,000 people live year-round on the island, but it is a very popular tourist destination with about 2.5 million visitors each year.

GOD IN MAINE'S CONSTITUTION (PREAMBLE)

We the people of Maine. . .acknowledging with grateful hearts the goodness of the Sovereign Ruler of the Universe. . .do agree to form ourselves into a free and independent State. . .and do ordain and establish the following Constitution for the government of the same.

WEIRDNESS IN MAINE

THE UMBRELLA COVER MUSEUM: Of all the things a person can collect, Nancy Hoffman of Peak's Island, Maine, may have chosen one of the strangest—umbrella covers, as in the fabric cover that comes on nearly every new umbrella. The Umbrella Cover Museum was founded in 1996, and today it features more than 730 umbrella covers of all colors, fabrics, and patterns. Hoffman's museum started in her kitchen but was later moved to a larger location when the collection grew.

SOME MAINE VIPS

GIOVANNI DA VERRAZZANO (1485–1528): Giovanni da Verrazzano is believed to be the first European to explore what would be the Pine Tree State's coast. Verrazzano was from Florence (in modern-day Italy), but he sailed in the service of King Francis I of France. In 1524 he explored the Atlantic coast of North America between what would be the Carolinas and Newfoundland. Historians believe his first landfall in Maine was at Cape Small at Casco Bay.

JOHN FORD (1894–1973): John Ford, who was born in Cape Elizabeth, Maine, is considered one of the greatest movie directors of all time. He is well known for his Westerns. He won a record four Academy Awards for best director (in 1935, 1940, 1941, and 1952). His 1941 movie How Green Was My Valley also won an Oscar for best picture. Ford's career as a director lasted more than 50 years. He directed more than 140 movies.

FRANK CHURCHILL (1901–1942): Frank Churchill was an American composer who is best known for writing the music for the 1937 Disney movie Snow White and the Seven Dwarfs. Churchill also wrote music for other Disney films, including Dumbo, Bambi, and The Adventures of Ichabod and Mr. Toad, as well as several animated shorts. Frank Churchill, who joined Disney studios in 1930, was born in Rumford, Maine.

MAINE'S CHRISTIAN CONNECTION

ELIJAH PARISH LOVEJOY (1802–1837): Born in Albion, Maine, Elijah Parish Lovejoy was a Presbyterian minister and journalist who was very active in the abolitionist movement, which worked to outlaw slavery in the United States. After attending what is now Colby College in Maine, he traveled west and settled in St. Louis, Missouri, in 1827. He later became an ordained minister, started a church, and continued his work against slavery. He started an abolitionist newspaper called the Alton Observer in 1937. On November 7 of that year, a mob who opposed his work and his views attacked the warehouse where he operated a printing press and shot him to death. ★

TWENTY-FOUR

MISSOURI

The Show Me State

MO

LIST OF COUNTIES: Adair, Andrew, Atchison, Audrain, Barry, Barton, Bates, Benton, Bollinger, Boone, Buchanan, Butler, Caldwell, Callaway, Camden, Cape Girardeau, Carroll, Carter, Cass, Cedar, Chariton, Christian, Clark, Clay, Clinton, Cole, Cooper, Crawford, Dade, Dallas, Daviess, DeKalb, Dent, Douglas, Dunklin, Franklin, Gasconade, Gentry, Greene, Grundy, Harrison, Henry, Hickory, Holt, Howard, Howell, Iron, Jackson, Jasper, Jefferson, Jefferson City, Johnson, Kansas City, Knox, Laclede, Lafayette, Lawrence, Lewis, Lincoln, Linn, Livingston, Macon, Madison, Maries, Marion, McDonald, Mercer, Miller, Mississippi, Moniteau, Monroe, Montgomery, Morgan, New Madrid, Newton, Nodaway, Oregon, Osage, Ozark, Pemiscot, Perry, Pettis, Phelps, Pike, Platte, Polk, Pulaski, Putnam, Ralls, Randolph, Ray, Reynolds, Ripley, Rives, Saline, Schuyler, Scotland, Scott, Shannon, Shelby, St. Charles, St. Clair, St. Francois, St. Louis, St. Louis City, State Level Sites, Ste. Genevieve, Stoddard, Stone, Sullivan, Taney, Texas, Van Buren, Vernon, Warren, Washington, Wayne, Webster, Worth, Wright

BECAME A STATE ON: August 10, 1821

NICKNAME: the Show Me State

STATE BIRD: bluebird

STATE FLOWER: white hawthorn

STATE SONG: "Missouri Waltz"

STATE MOTTO: *Salus populi suprema lex esto* (The welfare of the people shall be the supreme law)

POPULATION/RANK: 6,021,988/18

FUNNY TOWN NAMES: Bean Lake Station, Monkey Run, Possum Trot

SOME IMPORTANT MISSOURI HISTORY

> In 1682 French explorer Robert Cavalier travels the Mississippi River, claiming the valley for France and naming the region "Louisiana" in honor of King Louis XIV.

> In 1700 Jesuit missionaries establish the Mission of St. Francis Xavier near present-day St. Louis.

> In 1724 French build Fort Orleans on the north bank of the Missouri River near present-day Brunswick.

> In 1762 Spain gains control of the Louisiana Territory in the Treaty of Fontainebleau.

> In 1764 Frenchmen Pierre Laclède and Auguste Chouteau found St. Louis.

> In 1769 French-Canadian explorer Louis Blanchette establishes St. Charles as a trading post.

> In 1770 Spain officially assumes control of the territory of Louisiana.

> In 1796 Daniel Boone moves to Missouri and builds a cabin at Femme Osage Creek.

> In 1800 French leader Napoleon Bonaparte forces Spain to return territory west of the Mississippi to France.

> In 1803 the Louisiana Purchase grants land that would become Missouri to the US.

> In 1804 the Lewis and Clark Expedition starts from St. Louis.

> In 1812 a portion of the territory of Louisiana becomes the territory of Missouri.

> In 1820 Missouri adopts its first constitution.

> On August 10, 1821, Missouri becomes the 24th US state; the state capital is temporarily located in St. Charles.

> In 1826 Jefferson City is designated Missouri state capital.

> In 1837 fire destroys Missouri's capitol building in Jefferson City.

> In 1860 the Pony Express starts its first run from St. Joseph, Missouri.

> In 1911 the state capitol building is destroyed by fire after being struck by lightning.

> In 1919 Missouri becomes 11th state to ratify the 19th Amendment, granting women the right to vote.

The Gateway Arch in St. Louis, Missouri, is one of the most recognizable landmarks in the United States.

ST. LOUIS: Situated in eastern Missouri on the banks of the Mississippi River, St. Louis is the second largest city in the state and is a major port city. The best-known landmark of St. Louis is the 630-foot-tall Gateway Arch, which is a monument to the westward expansion of the United States.

JEFFERSON CITY: Missouri's capital city, Jefferson City is the 15th largest city in Missouri. Located in central Missouri on the banks of the Missouri River, it was incorporated as a city in 1825. Jefferson City was named after Thomas Jefferson, the Founding Father and third US president. When the Missouri Territory was first established in 1812, St. Louis was its capital. St. Charles served as the capital before Jefferson City was chosen as Missouri's capital in 1821—mostly because it is located in the middle of the state.

IMPORTANT CITIES IN MISSOURI

KANSAS CITY: The largest city in Missouri, Kansas City is located in the western part of the state. The city was founded in 1838 and called the "Town of Kansas." It was incorporated as a city in 1850 and renamed Kansas City in 1889. Kansas City is known as a major center for jazz music and Kansas City barbecue. It is home to dozens of barbecue restaurants.

RIVERS, MOUNTAINS, AND OTHER NATURAL STUFF

MISSOURI RIVER: At 2,341 miles in length, the Missouri River is the longest river in North America and the 15th longest in the world. The Missouri is a tributary of the Mississippi River, but it is actually about 140 miles longer than the river it empties into. It flows through seven states: Montana, North Dakota, South Dakota, Nebraska, Iowa, Kansas, and Missouri.

CREVE COEUR LAKE: The largest natural lake in Missouri, Creve Coeur Lake is an oxbow lake,

GOD IN MISSOURI'S CONSTITUTION (PREAMBLE)

We the people of Missouri, with profound reverence for the Supreme Ruler of the Universe, and grateful for His goodness, do establish this constitution for the better government of the State.

meaning a lake that remains in a river channel after the river changes course. The lake covers 320 acres and is part of Creve Coeur Memorial Park (also called Creve Coeur County Park), a 2,145-acre St. Louis County park located in Maryland Heights.

TAUM SAUK MOUNTAIN: Taum Sauk isn't that impressive of a mountain, but in a relatively flat state like Missouri, it stands out as the highest spot in the state. Taum Sauk Mountain, which stands 1,772 feet above sea level, is for the most part a high, flat ridge.

WEIRDNESS IN MISSOURI

JESSE JAMES WAX MUSEUM: Most historians will tell you that the notorious outlaw Jesse James was gunned down on April 3, 1882, by a man named Bob Ford. But some folks who live in Stanton, Missouri, aren't so sure. The Jesse James Wax Museum contains proof, its curator says, that James actually survived the shooting and escaped to live until 1951.

SOME MISSOURI VIPS

The great American writer Mark Twain.

MARK TWAIN (1835–1910): Mark Twain is the pen name of the 19th-century American author Samuel Langhorne Clemens. Clemens was born in Florida, Missouri. Many of his books—including *The Adventures of Tom Sawyer* (1876) and *Adventures of Huckleberry Finn* (1885)—are still popular and considered literary classics. Mark Twain grew up in Hannibal, Missouri, and he used the area as the setting for *Tom Sawyer* and *Huckleberry Finn*. Before establishing his fame as a novelist, Twain worked as a typesetter, a newspaper writer, and a riverboat pilot on the Mississippi River.

GEORGE WASHINGTON CARVER (C. 1864–1943): Born into slavery in what is now Diamond, Missouri, George Washington Carver later became a famous scientist who is best known for developing dozens of uses for peanuts. He developed about 100 products made from peanuts. Carver's work actually went far beyond uses for peanuts (though he developed 105 food recipes for them). He also promoted peanuts, soybeans, and sweet potatoes as cash crop alternatives to cotton.

American scientist George Washington Carver was a native of Missouri.

HARRY S. TRUMAN (1884–1972): Harry Truman, who was born in Lamar, Missouri, was the 33rd president of the United States (1945–1953). Truman was Franklin D. Roosevelt's vice president and became president when Roosevelt died in office on April 12, 1945. Under Truman's leadership, the US successfully concluded its part in World War II.

MISSOURI'S CHRISTIAN CONNECTION

OZARK CHRISTIAN COLLEGE: Located in Joplin, Missouri, Ozark Christian College is a private, not-for-profit college whose motto is "Not to be served, but to serve." Ozark Christian College was originally established in Bentonville, Arkansas, in June of 1942 as a training ground for Christian workers, including ministers, missionaries, and Christian educational directors. Ozark Bible College moved to Joplin in 1944. In 1985 Midwest Christian College merged with Ozark Bible under the name Ozark Christian College. ★

★★★ TWENTY-FIVE ★★★
ARKANSAS
The Land of Opportunity

BECAME A STATE ON: June 15, 1836	
NICKNAMES: the Natural State, the Land of Opportunity	
STATE BIRD: northern mockingbird	
STATE FLOWER: apple blossom	
STATE SONG: "Arkansas (You Run Deep in Me)"	
STATE MOTTO: *Regnat populus* (The People Rule)	
POPULATION/RANK: 2,949,131/32	
TOTAL AREA/RANK: 53,178.62 square miles/29	
LIST OF COUNTIES: Arkansas, Ashley, Benton, Boone, Bradley, Calhoun, Carroll, Chicot, Clark, Clay, Cleburne, Cleveland, Columbia, Conway, Craighead, Crawford, Crittenden, Cross, Dallas, Desha, Dorsey (now Cleveland County), Drew, Faulkner, Franklin, Fulton, Garland, Grant, Greene, Hempstead, Hot Spring, Howard, Independence, Izard, Jackson, Jefferson, Johnson, Lafayette, Lawrence, Lee, Lincoln, Little River, Logan, Lonoke, Lovely (now Washington County), Madison, Marion, Miller, Mississippi, Monroe, Montgomery, Nevada, Newton, Ouachita, Perry, Phillips, Pike, Poinsett, Polk, Pope, Prairie, Pulaski, Randolph, Saline, Scott, Searcy, Sebastian, Sevier, Sharp, St. Francis, State Level Sites, Stone, Union, Van Buren, Washington, White, Woodruff, Yell	
FUNNY TOWN NAMES: Bullfrog Valley, Goobertown	

SOME IMPORTANT ARKANSAS HISTORY

> In 1541 Spanish conqueror Hernando de Soto leads first European expedition into Arkansas.

> In 1682 French explorer René-Robert Cavelier claims Mississippi Valley for King Louis XIV of France.

> In 1762 France yields Louisiana Territory to Spain.

> In 1803 Louisiana Purchase gives US land that would become Arkansas.

> In 1812 the US Congress creates Missouri Territory, which includes Arkansas.

> In 1818 Quapaw Indians yield land between Red River and Arkansas River.

> In 1819 the Territory of Arkansas is created.

> In 1821 the Arkansas capital is moved from Arkansas Post to Little Rock.

> In 1824 Quapaw Indians are forced to yield lands south of Arkansas River.

> On June 15, 1836, Arkansas became 25th US state.

> In 1861 Arkansas secedes from Union and is admitted to the Confederate States of America.

> In 1867 the US Congress passes Reconstruction Act and voids government of Arkansas and nine other southern states.

> In 1868 Arkansas is readmitted to Union.

> In 1957 the Little Rock Nine, a group of African-American students, make history by braving a hostile crowd to reach the front door of Little Rock Central High School.

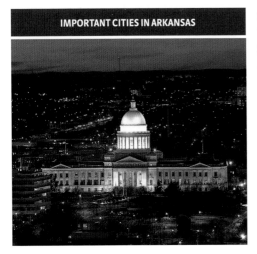

IMPORTANT CITIES IN ARKANSAS

The Arkansas State Capitol and the lights of Little Rock, just after sunset.

LITTLE ROCK: The state capital of Arkansas, Little Rock is located in central Arkansas on the south bank of the Arkansas River and is the largest city in the state. The city gets its name from a rock formation on the banks of the Arkansas River called *la Petite Rouche* (a French term meaning "the little Rock"), which was once an important landmark for people traveling up and down the river. Little Rock was founded in 1821 and named capital of the Arkansas Territory that same year. It was incorporated as a city in 1831.

The Little Rock Nine Civil Rights Memorial is located on the grounds of the Arkansas State Capitol building.

FORT SMITH: Fort Smith is the second largest city in Arkansas. It is located in the central-western part of the state. Fort Smith started out in 1817 as a military post and was named after US Army general Thomas Adams Smith (1781–1844).

FAYETTEVILLE: Located in northwestern Arkansas, deep in the Ozark Mountains, Fayetteville is the third largest city in the state. It was called Washington until 1829, when local settlers from Fayetteville, Tennessee, renamed it. Fayetteville was first incorporated as a city in 1836.

RIVERS, MOUNTAINS, AND OTHER NATURAL STUFF

ARKANSAS RIVER: The Arkansas River is a major tributary of the Mississippi River that starts near Leadville, Colorado. It gets its water from the snowpack of the Collegiate Peaks in the Rocky Mountains. From there, it flows mostly to the east and southeast, through Colorado, Kansas, Oklahoma, and, finally, Arkansas. It flows a total of 1,469 miles, making it the sixth longest river in the United States. It empties into the Mississippi River near Napoleon, Arkansas.

LAKE CHICOT: Located near Lake Village, Arkansas, Lake Chicot is the largest natural lake in the state and the largest oxbow lake in North America. The name *Chicot* is a French word for "stumpy," and the lake was named that because there are many cypress stumps and trees along its banks. Lake Chicot is about three-quarters of a mile wide and about 22 miles long.

MOUNT MAGAZINE: At 2,753 feet above sea level at its highest peak, Mount Magazine is the highest natural point in Arkansas. It is a flat-topped plateau with two peaks: Signal Hill (the highest point in Arkansas) and Mossback Ridge, which reaches 2,700 feet above sea level. Mount Magazine is located in the eastern-central part of the states. The mountain got its name when French explorers passing through the area heard a loud noise made by a landslide on the mountain. The noise was so loud that one of them said it sounded like an ammunition magazine exploding.

WEIRDNESS IN ARKANSAS

SNAKE WORL: A lot of people collect a lot of different things. Dale Ertel of Berryville, Arkansas, collects snakes. As of the latest count, he has more than 70 of them—more than the reptile house at the Little Rock Zoo, he claims. Dale's collection includes poisonous and nonpoisonous snakes alike, and for the past 45 years he has made it his life's work to know everything there is to know about every species.

SOME ARKANSAS VIPS

DOUGLAS MACARTHUR (1880–1964): Douglas MacArthur, who was born in Little Rock, Arkansas, was an American army five-star general who served as the supreme commander of the Allied Forces in the Pacific theater of World War II (where the US was at war with Japan). On September 2, 1945, aboard the USS *Missouri*, MacArthur accepted the Japanese surrender, ending the war between the US and Japan.

World War II hero General Douglas MacArthur was born in Little Rock, Arkansas.

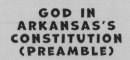

GOD IN ARKANSAS'S CONSTITUTION (PREAMBLE)

We, the people of the State of Arkansas, grateful to Almighty God for the privilege of choosing our own form of government, for our civil and religious liberty. . .do ordain and establish this Constitution.

LOU BROCK (1939–2020): Lou Brock, who was born in El Dorado, Arkansas, was a Hall of Fame Major League baseball player who was one of the greatest base stealers of all time. Brock played his first three MLB seasons with the Chicago Cubs, then joined the St. Louis Cardinals in 1964. During Brock's 19-year career as an MLB outfielder, he stole what was then a career record 938 bases, a record that stood until 1991.

BILL CLINTON (BORN 1946): William Jefferson Clinton was the 42nd president of the United States. Born in Hope, Arkansas, he was elected to two terms (1992 and 1996). Before he became president, Clinton served as governor of Arkansas from 1979 to 1981 and from 1983 to 1992. He also served as Arkansas attorney general from 1977 to 1979.

ARKANSAS'S CHRISTIAN CONNECTION

JOHN BROWN UNIVERSITY (JBU) is a private Christian college located in Siloam Springs, Arkansas, in the northwest corner of the state. The school was founded in 1919 by a Methodist evangelist named John E. Brown (1879–1957), whose travels took him through Arkansas, Missouri, and Kansas. JBU serves about 2,200 students. Its motto is "Christ over all." ★

TWENTY-SIX

MICHIGAN

The Wolverine State

LIST OF COUNTIES: Alcona, Alger, Allegan, Alpena, Antrim, Arenac, Baraga, Barry, Bay, Benzie, Berrien, Branch, Brown, Calhoun, Cass, Charlevoix, Cheboygan, Chippewa, Clare, Clinton, Crawford, Delta, Dickinson, Eaton, Emmet, Genesee, Gladwin, Gogebic, Grand Traverse, Gratiot, Hillsdale, Houghton, Huron, Ingham, Ionia, Iosco, Iowa, Iron, Isabella, Isle Royal, Jackson, Kalamazoo, Kalkaska, Kent, Keweenaw, Lake, Lapeer, Leelanau, Lenawee, Livingston, Luce, Mackinac, Macomb, Manistee, Manitou, Marquette, Mason, Mecosta, Menominee, Michilimackinac, Midland, Missaukee, Monroe, Montcalm, Montmorency, Muskegon, Newaygo, Oakland, Oceana, Ogemaw, Ontonagon, Osceola, Oscoda, Otsego, Ottawa, Presque Isle, Roscommon, Saginaw, Sanilac, Schoolcraft, Shiawassee, St. Clair, St. Joseph, State Level Sites, Tuscola, Van Buren, Washtenaw, Wayne, Wexford

BECAME A STATE ON: January 26, 1837

NICKNAMES: the Wolverine State, the Great Lakes State

STATE BIRD: American robin

STATE FLOWER: apple blossom

STATE SONG: "Michigan, My Michigan"

STATE MOTTO: *Si quaeris peninsulam amoenam circumspice* (If you seek a pleasant peninsula, look about you)

POPULATION/RANK: 9,883,360/9

TOTAL AREA/RANK: 96,716.11 square miles/11

FUNNY TOWN NAMES: Hard Luck, Paw Paw, Seewhy

SOME IMPORTANT MICHIGAN HISTORY

> In 1620 French-Canadian explorers arrive in upper region of Michigan.

> In 1634 Frenchman Jean Nicolet passes through Straits of Mackinac while exploring the area.

> In 1668 French missionaries establish the first permanent European settlement, Sault Ste. Marie.

> In 1679 Robert de La Salle establishes Fort Miami, near present-day St. Joseph, Michigan.

> In 1686 French explorer Daniel Greysolon establishes Fort St. Joseph (now Port Huron).

> In 1701 French army officer Antoine de la Mothe Cadillac founds Detroit.

> In 1760 British capture Detroit, ending French rule.

> In 1763 France concedes all lands in North America east of Mississippi River to Great Britain in Treaty of Paris.

> In 1787 Michigan becomes part of Northwest Territory.

> In 1796 the British evacuate Detroit.

> In 1805 the Michigan Territory is created and the seat of government is established in Detroit.

> In 1812 Fort Mackinac is surrendered to British in War of 1812.

> In 1813 American forces retake Detroit.

> In 1819 Potawatomi Indians surrender more than 6 million acres in Lower Peninsula to United States.

> On January 26, 1837, Michigan becomes 26th US state.

> In 1847 Lansing is named Michigan's state capital.

> In 1896 Charles King of Detroit becomes first person to design, build, and test-drive gasoline-powered automobile.

> In 1899 Ransom E. Olds establishes first automobile factory in Detroit.

> In 1908 the first Ford Model T is manufactured.

An aerial view of Detroit, Michigan's largest city.

IMPORTANT CITIES IN MICHIGAN

DETROIT: Michigan's largest city, Detroit is located in southeastern Michigan, along the Detroit River. Detroit was once the fourth largest city in the US. Around the year 2000, it was the nation's 10th largest city, but its population fell by 25 percent between 2000 and 2010, making it the nation's 18th largest city. Detroit is nicknamed "Motor City" because it is the center of the American automobile industry.

GRAND RAPIDS: Located in the central part of western Michigan, Grand Rapids is the second largest city in the state. It sits on the banks of the Grand River, so it is often called "River City." Grand Rapids's other nickname is "Furniture City" because it is home to several of the world's top office furniture companies.

LANSING: Michigan's state capital, Lansing, is the sixth largest city in the state. In 1835 two brothers from Lansing, New York, sold plots of land in the area that would become Lansing, Michigan, to buyers in New York. They named the area "Biddle Town." Some of the buyers stayed in the area and called the town "Lansing Township" after their hometown in New York. Lansing Township became the capital of Michigan in 1847, replacing Detroit as the state's seat of government.

RIVERS, MOUNTAINS, AND OTHER NATURAL STUFF

GRAND RIVER: Flowing 252 miles, the Grand River is the longest river in Michigan. It flows through seven Michigan counties before emptying into Lake Michigan. Along the way it flows through the cities of Jackson, Eaton Springs, Lansing, Grand Ledge, Portland, Ionia, Lowell, Grand Rapids, and Grand Haven.

LAKE MICHIGAN: The state of Michigan borders on four of the five Great Lakes (Michigan, Superior, Huron, and Erie), but nearly the entire eastern shore of Lake Michigan is part of the state. Lake Michigan is the only one of the five Great Lakes that is located entirely within the United States (the other four are shared by the US and Canada). By water volume, it is the second largest of the Great Lakes. By surface area, it is the third largest—after Superior and Huron. Lake Michigan has a maximum length of 307 miles, a maximum width of 118 miles, and a surface area of 22,300 square miles.

WEIRDNESS IN MICHIGAN

THE KALEVA BOTTLE HOUSE MUSEUM: In the 1940s John Maninen of Kaleva, Michigan, had his moment of inspiration: build a house out of bottles. He worked for a company called Northwest Bottle Works, with access to plenty of material, so he got to work. He used about 60,000 bottles (most of them from Northwestern Bottle Works), laying them on their sides with the bottoms facing outside. Maninen finished the house in 1941 but passed away before he and his family could move in. Since 1980, Maninen's creation has been a museum featuring items related to lumbering, farming, office machines, homemaking, and other subjects.

SOME MICHIGAN VIPS

THOMAS EDISON (1847–1931): America's best-known inventor, Thomas Alva Edison, was born in Milan, Ohio, but grew up in Port Huron, Michigan. He is best known as the inventor of a commercially viable, longer-lasting light bulb, but he also invented the phonograph (a device that played audio recordings long before the introduction of compact discs or digital recordings) and the motion picture camera. Edison patented almost 1,100 of his inventions.

In 1908, Henry Ford introduced the Model T, a mass-produced automobile that was affordable to many Americans.

HENRY FORD (1863–1947): Born in Greenfield Township in Michigan, Henry Ford was an American businessman and industrialist who is best known as the founder of the Ford Motor Company. He is also credited with helping develop the assembly line method of mass production, which helped make cars affordable to middle-class people. In 1908 he introduced the Model T, which revolutionized transportation in the United States because so many people could afford to buy one.

EARVIN "MAGIC" JOHNSON (BORN 1959): Few athletes have made as big an impact on their sport as Earvin "Magic" Johnson, who played point guard for the Los Angeles Lakers of the NBA for 13 seasons. Johnson, the first pick in the 1979 NBA Draft, was named the NBA Finals MVP after leading the Lakers to the championship during his first season in the league. He won four more championships with the Lakers during the 1980s.

MICHIGAN'S CHRISTIAN CONNECTION

CORNERSTONE THEOLOGICAL SEMINARY

Formerly known as Grand Rapids Theological Seminary, this graduate school of the Christian college Cornerstone University is a interdenominational seminary in Grand Rapids. Joseph M. Stowell III, who was the college president from 2008 to 2021, is author of more than 20 books and the former president of Moody Bible Institute. ★

GOD IN MICHIGAN'S CONSTITUTION (PREAMBLE)

We, the people of the State of Michigan, grateful to Almighty God for the blessings of freedom, and earnestly desiring to secure these blessings undiminished to ourselves and our posterity, do ordain and establish this constitution.

★★★ TWENTY-SEVEN ★★★

FLORIDA

Lots of Sunshine

BECAME A STATE ON: March 3, 1845

NICKNAME: the Sunshine State

STATE BIRD: mockingbird

STATE FLOWER: orange blossom

STATE SONG: "The Swanee River (Old Folks at Home)"

STATE MOTTO: In God We Trust

POPULATION/RANK: 19,552,860/4

TOTAL AREA/RANK: 65,754.59/22

LIST OF COUNTIES: Alachua, Baker, Bay, Benton (now Hernando County), Bradford, Brevard, Broward, Calhoun, Charlotte, Citrus, Clay, Collier, Columbia, DeSoto, Dixie, Duval, Escambia, Flagler, Franklin, Gadsden, Gilchrist, Glades, Gulf, Hamilton, Hardee, Hendry, Hernando, Highlands, Hillsborough, Holmes, Indian River, Jackson, Jefferson, Key West, Lafayette, Lake, Lee, Leon, Levy, Liberty, Madison, Manatee, Marion, Martin, Miami-Dade, Monroe, Mosquito (now Orange County), Nassau, New River (now Bradford County), Okaloosa, Okeechobee, Orange, Osceola, Palm Beach, Pasco, Pinellas, Polk, Putnam, Santa Rosa, Sarasota, Seminole, St. Johns, St. Lucie, State Level Sites, Sumter, Suwannee, Taylor, Union, Volusia, Wakulla, Walton, Washington

FUNNY TOWN NAMES: Sopchoppy, Weeki Wachee

SOME IMPORTANT FLORIDA HISTORY

> In 1513 Spanish explorer Juan Ponce de León lands near present-day St. Augustine and claims it for Spain.

> In 1539 Spanish explorer Hernando de Soto explores central and northern Florida.

> In 1565 the Spanish establish St. Augustine, the first permanent European settlement.

> In 1803 the United States claims West Florida and Pensacola as part of Louisiana Purchase.

> In 1822 a unified government of Florida is established and William Duval becomes its first governor.

> On March 3, 1845, Florida becomes 27th US state.

> In 1861 the American Civil War begins, and Florida secedes from the Union and joins the Confederacy.

> In 1868, following the Civil War, Florida is readmitted to Union.

> In 1947 President Harry Truman dedicates the Everglades National Park.

> In 1958 the National Aeronautics and Space Administration (NASA) begins operations at Cape Canaveral.

The Space Shuttle *Discovery* launches from Kennedy Space Center in Florida in 1990.

IMPORTANT CITIES IN FLORIDA

JACKSONVILLE: The largest city in Florida, Jacksonville is located in northeastern Florida. European explorers first arrived in the area that would become Jacksonville in 1562. The city was founded in 1791 and officially became a city in 1832. It is named after Andrew Jackson, the seventh president of the United States.

MIAMI: Miami is located in southeastern Florida, on the coast of the Atlantic Ocean. It is the second largest city in Florida. The area that would become Miami was first settled in 1825, and Miami was incorporated as a city in 1896. It is named for the Native American name for Lake Okeechobee: *Mayaimi*.

TALLAHASSEE: The capital of Florida, Tallahassee is located in the central part of northern Florida. It is the eighth largest city in Florida. Tallahassee became the capital of the Florida Territory in 1824.

RIVERS, MOUNTAINS, AND OTHER NATURAL STUFF

THE EVERGLADES: The Everglades is an enormous wetland area in Florida that is home to many unique (and some endangered) animal species like manatees, American crocodiles, and Florida panthers. The Everglades is basically a 50-mile-wide slow-moving river filled with saw grass, which is why it is nicknamed "River of Grass." The Everglades got its name when early European explorers saw the large fields of grass and combined the Old English words *ever* (forever) and *glades* (an open, grassy place).

The Florida Everglades are home to many kinds of animals and birds, including flamingos.

GOD IN FLORIDA'S CONSTITUTION (PREAMBLE)

We, the people of the State of Florida, being grateful to Almighty God for our constitutional liberty. . .do ordain and establish this constitution.

THE KEYS: The Florida Keys are a chain of coral cay islands that begin at the southeastern tip of Florida, about 15 miles south of Miami. From there, they form an arc that goes westward to Key West, which is just 90 miles of Cuba. The Calusa and Tequesta Indians inhabited the Keys before they were "discovered" by Juan Ponce de León in 1513.

LAKE OKEECHOBEE: Lake Okeechobee is the largest (by surface area) freshwater lake in Florida and the seventh largest in the US. Okeechobee covers 730 square miles but is very shallow for such a large lake. Its average depth is just nine feet.

WEIRDNESS IN FLORIDA

Kissimmee, the county seat of Osceola County, Florida, is home to one of the most impressive—and most famous—rock piles in the Unites States. The Monument of the States is a 40-foot tall, 30-ton creation that includes a rock from every state in the Union, as well as rocks from 22 other countries. Not only that, it features a petrified apple, a rock from the Sahara Desert, a meteorite (a rock from outer space!), eggs found in a glacier, a cannon ball, a human skull, buffalo horns, and a map of Holland.

SOME FLORIDA VIPS

A statue of Juan Ponce de León, the first European to see what would later be known as Florida.

JUAN PONCE DE LEÓN (1474–1521): Ponce de León, who sailed with Christopher Columbus on his second voyage, is best known as the first known European to see what is now Florida. He lived in what is now Puerto Rico and became governor of that island before exploring the Caribbean in 1513, searching for gold.

He landed at present-day St. Augustine and claimed the area for his home country of Spain. He embarked on another voyage in 1521 and landed on the southwest coast of Florida. He died in Cuba after being wounded in a battle with Native Americans.

WILLIAM POPE DUVAL (1784–1854): In 1822, the year after Florida became a US territory, William Pope Duval was named its first civilian governor when President James Monroe appointed him to succeed General Andrew Jackson as governor of the territory. Duval established the Florida Territory's capital at Tallahassee, where it remains to this day. Florida's Duval County is named after him.

DAVID ROBINSON (BORN 1965): One of the greatest players in NBA history, David Robinson was born in Key West, Florida. Robinson played college basketball for the Naval Academy and served as an officer in the US Navy. He is the only player from Navy to play in the NBA. He played his entire professional career with the San Antonio Spurs and won two championships with the team. He retired after the 2002–2003 season after playing 14 seasons in the NBA. He was inducted into the Basketball Hall of Fame in 2009.

FLORIDA'S CHRISTIAN CONNECTION

The ministry of one of the greatest evangelists of all time—Billy Graham—has some Florida roots. In 1940 Graham graduated from Trinity College in New Port Richey, Florida. The school, which was founded in 1932, was known as Florida Bible Institute at the time. ★

★★★ TWENTY-EIGHT ★★★

TEXAS

The Country That Became a US State

BECAME A STATE ON: December 29, 1845	
NICKNAME: the Lone Star State	
STATE BIRD: mockingbird	
STATE FLOWER: bluebonnet	
STATE SONG: "Texas, Our Texas"	
STATE MOTTO: Friendship	
POPULATION/RANK: 26,448,193/2	
FUNNY TOWN NAMES: Granny's Neck, Ding Dong, Big Stinking Creek	
TOTAL AREA/RANK: 268,580.82 square miles/2	

SOME IMPORTANT TEXAS HISTORY

> In 1519 Spanish explorer Alonso Álvarez de Pineda maps the Texas coastline.

> In 1528 Spanish explorer Alvar Núñez Cabeza de Vaca and crew shipwreck near present-day Galveston and begin exploration.

> In 1682 Corpus Christi de la Isleta, the first Spanish mission in Texas, is established near present-day El Paso.

> In 1830 the Mexican government bars almost all immigration into Texas from the United States.

> In 1832 the Texas Revolution begins.

> In 1836 the Texas Declaration of Independence is adopted, the first president (Sam Houston) and vice president (Lorenzo de Zavala) of the Republic of Texas are elected, and the first congress of the republic convenes.

> In 1837 the United States officially recognizes the Republic of Texas.

> In 1845 the United States Congress passes a resolution annexing Texas into the US, making Texas the 28th US state.

> In 1846 the Battle of Palo Alto, the first major battle of the two-year Mexican War, takes place near Brownsville.

> In 1850 the Treaty of Guadalupe Hidalgo is signed, ending the war with Mexico. Texas gives up claim to land that includes more than half of what is now New Mexico, about a third of what is now Colorado, as well as portions of Oklahoma and Wyoming.

> In 1861 Texas secedes from the Union.

> In 1865 the Battle of Palmito Ranch is fought near Brownsville—after the official end of the Civil War.

> In 1869 Texas adopts a new state constitution.

> In 1888 the state capitol in Austin is dedicated.

> In 1953 Dwight D. Eisenhower becomes the first Texas-born US president.

> On November 22, 1963, President John F. Kennedy is assassinated in Dallas.

LIST OF COUNTIES: Anderson, Andrews, Angelina, Aransas, Archer, Armstrong, Atascosa, Austin, Bailey, Bandera, Bastrop, Baylor, Bee, Bell, Bexar, Blanco, Borden, Bosque, Bowie, Brazoria, Brazos, Brewster, Briscoe, Brooks, Brown, Buchanan, Buchel, Burleson, Burnet, Caldwell, Calhoun, Callahan, Cameron, Camp, Carson, Cass, Castro, Chambers, Cherokee, Childress, Clay, Cochran, Coke, Coleman, Collin, Collingsworth, Colorado, Comal, Comanche, Concho, Cooke, Coryell, Cottle, Crane, Crockett, Crosby, Culberson, Dallam, Dallas, Dawson, Deaf Smith, Delta, Denton, DeWitt, Dickens, Dimmit, Donley, Duval, Eastland, Ector, Edwards, El Paso, Ellis, Encinal, Erath, Falls, Fannin, Fayette, Fisher, Floyd, Foard, Foley, Fort Bend, Franklin, Freestone, Frio, Gaines, Galveston, Garza, Gillespie, Glasscock, Goliad, Gonzales, Gray, Grayson, Greer, Gregg, Grimes, Guadalupe, Hale, Hall, Hamilton, Hansford, Hardeman, Hardin, Harris, Harrison, Hartley, Haskell, Hays, Hemphill, Henderson, Hidalgo, Hill, Hockley, Hood, Hopkins, Houston, Howard, Hudspeth, Hunt, Hutchinson, Irion, Jack, Jackson, Jasper, Jeff Davis, Jefferson, Jim Hogg, Jim Wells, Johnson, Jones, Karnes, Kaufman, Kendall, Kenedy, Kent, Kerr, Kimble, King, Kinney, Kleberg, Knox, La Baca, La Salle, Lamar, Lamb, Lampasas, Lavaca, Lee,   Leon, Liberty, Limestone, Lipscomb, Live Oak, Llano, Loving, Lubbock, Lynn, Madison, Marion, Martin, Mason, Matagorda, Maverick, McCulloch, McLennan, McMullen, Medina, Menard, Midland, Milam, Mills, Mitchell, Montague, Montgomery, Moore, Morris, Motley, Nacogdoches, Navarro, Newton, Nolan, Nueces, Ochiltree, Oldham, Orange, Palo Pinto, Panola, Parker, Parmer, Pecos, Polk, Potter, Presidio, Rains, Randall, Reagan, Real, Red River, Reeves, Refugio, Roberts, Robertson, Rockwall, Runnels, Rusk, Sabine, San Augustine, San Jacinto, San Patricio, San Saba, Schleicher, Scurry, Shackelford, Shelby, Sherman, Smith, Somervell, Starr, State Level Sites, Stephens, Sterling, Stonewall, Sutton, Swisher, Tarrant, Taylor, Terrell, Terry, Throckmorton, Titus, Tom Green, Travis, Trinity, Tyler, Upshur, Upton, Uvalde, Val Verde, Van Zandt, Victoria, Walker, Waller, Ward, Washington, Webb, Wegefarth, Wharton, Wheeler, Wichita, Wilbarger, Willacy, Williamson, Wilson, Winkler, Wise, Wood, Yoakum, Young, Zapata, Zavala

IMPORTANT CITIES IN TEXAS

HOUSTON: Houston is the largest city in Texas and the fourth largest in the United States. It is located on the Gulf Coast of Texas. Houston was founded in 1836 and incorporated as a city in 1837, and it is named after Sam Houston, the president of the Republic of Texas. Houston is home of NASA's Johnson Space Center, where the Mission Control Center is located.

DALLAS: Dallas is the third largest city in Texas and the ninth largest in the United States. Dallas was founded in 1841 and officially became a city in 1856. Early on, it was a major center for the oil and cotton industries.

Everything is big in Texas—including the colorful nighttime skyline of Dallas.

AUSTIN: Austin is the fourth largest city in Texas and the state's capital. Pioneers began settling the area that became Austin in the 1830s. The city was chosen as the capital of the Republic of Texas in 1839. Not long after that, the city was named after Stephen F. Austin, the "Father of Texas."

RIVERS, MOUNTAINS, AND OTHER NATURAL STUFF

GUADALUPE PEAK: With an elevation of 8,751 feet above sea level, Guadalupe Peak is the highest point in Texas. It is part of the Guadalupe Mountains range in southeastern New Mexico and west Texas..

COLORADO RIVER: The 18th longest river the United States at 862 miles, Texas's Colorado River begins and ends in Texas. It is the longest river completely within Texas. The river starts south of Lubbock, Texas, and flows mostly southeast before it dumps into the Gulf of Mexico at Matagorda Bay.

GULF OF MEXICO: The Gulf of Mexico is a huge body of water that is part of the Atlantic Ocean. Its eastern, northern, and northwestern shores are part of the United States—Florida, Alabama, Mississippi, Louisiana, and Texas. The Texas cities of Houston, Corpus Christi, Galveston, and Brownsville are all on or near the Gulf Coast.

WEIRDNESS IN TEXAS

Some artists work with paint and canvas, others with clay, and still others with wood or metal. But San Antonio, Texas, resident Barney Smith, a retired plumber in his 90s, chose as his medium. . .toilet seats. Smith's garage in Alamo Heights is his personal art museum, and it is home to more than 1,000 toilet seats, all painted and decorated in unique and sometimes strange ways.

SOME TEXAS VIPS

SAM HOUSTON (1793–1863): Sam Houston was a 19th-century politician and soldier who is best known as a leading figure in bringing Texas into the United States. Houston was born in Virginia, but he served as the first and third president of the Republic of Texas and as a US Senator for Texas after it joined the United States. He was later elected as governor of the state of Texas. He was removed from office when he refused to

---

GOD IN TEXAS'S CONSTITUTION (PREAMBLE)

We, the people of the State of Texas, acknowledging, with gratitude, the grace of God, in permitting us to make choice of our form of government, do ordain and establish this Constitution.

---

swear loyalty to the Confederacy when Texas seceded from the Union in 1861.

SANDRA DAY O'CONNOR (1930-2023): The first woman to serve as an associate justice on the US Supreme Court, Sandra Day O'Connor was born in El Paso, Texas. President Ronald Reagan appointed her to the nation's highest court in 1981, and she served until her retirement in 2006. She was 93 when she died in Phoenix, Arizona.

GEORGE W. BUSH (BORN 1946): The 43rd president of the United States, George W. Bush was born in New Haven, Connecticut, but later became the 46th governor of Texas (1995–2000). He is the eldest son of George H. W. Bush, the 41st US president. He was the co-owner of the Texas Rangers baseball team before defeating Ann Richards in 1994 to become governor of Texas. Bush was elected president in 2000 after a close election. He was in his first term as president when the September 11, 2001, terrorist attacks took place. He was reelected in 2004.

TEXAS'S CHRISTIAN CONNECTION

The term "Bible Belt" refers to a large section in the southern part of the United States where a high percentage of people believe in the Bible and make it a big part of their lives. A few spots within the Bible Belt are called "the Buckle of the Bible Belt." Among these is Dallas, Texas, which is home to several seminaries, including Brite Divinity School, Dallas Theological Seminary, Southwestern Baptist Theological Seminary, and Criswell College. ★

★★★ TWENTY-NINE ★★★

IOWA

The Hawkeye State

BECAME A STATE ON: December 28, 1846

NICKNAME: the Hawkeye State

STATE BIRD: American goldfinch

STATE FLOWER: wild rose

STATE SONG: "Iowa State Song"

STATE MOTTO: Our liberties we prize and our rights we will maintain

POPULATION/RANK: 3,074,186/30

TOTAL AREA/RANK: 56,271.55 square miles/26

FUNNY TOWN NAMES: Oskaloosa, Skunk River

LIST OF COUNTIES: Adair, Adams, Allamakee, Appanoose, Audubon, Benton, Black Hawk, Boone, Bremer, Buchanan, Buena Vista, Buncombe, Butler, Calhoun, Carroll, Cass, Cedar, Cerro Gordo, Cherokee, Chickasaw, Clarke, Clay, Clayton, Clinton, Crawford, Dallas, Davis, Decatur, Delaware, Des Moines, Dickinson, Dubuque, Emmet, Fayette, Floyd, Franklin, Fremont, Greene, Grundy, Guthrie, Hamilton, Hancock, Hardin, Harrison, Henry, Howard, Humboldt, Ida, Iowa, Jackson, Jasper, Jefferson, Johnson, Jones, Keokuk, Kossuth, Lee, Linn, Louisa, Lucas, Lyon, Madison, Mahaska, Marion, Marshall, Mills, Mitchell, Monona, Monroe, Montgomery, Muscatine, O'Brien, Osceola, Page, Palo Alto, Plymouth, Pocahontas, Polk, Pottawattamie, Poweshiek, Ringgold, Sac, Scott, Shelby, Sioux, State Level Sites, Story, Tama, Taylor, Union, Van Buren, Wapello, Warren, Washington, Wayne, Webster, Winnebago, Winneshiek, Woodbury, Worth, Wright

SOME IMPORTANT IOWA HISTORY

> In 1673 French explorers Louis Jolliet and Jacques Marquette explore area for the king of France.

> In 1682 LaSalle explores Mississippi River and claims the river and land for king of France.

> In 1762 France transfers claim to the land to Spain.

> In 1788 Julien Dubuque becomes first white settler in Iowa.

> In 1800 Spain transfers land back to France.

> In 1803 the US acquires Iowa in Louisiana Purchase.

> In 1808 the US Army builds Fort Madison.

> In 1820 the Missouri Compromise makes Iowa a non-slave territory.
> In 1833 the Iowa Territory is opened for settlement.
> On December 28, 1846, Iowa becomes 29th US state.

A nighttime view of the skyline of Des Moines, Iowa's capital city.

IMPORTANT CITIES IN IOWA

DES MOINES: Des Moines is the largest city in Iowa and the state's capital city. It is located in central Iowa. Des Moines got its start in 1843, when James Allen, a US Army captain, undertook the construction of a military fort. It was incorporated in 1851 and called Fort Des Moines, which was shortened to "Des Moines" in 1857. That same year, the Iowa state capital was moved there from Iowa City.

CEDAR RAPIDS: About 100 miles east of Des Moines is Cedar Rapids, the second largest city in Iowa. The first permanent settler of the area arrived there in 1838. When the town was first established, it was called Columbus. It was renamed Cedar Rapids in 1841, after the rapids of the Cedar River at the town's site. Cedar Rapids was incorporated as a city in 1849. It is nicknamed the "City of Five Seasons."

SIOUX CITY: Located in far western Iowa, Sioux City is the fourth largest city in the state. The first known US citizens to see the area that is now Sioux City were Meriwether Lewis and William Clark, who traveled through the area in the summer of 1804 during their famous expedition. The town of Sioux City was established in 1854. It grew very quickly and was incorporated as a city in 1857.

RIVERS, MOUNTAINS, AND OTHER NATURAL STUFF

DES MOINES RIVER: A tributary of the Mississippi River, the Des Moines River is the largest river flowing across Iowa. The river is about 525 miles long and starts in southern Minnesota. It flows through Iowa from the northwest to the southeast, passing by the city of Des Moines, which is named after the river. The Des Moines River empties into the Mississippi near Missouri's Clark County and Iowa's Lee County.

Located about 55 miles southeast of Des Moines, Red Rock Lake is a reservoir created in 1969, when the Army Corp of Engineers constructed the Red Rock Dam on the Des Moines River.

IOWA GREAT LAKES: Located in Dickinson County in northwestern Iowa, the Iowa Great Lakes are a group of natural lakes, including Spirit Lake, the largest natural lake in the state. Spirit Lake has a surface area of about 5,684 acres. The two other main lakes in the group are West Okoboji Lake (the deepest lake in Iowa and the second largest by surface area, after Spirit Lake) and East Okoboji Lake (which covers about 1,835 acres in area). The area is a popular destination for fishermen.

GOD IN IOWA'S CONSTITUTION (PREAMBLE)

We, the people of the State of Iowa, grateful to the Supreme Being for the blessings hitherto enjoyed, and feeling our dependence on Him for a continuance of those blessings, do ordain and establish a free and independent government. . . .

HAWKEYE POINT: The highest natural point in Iowa, Hawkeye Point reaches 1,670 feet above sea level. It is located in Osceola County in northwestern Iowa, about three and a half miles south of the Iowa-Minnesota border.

WEIRDNESS IN IOWA

THE WORLD'S LARGEST—OR AT LEAST ONE OF THEM—CONCRETE GNOME: Garden gnomes usually stand a few feet tall, but the one standing in Iowa State University's Reiman Gardens stands 15 feet tall and weighs more than 3,500 pounds. When the gnome was made, it was hoped he'd be a new world record, beating a gnome named Chomsky who is located in upstate New York. But rumor has it that someone in Poland built a gnome that stands around 17 feet tall. Still, if you're ever in Ames, Iowa, and would like a fun photo background, it would be hard to beat a 15-foot-tall gnome!

SOME IOWA VIPS

BILLY SUNDAY (1862–1935): Born near Ames, Iowa, Billy Sunday was a Major League Baseball outfielder who is better known as one of the most important Christian evangelists of the first two decades of the 1900s. Sunday played in the major leagues for eight seasons but left baseball to become a minister after he became a Christian in the 1880s. Sunday began his preaching in the Midwest but expanded his area of influence by holding campaigns in some of the largest cities in the United States.

WILLIAM CODY (1846–1917): Better known by his nickname "Buffalo Bill," William Cody was a Pony Express rider, US cavalry scout, buffalo hunter, and Wild West showman in the late 1880s. He was born in Le Claire, Iowa, and lived in Canada with his family for several years before his family moved to the Kansas Territory. He is well known for his cowboy-themed entertainment shows, which he took on the road to cities and town in the United States and Europe.

Pony Express rider, US cavalry scout, buffalo hunter, and Wild West showman William Cody was born in Claire, Iowa.

BOB FELLER (1918–2010): Bob Feller, who was born in Van Meter, Iowa, was a Hall of Fame Major League Baseball player whom many people consider the best right-handed pitcher in baseball history. Feller pitched 18 seasons for the Cleveland Indians and won the Triple Crown as a pitcher in 1940. He was inducted into the Baseball Hall of Fame in 1962.

IOWA'S CHRISTIAN CONNECTION

NORTHWESTERN COLLEGE (ORANGE CITY): Northwestern College is a private Christian college in Orange City, Iowa. It started out as a small academy in 1882, and then became a junior college in 1928. It became a four-year college in 1961. Northwestern College offers more than 40 majors as well as a minor in Christian missions. It keeps its Christian identity by holding weekly chapel services and student-led praise and worship services. Its motto is "Building Minds, Building Faith." ★

★★★ THIRTY ★★★
WISCONSIN
America's Dairyland

BECAME A STATE ON: May 29, 1848	
NICKNAME: the Badger State, America's Dairyland	
STATE BIRD: American robin	
STATE FLOWER: common blue violet	
STATE SONG: "On, Wisconsin!"	
STATE MOTTO: Forward	
POPULATION/RANK: 5,726,398/20	
TOTAL AREA/RANK: 65,497.82 square miles/23	
LIST OF COUNTIES: Adams, Ashland, Bad Ax, Barron, Bayfield, Brown, Buffalo, Burnett, Calumet, Chippewa, Clark, Columbia, Crawford, Dallas, Dane, Dodge, Door, Douglas, Dunn, Eau Claire, Florence, Fond Du Lac, Forest, Grant, Green, Green Lake, Iowa, Iron, Jackson, Jefferson, Juneau, Kenosha, Kewaunee, La Crosse, La Pointe, Lafayette, Langlade, Lincoln, Manitowoc, Marathon, Marinette, Marquette, Menominee, Milwaukee, Monroe, Oconto, Oneida, Outagamie, Ozaukee, Pepin, Pierce, Polk, Portage, Price, Racine, Richland, Rock, Rusk, Sauk, Sawyer, Shawano, Sheboygan, St. Croix, State Level Sites, Taylor, Trempealeau, Vernon, Vilas, Walworth, Washburn, Washington, Waukesha, Waupaca, Waushara, Winnebago, Wood	
FUNNY TOWN NAMES: Mukwonago, Vinnie Ha Ha	

SOME IMPORTANT WISCONSIN HISTORY

> In 1634 French explorer Jean Nicolet arrives in the Green Bay area.

> In 1673 the water route from Lake Michigan to the Mississippi River is explored by Louis Jolliet and Father Jacques Marquette.

> In 1678 Daniel Greysolon explores western end of Lake Superior.

> In 1763 control of Wisconsin area is transferred to England under Treaty of Paris at end of French and Indian War.

> In 1764 French-Canadian fur trader Charles Langlade establishes first permanent Euro-American settlement at Green Bay.

> In 1774 the Quebec Act incorporates all of Wisconsin lands into the Province of Quebec.

> In 1783 the US takes control of Wisconsin region.

> In 1787 Wisconsin becomes part of US Northwest Territory.

> In 1816 Astor's American Fur Company begins operating in Wisconsin.

> In 1818 Wisconsin area is included in Michigan Territory.

> In 1836 US Congress creates territory of Wisconsin; Madison is selected as territorial capital.

> On May 29, 1848, Wisconsin becomes 30th US state.

> In 1854 the Republican Party is founded in Ripon.

> In 1871 a forest fire devastates Peshtigo area.

Dairy cows, some of Wisconsin's very important residents, relax in a pasture.

IMPORTANT CITIES IN WISCONSIN

MILWAUKEE: Located in southeastern Wisconsin along the southwestern shores of Lake Michigan, Milwaukee is the state's largest city. The first Europeans to see the area that would become Milwaukee were French missionaries and fur traders. French-Canadian explorer Solomon Juneau settled the area in 1818. In 1846 his settlement combined with two nearby towns to form the city of Milwaukee.

The Wisconsin State Capitol building in Madison.

MADISON: Situated in the south-central part of Wisconsin, Madison is the second largest city in the state and the state's capital city. Madison got its start in 1829 and was named after James Madison, the Founding Father and the fourth president of the United States. Madison became the capital of the Wisconsin Territory in 1836 and remained Wisconsin's capital after it became a US state in 1848. Madison is called "the City of Four Lakes" after four lakes along the Yahara River: Lake Mendota, Lake Monona, Lake Waubesa, and Lake Kegonsa.

GREEN BAY: Green Bay is located in northeastern Wisconsin on Green Bay (a bay of Lake Michigan) at the mouth of the Fox River. It is the third largest city in Wisconsin. It is best known as the home of the NFL's Green Bay Packers. Green Bay was incorporated as a town in 1754 and is Wisconsin's oldest city. Today, Green Bay is an industrial city with several meatpacking and paper plants.

RIVERS, MOUNTAINS, AND OTHER NATURAL STUFF

WISCONSIN RIVER: At 430 miles long, the Wisconsin River is the longest river in the state of Wisconsin. It is a tributary of the Mississippi River. The Wisconsin River originates in the lake district of northern Wisconsin. From there, it flows south across central Wisconsin before turning in a southwesterly direction and flowing into the Mississippi River near the city of Prairie du Chien in southwestern Wisconsin.

LAKE SUPERIOR: Lake Superior is the largest of the Great Lakes of North America and the largest lake by volume in the entire United States. By surface area, it is considered the largest freshwater lake in the world, at 31,700

The Apostle Island Ice Cave on the shores of Lake Superior in Wisconsin.

square miles. At its longest, it stretches 350 miles with a maximum width of 160 miles. It has an average depth of 483 feet and a maximum depth of 1,332 feet. Lake Superior borders Ontario and Minnesota to the north and west and Wisconsin and Michigan to the south. The Wisconsin cities of Superior, Bayfield, Washburn, Ashland, Marquette, and Munising are located on the shore of Lake Superior.

TIMMS HILL: Timms Hill, which is located in north-central Wisconsin in Timms Hill County Park, is the highest point in the state. It is located less than a mile from Highway 86, about halfway between the towns of Omega and Spirit. Its maximum elevation is 1,952 feet above sea level. At the top of Timms Hill is a tall lookout tower offering views of the surrounding area.

WEIRDNESS IN WISCONSIN

NATIONAL MUSTARD MUSEUM: In downtown Middleton, Wisconsin, the National Mustard Museum features more than 5,000 bottles, tubes, and jars of prepared mustard from every state in the US and more than 60 countries. The museum was founded by Barry Levinson, the former assistant attorney general of Wisconsin. He started his collection of mustards in 1986 and opened the doors to his museum in 1992. By the way, the museum also includes some history about. . .mustard.

SOME WISCONSIN VIPS

FRANK LLOYD WRIGHT (1867–1959): Considered by many to be the greatest American architect of all time, Frank Lloyd Wright designed more than 1,000 structures during his career as an architect. Born in Richland Center, Wisconsin, Wright designed many types of buildings, including churches, offices, museums, schools, and hotels.

JOYCE CARLSON (1923–2008): Born in Racine, Wisconsin, Joyce Carlson was a designer and artist who

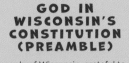

GOD IN WISCONSIN'S CONSTITUTION (PREAMBLE)

We, the people of Wisconsin, grateful to Almighty God for our freedom. . .do establish this constitution.

spent 56 years of her life working on Disney's animated films and on its theme park attractions. She created the universe of singing children in the popular "It's a Small World" rides at Walt Disney theme parks. She worked on films like *Cinderella*, *Peter Pan*, and *Sleeping Beauty*. She was also the lead ink artist for the 1955 animated movie *Lady and the Tramp*.

ERIC HEIDEN (BORN 1958): Eric Heiden is an Olympic record–setting speed skater who was born in Madison, Wisconsin. At the 1980 Winter Olympics in Lake Placid, New York, Heiden won all five men's speed skating races to take an Olympic record five gold medals in one Olympic Games. After he finished his career as a speed skater, Heiden became a professional racing cyclist. He now works as a physician in Utah.

WISCONSIN'S CHRISTIAN CONNECTION

MARANATHA BAPTIST UNIVERSITY

In Watertown, Wisconsin, is a Christian college called Maranatha Baptist University. Students at Maranatha can major in a wide variety of subjects. The school also offers graduate degrees in education, biblical studies, biblical counseling, and church music. The college was founded in 1968 and was named after the Aramaic phrase *Maranatha*, which means "Come, Lord!" and which appears in 1 Corinthians 16:22. The school's motto is "To the Praise of His Glory." ★

★★★ THIRTY-ONE ★★★
CALIFORNIA
This State Is Golden

BECAME A STATE ON: September 9, 1850	
NICKNAME: the Golden State	
STATE BIRD: California quail	
STATE FLOWER: California poppy	
STATE SONG: "I Love You, California"	
STATE MOTTO: *Eureka* (I have found it)	
POPULATION/RANK: 37,253,956/1	
TOTAL AREA/RANK: 163,695.57 square miles/3	
LIST OF COUNTIES: Alameda, Alpine, Amador, Butte, Calaveras, Colusa, Contra Costa, Del Norte, El Dorado, Fresno, Glenn, Humboldt, Imperial, Inyo, Kern, Kings, Lake, Lassen, Los Angeles, Madera, Marin, Mariposa, Mendocino, Merced, Modoc, Mono, Monterey, Napa, Nevada, Orange, Placer, Plumas, Riverside, Sacramento, San Benito, San Bernardino, San Diego, San Francisco, San Joaquin, San Luis Obispo, San Mateo, Santa Barbara, Santa Clara, Santa Cruz, Shasta, Sierra, Siskiyou, Solano, Sonoma, Stanislaus, Sutter, Tehama, Trinity, Tulare, Tuolumne, Ventura, Yolo, Yuba	
FUNNY TOWN NAMES: Angel Camp, Badwater, Nipinnawasee, Prunedale, Pumpkin Center, Skidoo	

SOME IMPORTANT CALIFORNIA HISTORY

> In 1542 Juan Cabrillo, a Portuguese explorer sailing on behalf of Spain, becomes the first European to sail the coast of what would later become California.

> In 1579 British explorer Francis Drake lands north of San Francisco Bay and claims the territory for England.

> Between 1769 and 1823, Spanish Franciscan missionaries found the California Missions, a series of Christian outposts used to spread Christianity to the natives.

> In 1821 the Mexican War of Independence gives Mexico the northern province of Alta, California, which includes what would become the US states of California, Nevada, Arizona, Utah, and parts of Colorado and Wyoming.

> In 1848 the US Senate ratifies the Treaty of Guadalupe Hidalgo, which ends the Mexican-American War (1846–1848) and gives the US possession of California and other territories.

> The California Gold Rush begins in 1849. Over the next several years, around 300,000 people travel to California from the rest of the United States and from other countries.

> On September 9, 1850, California becomes the 31st state—and without ever having been a US territory.

> On April 18, 1906, a major earthquake strikes the San Francisco area. The quake and the resulting fires kills more than 3,000 people and leaves nearly a quarter million others homeless.

IMPORTANT CITIES IN CALIFORNIA

The skyline of downtown Los Angeles set against a background of snow-covered mountaintops.

LOS ANGELES: Los Angeles is the largest city in California—in terms of both population and land area. It is the second most populous city in the US, behind New York City. Los Angeles, which is located in Southern California, was founded on September 4, 1781, by Spanish governor Filipe de Neve. With about 200,000 small businesses operating in Los Angeles, it is considered the entrepreneurial capital of the world. Its economy is larger than 46 of the 50 states.

SAN DIEGO: The second most populous city in California, San Diego is located about 120 miles south of Los Angeles, right at the US-Mexico border. San Diego is the eighth largest city in the United States. In 1542 explorer Juan Cabrillo landed in San Diego Bay and claimed the entire area for Spain. In 1769 the first European settlement in what is now California was started in San Diego.

SACRAMENTO: The capital of California, Sacramento is the state's sixth most populous city. It got its start in 1848 when Samuel Brannan and John Augustus Sutter Jr. founded the city. Sacramento became California's state capital in 1854, when the California state legislature moved operations to the city. At the 1879 California Constitutional Convention, Sacramento was named the permanent state capital.

SAN FRANCISCO: Located on the northern end of the San Francisco Peninsula in San Francisco Bay, the city of San Francisco is California's fourth most populous city and the second most densely populated city in the United States. San Francisco, which was named after the 13th-century Italian preacher Francis of Assisi, was founded in 1776 when Spanish colonists established a fort at the Golden Gate.

RIVERS, MOUNTAINS, AND OTHER NATURAL STUFF

MOJAVE DESERT: The Mojave Desert is a huge desert covering almost 48,000 square miles in southeastern California and parts of central California, southern Nevada, southwestern Utah, and northwestern Arizona. The Mojave includes Death Valley, which is the lowest elevation in North America at 282 feet below sea level.

MOUNT WHITNEY: At 14,505 feet, Mount Whitney is the highest summit in the contiguous United States (meaning states other than Alaska or Hawaii, also known as the "Lower 48"). It is about 85 miles west-northwest of Death Valley, the lowest point in North America.

SAN ANDREAS FAULT: The San Andreas Fault (a fault is a boundary between tectonic plates, which are massive rocks that make up the surface of the earth) is about 800 miles long and runs south to north in California. The fault was first identified in 1895. The best-known earthquake caused by the San Andreas Fault was the San Francisco Earthquake in 1906.

GOD IN CALIFORNIA'S CONSTITUTION (PREAMBLE)

We, the People of the State of California, grateful to Almighty God for our freedom, in order to secure and perpetuate its blessings, do establish this Constitution.

YOSEMITE NATIONAL PARK: Covering 761,263 acres and reaching across the western slopes of the Sierra Nevada mountain chain, Yosemite National Park is visited by more than 3.7 million people each year. Many come to see the park's many granite cliffs, waterfalls, streams, and giant Sequoia forests. Most of the visitors spend their time in Yosemite Valley, which runs about eight miles long and up to a mile deep and is surrounded by spectacular granite mountains.

WEIRDNESS IN CALIFORNIA

CABAZON DINOSAURS: The Cabazon Dinosaurs, also known as Claude Bell's Dinosaurs, are huge sculptures of two dinosaurs located in Cabazon, California. One is a likeness of an Apatosaurus measuring 150 feet long and 45 feet high and weighing 150 tons, holding a gift shop and a creationism museum.

The Cabazon Dinosaurs are a prominent tourist attraction in California.

SOME CALIFORNIA VIPS

WILLIAM RANDOLPH HEARST (1863–1951): William Randolph Hearst, who was born in San Francisco, was a newspaper publisher who is credited with having huge influence on print journalism in America.

He built the nation's largest newspaper chain and later expanded to magazine publishing. Hearst served two terms in the US House of Representatives and twice ran unsuccessfully for mayor of New York City.

RONALD REAGAN (1911–2004): Ronald Reagan, the 40th president of the United States, wasn't born in California (he was born in Tampico, Illinois), but he served as California's 33rd governor before being elected president in 1980. Ronald Reagan served two terms as president (1981–1989) and is still considered one of the most important presidents in US history.

JOE DiMAGGIO (1914–1999): Born in Martinez, California, Joe DiMaggio was a legendary Major League Baseball player who played centerfield for the New York Yankees from the 1936 through the 1942 seasons and from the 1946 through the 1951 seasons (he served in the US Army from 1947 to 1950). DiMaggio was named MVP three times. He was a member of nine Yankee World Series championship teams. DiMaggio was voted into the Baseball Hall of Fame in 1955.

CALIFORNIA'S CHRISTIAN CONNECTIONS

On September 25, 1949, the great evangelist Billy Graham began preaching his first sermon at what was to be a three-week Los Angeles Crusade—the first of many he would preach in the decades to follow.

The event was held in a circus tent erected in a parking lot. Each night, Graham, then 30 years old, preached to overflow crowds of more than 9,000 people. Eventually, the event was extended another five weeks. By the time the Los Angeles Crusade ended on November 20, Billy Graham had preached to more than 350,000 people—at least 3,000 of whom committed their lives to Christ. ★

THIRTY-TWO

MINNESOTA

Land of 10,000 Lakes

MN

BECAME A STATE ON: May 11, 1858
NICKNAMES: the Gopher State, the North Star State, Land of 10,000 Lakes
STATE BIRD: common loon
STATE FLOWER: the pink and white lady's slipper (also known as the showy lady's slipper or queen's lady slipper)
STATE SONG: "Hail Minnesota"
STATE MOTTO: *L'Etoile du nord* (The Star of the North)
POPULATION/RANK: 5,379,139/21
TOTAL AREA/RANK: 86,938.87 square miles/12
LIST OF COUNTIES: Aitkin, Anoka, Becker, Beltrami, Benton, Big Stone, Blue Earth, Breckenridge, Brown, Buchanan, Carlton, Carver, Cass, Chippewa, Chisago, Clay, Clearwater, Cook, Cottonwood, Crow Wing, Dakota, Dodge, Douglas, Faribault, Fillmore, Freeborn, Goodhue, Grant, Hennepin, Houston, Hubbard, Isanti, Itasca, Jackson, Kanabec, Kandiyohi, Kittson, Koochiching, Lac Qui Parle, Lake, Lake of the Woods, Le Sueur, Lincoln, Lyon, Mahnomen, Mankahta, Marshall, Martin, McLeod, Meeker, Mille Lacs, Monongalia, Morrison, Mower, Murray, Nicollet, Nobles, Norman, Olmsted, Otter Tail, Pembina, Pennington, Pierce, Pine, Pipestone, Polk, Pope, Ramsey, Red Lake, Redwood, Renville, Rice, Rock, Roseau, Scott, Sherburne, Sibley, St. Louis, State Level Sites, Stearns, Steele, Stevens, Swift, Todd, Toombs, Traverse, Wabasha, Wadena, Wahnata, Waseca, Washington, Watonwan, Wilkin, Winona, Wright, Yellow Medicine
FUNNY TOWN NAMES: Ah-Gwah-Ching, Looneyville, Oxlip

SOME IMPORTANT MINNESOTA HISTORY

> From 1659 to 1660 French fur traders Médard Chouart des Groseilliers and Pierre-Esprit Radisson explore western end of Lake Michigan and surrounding area.

> In 1673 French explorers Marquette and Jolliet discover upper portion of Mississippi River.

> In 1763 Spain receives Louisiana Territory from France, including Minnesota west of the Mississippi.

> In 1783 the US gains eastern portion of Minnesota from Great Britain during American Revolution.

> In 1787 eastern Minnesota is designated part of American Northwest Territory.

> In 1803 the US gains western portion of Minnesota in Louisiana Purchase.

> In 1805 Lieutenant Zebulon Montgomery Pike leads first US expedition through Minnesota.

> In 1818 the northern boundary of Minnesota is established at the 49th parallel.

> In 1832 Henry Schoolcraft finds source of Mississippi River at Lake Itasca.

> In 1836 the Wisconsin Territory, which includes Minnesota, is established.

> In 1849 the Minnesota Territory is formed with present-day eastern and southern boundaries set.

> On May 11, 1858, Minnesota becomes 32nd US state.

> In 1862 the first railroad between Minneapolis and St. Paul is completed.

> In 1881 fire destroys St. Paul.

IMPORTANT CITIES IN MINNESOTA

The Minneapolis skyline at sunset. Minneapolis is Minnesota's largest city.

MINNEAPOLIS: Minnesota's largest city, Minneapolis, is located in the southeastern-central part of the state. There are more than 20 lakes and wetlands in and around the city of Minneapolis, and the Mississippi River runs through it. It also borders on Saint Paul, the state capital of Minnesota and the other half of the state's "Twin Cities." It is believed that the name "Minneapolis" was coined by the city's first schoolteacher, who combined the Dakota Sioux word for waterfall (*minnehaha*) with the Greek word for city (*polis*). Min-

neapolis became a town in 1856 and was incorporated as a city in 1867.

SAINT PAUL: Located in the southeastern part of central Minnesota, just east of Minneapolis, Saint Paul is the state's capital and its second largest city. It was founded as a trading and transportation center. In 1849 it became the capital of the Minnesota Territory.

ROCHESTER: Located in southeastern Minnesota, on the banks of the Zumbro River, Rochester is the third largest city in the state. Rochester was founded in 1854 and was named after Rochester, New York. Rochester's main claim to fame is that it is the birthplace of the world-famous Mayo Clinic, a not-for-profit medical practice and research organization that employs more than 3,800 physicians and researchers and 51,000 other staff.

RIVERS, MOUNTAINS, AND OTHER NATURAL STUFF

MINNESOTA RIVER: At 332 miles long, the Minnesota River is one of the longest rivers in Minnesota. It is a tributary of the Mississippi River. The river starts in southwestern Minnesota, at Big Stone Lake at the Minnesota-South Dakota border. From there, it flows in a southeasterly direction before turning northeast. It empties into the Mississippi River south of the Twin Cities area (Minneapolis and Saint Paul).

RED LAKE: The largest natural freshwater lake located entirely in Minnesota (which is called the "Land of 1,000 Lakes), Red Lake covers a surface area of about 427 square miles. Red Lake is divided into two sections by a peninsula on the eastern side of the lake. The two parts of the lake are called the Upper Red Lake and the Lower Red Lake. Red Lake is the 16th largest lake in the United States.

LAKE ITASCA: In a state known for its lakes, Lake Itasca doesn't stand out among the largest. In fact, it covers a surface area of just 1.8 square miles. But Lake Itasca is an important lake because it is the primary source of the headwaters of the Mississippi River,

261

GOD IN MINNESOTA'S CONSTITUTION (PREAMBLE)

We, the people of the state of Minnesota, grateful to God for our civil and religious liberty, and desiring to perpetuate its blessings and secure the same to ourselves and our posterity, do ordain and establish this Constitution.

which flows north-to-south through the center of the United States before emptying into the Gulf of Mexico. Lake Itasca is located in north-central Minnesota, in southeastern Clearwater County. An American geographer named Henry Schoolcraft identified the lake as the Mississippi River's source in 1832.

WEIRDNESS IN MINNESOTA

THE SPAM MUSEUM: Are you at all curious about the canned meat product called SPAM? If you are—and if you're ever in Austin, Minnesota—then you can't afford not to take a trip to the SPAM Museum. The museum features a wall lined with 3,390 cans of SPAM, as well as several exhibits explaining the history of SPAM. Yes, the SPAM Museum has a gift shop, and yes, it sells SPAM. In fact, it sells 12 different varieties (who knew). Come lunchtime, you can head across the street from the museum to Johnny's Diner and take your pick of SPAM-related items on the menu.

SOME MINNESOTA VIPS

JUDY GARLAND (1922–1969): Judy Garland was an actress and singer who is best known for her role as Dorothy in the classic movie *The Wizard of Oz*. She was also nominated for the Academy Award for Best Actress for her role in the 1954 movie *A Star Is Born* and for Best Supporting Actress for her performance in the 1961 movie *Judgment at Nuremberg*. Garland made more than two dozen movies with Metro-Goldwyn-Mayer. She was born in Grand Rapids, Minnesota.

CHARLES SCHULZ (1922–2000): Born in Minneapolis, Minnesota, Charles Schulz was a cartoonist who is best known as the creator of the comic strip *Peanuts*. Peanuts is still popular in newspaper reruns, and the characters still appear every year in holiday specials. Schulz actually debuted

A young Charles Schulz sketching the Peanuts character Charlie Brown.

Peanuts's most famous character—Charlie Brown—in an earlier cartoon called *Li'l Folks*, which was published from 1947 to 1950.

HERB BROOKS (1937–2003): Born in Saint Paul, Minnesota, Herb Brooks was an ice hockey coach best remembered for being the coach of the 1980 US Olympic hockey team that won the gold medal at the 1980 games in Lake Placid, New York. The team's Olympic semifinal game was against a heavily favored Soviet team that had beaten the Americans 10-3 in an exhibition game in New York City. On February 22, 1980, Team USA pulled off one of the greatest upsets in sports history, beating the Soviets 4–3 to earn a spot in the gold medal game.

MINNESOTA'S CHRISTIAN CONNECTION

BETHEL UNIVERSITY: Located in the Saint Paul, Minnesota, suburb of Arden, Bethel University is a Christian college that serves about 6,000 students from 36 countries. ★

★★★ THIRTY-THREE ★★★

OREGON

Flying with Her Own Wings

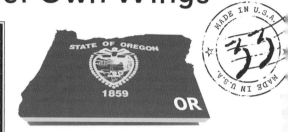

BECAME A STATE ON: February 14, 1859	
NICKNAME: the Beaver State	
STATE BIRD: western meadowlark	
STATE FLOWER: Oregon grape	
STATE SONG: "Oregon, My Oregon"	
STATE MOTTO: *Alis Volat Propiis*—"She Flies with Her Own Wings"	
POPULATION/RANK: 3,831,074/27	
TOTAL AREA/RANK: 98,380.64 square miles/9	
LIST OF COUNTIES: Baker, Benton, Clackamas, Clatsop, Columbia, Coos, Crook, Curry, Deschutes, Gilliam, Grant, Harney, Hood River, Jackson, Jefferson, Josephine, Klamath, Lake, Lane, Lincoln, Linn, Malheur, Marion, Morrow, Multnomah, Polk, Sherman, Tillamook, Umatilla, Union, Wallowa, Wasco, Washington, Wheeler, Yamhill	
FUNNY TOWN NAMES: Zigzag, Noon, Bakeoven, Boring	

SOME IMPORTANT OREGON HISTORY

> In 1805 the Lewis and Clark Expedition navigates the Snake and Columbia Rivers and establishes Fort Clatsop near modern-day Astoria, Oregon.

> In 1811 the first permanent white settlement is established in Oregon.

> In 1818 and 1827 the US and Great Britain enter into joint-occupancy treaties over what would become Oregon as well as other territory.

> In 1834 the Oregon Mission is established as a missionary effort by the Methodist Episcopal Church to take the gospel message to the natives living in Oregon. The mission was located about 10 miles north of present-day Salem.

> In 1843 the first group of settlers (pioneers) arrives via the Oregon Trail. Many thousands more would arrive over the next 25 years or so.

> In 1848 the Oregon Territory is established.

> On February 14, 1859, Oregon becomes the 33rd state of the Union.

> In 1937 the Bonneville Dam hydroelectric project on the Columbia River is completed.

IMPORTANT CITIES IN OREGON

PORTLAND: With just under 590,000 people, Portland is the most populous city in Oregon and the 28th most populous in the United States. It is located 70 miles east of the Pacific Ocean. The city is bordered on the north by the Columbia River, and the Willamette

People living in Portland, Oregon's largest city, have a beautiful view of Mount Hood to the east.

gene is named after its founder, Eugene Franklin Skinner, who built the first cabin in the area in 1846. It was fully incorporated as a city in 1862.

RIVERS, MOUNTAINS, AND OTHER NATURAL STUFF

CRATER LAKE: Crater Lake was formed after a huge eruption and collapse of a volcano called Mount Mazama. The crater left at the top of the mountain filled with about 4.6 trillion gallons of rainwater and snow melt to create a lake that is up to 1,932 feet deep.

River flows through the middle of it. It was incorporated as a city in 1851.

SALEM: Salem is Oregon's third largest city in Oregon and the state's capital. It is located in the center of the Willamette Valley, and the Willamette River runs through the city. In 1812 the first European settlers arrived in the area that would become Salem. It was founded in 1842 and became the capital of the Oregon Territory in 1851.

WILLAMETTE RIVER: The Willamette River is a major tributary of the Columbia River. The river's main stem runs 187 miles from its mouth at the Columbia River at Portland, Oregon. The Willamette flows northward between the Oregon Coast Range and the Cascade Range and has formed the Willamette Valley, which is home to two-thirds of Oregon's population.

EUGENE: Eugene is the second largest city in Oregon. It is located about 50 miles east of the Oregon Coast at the south end of the Willamette Valley. Eu-

MOUNT HOOD: Mount Hood, which is located about 50 miles east-southeast of Portland, is Oregon's highest mountain peak at about 11,240 feet. Mount Hood is the highest point in Oregon and the fourth highest in the Cascade Range. It is a dormant volcano

Oregon's beautiful Crater Lake (including Wizard Island) as it looks in the middle of winter.

that has erupted in the past and could erupt in the future, though scientists don't think that will happen anytime soon.

A replica of historic Fort Clatsop in the northwestern corner of Oregon.

WEIRDNESS IN OREGON

OREGON VORTEX: In the southern Oregon community of Gold Hill is a strange tourist attraction in which a rumored gravitational abnormality causes people who visit to appear to "lean" at an angle as they walk around. Visitors there also appear taller or shorter, depending on where they stand in relation to the magnetic north and south poles. There are several theories about how it works, and some skeptics believe it's simply a manmade optical illusion.

SOME OREGON VIPS

JASON LEE (1803–1845): In 1834 Christian missionary Jason Lee arrived in Oregon's Willamette Valley, near present-day Salem. He left Oregon for a time but returned in 1840 with 50 settlers and assistants. In 1842 the missionaries the Oregon Institute, which was a forerunner to Willamette University, the first university in the West.

DICK FOSBURY (1947–2023): Dick Fosbury, who was born in Portland, Oregon, and attended college at Oregon State University in Corvallis, revolutionized the high jump event. He invented the "back-first" high jump technique, also known as the "Fosbury Flop."

Today, nearly all high jumpers at every level of competition use his technique. Fosbury won the NCAA championship and the gold medal at the 1968 Olympics in Mexico City with an Olympic record of 7 feet, 4.25 inches.

PHIL KNIGHT (BORN 1938): After graduating from the University of Oregon, where he ran middle-distance races on the UO track team for coach Bill Bowerman, Phil Knight and his coach cofounded Nike, Inc., the multi-billion sports shoe and apparel company known for its trademark "swoosh." Knight has donated millions of dollars to the University of Oregon and the Stanford Graduate School of Business, as well as millions more to other causes and organizations.

GOD IN OREGON'S CONSTITUTION (BILL OF RIGHTS, ARTICLE I. SECTION 2)

All men shall be secure in the Natural right, to worship Almighty God according to the dictates of their consciences.

OREGON'S CHRISTIAN CONNECTION

In Beaverton, Oregon—a suburb west of Portland—is the headquarters of the Luis Palau Association, an organization devoted to preaching the gospel message around the world. Evangelist Luis Palau was born in Argentina in 1934 and, like his friend Billy Graham, preached to millions of people in many countries around the world. Palau died in 2023 at the age of 86. ★

★★★ THIRTY-FOUR ★★★
KANSAS
The Sunflower State

KANSAS   KS

BECAME A STATE ON: January 29, 1861
NICKNAME: the Sunflower State, the Wheat State
STATE BIRD: western meadowlark
STATE FLOWER: wild sunflower
STATE SONG: "Home on the Range"
STATE MOTTO: *Ad astra per aspera* (To the stars through difficulties)
POPULATION/RANK: 2,885,905/33
TOTAL AREA/RANK: 82,276.84 square miles/15
FUNNY TOWN NAMES: Admire, Kickapoo, Spasticville

LIST OF COUNTIES: Allen, Anderson, Arapahoe, Atchison, Barber, Barton, Bourbon, Breckenridge, Brown, Butler, Chase, Chautauqua, Cherokee, Cheyenne, Clark, Clay, Cloud, Coffey, Comanche, Cowley, Crawford, Davis, Decatur, Dickinson, Doniphan, Dorn, Douglas, Edwards, Elk, Ellis, Ellsworth, Finney, Ford, Franklin, Geary, Godfrey, Gove, Graham, Grant, Gray, Greeley, Greenwood, Hamilton, Harper, Harvey, Haskell, Hodgeman, Howard, Hunter, Jackson, Jefferson, Jewell, Johnson, Kansas, Kearny, Kingman, Kiowa, Labette, Lane, Leavenworth, Lincoln, Linn, Logan, Lykins, Lyon, Madison, Marion, Marshall, McGee, McPherson, Meade, Miami, Mitchell, Montgomery, Morris, Morton, Nemaha, Neosho, Ness, Norton, Old Seward, Osage, Osborne, Otoe, Ottawa, Pawnee, Peketon, Phillips, Pottawatomie, Pratt, Rawlins, Reno, Republic, Rice, Riley, Rooks, Rush, Russell, Saline, Scott, Sedgwick, Sequoyah, Seward, Shawnee, Sheridan, Sherman, Smith, St. John, Stafford, Stanton, State Level Sites, Stevens, Sumner, Thomas, Trego, Wabaunsee, Wallace, Washington, Wichita, Wilson, Woodson, Wyandotte

SOME IMPORTANT KANSAS HISTORY

> In 1541 Spanish explorers, searching for gold, claim Kansas for Spain.

> In 1682 French explorer LaSalle claims all of the Kansas Territory for France.

> In 1803 the US acquires most of Kansas from France in the Louisiana Purchase.

> In 1827 Fort Leavenworth is established.

> In 1830s settlers arrive in Kansas by the thousands.

> In 1854 the Kansas Territory is organized.

> From 1855 to 1859 the Kansas-Nebraska Act leads to bloody fighting over slavery.

> In 1860 the first railroad reaches Kansas.

> On January 29, 1862, Kansas becomes 34th US state.

> In 1887 Susanna Salter is elected mayor of Argonia, Kansas, making her the first woman mayor in the country.

> In the 1930s severe dust storms destroyed millions of acres of Kansas crops.

IMPORTANT CITIES IN KANSAS

The downtown area of Wichita, Kansas, at night.

WICHITA: Kansas's largest city, Wichita is located in the south-central part of the state, on the Arkansas River. Wichita was founded in 1863 and incorporated as a city in 1870. It was called "Cowtown" because it was an important destination for cattle drives coming out of Texas. It later became a key center for the production of US aircraft, earning the nickname "the Air Capital of the World." Aircraft producers still operate production facilities in Wichita today.

KANSAS CITY: Located in northeastern Kansas, where the Missouri River and Kansas River meet (also called Kaw Point), Kansas City is the third largest city in the state. It was founded in 1868 and incorporated in 1872.

TOPEKA: Topeka was established as a city in 1857 and became the capital of the state of Kansas in 1861. The city was a major hub for railroads expanding to the West. It is located in northeastern Kansas, along the Kansas River. Topeka is Kansas's fourth largest city.

RIVERS, MOUNTAINS, AND OTHER NATURAL STUFF

KANSAS RIVER: The Kansas River is a 148-mile-long river that begins just east of Junction City in the northeastern portion of the state of Kansas. From there it flows mostly eastward and empties into the Missouri River in Kansas City. The Kansas River is an important river because the state is named after it. The name comes from the Kanza (or Kaw) Indians, who once lived in the area. Kansas City, Lawrence, Tecumseh, and Topeka are all located on the banks of the Kansas River.

MONUMENT ROCKS AND CASTLE ROCK: Monument Rocks is a series of large, fossil-rich chalk formations in Cove County. The formations stand up to 70 feet tall. About 31 miles east of Monument Rocks is Castle Rock, a pillar-like limestone formation that got its name because it kind of resembles an ancient

The Monument Rock limestone formation stands out in the Kansas prairie.

castle in the middle of the Kansas prairie. In 2008 Monument Rocks and Castle Rock were named one of the 8 Wonders of Kansas.

MOUNT SUNFLOWER: Here's a "mount" that isn't a mountain at all, just a high point that you can't really tell apart from the surrounding land. But at 4,039 feet above sea level and 3,300 feet above Kansas's natural low point (near Coffeyville), Mount Sunflower is the highest natural point in a state that is mostly flat. It is located in far western Kansas. Mount Sunflower is located on private land, but its owners encourage visitors to come to the site.

WEIRDNESS IN KANSAS

WORLD'S LARGEST BALL OF TWINE: In the early 1950s Cawker City, Kansas, resident Frank Stoeber realized that he just couldn't sit by and let the 12-foot-wide Johnson Twine Ball in Darwin, Minnesota, hold the distinction of being the world's largest ball of twine. So in 1953 he got busy. He started winding twine in his basement until his death in 1974—but finished one foot short of his goal. Since Stoeber's death, residents and Cawker City tourists have been adding to his twine ball at the "Twineathon," which is held every August. The behemoth now measures 40 feet in diameter and weighs in at nine tons.

SOME KANSAS VIPS

WALTER P. CHRYSLER (1875–1940): Walter P. Chrysler, who was born in Wamego, Kansas, was an early 20th-century executive in the automobile industry who founded Chrysler Corporation. Today, the Chrysler Corporation brands are Chrysler, Dodge, Ram, Jeep, Fiat, Mopar, and SRT.

The famous aviator Amelia Earhart was a native of Atchison, Kansas.

AMELIA EARHART (1897–1937/39): Born in Atchison, Kansas, Amelia Earhart was a famous aviator who was the 16th woman to be issued a pilot's license. In 1928 she became the first woman to fly across the Atlantic Ocean. She received the US Distinguished Flying Cross for that flight. Earhart wrote several books about her flying experiences and was key in forming

> # GOD IN THE KANSAS CONSTITUTION (PREAMBLE)
>
> We, the people of Kansas, grateful to Almighty God for our civil and religious privileges, in order to insure the full enjoyment of our rights as American citizens, do ordain and establish this constitution of the State of Kansas. . . .

The Ninety-Nines, an organization of women pilots. In 1937 Earhart disappeared over the Pacific Ocean near Howland Island while attempting to circumnavigate the globe in a Lockheed Model 10 Electra. She was declared dead in 1939.

BARRY SANDERS (BORN 1968): On any list of the greatest athletes in Kansas history, former NFL running back Barry Sanders would have to be at or near the top. Sanders, who was born in Wichita, Kansas, spent his entire 10-year NFL career (1989–1998) with the Detroit Lions. Sanders averaged better than 1,500 yards rushing per season and never had a season with less than 1,115 yards. When he retired, he was just 1,457 yards short of setting the NFL record for career rushing yards. Sanders won the Heisman Trophy following the 1988 college football season. That year, he rushed for 2,628 yards and 37 touchdowns for Oklahoma State University.

KANSAS'S CHRISTIAN CONNECTION

MidAmerica Nazarene University (MNU) is a Christian college located in the northeastern Kansas city of Olathe, a suburb of Kansas City, Missouri. MNU was first established in 1966 by the Church of the Nazarene and was called Mid-America Nazarene College. In 1996, it formally changed its name to MidAmerica Nazarene University. MNU offers undergraduate degrees in 40 different majors. ★

★★★ THIRTY-FIVE ★★★
WEST VIRGINIA

Home of Some Free Mountaineers

BECAME A STATE ON: June 20, 1863

NICKNAME: the Mountain State

STATE BIRD: cardinal

STATE FLOWER: rhododendron

STATE SONG: "West Virginia Hills"

STATE MOTTO: *Montani semper liberi* (Mountaineers are always free)

POPULATION/RANK: 1,854,304/38

TOTAL AREA/RANK: 24,229.76/41

LIST OF COUNTIES: Barbour, Berkeley, Boone, Braxton, Brooke, Cabell, Calhoun, Clay, Doddridge, Fayette, Gilmer, Grant, Greenbrier, Hampshire, Hancock, Hardy, Harrison, Jackson, Jefferson, Kanawha, Lewis, Lincoln, Logan, Marion, Marshall, Mason, McDowell, Mercer, Mineral, Mingo, Monongalia, Monroe, Morgan, Nicholas, Ohio, Pendleton, Pleasants, Pocahontas, Preston, Putnam, Raleigh, Randolph, Ritchie, Roane, State Level Sites, Summers, Taylor, Tucker, Tyler, Upshur, Wayne, Webster, Wetzel, Wirt, Wood, Wyoming

FUNNY TOWN NAMES: Big Ugly, Booger Hole, Looneyville

SOME IMPORTANT WEST VIRGINIA HISTORY

> In 1607 England establishes the Virginia Colony.

> In 1669 German explorer John Lederer and traveling companions reach the crest of Blue Ridge Mountains and became first Europeans to see what is now West Virginia.

> In 1671 Thomas Batts and Robert Fallam claim land that is now West Virginia for England.

> In 1732 German, Welsh, and Scotch-Irish pioneers settle in western Virginia.

> In 1755 English General Edward Braddock leads army through West Virginia counties on his way to Pittsburgh.

> In 1791 Daniel Boone is elected as a delegate to Virginia Assembly.

> In 1818 the Cumberland Road, the first major improved highway, is completed from Cumberland, Maryland, to Wheeling, West Virginia.

> In 1859 abolitionist John Brown conducts raids on federal arsenal at Harpers Ferry to end slavery.

> In 1861 the American Civil War begins; several counties in western Virginia refuse to secede from Union and separate from Virginia.

> On June 20, 1863, West Virginia becomes the 35th US state.

> In 1872 West Virginia voters ratify new state constitution.

> In 1863 Wheeling becomes West Virginia's state capital.

> In 1870 Charleston becomes West Virginia's state capital.

GOD IN WEST VIRGINIA'S CONSTITUTION (PREAMBLE)

Since through Divine Providence we enjoy the blessings of civil, political, and religious liberty, we, the people of West Virginia, in and through the provisions of this Constitution, reaffirm our faith in and constant reliance upon God and seek diligently to promote. . .good government in the state of West Virginia. . . .

IMPORTANT CITIES IN WEST VIRGINIA

The West Virginia State Capitol building on a beautiful spring day.

HUNTINGTON: The second largest city in West Virginia, Huntington is a major river port in the state. It is located in southwestern West Virginia. It was founded in 1871 and was named after one of its founders, Collis P. Huntington.

PARKERSBURG: Parkersburg is the third largest city in West Virginia. When it was settled following the American Revolutionary War, Parkersburg was named Newport. It was renamed Parkersburg in 1810.

RIVERS, MOUNTAINS, AND OTHER NATURAL STUFF

A view of West Virginia's Allegheny Mountains from Spruce Mountain.

CHARLESTON: Charleston is West Virginia's largest city and the state capital. It is located in Kanawha County, where the Elk and Kanawha Rivers meet. Charleston began to grow in the early 1800s, when pioneers leaving early settlements migrated to what was then the western part of Virginia. Charleston grew mostly because of its many natural resources.

SPRUCE MOUNTAIN: In eastern West Virginia is the highest ridge in the Allegheny Mountains, Spruce Mountain. Spruce Mountain is actually a "whale-backed" ridge (a ridge with more than one peak) that extends northeast to southwest for about 16 miles. Several of its peaks are higher than 4,500 feet, including Spruce Knob, Spruce Mountain's summit and the highest natural point (4,863 feet above sea level) in West Virginia and the highest peak in the Allegheny Mountains.

NEW RIVER GORGE: Located in southern West Virginia, the New River Gorge averages between 700 and 1,300 feet deep. The Gorge was formed by the erosion caused by the New River. The New River Gorge is a beautiful natural feature of West Virginia that includes steep canyon walls, beautiful rock formations, and, of course, the New River, which is a major whitewater rafting and fishing stream.

LOST WORLD CAVERNS: Just outside of Lewisburg, West Virginia, is a series of underground caves called Lost World Caverns. This amazing natural attraction includes stalagmites, vertical caves, waterfalls, and other features. It is an easily accessible large chamber at 1,000 feet long and 120 feet high.

WEIRDNESS IN WEST VIRGINIA

George and Pam Farnham of Unger, West Virginia, collect all kinds of things, but their home is best known for its collection of giant fiberglass statues. Their collection includes likenesses of the Muffler Man, Santa Claus, the Uniroyal Gal, and a character called "Hamburger Man" (not to be confused with Bob's Big Boy). This strange attraction is called "Land of the Giants," or the "Farnham Colossi."

SOME WEST VIRGINIA VIPS

DANIEL BOONE (1734–1820): Daniel Boone was a famous explorer, scout, and trailblazer who lived in what is now Charleston, West Virginia. Boone served as a militia officer during the American Revolutionary War. In 1775 he blazed the Wilderness Road through the Cumberland Gap in the Appalachian Mountains. He founded the village of Boonesborough, Kentucky, one of the first American settlements west of the Appalachian Mountains.

THOMAS "STONEWALL" JACKSON (1824–1863): Born in what became Clarksburg, West Virginia, General Thomas "Stonewall" Jackson was one of the best known Confederate military leaders. Experts consider him one of the greatest military tacticians in US history. He led his troops to victory in the First Battle of Bull Run, as well as other battles. Jackson died eight days after being accidentally shot by one of his own soldiers at Chancellorsville. Historians consider his death one of the biggest setbacks for the Confederacy.

A statue of Thomas "Stonewall" Jackson at his grave in Lexington, Virginia.

BOOKER T. WASHINGTON (1856–1915): Booker T. Washington, who grew up in Malden, West Virginia, was an African-American educator, author, and civil rights leader who also served as an advisor to US presidents. Washington, who was a Christian man, was part of the last generation of black American leaders born into slavery. He believed that black people in America should work to educate themselves and to better themselves through work. In 1881 Washington traveled to Tuskegee, Alabama, to help establish a new school for black students called the Tuskegee Institute. He spent the rest of his life building the institute into a major American university.

WEST VIRGINIA'S CHRISTIAN CONNECTION

ALEXANDER CAMPBELL (1788–1866) was an immigrant from Ireland who served as a minister in what is now West Virginia and who led what is now called the "Restoration Movement," which emphasized stronger reliance on scripture. The Restoration Movement resulted in the rise of nondenominational churches. Campbell believed that ministers should be college educated, so he founded Bethany College in Bethany, West Virginia. ★

★★★ THIRTY-SIX ★★★

NEVADA

The Silver State

BECAME A STATE ON: October 31, 1864

NICKNAMES: Sagebrush State, Silver State, Battle Born State

STATE BIRD: mountain bluebird

STATE FLOWER: sagebrush

STATE SONG: "Home Means Nevada"

STATE MOTTO: All for Our Country

POPULATION/RANK: 2,758,931/35

TOTAL AREA/RANK: 110,560.72 square miles/7

LIST OF COUNTIES: Carson City, Churchill, Clark, Douglas, Elko, Esmeralda, Eureka, Humboldt, Lake, Lander, Lincoln, Lyon, Mineral, Nye, Ormsby, Pah Ute, Pershing, Roop, State Level Sites, Storey, Washoe, White Pine

FUNNY TOWN NAMES: Bungy, Pahrump, Sandwich Landing

SOME IMPORTANT NEVADA HISTORY

> In 1519 Spain claims area that would become Nevada.

> In 1609 the town of Santa Fe is established as Spanish-Indian trade center.

> In 1776 Spanish missionaries arrive in southern Nevada.

> In 1821 Mexico takes control of the Nevada area.

> In 1842 Captain John Fremont and party are first white men to view Lake Tahoe.

> In 1843 Joseph Walker leads first group of wagons across the Sierras.

> In 1848 the US gains control of Nevada after the Mexican-American War ends.

> In 1849 more than 60,000 settlers in covered wagons (called 49ers) pass through Nevada on their way west.

> In 1859 the discovery of silver brings thousands of prospectors into the state.

> In 1860 the Nevada Territory is created.

> On October 31, 1864, Nevada becomes 36th US state.

> In 1869 the transcontinental railroad crosses Nevada for the first time.

IMPORTANT CITIES IN NEVADA

A view of Nevada's largest city, Las Vegas, against a backdrop of mountains.

LAS VEGAS: Las Vegas, which is located in the Mojave Desert in southeastern Nevada, is the state's largest city. It is known as a major tourist destination and for its resorts, hotels, and gambling casinos. Las Vegas was established in 1905 and incorporated as a city in 1911.

HENDERSON: Henderson is located in southeastern Nevada and is the second largest city in the state. The township of Henderson got its start during World War II, when it became a major supplier of magnesium, an important metal used for military purposes. Henderson was officially incorporated as a city in 1953.

RENO: Reno, the third largest city in Nevada, is located in the central-western part of the state, at the foot of the Sierra Nevada mountain range. Reno is often called "the Biggest Little City in the World." It was founded in 1868.

RIVERS, MOUNTAINS, AND OTHER NATURAL STUFF

HUMBOLDT RIVER: At 330 miles long, the Humboldt River is the fourth largest river in the US that does not eventually flow into an ocean. The Humboldt runs through northern Nevada and empties into an area called the Humboldt Sink, a sometimes-dry lake bed in northwestern Nevada. The body of water in Humboldt Sink is called Humboldt Lake. The Humboldt River and its tributaries drain most of northern Nevada, a sparsely populated area.

PYRAMID LAKE: Pyramid Lake is located about 40 miles northeast of Reno, between the Virginia Mountains to the west and the Lake Range to the east. It is a geographic sink, meaning it has no outlet. Water leaves the lake only through evaporation or by seeping into the ground under the lake's bed. Pyramid Lake is fed by the Truckee River, which empties into the lake at its southern end. The water in Pyramid Lake is about one-sixth as salty as sea water, but several species of freshwater fish live in it. The lake measures 29.8 miles long and 8.7 miles wide and has a surface area of 188 square miles.

VALLEY OF FIRE: The Valley of Fire is located 50 miles northeast of Las Vegas and gets its name from the red sandstone formations in the area that often

Elephant Rock is an amazing formation in Nevada's Valley of Fire.

look like they are on fire when they reflect the sun's rays. The landscape of the Valley of Fire was created by uplifting and faulting in the area, as well as erosion. The Valley of Fire features beautiful sandstone and limestone formations. The Valley of Fire State Park is the oldest state park in Nevada and covers an area of almost 42,000 acres.

WEIRDNESS IN NEVADA

THE CLOWN MOTEL: In the southern Nevada town of Tonopah is one of the strangest attractions in the states—and it's a motel! Tonopah's Clown Motel has the same accommodations as any roadside motel, but it qualifies as really weird because it is full of clowns. The Clown Motel has clowns on its doors, on its walls, and on the ceilings. In the lobby, you can see shelves filled with clown dolls and clown-related memorabilia. If you don't mind clowns, or if you think they're kind of funny, then a night in the Clown Motel could be a fun experience for you.

SOME NEVADA VIPS

JAMES E. CASEY (1888–1983): James E. Casey, who was born in Candelaria, Nevada, is an American businessman who is best known as the founder of the United Parcel Service (UPS), which he began in Seattle, Washington.

HARRY REID (1939–2021): Harry Reid, who was born in Searchlight, Nevada, was a member of the US Senate. He was first elected in 1986, and became the Senate majority leader in 2007, making him one of the most powerful people in Washington, DC. Before joining the Senate, Reid represented Nevada's first congressional district in the US House of Representatives. Before that, he served in several political positions in Nevada.

GOD IN NEVADA'S CONSTITUTION (PREAMBLE)

We the people of the State of Nevada, grateful to Almighty God for our freedom, in order to secure its blessings, insure domestic tranquility, and form a more perfect government, do establish this Constitution.

ANDRE AGASSI (BORN 1970): Andre Agassi, who was born in Las Vegas, Nevada, was one of the most dominant players in professional tennis during the early 1990s to the mid-2000s. As a singles player, Agassi won the Grand Slam championship—which is determined through the world's four major professional tennis tournaments: the Australian Open, the French Open, Wimbledon, and the US Open—eight times. He also won the gold medal in the 1996 Olympics in Atlanta, Georgia.

NEVADA'S CHRISTIAN CONNECTION

THE SCHOOL OF MINISTRY is located in Las Vegas, Nevada, as part of The Church LV. It is designed for students ages 17 to 30, "to develop spirit-filled leaders of character and competence to make an eternal impact in their world." ★

★★★ THIRTY-SEVEN ★★★

NEBRASKA

Equality before the Law

NE

SOME IMPORTANT NEBRASKA HISTORY

> In 1541 explorers claim area that would become Nebraska for Spain.

> In 1682 French explorer Robert Cavelier de La Salle claims area for France.

> In 1803 the US acquires Nebraska from France as part of the Louisiana Purchase.

> In 1804 Lewis and Clark travel up the Missouri River.

> In 1823 the first permanent white settlement is built at what is now Bellevue.

> In 1833 the US government purchases Pawnee Indian lands south of the Platte River.

> In the 1840s tens of thousands of settlers travel across Nebraska on the Oregon Trail.

> In 1854 the Nebraska Territory is organized.

> On March 1, 1867, Nebraska becomes 37th US state.

BECAME A STATE ON: March 1, 1867	
NICKNAME: Cornhusker State	
STATE BIRD: western meadowlark	
STATE FLOWER: goldenrod	
STATE SONG: "Beautiful Nebraska"	
STATE MOTTO: Equality before the Law	
POPULATION/RANK: 1,855,525/37	
TOTAL AREA/RANK: 77,353.73/16	

LIST OF COUNTIES: Adams, Antelope, Arthur, Banner, Blackbird, Blaine, Boone, Box Butte, Boyd, Brown, Buffalo, Burt, Butler, Calhoun, Cass, Cedar, Chase, Cherry, Cheyenne, Clay, Colfax, Cuming, Custer, Dakota, Dawes, Dawson, Deuel, Dixon, Dodge, Douglas, Dundy, Fillmore, Fort Laramie, Franklin, Frontier, Furnas, Gage, Garden, Garfield, Gosper, Grant, Greeley, Greene, Hall, Hamilton, Harlan, Hayes, Hitchcock, Holt, Hooker, Howard, Izard, Jefferson, Johnson, Jones, Kearney, Keith, Keya Paha, Kimball, Knox, L'Eau Qui Court, Lancaster, Lincoln, Logan, Loup, Madison, McPherson, Merrick, Morrill, Nance, Nemaha, Nuckolls, Otoe, Pawnee, Perkins, Phelps, Pierce, Platte, Polk, Red Willow, Richardson, Rock, Saline, Sarpy, Saunders, Scotts Bluff, Seward, Sheridan, Sherman, Shorter, Sioux, Stanton, State Level Sites, Thayer, Thomas, Thurston, Valley, Washington, Wayne, Webster, Wheeler, Winnebago Reservation, York

FUNNY TOWN NAMES: Crab Orchard, Moomaw Corner, Mumper

A waterfront view of downtown Omaha, Nebraska.

IMPORTANT CITIES IN NEBRASKA

OMAHA: Omaha, the largest city in Nebraska, is located in the central-eastern edge of the state, along the Missouri River. The Lewis and Clark Expedition passed through the area in 1804. Omaha was founded in 1854. That same year, Omaha was chosen as the capital of the Nebraska Territory, but when Nebraska became a state in 1867, Lincoln became the new capital. In 1863 Omaha became the starting point of the Union Pacific Railroad.

LINCOLN: The second largest city in Nebraska, Lincoln is the state's capital. Lincoln is located in southeastern Nebraska. It was founded in 1856 but was called Lancaster at the time. When Nebraska became a state, the city was chosen as the capital and renamed Lincoln in honor of President Abraham Lincoln, who had recently been assassinated.

BELLEVUE: Located in the central part of eastern Nebraska, on the western banks of the Missouri River, Bellevue is the fourth largest city in the state. The area that would become Bellevue was first settled in the 1830s. Bellevue was incorporated in 1855.

RIVERS, MOUNTAINS, AND OTHER NATURAL STUFF

PLATTE RIVER: The Platte River is an important river that flows from the west to the east in Nebraska. It is formed where the North Platte and South Platte Rivers meet. It is mostly a slow-moving, muddy, shallow stream with a lot of islands, making it a poor choice for travel for 17th-century trappers and explorers. The Platte River itself is about 310 miles long.

PANORAMA POINT: At 5,429 feet above sea level, Panorama Point is the highest natural point in Nebraska. It is situated in southwestern Kimball County, near the Nebraska-Wyoming-Colorado boundary. Panorama Point isn't a mountain or even a hill, just a high point in the High Plains of Nebraska.

NEBRASKA SAND HILLS: Covering about one-quarter of the state, the Nebraska Sand Hills is an area of grassland prairie and dunes in north-central Nebraska that covers an area of 23,000 square miles. The

Nebraska grasslands near the Agate Fossil Bed National Monument.

area was formed by windblown sand from the west, but it is covered by a variety of grasses common to North America. Most of the area has never been cultivated and very few people live there, but it is used for cattle ranching.

WEIRDNESS IN NEBRASKA

THE KOOL-AID MUSEUM

Unless you grew up in or around Hastings, Nebraska, you probably didn't know that the town is the birthplace of the sugary soft drink Kool-Aid. In the late 1920s a man named Edwin Perkins figured out a way to ship flavored drinks in powdered form. His invention was called Kool-Aid. Hastings is now home to the Kool-Aid Museum, where you can learn everything there is to know about the drink. Hastings hosts the annual festival called Kool-Aid Days every August. Kool-Aid is also Nebraska's official soft drink.

SOME NEBRASKA VIPS

RED CLOUD (1822–1909): Red Cloud was a very important warrior and chief of the Oglala Lakota tribe. He was chief from 1868 to 1909. Red Cloud was one of the most formidable Native American military leaders the US Army ever faced. He led a very effective campaign known as Red Cloud's War, which was fought from 1866 to 1868 over control of the Powder River Country in northeastern Wyoming and southern Montana. After he signed the Treaty of Fort Laramie in 1868, Red Cloud worked to help his people transition to life on the reservations.

GERALD FORD (1913–2006): Gerald Ford was the 38th president of the United States and the only president born in Nebraska (he was born in Omaha). Ford served as president from 1974 to 1977. Before becoming president, he served as the 40th vice president of the United States after Spiro Agnew resigned in 1973. He became president on August 9, 1974, after President Richard Nixon resigned due to the Watergate Scandal. He was the first and only person to serve as both vice president and president of the United States without being elected.

BOB GIBSON (1935–2020): Considered one of Nebraska's all-time greatest athletes, Bob Gibson was a pitcher who played 17 seasons of Major League Baseball, all with the St. Louis Cardinals. Gibson, who was born in Omaha, began his Major League career in 1959 and retired in 1975. Gibson played in nine All-Star games and also helped the Cardinals to two World Series championships. He won two Cy Young Awards and was named the 1968 National League Most Valuable Player after recording a 1.12 ERA for the season. He was elected to the Baseball Hall of Fame in 1981.

GOD IN NEBRASKA'S CONSTITUTION (PREAMBLE)

We, the people, grateful to Almighty God for our freedom, do ordain and establish the following declaration of rights and frame of government, as the Constitution of the State of Nebraska.

NEBRASKA'S CHRISTIAN CONNECTION

Though born in Illinois, William Jennings Bryan moved to Lincoln, Nebraska, as a young man to practice law. He served in the US Congress and as US Secretary of State, and ran for president (unsuccessfully) three times. But he is perhaps best known for his role in the "Scopes monkey trial," defending a Tennessee law that prohibited the teaching of evolution in public schools. Bryan was a strong believer in reading the Bible literally. ★

★★★ THIRTY-EIGHT ★★★

COLORADO

Nothing without Providence

BECAME A STATE ON: August 1, 1876

NICKNAME: the Centennial State

STATE BIRD: lark bunting

STATE FLOWER: Rocky Mountain columbine

STATE SONG: "Where the Columbines Grow"

STATE MOTTO: *Nil sine Numine* (Nothing without Providence)

POPULATION/RANK: 5,187,582/22

TOTAL AREA/RANK: 104,093.57 square miles/8

LIST OF COUNTIES: Adams, Alamosa, Arapahoe, Archuleta, Baca, Bent, Boulder, Broomfield, Chaffee, Cheyenne, Clear Creek, Conejos, Costilla, Crowley, Custer, Delta, Denver, Dolores, Douglas, Eagle, El Paso, Elbert, Fremont, Garfield, Gilpin, Grand, Greenwood (now Elbert County and Bent County), Gunnison, Hinsdale, Huerfano, Jackson, Jefferson, Kiowa, Kit Carson, La Plata, Lake, Larimer, Las Animas, Lincoln, Logan, Mesa, Mineral, Moffat, Montezuma, Montrose, Morgan, Otero, Ouray, Park, Phillips, Pitkin, Platte (now Weld County), Prowers, Pueblo, Rio Blanco, Rio Grande, Routt, Saguache, San Juan, San Miguel, Sedgwick, State Level Sites, Summit, Teller, Washington, Weld, Yuma

FUNNY TOWN NAMES: Buckskin Joe, Goodnight, Horsetooth Heights

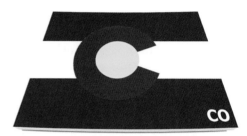

SOME IMPORTANT COLORADO HISTORY

> In 1682 French explorer La Salle claims area east of the Rocky Mountains, now known as Colorado, for France.

> In 1765 Spanish explorer Juan Rivera leads an expedition into the San Juan and Sangre de Cristo Mountains in Colorado in search of gold and silver.

> In 1803 the US acquires eastern Colorado from France as part of the Louisiana Purchase.

> In 1806 Lieutenant Zebulon M. Pike and a small party of US soldiers discover the peak that bears his name.

> In 1848 Mexico grants western Colorado to United States under terms of Treaty of Guadalupe Hidalgo, which ended the Mexican-American War.

> In 1851 the first permanent settlement is founded at San Luis, Colorado.

> In 1861 the United States Congress establishes the Colorado Territory.

> In 1867 Denver is named permanent seat of government for Colorado.

> On August 1, 1876, Colorado becomes the 38th US state.

IMPORTANT CITIES IN COLORADO

DENVER: Colorado's state capital and largest city, Denver is located in the north-central part of the state. Denver sits just east of what is called the Front Range of the Rocky Mountains. Denver is nicknamed the "Mile High City" because its elevation is 5,280 feet (exactly one mile) above sea level. It is one of the highest major cities in the United States. It was incorporated as a city in 1861 and was named after James William Denver, a 19th-century American politician and soldier.

COLORADO SPRINGS: Located 65 miles south of Denver in east-central Colorado, Colorado Springs is the second largest city in the state. Like Denver, Colorado Springs sits at a very high elevation—6,035 feet above sea level. Colorado Springs started out as a gold mining town and was incorporated as a city in 1886.

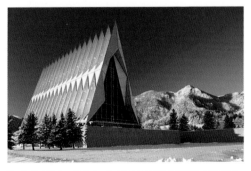

The United States Air Force Academy chapel in Colorado Springs.

FORT COLLINS: Located 65 miles north of Denver, Fort Collins is the fourth largest city in Colorado. Fort Collins was founded in 1864 as a base of the US Army. Camp Collins was erected during the Indian Wars of the mid-1860s. The camp (as well as the city that sprang from it) was named after Colonel William O. Collins, the commander of the outpost. Fort Collins was incorporated as a city in 1883.

RIVERS, MOUNTAINS, AND OTHER NATURAL STUFF

COLORADO RIVER: The Colorado River is a major river that starts in the Rocky Mountains of north-central Colorado and flows mostly southwest for 1,450 miles. The headwaters of the Colorado River start at La Poudre Pass Lake in the Rocky Mountain National Park. It flows through the states of Colorado, Utah, and Arizona before flowing into northwestern Mexico and emptying into the Gulf of California.

An autumn view of Mount Elbert, the highest peak in North America's Rocky Mountains.

MOUNT ELBERT: At 14,440 feet above sea level, Mount Elbert is the highest peak in the Rocky Mountains, the second highest mountain in the contiguous United States (all states except Hawaii and Alaska), and the highest of Colorado's "fourteeners"—the list of more than 50 Colorado mountains with peaks over 14,000 feet above sea level. It is located in west-central Colorado.

PIKES PEAK: Located about 10 miles west of Colorado Springs and measuring 14,115 feet above sea level, Pikes Peak is one of Colorado's 54 peaks that rise more than 14,000 feet above sea level. Spanish settlers called the mountain *El Capitán*, but it was renamed after Zebulon Pike, an explorer who led an expedition into southern Colorado in 1806.

GOD IN COLORADO'S CONSTITUTION (PREAMBLE)

We, the people of Colorado, with profound reverence for the Supreme Ruler of the Universe. . .do ordain and establish this constitution for the "State of Colorado."

WEIRDNESS IN COLORADO

THE CANO CASTLE

Ever hear the old saying "a man's home is his castle"? Well, one southern Colorado man's castle is made of. . .junk. Cano Espinoza of Antonito, Colorado, a tiny town less than 10 miles from the New Mexico border, began building his "castle" more than 30 years ago, using trash—aluminum cans, tires, hubcaps, wire, and other items you might find in a recycling center. Espinoza is still adding to his castle to this day. The Cano Castle is certainly creative and labor-intensive, and it's also a strange, world-famous roadside attraction in Colorado.

SOME COLORADO VIPS

ZEBULON PIKE (1779–1813): In 1806 Zebulon Pike became one of the first men of European descent to explore the area that would become Colorado. Pike was a soldier and explorer who discovered and named Pikes Peak. Pike's discovery of Pikes Peak came during the Pike Expedition of 1806–1807. He led a party of men to explore the southern part of the Louisiana Territory and to find the source of the Red River. Pike later served as a brigadier general in the US Army during the War of 1812.

JACK DEMPSEY (1895–1983): One of the greatest heavyweight boxers in the first half of the 20th century, Jack Dempsey held the World Championship from 1919 to 1926. Dempsey was born in Manassa, Colorado, and was named William Harrison Dempsey. His aggressive style and hard punching earned him the nickname "the Manassa Mauler." Dempsey is a member of the International Boxing Hall of Fame.

BYRON WHITE (1917–2002): Byron White, who was born in Fort Collins, Colorado, was both a famous football player and an important American lawyer. White was an All-American halfback at the University of Colorado. After college he led the NFL in rushing yardage in 1938 and 1940 for the Pittsburgh Pirates (now the Steelers). His football career ended when he entered the US Navy during World War II. In 1962 President John F. Kennedy appointed White to the US Supreme Court. He served until his retirement in 1993, writing 994 opinions during his Supreme Court career.

Former United States Supreme Court Justice Byron White.

COLORADO'S CHRISTIAN CONNECTION

COLORADO SPRINGS–BASED MINISTRIES

If you're looking to work for a Christian ministry, the Colorado Springs area is a good place to consider. "The Springs," as locals often call it, is home to dozens of headquarters for evangelical Christian ministries, including Compassion International, Focus on the Family, the Navigators, Young Life, and Biblica. ★

★★★ THIRTY-NINE ★★★

NORTH DAKOTA

Liberty and Union, Now and Forever

BECAME A STATE ON: November 2, 1889

NICKNAMES: Peace Garden State, Flickertail State, Roughrider State, The 701, Heaven, Norse Dakota

STATE BIRD: western meadowlark

STATE FLOWER: wild prairie rose

STATE SONG: "North Dakota Hymn"

STATE MOTTO: Liberty and union, now and forever, one and inseparable

POPULATION/RANK: 699,628/48

TOTAL AREA/RANK: 70,699.79 square miles/19

LIST OF COUNTIES: Adams, Barnes, Benson, Billings, Bottineau, Bowman, Burke, Burleigh, Cass, Cavalier, Dickey, Divide, Dunn, Eddy, Emmons, Foster, Golden Valley, Grand Forks, Grant, Griggs, Hettinger, Kidder, La Moure, Logan, McHenry, McIntosh, McKenzie, McLean, Mercer, Morton, Mountrail, Nelson, Oliver, Pembina, Pierce, Ramsey, Ransom, Renville, Richland, Rolette, Sargent, Sheridan, Sioux, Slope, Stark, State Level Sites, Steele, Stutsman, Towner, Traill, Walsh, Ward, Wells, Williams

FUNNY TOWN NAMES: Can Do, Zap

SOME IMPORTANT NORTH DAKOTA HISTORY

> In 1610 Henry Hudson claims Hudson Bay watershed, including eastern North Dakota, for England.

> In 1682 LaSalle claims Mississippi River drainage, including Missouri River drainage in North Dakota, for France.

> In 1713 France gives England northern North Dakota.

> In 1762 France gives land claimed by LaSalle to Spain.

> In 1801 the first white settlement in North Dakota is established in Pembina.

> In 1803 Spain returns Missouri River watershed to France; Louisiana Purchase transfers area from France to the United States.

> In 1804 Lewis and Clark arrive and build Fort Mandan.

> In 1818 North Dakota becomes part of Missouri Territory.

> In 1861 the Dakota Territory is officially organized; William Jayne is appointed first governor.

> In 1876 General George Custer is defeated at Little Big Horn River.

> In 1883 the capital of the North Dakota Territory is moved from Yankton to Bismarck.

> On November 2, 1889, North Dakota becomes 39th US state.

GOD IN NORTH DAKOTA'S CONSTITUTION (PREAMBLE)

We, the people of North Dakota, grateful to Almighty God for the blessings of civil and religious liberty, do ordain and establish this constitution.

IMPORTANT CITIES IN NORTH DAKOTA

FARGO: Fargo is the largest city in North Dakota. It was founded in 1871 and was originally called "Centralia." It was renamed after William Fargo (1818–1881), who was director of Northern Pacific Railway and founder of the Wells Fargo Express Company. Fargo sits on the Red River of the North in the Red River Valley. Early in its history, it was a stopping point for steam-powered boats navigating the Red River.

Bismarck is the capital of North Dakota.

BISMARCK: The capital of North Dakota, Bismarck is the second largest city in the state. It was founded in 1872 but was originally called "Edwinton" after Edwin M. Johnson, a well-known engineer for the Northern Pacific Railway. A year later the Northern Pacific Railway renamed the city Bismarck after German chancellor Otto von Bismarck, in hopes of attracting German immigrants and trade to the town. It became the capital of the Dakota Territory in 1883 and of the state of North Dakota in 1889.

GRAND FORKS: Located in northeastern North Dakota on the western banks of the Red River of the North, Grand Forks is the third largest city in the state. Grand Forks was founded in 1870 by Alexander Griggs, a steamboat captain who worked in the area. It was called Grand Forks because it is located at the "fork" of the Red River and the Red Lake River. The city was incorporated in 1881.

RIVERS, MOUNTAINS, AND OTHER NATURAL STUFF

RED RIVER OF THE NORTH: Stretching 550 miles in length, the Red River of the North (so called to avoid confusion with the Red River that forms part of the Texas-Oklahoma border), flows from its starting point where the Bois de Sioux and Otter Tail Rivers meet between Minnesota and North Dakota. From there it flows north through the Red River Valley and forms the border between Minnesota and North Dakota, then continues into Manitoba, Canada, where it empties into Lake Winnipeg. The Red River flows through Fargo and Grand Forks on its way to Canada.

WHITE BUTTE: In the southwestern part of the state is White Butte, the highest natural point in North Dakota at 3,506 feet above sea level. It is within the Little Missouri National Grassland but is on private property.

DEVILS LAKE: Devils Lake is the largest natural body of water in North Dakota and second largest body of

A beautiful shot of Devils Lake, the largest natural body of water in North Dakota.

water in the state, behind Lake Sakakawea, a manmade reservoir. It is located in northeastern North Dakota. The city of Devils Lake, North Dakota, gets its name from the lake, which gets its name from the Lakota tribe name *Ble Waka Sica*, which means "Lake of the Spirits." Devils Lake is a popular fishing destination and home to large numbers of freshwater fish that live in colder water.

WEIRDNESS IN NORTH DAKOTA

THAT'S ONE TALL TOWER: The KVLY TV mast, located three miles west of Blanchard, North Dakota, may not qualify as "weird," but it's pretty amazing. In a state that is pretty much flat from border to border, the mast stands out at 2,063 feet tall. At one time, it was the world's tallest manmade structure. It was surpassed in 2010 by the 2,722-foot-tall Burj Khalifa skyscraper in the middle eastern city of Dubai, United Arab Emirates. The KVLY tower is still the tallest structure in the western hemisphere.

SOME NORTH DAKOTA VIPS

PIERRE GAULTIER DE VARENNES ET DE LA VÉREN-DRYE (1685–1749): A French-Canadian soldier, fur trader, and explorer, Pierre Gaulitier de Varennes et de la Vérendrye was the first European to see what is now North Dakota. During their explorations, he and his four sons set up a string of important trading posts between 1731 and 1738. He spent a lot of his time looking for a "great river" that would lead to the Pacific Ocean. In the fall of 1738, la Vérendrye arrived at the Mandan Indian villages on the banks of the Missouri River in what is now North Dakota.

JOHN MILLER (1843–1908): John Miller, who was born and raised in Dryden, New York, became the first governor of the state of North Dakota in 1889. During his tenure as governor, the North Dakota state govern-ment was formed. Miller declined to run for reelection as governor (or for any other public office) and returned to his farming interests.

ROGER MARIS (1934–1985): Roger Maris, a Major League Baseball player who set what was then a record 61 home runs in 1961, was born in Hibbing, Minnesota, but grew up in Fargo, North Dakota. He started his Major League career in 1956 and played in the Big Leagues for 12 seasons on four teams— the Cleveland Indians, the Kansas City Athletics, the New York Yankees, and the St. Louis Cardinals. Maris played in seven World Series, five with the Yankees and two with the Cardinals. He won the American League Most Valuable Player in 1960 and 1961 as a member of the Yankees.

NORTH DAKOTA'S CHRISTIAN CONNECTION

RICHARD CHRISTIAN HALVERSON (1916–1995) was a North Dakota native who served as the chaplain of the US Senate from 1981 through 1994. He also served as senior pastor of Fourth Presbyterian Church in Bethesda, Maryland, as a member of the board of directors of World Vision and later as their chairman, and as president of Concern Ministries, a charitable organization based in Washington, DC. ★

★★★ FORTY ★★★

SOUTH DAKOTA

Under God the People Rule

BECAME A STATE ON: November 2, 1889	
NICKNAME: the Mount Rushmore State	
STATE BIRD: ring-necked pheasant	
STATE FLOWER: Pasque flower	
STATE SONG: "Hail! South Dakota!"	
STATE MOTTO: Under God the People Rule	
POPULATION/RANK: 833,354/46	
TOTAL AREA/RANK: 77,116.49/17	
LIST OF COUNTIES: Hamlin, Hand, Hanson, Harding, Hughes, Hutchinson, Hyde, Jackson, Jayne, Jerauld, Jones, Kingsbury, Lake, Lawrence, Lincoln, Lugenbeel, Lyman, Marshall, Martin, McCook, McPherson, Meade, Mellette, Meyer, Miner, Minnehaha, Moody, Nowlin, Pennington, Perkins, Potter, Pratt, Presho, Rinehart, Roberts, Rusk, Sanborn, Schnasse, Scobey, Shannon, Spink, Stanley, State Level Sites, Sterling, Sully, Todd, Tripp, Turner, Union, Wagner, Walworth, Washabaugh, Washington, Yankton, Ziebach	
FUNNY TOWN NAMES: Bison, Bonesteel, Pukwana	

SOME IMPORTANT SOUTH DAKOTA HISTORY

> In 1743 the La Vérendrye brothers, French explorers, claim area for France.

> In 1803 the US acquires South Dakota from France as part of the Louisiana Purchase.

> In 1804 the Lewis and Clark Expedition arrives in South Dakota.

> In 1861 the Dakota Territory is established and William Jayne is appointed governor.

> On November 2, 1889, South Dakota becomes 40th US state.

> In 1890 the Seventh Cavalry kills more than 250 Lakota Indians in the Wounded Knee Massacre.

> In 1927 Gutzon Borglam begins work on Mount Rushmore National Monument.

> In 1941 the Mount Rushmore National Monument is completed.

> In 1960 Ben Reifel becomes first American Indian elected to serve in the United States Congress.

IMPORTANT CITIES IN SOUTH DAKOTA

SIOUX FALLS: Located in southeast South Dakota, Sioux Falls is the largest city in the state. It was chartered in 1856, when the Western Town Company began developing the site. The Dakota Land Company moved

Waterfalls on the Big Sioux River from which the city of Sioux Falls takes its name.

more. The Mount Rushmore National Memorial is a sculpture of four US presidents—George Washington, Thomas Jefferson, Theodore Roosevelt, and Abraham Lincoln—carved into the granite face of the mountain. The memorial is 5,725 feet above sea level and attracts about 3 million visitors each year. Carving on the monument began in 1927 and ended in 1941.

South Dakota's Mount Rushmore is one of the most famous landmarks in the entire United States.

into the area the following year and worked with the Western Town Company to develop the area.

RAPID CITY: Located in the central part of western South Dakota, Rapid City is best known as home to the Mount Rushmore National Monument, which is located just outside the city limits. Rapid City is the second largest city in the state and was named after Rapid Creek, which flows through the city. Rapid City's nicknames are "the Gateway to the Black Hills" and "the City of Presidents." Rapid City was founded in 1876, a few years after the discovery of gold in the Black Hills region of South Dakota.

RIVERS, MOUNTAINS, AND OTHER NATURAL STUFF

JAMES RIVER: Also known as the Jim River or the Dakota River, the James River is a tributary of the Missouri River located in North and South Dakota. The James River is about 710 miles long and starts in Wells County, North Dakota. Downstream, it flows across eastern South Dakota and joins the Missouri River east of Yankton.

MOUNT RUSHMORE: Without a doubt, South Dakota's best-known attraction is Mount Rush-

HARNEY PEAK: At 7,242 feet above sea level, Harney Peak is the highest natural point in South Dakota and the highest US summit east of the Rocky Mountains. Harney Peak is located in the Black Elk Wilderness Area, in the southern part of Pennington County in western South Dakota. The peak is named after General William S. Harney, a US military commander who served in the Black Hills area in the late 1870s.

A beautiful view of Harney Peak, South Dakota's highest natural point.

WEIRDNESS IN SOUTH DAKOTA

FLINTSTONES BEDROCK CITY: If you're a fan of the old cartoon show *The Flintstones* (and if you're not, check it out sometime), then you'd enjoy a trip to Flintstones Bedrock City, a theme park near Custer, South Dakota. The 30-acre park features the Stone Age homes of Fred and Wilma Flintstone, Barney and Betty Rubble, and the whole downtown area of Fred Flintstone's hometown, Bedrock. It also includes a gift shop, the Bronto Rib (a drive-in restaurant), and a huge statue of Dino, Fred and Wilma's pet dinosaur.

SOME SOUTH DAKOTA VIPS

CRAZY HORSE (1840–1877): Crazy Horse was an Oglala Sioux Indian chief and warrior who fought against the US government when white settlers began encroaching on Lakota territories in the 1800s and when his people were being moved to Indian reservations. In 1876 he joined with Cheyenne warriors to launch a surprise attack on General George Cook. He also joined with Chief Sitting Bull and other leaders in the 1876 Battle of the Little Big Horn, which is also called "Custer's Last Stand." It was a huge victory for Crazy Horse over the US Seventh Cavalry, which lost 268 men, including Custer himself. Crazy Horse was born around 1840 near what is now Rapid Springs, South Dakota.

SPARKY ANDERSON (1934–2010): Sparky Anderson, who was born in Bridgewater, South Dakota, was a Major League Baseball manager who led the Cincinnati Reds of the National League to World Series championships in 1975 and 1976, and the American League's Detroit Tigers to the championship in 1984. Anderson was the first manager to win the World Series in both leagues. He was named American League Manager of the Year in 1984 and 1987. In 2000 he was elected to the Baseball Hall of Fame.

TOM BROKAW (BORN 1940): Tom Brokaw, who was born in Webster, South Dakota, is a famous American television news journalist and author. He is best known as managing editor and anchor of *NBC Nightly News* from 1982 to 2004. He is also an award-winning author of several books, including 2008's *The Greatest Generation*. Brokaw is the only newsman to host all three of NBC News's major programs—*The Today Show*, *NBC Nightly News*, and *Meet the Press*. He is now a special correspondent for NBC.

GOD IN SOUTH DAKOTA'S CONSTITUTION (PREAMBLE)

We, the people of South Dakota, grateful to Almighty God for our civil and religious liberties...do ordain and establish this Constitution for the State of South Dakota.

SOUTH DAKOTA'S CHRISTIAN CONNECTION

Founded in 1977 and originally called Great Plains Baptist College, Great Plains Baptist Divinity School is a Christian institution of higher learning that offers training for ministries and careers within Baptist churches. The school's campus is located in Sioux Falls, South Dakota, and offers multiple courses of study. ★

★★★ FORTY-ONE ★★★

MONTANA
A True Treasure

BECAME A STATE ON: November 8, 1889	

NICKNAMES: Big Sky Country, the Treasure State

STATE BIRD: western meadowlark

STATE FLOWER: bitterroot

STATE SONG: "Montana"

STATE MOTTO: *Oro y plata* (Spanish for gold and silver)

POPULATION/RANK: 989,415/44

TOTAL AREA/RANK: 147,042.40 square miles/4

LIST OF COUNTIES: Beaverhead, Big Horn, Blaine, Broadwater, Carbon, Carter, Cascade, Chouteau, Custer, Daniels, Dawson, Deer Lodge, Fallon, Fergus, Flathead, Gallatin, Garfield, Glacier, Golden Valley, Granite, Hill, Jefferson, Judith Basin, Lake, Lewis And Clark, Liberty, Lincoln, Madison, McCone, Meagher, Mineral, Missoula, Musselshell, Park, Petroleum, Phillips, Pondera, Powder River, Powell, Prairie, Ravalli, Richland, Roosevelt, Rosebud, Sanders, Sheridan, Silver Bow, Stillwater, Sweet Grass, Teton, Toole, Treasure, Valley, Wheatland, Wibaux, Yellowstone, Yellowstone National Park

FUNNY TOWN NAMES: Bear Dance, Hog Heaven, Hungry Horse, Hungry Joe, Muddy

SOME IMPORTANT MONTANA HISTORY

> In 1803 the United States acquires most of what would become the state of Montana in the Louisiana Purchase. The US acquires the rest of Montana in the Oregon Treaty of 1846.

> In 1852 the first gold discovered in Montana is found at Gold Creek, near present-day Garrison, Montana. Starting in 1862, a series of major mining discoveries (gold, silver, copper, lead, and coal) in the western third of the state attracts tens of thousands of miners.

> On May 28, 1864, Montana becomes an official territory of the United States. Before the Montana Territory was created, parts of what is now the state of Montana were parts of the Oregon Territory, the Washington Territory, the Idaho Territory, and the Dakota Territory.

> In 1872 the United States Congress creates Yellowstone National Park.

> On June 25–26, 1876, General George Custer, two of his brothers, and more than 260 other US military personnel die in the Battle of Little Big Horn, a battle between the combined forces of the Lakota, Northern Cheyenne, and

Arapaho tribes and the Seventh Cavalry Regiment of the United States Army.

> On November 8, 1889, Montana is admitted into the Union as the 41st state. Montana's first state governor is Joseph K. Toole.

GOD IN MONTANA'S PREAMBLE

We, the people of Montana, grateful to God for the quiet beauty of our state. . .do ordain and establish this constitution.

IMPORTANT CITIES IN MONTANA

BILLINGS: Located in the south-central part of Montana, Billings is the most populous city in the state and the only city in Montana with more than 100,000 residents.

The Montana State Capitol building in Helena.

The summit of breathtaking Granite Peak is Montana's highest natural point.

HELENA: Helena is the capital of the state of Montana and the sixth largest city in Montana by population. It was founded in July 1864 with the discovery of gold in the area.

MISSOULA: The second most populous city in Montana, Missoula is often called the "Hub of Five Valleys" because it sits at the meeting point of five mountain ranges. Missoula was part of the Washington Territory when it was founded in 1860.

RIVERS, MOUNTAINS, AND OTHER NATURAL STUFF

YELLOWSTONE RIVER: A tributary of the Missouri River, the Yellowstone River is about 692 miles long. It is considered one of the greatest trout streams not just in North America but in the entire world.

GRANITE PEAK: At an elevation of 12,807 feet above sea level, Granite Peak is the highest natural point in Montana. It is located in the Absaroka-Beartooth Wilderness.

GLACIER NATIONAL PARK: The most visited place in Montana is Glacier National Park. The park, which has been called the "Crown of the Continent Ecosystem," covers more than 16,000 square miles and includes two mountain ranges and more than 130 named lakes. More than 1,000 species of plants and hundreds of species of animals live there.

WEIRDNESS IN MONTANA

THE WORLD'S LARGEST STEER: At the Baker, Montana's O'Fallon Museum is a stuffed steer named Steer Montana that was the largest on record. The enormous bovine was born near Baker in 1923 and grew (and grew, and grew, and grew) to 5 feet, 9 inches tall, 10 feet, 4 inches long, and 3,980 pounds. When he was alive, Steer Montana toured local stock shows and circuses. After he died, his hide was preserved but was lost for many years. It was discovered in a storage facility in Billings and donated to the O'Fallon Museum.

SOME MONTANA VIPS

MARCUS DALY (1841–1900): Marcus Daly was born in Ireland but became a successful American businessman and political figure in Montana. He made his fortune with the Anaconda Copper Mine in Butte, Montana, which he purchased in 1880. By the late 1920s, a company called Anaconda Copper became the fourth largest company in the world. Daly also founded the town of Anaconda, Montana.

JEANNETTE RANKIN (1880–1973): Born in Missoula, Montana, Jeannette Rankin was the first woman to serve in the US Congress. She was elected to the US House of Representatives in 1916 and again in 1940. She was the only member of Congress who voted against a declaration of war on Japan following the 1941 attack on Pearl Harbor.

PHIL JACKSON (BORN 1945): Born in Deer Lodge, Montana, retired basketball coach Phil Jackson holds the record for most NBA championships by a coach. He coached the Chicago Bulls from 1989 through 1998, winning six championships. He later coached the Los Angeles Lakers, who won five championships for him between 2000 and 2010. He also won two championships as a player for the New York Knicks, in 1970 and 1973.

MONTANA'S CHRISTIAN CONNECTION

In Stevensville, Montana, near the Montana-Idaho border is a historic exhibit called the St. Mary's Mission, which was founded in 1841 by a Jesuit priest named Pierre De Smet. The state of Montana got its start at the St. Mary's Mission, and to this day the town of Stevensville is called the place "Where Montana Began."

The Salish and Nez Perce Indian tribes had learned about Christianity and about the Jesuit missionaries who worked among the Iroquois, and between 1831 and 1841, the Salish and Nez Perce tribes sent four separate delegations to St. Louis, Missouri, with requests for missionaries to be sent to them. In response to those requests, De Smet and five other Jesuits traveled to what would become Stevensville. They arrived on September 24, 1841, named the settlement St. Mary's, and immediately began constructing a chapel, which would be the first church in the region and the first white settlement in Montana. ★

Montana's Flathead Lake and Swan Mountain Range in winter.

★★★ FORTY-TWO ★★★

WASHINGTON

Hope for the Future

BECAME A STATE ON: November 11, 1889	
NICKNAME: the Evergreen State	
STATE BIRD: willow goldfinch	
STATE FLOWER: coast rhododendron	
STATE SONG: "Washington, My Home"	
STATE MOTTO: *Al-ki* or *Alki*, a Chinook Indian word meaning "bye and bye" or "hope for the future"	
POPULATION/RANK: 6,724,540/13	
TOTAL AREA/RANK: 71,299.64 square miles/18	
LIST OF COUNTIES: Adams, Asotin, Benton, Chelan, Clallam, Clark, Columbia, Cowlitz, Douglas, Ferry, Franklin, Garfield, Grant, Grays Harbor, Island, Jefferson, King, Kitsap, Kittitas, Klickitat, Lewis, Lincoln, Mason, Okanogan, Pacific, Pend Oreille, Pierce, San Juan, Skagit, Skamania, Snohomish, Spokane, Stevens, Thurston, Wahkiakum, Walla Walla, Whatcom, Whitman, Yakima	
FUNNY TOWN NAMES: Walla Walla, Chnak'wa'qn Breaks, Hamma Hamma, Kooskooskie, Loop Loop	

SOME IMPORTANT WASHINGTON HISTORY

> From 1774 to 1775, two Spanish explorers—Juan Perez and Don Bruno de Heceta—lead expeditions to explore the northwest coast of what would be the United States. While Perez never went ashore and therefore could not claim the land for Spain, de Heceta, who was with the Spanish Royal Navy and sailing on board the *Santiago*, claimed the land for Spain in 1775.

> In 1792 three historic events take place in what would later be called Washington. First, American explorer Robert Gray (1755–1806), sailing from Boston, Massachusetts, names the Columbia River after his ship. That same year, British explorer George Vancouver (1758–1798) leads an expedition into the area. Also in 1792, Spain establishes the first European settlement in Washington—at Neah Bay.

> In 1819 Spain gives up all claims to the territory to the US, beginning a time of joint occupancy by the Americans and the British that ends in 1846 with the Treaty of Oregon.

> In 1853 the Washington Territory is created out of a portion of the Oregon Territory. It includes all of what is now Washington and Idaho and parts of Montana and Wyoming and exists until Washington becomes a state on November 11, 1889.

> On the morning of May 18, 1980, one of Washington's volcanic mountains, Mount St. Helens, erupts. It is the deadliest and most costly volcanic eruption in the his-

tory of the United States. Fifty-seven people die, and 250 homes, 47 bridges, and miles of railways and highways are destroyed.

IMPORTANT CITIES IN WASHINGTON

The beautiful waterfront and skyline of Seattle, Washington's largest city.

SEATTLE: The largest city in the Pacific Northwest and the 22nd largest in the United States, Seattle is a seaport city located on a narrow strip of land between Puget Sound and Lake Washington. It is a major seaport for trade with Asia and with other world trading partners.

OLYMPIA: The state of Washington's capital city and the county seat of Thurston County, Olympia was incorporated as a city in 1859. The area that later became Olympia was first visited by Europeans in 1792. The town settled on the name Olympia in 1853 because of the view of the Olympic Mountains to the northwest.

SPOKANE: Spokane is the second largest city in Washington—behind only Seattle—and the largest east of Seattle and west of Minneapolis, Minnesota. Spokane was first settled in 1871 and was officially incorporated

as a city in 1881. The city's name comes from a local American Indian tribe known as the Spokane, which means "children of the sun" in the Salishan language.

RIVERS, MOUNTAINS, AND OTHER NATURAL STUFF

PUGET SOUND: Puget Sound is a large seaway in the state of Washington. It is an inlet of the Pacific Ocean and part of the Salish Sea. Puget Sound extends about 100 miles from Deception Pass in the north to Olympia, Washington, in the south. Puget Sound has an average depth of about 205 feet. It is at its deepest, about 930 feet deep, at Point Jefferson. George Vancouver explored Puget Sound and claimed it for Great Britain in 1792. The area's first European settlement was called Fort Nisqually.

MOUNT RAINIER: The fifth highest mountain peak in the continental United States—meaning a peak in states other than Alaska and Hawaii—Mount Rainier stands 14,417 feet above sea level and is part of the Cascade Range. It is a very important mountain since it is considered one of the most dangerous volcanoes in the world—because it is so large and because it is located just 54 miles southeast of the Seattle Metropolitan Area. Mount Rainier's most recent recorded volcanic eruption was between 1820 and 1854, but there were eyewitness reports of eruptions in 1858, 1870, 1879, 1882, and 1894.

Mount Rainier is pretty but dangerous—because it's a volcano that has erupted in the past.

GOD IN WASHINGTON'S CONSTITUTION (PREAMBLE)

We, the people of the State of Washington, grateful to the Supreme Ruler of the Universe for our liberties, do ordain this constitution.

The 1980 eruption of Mount St. Helens in southwestern Washington.

MOUNT ST. HELENS: Located 96 miles south of Seattle and 50 miles northeast of Portland, Oregon, Mount St. Helens is an active volcano that famously erupted in 1980. It is part of the Cascade Range.

WEIRDNESS IN WASHINGTON

CAMLANN MEDIEVAL VILLAGE: Four miles north of the tiny King County town of Carnation, Washington, sits Camlann Medieval Village, a historical replica of 1376 England. The village is open to the public each weekend from May through the end of September. Visitors can witness and talk to volunteers playing the parts of 14th-century villagers going about their daily tasks. The village also includes the Bors Hede Inne, a restaurant that serves recipes found in actual medieval cookbooks. During the meal, visitors are visited by minstrels who play 14th-century music.

SOME WASHINGTON VIPS

WILLIAM BOEING (1881–1956): In 1903 William Boeing, who was born in Detroit, Michigan, left Yale University to go into the lumber industry. He purchased timberlands around Grays Harbor, Washington, and began his business. In 1916 he went into business with a man named George Conrad Westervelt, starting a company that would eventually be named the Boeing Airplane Company.

BILL GATES (BORN 1955): Along with Paul Allen, Bill Gates cofounded Microsoft, the world's largest personal computer software company. Since the mid-1990s, Bill Gates has regularly been listed as one of the world's wealthiest people.

JOHN ELWAY (BORN 1960): Legendary NFL quarterback John Elway was born and raised in Port Angeles, Washington, before starring at Stanford University in California and then playing 15 years for the Denver Broncos. After leading Denver to two Super Bowl victories, he retired from professional football in 1999. He was inducted into the Pro Football Hall of Fame in 2004.

WASHINGTON'S CHRISTIAN CONNECTION

GEORGE F. WHITWORTH (1816–1907) was a Presbyterian missionary who was born in Great Britain and educated in Indiana. He worked as a minister in the Ohio Valley until 1853, when he and his family became some of the earliest pioneers to settle in the Puget Sound area of Washington. After helping start several Washington churches, Whitworth became known as "the Father of the Presbyterian Church in the state of Washington." Whitworth served as president of the University of Washington and also started Whitworth College (now Whitworth University), a Christian school now located in Spokane. ★

★★★ FORTY-THREE ★★★

IDAHO

America's Gem

BECAME A STATE ON: July 3, 1890	
NICKNAME: the Gem State	
STATE BIRD: mountain bluebird	
STATE FLOWER: syringa	
STATE SONG: "Here We Have Idaho"	
STATE MOTTO: *Esto Perpetua*—"Let it be perpetual"	
POPULATION/RANK: 1,567,582/39	
TOTAL AREA/RANK: 83,570.08 square miles/14	
LIST OF COUNTIES: Ada, Adams, Bannock, Bear Lake, Benewah, Bingham, Blaine, Boise, Bonner, Bonneville, Boundary, Butte, Camas, Canyon, Caribou, Cassia, Clark, Clearwater, Custer, Elmore, Franklin, Fremont, Gem, Gooding, Idaho, Jefferson, Jerome, Kootenai, Latah, Lemhi, Lewis, Lincoln, Madison, Minidoka, Nez Perce, Oneida, Owyhee, Payette, Power, Shoshone, Teton, Twin Falls, Valley, Washington	
FUNNY TOWN NAMES: Bingo Creek Landing, Comical Turn, Good Grief, Underkoflers Corner	

SOME IMPORTANT IDAHO HISTORY

> In 1803 representatives of the United States negotiate with France for what would come to be known as the Louisiana Purchase. The new territory includes parts of what would later become known as the Idaho Territory.

> In 1818 a treaty between the United States and Great Britain allows citizens from both nations to settle in the Oregon Territory, which includes Oregon at the time. That ends in 1846 with the Oregon Treaty, which gives America undisputed ownership of all of the land, making Idaho a part of the US.

> On March 4, 1863, President Abraham Lincoln signs an act creating the Idaho Territory out of portions of the Washington Territory and the Dakota Territory. The Idaho Territory includes most of the land that would become the states of Idaho, Montana, and Wyoming.

> On July 3, 1890, President Benjamin Harrison signs the law admitting Idaho to the US as a state.

IMPORTANT CITIES IN IDAHO

BOISE: The city of Boise is the Idaho state capital, the most populous city in the state, and the 99th largest city in the United States. Boise is located in southwestern Idaho.

A winter view of Boise, Idaho's state capital.

NAMPA: Nampa is the second largest city in Idaho, but it is less than half the size of Boise. It is located about 20 miles west of Boise. The Shoshone word *Nampa* means "moccasin" or "footprint." Nampa got its start in the early 1880s as an important railroad town.

MERIDIAN: Meridian is Idaho's third most populous city. It was founded in 1891 and incorporated as a city in 1903.

RIVERS, MOUNTAINS, AND OTHER NATURAL STUFF

SALMON RIVER MOUNTAINS: Part of the Rocky Mountains, the Salmon River Mountain Range is more than 120 miles long, covering most of the central part of Idaho. The highest peak of the Salmon River Mountains is White Mountain, which stands 10,442 feet above sea level at its peak. The Salmon River Mountains include five peaks standing taller than 10,000 feet.

SHOSHONE FALLS: About five miles east of the city of Twin Falls on the Snake River is an amazing waterfall called Shoshone Falls. Rising 212 feet high and flowing over a rim 1,000 feet wide, Shoshone Falls is sometimes called the "Niagara of the West."

LAKE PEND OREILLE: The largest and deepest lake in Idaho, Lake Pend Oreille is 43 miles long and has 143 miles of shoreline. It's a very deep lake, being more than 1,170 deep in places. The city of Sandpoint is located on the banks of the lake, which is a very popular recreation destination.

WEIRDNESS IN IDAHO

THE BALANCED ROCK: South of Buhl, a small town located in southern Idaho, is the famous Balanced Rock. The rock is 48 feet tall and weighs 40 tons but is balanced on a rock pedestal only 3 feet long and 17 inches wide.

How does that stay up there? A photograph of Idaho's Balanced Rock.

GOD IN IDAHO'S CONSTITUTION (PREAMBLE)

We, the people of the state of Idaho, grateful to Almighty God for our freedom, to secure its blessings and promote our common welfare, do establish this Constitution.

SOME IDAHO VIPS

SACAGAWEA (1790–1884): Sacagawea, who was born near Salmon, Idaho, was a Lemhi Shoshone woman who accompanied the Lewis and Clark Expedition, serving as an interpreter and guide. Between 1804 and 1806, she traveled thousands of miles from North Dakota to the Pacific Ocean. The Sacagawea Dollar was designed and minted in her honor.

GUTZON BORGLUM (1867–1941): Born in St. Charles in what was then the Idaho Territory, Gutzon Borglum gained fame as the artist/sculptor who, with assistance from his son Lincoln Borglum, sculpted the presidents' heads on Mount Rushmore in South Dakota.

HARMON KILLEBREW (1936–2011): One of the greatest home run hitters in Major League Baseball history, Harmon Killebrew was born in Payette, Idaho, in 1936. Killebrew played first base, left field, and third base for the Washington Senators/Minnesota Twins. During the 1960s, Killebrew hit 40 home runs in eight different seasons and ended his career with 573 homers. He was inducted into the Baseball Hall of Fame in 1984.

IDAHO'S CHRISTIAN CONNECTION

On Christmas Day in 1871, the first Indian Presbyterian Church in the United States opened its doors in Kamiah, Idaho—a small town in northern Idaho. The church, which is still holding services, owes much of its history to the McBeth Sisters—Kate (1833–1915) and Susan (1830–1893)—Presbyterian Christian missionaries who came to Kamiah in the 1870s to teach the Nez Perce Indians. Susan arrived in Kamiah in 1873 and immediately began teaching the Nez Perce men, and Kate arrived in 1879 and began her work as a missionary to the Nez Perce women. The sisters worked among the Nez Perce people for the rest of their lives.
★

Potatoes are Idaho's biggest cash crop; in fact, Idaho is by far the biggest producer of potatoes in the United States.

★★★ FORTY-FOUR ★★★
WYOMING
The Cowboy State

BECAME A STATE ON: July 10, 1890	
NICKNAMES: the Equality State, the Cowboy State	
STATE BIRD: western meadowlark	
STATE FLOWER: Indian paintbrush or painted cup	
STATE SONG: "Wyoming"	
STATE MOTTO: Equal Rights	
POPULATION/RANK: 582,658/50	
TOTAL AREA/RANK: 97,813.56/10	
LIST OF COUNTIES: Albany, Big Horn, Campbell, Carbon, Carter (Renamed Sweetwater on December 1, 1869), Converse, Crook, Fremont, Goshen, Hot Springs, Johnson, Laramie, Lincoln, Natrona, Niobrara, Park, Platte, Sheridan, State Level Sites, Sublette, Sweetwater, Teton, Uinta, Washakie, Weston, Yellowstone National Park	
FUNNY TOWN NAMES: Jackson Hole, Muddy Gap, Scott's Bottom	

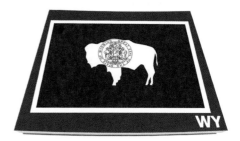

> In 1867 the town of Cheyenne is founded; the transcontinental railroad enters Wyoming.
> In 1868 the Wyoming Territory is created.
> In 1872 Yellowstone Park becomes the first US national park.
> On July 10, 1890, Wyoming is admitted as the 44th US state.

IMPORTANT CITIES IN WYOMING

CHEYENNE: The largest city in Wyoming, Cheyenne is the state capital. Founded in 1867, it is located along Crow Creek and Dry Creek.

CASPER: Casper, Wyoming's second largest city, is nicknamed "The Oil City" because it has a long history as an oil boomtown. Casper is located in east-central Wyoming at the foot of Casper Mountain, at the north end of the Laramie Mountain Range.

LARAMIE: Laramie is Wyoming's third largest city and sits along the Laramie River in the southeastern

SOME IMPORTANT WYOMING HISTORY

> In 1742–1743 François de La Vérendrye enters Wyoming and discovers Big Horn Mountains.
> In 1803 the Louisiana Purchase gives the US possession of what is now Wyoming.
> In 1806 American John Colter, a member of the Lewis and Clark expedition, discovers Yellowstone.

GOD IN WYOMING'S CONSTITUTION (PREAMBLE)

We, the people of the State of Wyoming, grateful to God for our civil, political, and religious liberties. . .establish this Constitution.

THE TETON RANGE: Located mostly on the Wyoming side of the Idaho-Wyoming border, the Teton Range is part of the Rocky Mountains. It runs north to south. The Teton Range includes a group of mountains called the "Cathedral Group"—Grand Teton (13,770 feet), Mount Owen (12,928 feet), Teewinot (12,325 feet), Middle Teton (12,804 feet), and South Teton (12,514 feet).

part of Wyoming. Laramie was first settled in the mid-1860s and was named after Jacques LaRamie, a French or Canadian trapper who disappeared in the Laramie Mountains in the 1810s and was never seen or heard from again.

RIVERS, MOUNTAINS, AND OTHER NATURAL STUFF

YELLOWSTONE NATIONAL PARK: Covering about 2.2 million acres (3,468.4 miles), Yellowstone National Park is located mostly in Wyoming. It includes mountains, lakes, canyons, rivers, geysers, forests, and other natural attractions. The Old Faithful Geyser, Mammoth Hot Springs, the Grand Canyon of the Yellowstone, West Thumb Geyser Basin, and Lamar Valley are all located within Yellowstone National Park. The park is larger than the states of Rhode Island and Delaware.

The Grand Tetons Range in Wyoming.

GANNETT PEAK: At 13,804 feet, Gannett Peak is the highest point in the state of Wyoming. It is located in the Wind River Range of the Rocky Mountains in west-central Wyoming. It is the highest peak in the Rocky Mountains outside of Colorado and home to Gannett Glacier, which is considered to be the largest glacier in the US portion of the Rocky Mountains.

WEIRDNESS IN WYOMING

JACKALOPES, mythical creatures in North American folklore that can be described as jackrabbits with antelope horns or deer antlers on their heads, are a big deal in Wyoming—so big that in 2005 the Wyoming state legislature declared it the state's "Official Mythical Creature." The jackalope got its start in the 1930s when

The Old Faithful Geyser erupts so regularly that these bison don't even seem to notice.

Jackalopes aren't real, but they're still a pretty big deal in Wyoming.

a hunter/taxidermist named Douglas Herrick, who lived in Douglas, Wyoming, grafted deer antlers onto a jackrabbit carcass. Douglas proudly calls itself "Home of the Jackalope," and it features an eight-foot-tall concrete jackalope statue that is among the world's largest.

SOME WYOMING VIPS

JOSEPH MAULL CAREY (1845–1924): Joseph Carey was born in Milton, Delaware, but he became well known for his work as a lawyer and politician in Wyoming. He served as the first US attorney for the territory, as a justice on the supreme court of the territory of Wyoming, as mayor of Cheyenne, and after that he served the territory in the US House of Representatives. After Wyoming became a state, he served in the US Senate. He was elected governor of Wyoming in 1911.

DICK CHENEY (BORN 1941): Dick Cheney was the 46th vice president of the United States. He held that position from 2001 to 2009, serving under President George W. Bush. Cheney was born in Lincoln, Nebraska, but was raised mostly in Sumner, Nebraska, and Casper, Wyoming. He attended the University of Wyoming before beginning his career in politics. He worked for the Nixon and Ford administrations before being elected to the US House of Representatives in 1978. He served as secretary of defense under President George H. W. Bush.

BOYD DOWLER (BORN 1937): Born in Rock Springs, Wyoming, Boyd Dowler is one of Wyoming's greatest athletes of all time. After playing college football at the University of Colorado, Dowler went on to be named the 1959 NFL Rookie of the Year as a wide receiver for the Green Bay Packers. He was an important part of the Packers' five NFL championships, including their wins in Super Bowl I and Super Bowl II. He played 12 seasons in the NFL.

WYOMING'S CHRISTIAN CONNECTION

Founded in 1867, the First United Methodist Church in Cheyenne is believed to be the oldest established church congregation in the state of Wyoming. Its current building was constructed in 1890 and is on the National Register of Historic Places. Before the congregation moved to its current location, the First United Methodist Church became a part of Old West history when it hosted the wedding between real-life folk character Wild Bill Hickok and 50-year-old businesswoman Agnes Thatcher Lake on March 5, 1876. ★

FORTY-FIVE

UTAH

This Is the Place!

BECAME A STATE ON: January 4, 1896	
NICKNAME: the Beehive State	
STATE BIRD: common American gull	
STATE FLOWER: sego lily	
STATE SONG: "Utah, This Is the Place"	
STATE MOTTO: Industry	
POPULATION/RANK: 2,900,872/33	
TOTAL AREA/RANK: 84,898.83/13	
LIST OF COUNTIES: Beaver, Box Elder, Cache, Carbon, Carson, Cedar, Daggett, Davis, Duchesne, Emery, Garfield, Grand, Great Salt Lake, Green River, Humboldt, Iron, Juab, Kane, Millard, Morgan, Piute, Rich, Rio Virgin, Salt Lake, San Juan, Sanpete, Sevier, Shambip, St. Marys, State Level Sites, Summit, Tooele, Uintah, Utah, Wasatch, Washington, Wayne, Weber	
FUNNY TOWN NAMES: Bullfrog, Mexican Hat, Orderville	

SOME IMPORTANT UTAH HISTORY

> In 1821 Mexico wins its independence from Spain and claims all of Utah.

> In 1824 mountain man Jim Bridger discovers Great Salt Lake.

> In 1841 Captain John Bartleson and John Bidwell lead settlers across Utah to California.

> In 1847 Brigham Young and Mormon pioneers arrive in Salt Lake Valley.

> In 1848 the Mexican-American War ends with the Treaty of Guadalupe; Utah becomes part of the US.

> In 1850 Utah becomes a US territory.

> On January 4, 1896, Utah becomes the 45th US state.

IMPORTANT CITIES IN UTAH

SALT LAKE CITY: Salt Lake City is the most populous city in Utah and the state's capital city. In 1847 Brigham Young and several other Mormon pioneers founded Salt Lake City and began farming the valley in the area. Due to its proximity to the Great Salt Lake, the city was originally named "Great Salt Lake City," but the word "great" was officially dropped from the name in 1868.

WEST VALLEY CITY: Located in Salt Lake County, West Valley City is the third largest city in Utah and is a suburb of Salt Lake City. The city incorporated in 1980.

PROVO: The third largest city in Utah, Provo is located about 43 miles south of Salt Lake City along the Wasatch Front. Provo was originally called "Fort Utah" when it was settled in 1849 but was renamed Provo in 1850.

Salt Lake City is located near the Wasatch Mountains in Utah.

RIVERS, MOUNTAINS, AND OTHER NATURAL STUFF

GREAT SALT LAKE: The Great Salt Lake is located in northern Utah and is the largest salt water lake in the Western Hemisphere. In an average rain year, the lake covers about 1,700 square miles. The Jordan, Weber, and Bear Rivers are the three major tributaries that flow into the lake, and they deposit about 1.1 million tons of minerals into the lake each year. Because the lake is so salty, it has been called "America's Dead Sea."

WASATCH MOUNTAIN RANGE: The Wasatch Range stretches about 160 miles from the Idaho-Utah border and south through central Utah. It is considered the western edge of the greater Rocky Mountains. The highest peak in the Wasatch Range is Mount Nebo, which stands 11,928 feet high.

WEIRDNESS IN UTAH

Utah's Great Salt Lake is sometimes called "America's Dead Sea" because it is so salty.

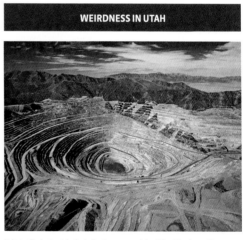

It is really just a big hole in the ground, but the Bingham Canyon Copper Mine is a popular tourist attraction in Utah.

ANTELOPE ISLAND: Antelope Island is the largest island in the Great Salt Lake. It is home to thousands of animals and many species of shore birds and wading birds. Visitors to Antelope Island State Park can catch a spectacular view of the Wasatch Mountains.

So how could a big hole in the ground become a major tourist attraction? By being so big that if it were a sports stadium, it could seat nine million people. At half a mile deep and 2.5 miles wide, the Bingham

Canyon Copper Mine in Copperton, Utah, which holds the title of the "Biggest Pit in the World," is one of the state's major tourist attractions. The Kennecott Copper Corporation, which has been digging the hole for a century, hauls about 250,000 tons of dirt, rock, and (of course) copper out of the pit every day, so it is still growing bigger and bigger as time goes on.

GOD IN UTAH'S CONSTITUTION (PREAMBLE)

Grateful to Almighty God for life and liberty, we establish this Constitution.

SOME UTAH VIPS

BRIGHAM YOUNG (1801–1877): Brigham Young was a leader in the Latter Day Saint (Mormon) Church who also founded Salt Lake City and served as the first governor of the Utah Territory. In 1846 Young organized a group of people who migrated to what would become Salt Lake Valley, Utah, which was part of Mexico at the time. He arrived in Salt Lake Valley on July 24, 1847—a date still recognized in Utah as "Pioneer Day." In 1847 Young—along with several others—founded Salt Lake City.

JON HUNTSMAN JR. (BORN 1960): Utah's 16th governor (he served from 2005 to 2009), Jon Huntsman Jr. has served under four US presidents and also ran as a candidate for the 2012 Republican presidential nomination. Huntsman began his career as a staff assistant for President Ronald Reagan and later held several positions under President George H. W. Bush. He has worked as a US ambassador, as the CEO of the Huntsman Corporation, and as the chairman of the Huntsman Cancer Foundation.

STEVE YOUNG (BORN 1961): One of Utah's greatest athletes of all time, Steve Young was a quarterback who played in the NFL for 15 seasons between 1985 and 1999. He spent his first two seasons with the Tampa Bay Buccaneers before moving on to the San Francisco 49ers. With the 49ers, Young was named NFL MVP in 1992 and 1994 and MVP of Super Bowl XXIX. Young, who was born in Salt Lake City and played college football at Brigham Young University, is a member of the College Football Hall of Fame and the Pro Football Hall of Fame.

UTAH'S CHRISTIAN CONNECTION

On July 24, 1847, Mormon pioneers, led by Brigham Young and others, arrived in the Salt Lake Valley. But it wasn't long before Protestant Christians began arriving in the area. The first non-Mormon church services held in the Salt Lake Valley were conducted in 1865 and led by the Reverend Norman McLeod, a Congregationalist missionary sent by the American Home Missionary Society to work as an evangelist in Utah. Later, Episcopals, Methodists, Presbyterians, and Baptists established congregations in Utah. ★

★★★ FORTY-SIX ★★★

OKLAHOMA
The Sooner State

BECAME A STATE ON: November 16, 1907	
NICKNAME: Sooner State	
STATE BIRD: Scissor-tailed flycatcher	
STATE FLOWER: mistletoe	
STATE SONG: "Oklahoma"	
STATE MOTTO: *Labor omnia vincit* (Labor Conquers All Things)	
POPULATION/RANK: 3,814,820/28	
TOTAL AREA/RANK: 69,898.19 square miles/20	
LIST OF COUNTIES: Adair, Alfalfa, Atoka, Beaver, Beckham, Blaine, Bryan, Caddo, Canadian, Carter, Cherokee, Choctaw, Cimarron, Cleveland, Coal, Comanche, Cotton, Craig, Creek, Custer, Day, Delaware, Dewey, Ellis, Garfield, Garvin, Grady, Grant, Greer, Harmon, Harper, Haskell, Hughes, Jackson, Jefferson, Johnston, Kay, Kingfisher, Kiowa, Latimer, LeFlore, Lincoln, Logan, Love, Major, Marshall, Mayes, McClain, McCurtain, McIntosh, Murray, Muskogee, Noble, Nowata, Okfuskee, Oklahoma, Okmulgee, Osage, Ottawa, Pawnee, Payne, Pittsburg, Pontotoc, Pottawatomie, Pushmataha, Roger Mills, Rogers, Seminole, Sequoyah, State Level Sites, Stephens, Texas, Tillman, Tulsa, Wagoner, Washington, Washita, Woods, Woodward	
FUNNY TOWN NAMES: Bowlegs, Bug Tussle, Cookietown	

SOME IMPORTANT OKLAHOMA HISTORY

> In 1682 French explorer Robert de La Salle claims area that would be Oklahoma for France.

> In 1803 US acquires most of Oklahoma from France in the Louisiana Purchase.

> In 1875 the Indian Wars end.

> In 1889 the US government opens all unclaimed Oklahoma lands for settlement.

> In 1890 the Oklahoma Territory is created.

> On November 16, 1907, Oklahoma becomes a state.

> In the 1930s a severe drought and the Great Depression combine to financially ruin most of Oklahoma's farmers.

IMPORTANT CITIES IN OKLAHOMA

OKLAHOMA CITY: The largest city in Oklahoma, Oklahoma City is located in the central part of the state and is the state capital of Oklahoma. Oklahoma City's economy is based in livestock, petroleum, and natu-

Oklahoma City is the largest city in Oklahoma. . .and the state's capital.

GOD IN OKLAHOMA'S CONSTITUTION (PREAMBLE)

Invoking the guidance of Almighty God. . .we, the people of the State of Oklahoma, do ordain and establish this Constitution.

ral gas. It was founded in the spring of 1889, during the Oklahoma Land Rush. Within hours of its founding, the city grew to more than 10,000 residents. It was named the capital of Oklahoma (replacing Guthrie) not long after Oklahoma became a US state in 1907.

TULSA: Tulsa, which is Oklahoma's second largest city, is located in the northeastern part of the state. The city of Tulsa was officially incorporated in January 1889. For most of the 1900s, Tulsa was known as the "Oil Capital of the World" because it was a major center of the US petroleum industry.

BROKEN ARROW: Broken Arrow is the largest suburb of Tulsa. It is located in northeastern Oklahoma and is the fourth largest city in the state. Broken Arrow was established in 1902 when a company called the Missouri-Kansas-Texas Railroad sold lots at the site of the town. The city was originally a farming community, but today it is the site of several manufacturers.

RIVERS, MOUNTAINS, AND OTHER NATURAL STUFF

CANADIAN RIVER: The Canadian River, which starts in Colorado, is the longest tributary of the Arkansas River. It starts at the east side of the Sangre de Cristo Mountains of Colorado (about 1.5 miles from the New Mexico border) then flows about 906 miles—through New Mexico, the Texas Panhandle, and Oklahoma. It flows into the Arkansas River about

20 miles downstream from Eufaula Lake (near Eufaula, Oklahoma).

BLACK MESA: Black Mesa is a 28-mile-long flat-topped mountain that is shared by the states of Colorado, New Mexico, and Oklahoma. It extends southeasterly from Mesa de Maya, Colorado, to the Oklahoma Panhandle, near a town called Kenton. In Oklahoma, Black Mesa reaches a height of 4,973 feet above sea level, the highest natural point in the whole state. Black Mesa's highest elevation is in Colorado, where it reaches 5,712 feet above sea level.

A pointy-topped hill near Black Mesa in Oklahoma.

THE GREAT PLAINS: Oklahoma is one of 10 US states that share what is called the Great Plains. Including the part of the Great Plains located in Canada (called "the Prairies" there), the region covers a total of 501,900 square miles. The Great Plains are a huge area of flat land—much of which is prairie and grassland—that stretches about 500 miles from the east to the west and about 2,000 miles from the north to the south. The area is important to ranching and agriculture in both the US and Canada.

WEIRDNESS IN OKLAHOMA

GRAVITY HILL, located south of Bartlesville, Oklahoma, is one of those places that seems to defy explanation. To hear the locals tell it, the hill turns the laws of gravity on their head. For example, if a visitor parks his car facing downhill and puts it in neutral, the car will roll backward—uphill! Also, if you pour water on the ground on the hill, it appears to flow uphill.

SOME OKLAHOMA VIPS

SAMUEL WALTON (1918–1992): Samuel Walton, who was born in Kingfisher, Oklahoma, was a businessman who is best known for founding the discount retail stores Walmart and Sam's Club. The first Walmart opened in Rogers, Arkansas, on July 2, 1962. Not long after that, many more Walmart stores opened. Walton's efforts included finding American manufacturers who would sell in large enough quantities to help the Walmart chain keep its prices low. At first, Walton located his stores in smaller towns and not larger cities. By the mid-1980s, more than 800 stores had opened nationwide.

THOMAS STAFFORD (BORN 1930): Born in Weatherford, Oklahoma, Thomas Stafford is a former NASA astronaut and retired US Air Force officer. Stafford flew aboard two Gemini space flights—in 1965 and 1966—and was the commander of Apollo 10, the second manned mission to orbit the moon. In 1975 he commanded the Apollo-Soyuz flight, the first joint space mission of the United States and the old Soviet Union. He was a brigadier general of the United States Air Force at the time, making him the first general to travel into space.

MICKEY MANTLE (1931–1995): Mickey Mantle was a great professional baseball player who played centerfield and first base for the New York Yankees from 1951 through 1968. He is considered one of the greatest players in MLB history. In 1956 he won the "triple crown"—meaning he led MLB in batting average, home runs, and runs batted in. He was named the American League MVP three times and was named an All-Star 16 times. He still holds multiple World Series records. Mantle was inducted into the Baseball Hall of Fame in 1974.

OKLAHOMA'S CHRISTIAN CONNECTION

OKLAHOMA CHRISTIAN UNIVERSITY: Charles William Kerr (1875–1951) was the longtime senior pastor at Tulsa, Oklahoma's First Presbyterian Church, then the second largest Presbyterian church in the US. Kerr, the first permanent Protestant Christian pastor in Tulsa (he arrived in 1900), distinguished himself in the city as a man who wanted to unite Christians who lived there, regardless of their race or social standing. Not long after he arrived in Tulsa, Kerr befriended many of the black pastors in Greenwood, who were mostly ignored by Tulsa's other white ministers. He was the only Protestant minister in the city who was individually recognized for his efforts to prevent the Tulsa Race Riot of 1921—and to provide safety to victims of the violence. Kerr also made frequent Friday and Saturday night visits to Tulsa's "skid row" to pray with drunk cowboys and to talk to them about salvation through Jesus Christ. ★

★★★ FORTY-SEVEN ★★★

NEW MEXICO

An Enchanting State

BECAME A STATE ON: January 6, 1912	
NICKNAME: the Land of Enchantment	
STATE BIRD: roadrunner	
STATE FLOWER: yucca	
STATE SONG: "O, Fair New Mexico"	
STATE MOTTO: *Crescit eundo* (It Grows as It Goes)	
POPULATION/RANK: 2,085,287/36	
TOTAL AREA/RANK: 121,589.48 square miles/5	
LIST OF COUNTIES: Bernalillo, Catron, Chaves, Cibola, Colfax, Curry, De Baca, Doña Ana, Eddy, Grant, Guadalupe, Harding, Hidalgo, Lea, Lincoln, Los Alamos, Luna, McKinley, Mora, Otero, Quay, Rio Arriba, Roosevelt, San Juan, San Miguel, Sandoval, Santa Ana, Santa Fe, Sierra, Socorro, State Level Sites, Taos, Torrance, Union, Valencia	
FUNNY TOWN NAMES: Pie Town, Truth or Consequences	

SOME IMPORTANT NEW MEXICO HISTORY

> From 1580 to1581 Agustin Rodriguez leads expedition to New Mexico; four members of his party are killed by Indians.

> In 1598 New Mexico becomes an official colony of Spain. The first capital is San Juan de los Caballeros.

> In 1600 San Gabriel, second capital of New Mexico, is founded where the Rio Grande River and Chama River meet.

> In 1609–1610 Governor Pedro de Peralta establishes a new capital at Santa Fe.

> In 1786 Governor Juan Bautista de Anza makes peace with the Comanches.

> In 1807 American explorer Zebulon Pike leads first Anglo-American expedition into New Mexico.

> In 1846 the Mexican-American War begins. US Army commander Stephen W. Kearny annexes New Mexico to the United States.

> In 1848 the Treaty of Guadalupe Hidalgo ends the Mexican-American War.

> In 1850 New Mexico—which included present-day Arizona, southern Colorado, southern Utah, and southern Nevada—is designated a US territory.

> In 1854 the Gadsden Purchase adds 45,000 square miles to the territory.

> In 1861 Confederate soldiers invade New Mexico; Confederate territory of Arizona is created with a capital at La Mesilla.

> In 1862 Confederate occupation of New Mexico ends after the Battles of Valverde and Glorieta Pass.

> In 1863 New Mexico is split into the territory of New Mexico and the territory of Arizona.

> In 1906 the people of New Mexico and Arizona vote on joint statehood, New Mexico voting in favor and Arizona against.

> In 1910 the New Mexico State Constitution is drafted.

> On January 6, 1912, New Mexico is admitted to the Union as the 47th state.

> On July 16, 1945, the world's first atomic bomb is tested at the Trinity Site in central New Mexico.

The San Miguel Mission, also known as the San Miguel Chapel, has been standing in New Mexico since the early 1600s.

IMPORTANT CITIES IN NEW MEXICO

ALBUQUERQUE: The most populous city in New Mexico, Albuquerque is located on the Rio Grande River in the central part of the state. It was founded in 1706 as the Spanish colonial settlement called Ranchos de Alburquerque.

SANTA FE: The fourth largest city in New Mexico, Santa Fe is the state's capital—and the oldest state capital in the United States. Santa Fe was founded in 1610 and was soon named the capital of a province. It is also at least the third oldest US city originally founded by Europeans. The name Santa Fe means "holy faith."

RIVERS, MOUNTAINS, AND OTHER NATURAL STUFF

CARLSBAD CAVERNS: Located in southeastern New Mexico in the Guadalupe Mountains, Carlsbad Caverns National Park includes several amazing natural attractions, including a large cave chamber called "the Big Room." The Big Room, the third largest cave chamber in the world, is

Some amazing formations in New Mexico's Carlsbad Caverns.

a limestone chamber measuring almost 4,000 feet long, 625 feet wide, and 255 feet high at its highest point.

WHITE SANDS NATIONAL MONUMENT: Located about 12 miles southwest of Alamogordo in south-central New Mexico, the White Sands National Monument is a field of white sand dunes, some up to 60 feet tall, made up of gypsum crystals. It is the biggest gypsum dune in the world. Gypsum sand dunes are very rare because gypsum is water soluble, meaning rainwater will dissolve the mineral. White Sands is far inland and in a very dry area, making it possible for the gypsum crystals to form the dunes.

RIO GRANDE RIVER: The Rio Grande River is the fourth or fifth longest river system in North America. It flows from southwestern Colorado in the Rio Grande National Forest, then south into New Mexico. It flows north to south through New Mexico before entering Texas at El Paso. The river forms a small part of the boundary between Mexico and New Mexico. It is also a natural border between Texas and the Mexican states of Chihuahua, Coahuila, Nuevo Leon, and Tamaulipas.

The deserts of New Mexico are home to colorful reptiles called Gila monsters.

WEIRDNESS IN NEW MEXICO

Since the early 1950s, when people hear the name "Roswell," their minds almost always go to stories of UFOs and extraterrestrial spacecraft. That's because in the summer of 1947, a strange, mysterious object from outer space allegedly crashed at a ranch near Roswell, New Mexico. The official story was that the landing was actually that of a high-altitude weather and surveillance balloon, but the rumors and conspiracy theories have lived on. Business owners in Roswell have cashed in on their city's notoriety. Roswell hosts an annual UFO Festival and is home of the International UFO Museum and Research Center, which is open to the public daily—except on major holidays.

SOME NEW MEXICO VIPS

KIT CARSON (1809–1868): Kit Carson was an American frontiersman and Indian fighter who was a leader of Union troops during the Civil War. During the war, both the Union and the Confederacy claimed New Mexico, and several battles resulted, including the Battle of Valverde in 1862. Carson also led the Union troops in battles against local Indian tribes. In 1863 he and his men forced the Navajo tribe to surrender.

CONRAD HILTON (1887–1979): Born in San Antonio, New Mexico, Conrad Hilton was an American businessman best known for founding the Hilton Hotels chain. He began his work life at his father's general store in Socorro County, New Mexico. He bought his first hotel in 1919 and formed the Hilton Hotels Corporation in 1946 and the Hilton International Company in 1948. Hilton eventually owned 188 hotels in 38 US cities as well as 54 hotels in other countries.

AL UNSER (1939–2021): Al Unser, who was born in Albuquerque, was a race car driver from a family of famous racers. He was the younger brother of fellow racers Jerry and Bobby, and the father of Al Unser, Jr. His nephews Johnny and Robby Unser also became race car drivers. Al Unser is one of only four drivers to have won the Indianapolis 500 four times and one of five to have won the race in consecutive years (1970 and 1971). He is the only racer with a sibling (Bobby) and a child (Al, Jr.) who also won the Indy 500.

NEW MEXICO'S CONSTITUTION PREAMBLE

We, the people of New Mexico, grateful to Almighty God for the blessings of liberty, in order to secure the advantages of a state government, do ordain and establish this constitution.

NEW MEXICO'S CHRISTIAN CONNECTION

Santa Fe, New Mexico, holds the distinction of being home to what is believed to be the oldest church in the United States. The San Miguel Mission, also called the San Miguel Chapel, is a Spanish mission church built between around 1610 and 1626. It has been repaired and rebuilt several times over the past three and a half centuries, and its original adobe walls are still mostly standing. The mission still holds Sunday mass once a week. ★

★★★ FORTY-EIGHT ★★★

ARIZONA

Home of the Grand Canyon

BECAME A STATE ON: February 14, 1912
NICKNAME: the Grand Canyon State
STATE BIRD: cactus wren
STATE FLOWER: saguaro
STATE SONG: "Arizona"
STATE MOTTO: *Ditat Deus* (God enriches)
POPULATION/RANK: 6,626,624/15
TOTAL AREA/RANK: 113,998.30 square miles/6
LIST OF COUNTIES: Apache, Cochise, Coconino, Gila, Graham, Greenlee, La Paz, Maricopa, Mohave, Navajo, Pima, Pinal, Santa Cruz, State Level Sites, Yavapai, Yuma
FUNNY TOWN NAMES: Catfish Paradise, Fort Misery, Nothing

SOME IMPORTANT ARIZONA HISTORY

> In 1539 Father Marcos de Niza, who was looking for cities of gold, explores Arizona and claims it for Spain.

> In 1752 Tubac becomes first permanent settlement in what would become Arizona.

> In 1821 all of Arizona is governed by Mexico.

> In 1846 the Mexican-American War begins. The war ends in 1848 with most of the land that would become Arizona now part of the US.

> In 1863 the United States Congress creates the Arizona Territory; Prescott is the territory's capital.

> On October 26, 1881, the famous Gunfight at the OK Corral takes place in Prescott.

> On September 4, 1886, Apache Chief Geronimo surrenders at Skeleton Canyon, ending fighting between the European settlers and the natives.

> In 1889 Phoenix becomes Arizona's capital city.

> On February 14, 1912, Arizona became the 48th state of the US.

IMPORTANT CITIES IN ARIZONA

PHOENIX: The largest city in Arizona, Phoenix is the state capital and was established as a city in 1881. It was

An aerial view of Phoenix, Arizona's capital and largest city.

GRAND CANYON: One of the most popular tourist attractions in America, the Grand Canyon is an amazing steep-sided canyon carved by the Colorado River. The Grand Canyon is 277 miles long, up to 18 miles wide, and in some spots is over a mile deep. It is one of the Seven Wonders of the World.

Beautiful Havasu Falls is a popular tourist destination in Arizona.

founded in 1861 near where the Salt River meets the Gila River.

TUCSON: Tucson is the second most populous city in Arizona, behind Phoenix. It was incorporated in 1877, making it the oldest incorporated city in Arizona. From 1867 to 1877, Tucson was capital of the Arizona Territory.

MESA: Behind Phoenix and Tucson, Mesa is the third largest city in Arizona. It is located about 20 miles east of Phoenix and is considered a suburb of Arizona's largest city. Mesa was incorporated in 1883 when only 300 people lived there.

RIVERS, MOUNTAINS, AND OTHER NATURAL STUFF

HAVASU FALLS: One of the most popular and photographed attractions in the Grand Canyon, Havasu Falls is a beautiful waterfall that plunges 120 feet into a pool of blue-green water. Reaching it means taking an eight-mile hike, horseback ride, or helicopter ride.

A view of the Grand Canyon from Cape Royal.

MONUMENT VALLEY: A region of the Colorado Plateau, Monument Valley is located on the Arizona-Utah border, near the Four Corners area (where the states of Colorado, Utah, Arizona, and New Mexico border one another). Monument Valley has been used as a shooting site for many movies. Monument Valley isn't technically a valley but a large, flat area interrupted by many beautiful rock formations.

WEIRDNESS IN ARIZONA

In a tiny town called Congress, Arizona, you can see what may be the biggest frog in the world. While it may seem strange that such a big amphibian would live in such a dry place, it makes sense when you understand that this frog, which weighs about 60 tons and stands more than 16 feet tall, is actually a frog-shaped boulder first painted green in the late 1920s. Since then, the boulder-frog has remained a landmark in Congress.

SOME ARIZONA VIPS

COCHISE (C. 1815–1874): Cochise, who was born in the Arizona Territory, was an Apache Indian chief who is known as the leader of a Native-American uprising that started in 1861. Cochise was friendly with white people until 1861, when US soldiers hanged several of his relatives for a crime they didn't commit. After that, he led a furious war effort against the US Army. Cochise was close friends with US Army scout Thomas Jeffords, and that friendship helped lead to an end to the hostilities between whites and Indians in the area.

JOHN MCCAIN (1936–2018): While John McCain wasn't born in Arizona (he was born at the Coco Solo Naval Air Station in the Panama Canal zone), he is best known as a US senator from that state and as the 2008 Republican presidential nominee. McCain served in the US Navy as an aviator during the Vietnam War. In October 1967 he was shot down and captured by the North Vietnamese. He was a prisoner of war until 1973. After he retired from the navy in 1981, he moved to Arizona and entered into politics. He served two terms in the US House of Representatives before being elected to the US Senate for the first time in 1986.

TY MURRAY (BORN 1969): Ty Murray, who was born in Glendale, is one of the greatest rodeo cowboys of all time. He joined the Professional Rodeo Cowboys Association (PRCA) when he was 18 years old and became the youngest PRCA All-Around Rodeo Cowboy of all time. He won the World All-Around Rodeo Champion title seven times (in 1989 through 1984 and in 1998). He also won the PRCA World Bull Riding Championship in 1993 and 1998.

GOD IN ARIZONA'S CONSTITUTION (PREAMBLE)

We the people of the State of Arizona, grateful to Almighty God for our liberties, do ordain this Constitution.

ARIZONA'S CHRISTIAN CONNECTION

In 1917, a Christian missionary and registered nurse named Ida Clouse moved from the Midwest and settled (under the Homestead Act) 160 acres of barren land in what was then called Cactus, Arizona. Clouse's ranch soon began hosting Christian conferences. Clouse passed away in 1946, but 13 years later 35 acres of her land were donated to the Arizona Baptist Convention so it could open a Christian college. Since that time, the college has undergone many name changes and even a physical move. Today it is known as Arizona Christian University in Glendale. ★

★★★ FORTY-NINE ★★★

ALASKA

America's Last Frontier

U.S.A. 49 MADE IN U.S.A.

BECAME A STATE ON: January 3, 1959
NICKNAMES: the Last Frontier, Land of the Midnight Sun
STATE BIRD: willow ptarmigan
STATE FLOWER: alpine forget-me-not
STATE SONG: "Alaska's Flag"
STATE MOTTO: North to the Future
POPULATION/RANK: 710,231/47
TOTAL AREA/RANK: 663,267.26 square miles/1
LIST OF COUNTIES: Aleutians East, Aleutians West, Anchorage, Bethel, Bristol Bay, Denali, Dillingham, Fairbanks, North Star, Haines, Juneau, Kenai Peninsula, Ketchikan Gateway, Kodiak Island, Lake And Peninsula, Matanuska-Susitna, Nome, North Slope, Northwest Arctic, Prince of Wales-Outer Ketchikan, Sitka, Skagway, Southeast Fairbanks, Valdez-Cordova, Wade Hampton, Wrangell, Yakutat
FUNNY TOWN NAMES: Chicken, Mary's Igloo, Humpy Creek, Funny River, Ungalikthluk

SOME IMPORTANT ALASKAN HISTORY

> In 1728 Danish explorer Vitus Bering discovers the Bering Strait between Asia and North America. Thirteen years later, in 1741, Bering and German botanist Georg Steller lead an expedition that first "discovers" Alaska when they land on or near what becomes known as Kayak Island.

> In 1794 eight Russian Orthodox missionaries arrive at Alaska's Kodiak Island. Within just a few months, several thousand people are baptized.

> In 1867 the United States purchases Alaska from Russia for $7.2 million dollars in gold—about two cents an acre. The deal is brokered by US Secretary of State William Seward, and critics, not knowing just how rich in natural resources the territory is, call it "Seward's Folly."

> Between 1896 and 1903 more than 100,000 prospectors seek their fortune in the Klondike Gold Rush.

> Starting on June 3, 1942, a small Japanese force occupies the Aleutian islands of Attu and Kiska, leading to the construction of the Alaska-Canada Highway to transport troops to Alaska.

> On January 9, 1959, Alaska becomes the 49th state.

> On March 27, 1964, one of the most powerful earthquakes in history, the Good Friday Earthquake, strikes south-central Alaska, causing terrible destruction and 139 deaths, most of which occur after tsunamis tear apart the towns of Valdez and Chenega.

The moon rises over Mount McKinley, the tallest mountain in Alaska—and the entire United States.

IMPORTANT CITIES IN ALASKA

ANCHORAGE: Alaska's largest city by population, Anchorage is the northernmost US city with more than 100,000 residents. More than 40 percent of Alaska's residents live in Anchorage. The city is located in south-central Alaska.

A community with an amazing view, Anchorage is Alaska's largest city.

FAIRBANKS: Fairbanks is Alaska's second largest city. It is located in the central Tanana Valley, a region in central Alaska. Elbridge Truman Barnette, a Yukon riverboat captain and banker, founded Fairbanks in 1901 and served as the city's first mayor.

JUNEAU: Alaska's capital city, Juneau is located at the foot of Mount Juneau across the Gastineau Channel from Douglas Island. The city is Alaska's second largest and has been the state's capital since 1906. In area, it is almost as large as the states of Rhode Island and Delaware.

RIVERS, MOUNTAINS, AND OTHER NATURAL STUFF

BERING SEA: The Bering Sea, which covers about 878,000 square miles, is located north of the Pacific Ocean, between Siberia and Alaska. It is separated from the Pacific by the Aleutian Islands and is connected with the Arctic Ocean by the Bering Strait. Even though the Bering Sea is considered one of the most dangerous bodies of water in the world, it is still home to a huge commercial fishing industry.

ALEUTIAN ISLANDS: A chain of 14 large volcanic islands and 57 smaller ones that separate the Bering Sea and the Pacific Ocean, the Aleutian Island chain extends southwest—then northwest—about 1,100 miles from the tip of the Alaska Peninsula to Attu Island. Nearly all of the islands are part of Alaska. The Aleutians are part of what is often called the "Ring of Fire," a horseshoe-shaped area around the basin of the

Pacific Ocean where a large number of earthquakes and volcanic eruptions take place.

MOUNT MCKINLEY: Alaska is home to the top 10 tallest mountain peaks in the United States, and none is taller than Mount McKinley, which stands 20,237 feet above sea level at its summit. McKinley, which is the tallest peak in North America, is located in the Alaska Range in the Denali National Park and Preserve.

A grizzly bear in Alaska needs a nap after hunting for food all morning.

WEIRDNESS IN ALASKA

STUFFED TOGO THE WONDER DOG: Way back in 1925, a musher named Gunnar Kassen drove a team of Siberian huskies through the Alaskan Wilderness to reach Nome. It was a true mission of mercy because the native population was threatened by an outbreak of diphtheria, and Kassen's sled was loaded with serum for the deadly disease. The team of 13 dogs was led by a now-famous husky named Balto. Another of the dogs was named Togo, and he's still in Wasilla, Alaska—stuffed and set up on exhibit at the Iditarod Trail Headquarters.

SOME ALASKA VIPS

VITUS BERING (C. 1681–1741): Several important places in and around Alaska go by the name "Bering"— the Bering Strait, the Bering Sea, Bering Island, Bering Glacier, and the Bering Land Bridge. All these places were named after Vitus Bering, a Danish explorer and officer of the Russian Navy. Bering is best known for his explorations of the northeastern coast of the Asian continent and of the west coast of the North American continent.

SARAH PALIN (BORN 1964): Sarah Palin served as Alaska's ninth governor, from 2006 to 2009, and was the Republican Party's nominee for vice president of the United States in the 2008 presidential election, running with Arizona Senator John McCain. She was the first Alaskan on a national ticket of a major political party and the first Republican woman nominated for the vice presidency.

CURT SCHILLING (BORN 1966): Born in Anchorage, Curt Schilling is a former Major League Baseball pitcher who helped lead the Philadelphia Phillies to the World Series championship in 1993 and also won World Series titles with the Arizona Diamondbacks in 2001 and the Boston Red Sox in 2004 and 2007. He retired from baseball in 2009 with a career postseason record of 11–2 and a career record of 216–146, a career 3.46 earned-run average, and 3,116 strikeouts.

GOD IN ALASKA'S CONSTITUTION (PREAMBLE)

We, the people of Alaska, grateful to God and to those who founded our nation and pioneered this great land, in order to secure and transmit to succeeding generations our heritage of political, civil, and religious liberty within the Union of States, do ordain and establish this constitution for the State of Alaska.

ALASKA'S CHRISTIAN CONNECTION

In 1823 a Russian Orthodox missionary named John Veniaminov traveled from his home in Irkutsk to the Aleutian Islands in Alaska to work as a missionary among the Aleuts. While there, Veniaminov learned the local language, opened a school, and translated the Gospel of Matthew. He also found time to write a book on the Aleut culture titled *Notes on the Island of Unalaska*. He later moved to Sitka, where he learned the Tlingit language, opened an orphanage, and built a beautiful church. ★

★★★ FIFTY ★★★

HAWAII

Say Aloha!

HI

BECAME A STATE ON: August 21, 1959	
NICKNAME: the Aloha State	
STATE BIRD: nene, also known as the Hawaiian goose	
STATE FLOWER: Hawaiian hibiscus	
STATE SONG: "Hawai'i Pono'i"	
STATE MOTTO: *Ua Mau ke Ea o ka 'Āina i ka Pono* (Hawaiian for "The life of the land is perpetuated in righteousness")	
POPULATION/RANK: 1,360,301/40	
TOTAL AREA/RANK: 10,930.98 square miles/43	
LIST OF COUNTIES: Hawaii, Honolulu, Kauai, Maui	
FUNNY TOWN NAMES: Laupahoehoe, Papaaloa	

SOME IMPORTANT HAWAIIAN HISTORY

> On January 20, 1778, British explorer James Cook lands at the mouth of the Waimea River on the island of Kauai. Cook is the first European known to have sighted the Hawaiian Islands. He names them the "Sandwich Islands," after the fourth Earl of Sandwich.

> In 1820 the first American Christian missionaries arrive in Hawaii.

> On January 17, 1893, American businessmen remove Hawaiian Queen Liliuokalani from power and establish a provisional government.

> On July 7, 1898, President McKinley signs the Newlands Resolution, which annexes Hawaii.

> In 1900, Hawaii becomes a territory of the United States.

> On the morning of December 7, 1941, the Imperial Japanese Navy attacks the United States Naval Base in Pearl Harbor, drawing the US into World War II.

> In 1959 the US Congress passes the Hawaii Admission Act, making Hawaii the 50th American state. Hawaii officially becomes a state on August 21, 1959.

IMPORTANT CITIES IN HAWAII

HONOLULU: Located on the island of Oahu, Honolulu is the capital of Hawaii and the largest city in the state of Hawaii. Honolulu is the southernmost and the westernmost major US city. Honolulu has been Hawaii's capital since 1845, when Kamehameha III moved the permanent capital of the Hawaiian Kingdom from Lahaina on Maui.

The skyline of Honolulu, capital of Hawaii.

PEARL CITY: Located on the north shore of Pearl Harbor on the island of Oahu, Pearl City is the second most populous city in Hawaii—and a distant second in that area to Honolulu.

HILO: Hilo is the largest city on the island of Hawaii and the third largest in the entire state. The town overlooks Hilo Bay, a large inlet on the east side of the island of Hawaii.

RIVERS, MOUNTAINS, AND OTHER NATURAL STUFF

DIAMOND HEAD: Diamond Head is a major tourist attraction near Waikiki on the island of Oahu. It is a volcanic cone that formed thousands of years ago. Nineteenth-century British sailors named it Diamond Head when they mistook calcite crystals embedded in its rocks for diamonds.

An overhead view of the Diamond Head Crater in Oahu.

GOD IN HAWAII'S CONSTITUTION (PREAMBLE)

We, the people of the State of Hawaii, grateful for Divine Guidance. . .do hereby ordain and establish this constitution for the State of Hawaii.

RAINBOW FALLS: Located in Hilo, Hawaii, Rainbow Falls is 80 feet tall and almost 100 feet in diameter. Rainbow Falls got is name from the fact that the mist thrown up by the falls creates rainbows around 10 o'clock every sunny morning.

MAUNA KEA: Mauna Kea is Hawaii's highest peak, standing 13,803 feet above sea level. But most of Mauna Kea is below sea level, and its actual height from its undersea base is 33,100 feet, making it twice as tall as Mount Everest.

WEIRDNESS IN HAWAII

WORLD'S LARGEST HEDGE MAZE: The town of Wahiawa on the island of Oahu is home to what is billed as the "World's Largest Hedge Maze." It's actually the Dole Plantation's giant Pineapple Garden Maze, and it stretches over three acres and features nearly two and a half miles of paths crafted out of 14,000 Hawaiian plants. Dole added the maze to its tourist attractions in 1999.

SOME HAWAII VIPS

HIRAM BINGHAM (1789–1869): Born in Bennington, Vermont, Hiram Bingham led the first group of American missionaries to Hawaii in 1820.

LILIUOKALANI (1838–1917): Queen Liliuokalani, who was born Lydia Lili'u Loloku Walania Wewehi Kamaka'eha, was the kingdom of Hawaii's last monarch and the only queen to hold that position.

Red hot lava flows into the Pacific Ocean from the Big Island of Hawaii.

BARACK OBAMA (BORN 1961): Born in Honolulu, Barack Obama served as the 44th president of the United States. He was the only Hawaiian-born citizen to hold that position, and the first African American to be elected president. Before that, he had served as a US Senator from Illinois.

HAWAII'S CHRISTIAN CONNECTION

HENRY OPUKAHA'IA (C. 1792–1818) didn't live very long, but he had a huge impact on Christian missions in his native home of Hawaii. At the age of 21, he left Hawaii and began an overseas journey that took him to China, New York, and Connecticut. While in the US, he began his formal education and eventually became a Christian. After training for ministry, he preached in several churches. But his heart was with his people back in Hawaii. But Henry never had a chance to teach and preach in Hawaii. He died after a long battle with typhus on February 17, 1818. Henry's diary was published shortly after his death, and it inspired many American missionaries to travel to the islands. ★

Not a State...but Part of the United States

The United States of America, the third largest country in the world (in area and in population) is divided into 50 states, each of which has its own laws and governments. But there are several places that are part of the United States but aren't part of any of the 50 states. These areas are Washington, DC, the nation's capital, and its 14 territories (places administered by the US that aren't officially claimed by any of the 50 states).

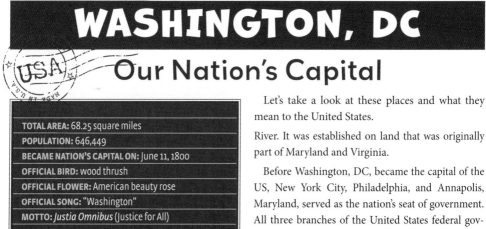

WASHINGTON, DC
Our Nation's Capital

TOTAL AREA: 68.25 square miles	
POPULATION: 646,449	
BECAME NATION'S CAPITAL ON: June 11, 1800	
OFFICIAL BIRD: wood thrush	
OFFICIAL FLOWER: American beauty rose	
OFFICIAL SONG: "Washington"	
MOTTO: *Justia Omnibus* (Justice for All)	

Washington, DC, the capital city of the United States, was named in honor of George Washington, the first president of the United States. The "DC" part of the city's name stands for "District of Columbia," in honor of Christopher Columbus.

On July 16, 1790, the US Congress passed the Residence Act, which approved the creation of a capital along the Potomac River on the east coast. In 1791 the city of Washington, DC, was founded to serve as that capital. The city is not a state or part of any state. It is a "federal district" created for the specific purpose of acting as the United States seat of government.

Washington, DC, is located in what is called the mid-Atlantic region, about 90 miles inland from the Atlantic Ocean. It is south of Maryland and north of Virginia. It is separated from Virginia by the Potomac

Let's take a look at these places and what they mean to the United States.

River. It was established on land that was originally part of Maryland and Virginia.

Before Washington, DC, became the capital of the US, New York City, Philadelphia, and Annapolis, Maryland, served as the nation's seat of government. All three branches of the United States federal government—the executive (the president and the president's administration), the legislative (the House of Representatives and the Senate), and the judicial (the US Supreme Court)—are based in Washington, DC.

Washington, DC, is home to many national monuments and museums. It also hosts 176 foreign embassies and the headquarters of many international organizations. ★

This view of Washington, DC, shows the Washington Monument to the left and the Capitol Building to the right.

Inhabited US Territories

Of the 14 territories claimed by the United States, only six are inhabited and only five have established government. Most of these territories depend on the United States for economic support and for defense. Here is a list of these territories and some interesting facts about them:

AMERICAN SAMOA

BECAME A US TERRITORY ON: April 17, 1900

OFFICIAL SONG: "Amerika Samoa"

MOTTO: *Samoa, Muamua Le Atua* (Samoan for "Samoa, Let God Be First")

CAPITAL: Pago Pago

POPULATION: 55,500 (approximate)

TOTAL AREA: 77 square miles

American Samoa is located in the South Pacific Ocean and is about 2,600 miles south of Hawaii. It is the only inhabited US territory located south of the equator.

American Samoa consists of five main islands and two coral atolls. The largest island—by land area and by population—is Tutuila. The Manu'a Islands (Ta'u, Ofu, and Olosega), Rose Atoll, and Swains Island are also included in the territory. The American Samoan capital of Pago Pago is on Tutuila. Most of the islands are heavily wooded, mountainous, and surrounded by coral reefs.

American Samoa became a territory of the United States on April 17, 1900, when the high chiefs of Tutuila signed the first of two Deeds of Cession for the islands to the US.

GUAM

Guam is located in the western Pacific Ocean. It is the largest and southernmost of the Mariana Islands and is one of five US territories that operates under an

BECAME A US TERRITORY IN: 1898

OFFICIAL BIRD: Marianas rose crown fruit dove

OFFICIAL FLOWER: great bougainvillea

OFFICIAL SONG: "Stand Ye Guamanians"

MOTTO: Where America's Day Begins

CAPITAL: Hagåtña

POPULATION: 175,900 (approximate)

TOTAL AREA: 212 square miles

established civilian government. The island's capital is Hagåtña.

The natives of Guam are called the Chamorros. Guam has two official languages: Chamorro and English.

The first European colony on Guam was established by Spain in 1668. The island was controlled by Spain in 1898. Spain surrendered it to the US during the Spanish-American War.

Guam was captured by Japan on December 8, 1941, just hours after the attack on Pearl Harbor in Hawaii. Japan occupied the island for two and a half years. The US recaptured the island on July 21, 1944. That date is celebrated every year in Guam and is called Liberation Day.

In Guam, Mount Lamlam rises 1,332 feet above sea level.

NORTHERN MARIANA ISLANDS

The Northern Mariana Islands are located in the western Pacific Ocean and are made up of 15 islands, but only three of them—Saipan, Tinian, and Rota—are permanently inhabited. More than 90 percent of the residents of the Northern Mariana Islands live on Saipan.

The Northern Mariana Islands were first sighted by Europeans in 1521, when Spanish explorer Ferdinand Magellan passed by the islands as he sailed for Spain. The islands were first settled by Europeans in 1668, when Spanish missionaries arrived. The islands were ruled by Spain, Germany, and Japan prior to World War II.

BECAME A US TERRITORY IN: 1986	
OFFICIAL BIRD: Marianas fruit dove	
OFFICIAL FLOWER: lumeria	
OFFICIAL SONG: "Gi Talo' Gi Halom Tasi"	
CAPITAL: Saipan (Capitol Hill)	
POPULATION: 54,000 (approximate)	
TOTAL AREA: 184 square miles	

PUERTO RICO

Puerto Rico, officially known as the Commonwealth of Puerto Rico, is located in the Caribbean Sea. It is made up of the main island of Puerto Rico plus the nearby small islands of Vieques, Culebra, and Mona.

When Christopher Columbus arrived in what would later be known as Puerto Rico in 1493, the island was inhabited by the peaceful Arawak Indians. Columbus claimed the island for Spain and named it San Juan Bautista (St. John the Baptist). In 1508 Spanish explorer Juan Ponce de León established the first Spanish settlement on the island. He was named governor of San Juan Bautista in 1509. The island was first called Puerto Rico in the 1520s.

After 1830, sugarcane, coffee, and tobacco plantations were developed in Puerto Rico. In 1897 Spain granted the island a great deal of independence. Puerto Rico became a US territory after the US invaded it during the Spanish-American War of 1898. It has remained a US territory since then, even though some Puerto Ricans want their island to be an independent nation.

In 1917 residents of Puerto Rico were granted full American citizenship under the Jones Act. Beginning in 1948, they were granted the right to elect their own governor.

BECAME A US TERRITORY IN: 1898	
NICKNAME: Isle of Enchantment	
OFFICIAL BIRD: Puerto Rican spindalis	
OFFICIAL FLOWER: Puerto Rican hibiscus	
OFFICIAL SONG: "La Borinqueña"	
MOTTO: Joannes Est Nomen Eius ("John is his name")	
CAPITAL: San Juan	
POPULATION: 3.6 million (would be 29th largest state by population)	
TOTAL AREA: 3,151 square miles	

US VIRGIN ISLANDS

The US Virgin Islands of the United States are a group of islands located in the Caribbean Sea and the Atlantic Ocean. They are made up of three main islands—St. Croix, St. John, and St. Thomas—in addition to Water Island and other small islands. St. Croix is the most populous of the islands, followed closely by St. Thomas.

The US Virgin Islands were a possession of Denmark, which called them the Danish West Indies. In 1916 the US purchased them for $25 million and they were renamed. The US Congress granted residents of the islands US citizenship. The economy of the US Virgin Islands is based mostly in tourism.

BECAME A US TERRITORY IN: 1916	
NICKNAME: the American Paradise	
OFFICIAL BIRD: bananaquit (yellow breast)	
OFFICIAL FLOWER: yellow elder	
OFFICIAL SONG: "Virgin Islands March"	
MOTTO: United in Pride and Hope	
CAPITAL: Charlotte Amalie (on St. Thomas Island)	
POPULATION: 109,666 (approximate)	
TOTAL AREA: 133.7 square miles	

WAKE ISLAND

Located about halfway between Midway and Guam, Wake Island is an atoll consisting of the three small islands of Wilkes, Peale, and Wake. Wake Island was discovered by the British in 1796 and was annexed by the United States in 1899. Pan American Airways established a seaplane base on Wake Island in 1938. On December 8, 1941, the Japanese attacked Wake Island and later took full possession of it on December 23. It was surrendered back to the US on September 4, 1945. Wake Island covers about 2.5 square miles of area and is inhabited by about 200 people. ★

Uninhabited US Territories

BAKER ISLAND: An atoll (a ring-shaped coral reef), Baker Island is located just north of the equator in the central Pacific Ocean. It is about 1,700 southwest of Honolulu, Hawaii. Baker Island's total area is about .63 square miles.

HOWLAND ISLAND: A geographical neighbor of Baker Island, Howland Island is a coral island just north of the equator in the central Pacific Ocean. It is about 1,700 miles south of Honolulu, almost halfway between Hawaii and Australia. Howland Island has a total area of about .69 square miles.

JARVIS ISLAND: Formerly known as Bunker Island, Jarvis Island is a 1.75-square-mile coral island located in the South Pacific Ocean, about halfway between Hawaii and the Cook Islands.

JOHNSTON ATOLL: Also known as Kalama Atoll to native Hawaiians, Johnston Atoll is located in the North Pacific Ocean, about 860 miles southwest of the island of Hawaii. Johnston Atoll's total area is about 1.02 square miles.

KINGMAN REEF: Kingman Reef is a mostly underwater reef that is located about halfway between the Hawaiian Islands and American Samoa, about 930 nautical miles (1,070 land miles) south of Honolulu. It measures 10.9 miles east-to-west and 5.75 miles north-to-south with about .01 square miles of area above sea level.

MIDWAY ISLAND: Also called Midway Atoll, Midway Island is an atoll in the north Pacific Ocean, about halfway between North America and Asia and one-third of the way between Honolulu, Hawaii, and Tokyo, Japan. Midway Island is about 2.4 square miles in area and is considered uninhabited, even though a few hundred people reside on the island from time to time.

NAVASSA ISLAND: Measuring about two square miles in area, Navassa Island sits in the Caribbean Sea, just west of Haiti. It is an American territory, but the nation of Haiti also claims the island as part of its territory.

PALMYRA ATOLL: Palmyra Atoll sits in the northern Pacific Ocean, directly south of the Hawaiian Islands, about halfway between Hawaii and American Samoa. The atoll is 4.6 square miles in area and is considered unoccupied, even though 4 to 20 "non-occupants" work there. ★